The Epic Trickster in American Literature

Just as Africa and the West have traditionally fit into binaries of Darkness/Enlightenment, Savage/Modern, Ugly/Beautiful, and Ritual/Art, among others, much of Western cultural production rests upon the archetypal binary of Trickster/Epic, with trickster aesthetics and commensurate cultural forms characterizing Africa. Challenging this binary and the exceptionalism that even underlies many anti-hegemonic efforts today, this book begins with the scholarly foundations that mapped out African trickster continuities in the United States and excavated the aesthetics of traditional African epic performances. Rutledge locates trickster-like capacities *within* the epic hero archetype (the "epic trickster" paradigm) and constructs an *Homeric Diaspora*, which is to say that the modern Homeric performance foundation lies at an absolute time and distance away from the ancient storytelling performance needed to understand the cautionary aesthetic inseparable from epic potential. As traditional epic performances demonstrate, unchecked epic trickster dynamism anticipates not only brutal imperialism and creative diversity, but the greatest threat to everyone, an eco-apocalypse. Relying upon the preeminent scholarship on African-American trickster-heroes, traditional African heroic performances, and cultural studies approaches to Greco-Roman epics, Rutledge traces the epic trickster aesthetic through three seminal African-American novels keenly attuned to the American Homeric Diaspora: Charles Chesnutt's *The Marrow of Tradition*, Richard Wright's *Native Son*, and Toni Morrison's *Beloved*.

Gregory E. Rutledge is Associate Professor with a joint appointment in the Department of English and the Institute for Ethnic Studies at the University of Nebraska, Lincoln, US.

Routledge Studies in Twentieth-Century Literature

The Epic Trickster in American Literature

From Sunjata to So(u)l

Gregory E. Rutledge

Routledge
Taylor & Francis Group
NEW YORK   LONDON

First published 2013
by Routledge
711 Third Avenue, New York, NY 10017

Simultaneously published in the UK
by Routledge
2 Park Square, Milton Park, Abingdon, Oxon OX14 4RN

*Routledge is an imprint of the Taylor & Francis Group,
an informa business*

Library of Congress Cataloging-in-Publication Data
Rutledge, Gregory E.
    The epic trickster in American literatue from Sunjata to So(u)l /
by Gregory E. Rutledge.
        p. cm. — (Routledge studies in twentieth-century literature ; 30)
    Includes index.
    1. American literature—African American authors—History and
criticism.   2. Tricksters in literature.   3. American literature—African
influences.   4. Epic literature—History and criticism.   I. Title.
    PS153.N5R88 2012
    810.9'896073—dc23
    2012033047

ISBN13: 978-0-415-63692-6 (hbk)
ISBN13: 978-0-203-08494-6 (ebk)

Typeset in Sabon
by IBT Global.

Printed and bound in the United States of America on sustainably sourced
paper by IBT Global.

To my mother (and Rutledge and McClendon families),
my wife (and Lee family), and my son, our epic trickster . . .
my Heart, S(e)oul, and Future.

Contents

Figures and Tables

FIGURES

TABLES

Preface

> *Epic.*
> *See It, hear It,*
> *smell It, read and study*
> *It to know It,*
> *and even practice It*
> *as is absolutely*
> *necessary to avoid*
> *being victimized by It . . .*
> *but, whatever you do,*
> *do not promote it or*
> *—and this is key—*
> *live It.*

Some might argue that this book may be worth publishing if only for the debate that it will inevitably create, much like Martin Bernal's *Black Athena* volumes, and the more than the usual number of copies that it will sell. Most epic specialists see the hero and trickster as two different figures, they argue.

While every scholar aims to produce a *magnum opus*, this study is, *and should be*, a failure—*not* because I failed to consider epic heroes and tricksters as the same, for a careful and close reading easily debunks such claims. No, neither grandiose ambition, fatalism, nor melancholia dictates my assessment and hope for *The Epic Trickster in American Literature: From Sunjata to So(u)l*. Like the traditional epic performance, insofar as my investigations and deliberations are correct, its success should be equaled—and probably exceeded—by its failure, which is still success, albeit in closure.

If this study helps the epic performance to conform to the timely performativity of a well-uttered proverb, which is context bound but nevertheless timeless and universal, then my successful failure will have been worth the years of study—and risks—I put into this.

This entire enterprise is possible because of my movement from a classical education and high literacy–based racial uplift strategy—founded on exceptional "firsts"—to a counterintuitive ethos that now envelops my former belief in a Mother's embrace. It originated back in 1996 when I first encountered and read W.E.B. Du Bois' *The Souls of Black Folk* (1903), which struck me, as Longinus says of sublime literature, like a flash of lightning. Finding my story (the African-American story) superbly and profoundly lyricized, I then, there, and immediately formulated a plan to leave the practice of law in Atlanta, Georgia. I had to respond to the call that I heard in Du Bois' *Souls*.

There were a lot of risks. Leave Atlanta and the South, *the* Black Metropolis after the 1996 Olympics and my home region, respectively? Leave your budding career as a young attorney—on the cusp of leisure and status if not fame and riches—full of dedication to fairness, justice, and the worth ethic? Go back to school, accrue more loans, to become, basically, a professor—a glorified teacher, many Americans would say—of literature when one had to ask, as Kurt Vonnegut indirectly did in *Slaughterhouse-Five* (1969), "whether the novel was dead or not."

In hindsight, the risk was the uplift strategy of staying the course, making the American Dream work. How could it when, in light of America's peculiar racial history, I'd been *privileged* to go through my entire formal education without once encountering an African-American novel? (This means a course in African-American culture was out of sight, out of mind in the most literal sense.) Instead of receiving the best education as an African American who had the highest stakes, I and tens of millions of members of the black community, over generations, had received educations that went in the opposite direction. The contradiction between the two educational goals easily engulfs the classical uplift strategy, which relies upon individual conquest of the very forms of knowledge—and material incentives—that have resulted in rapid brain drain for decades.

What chance did my maternal grandfather, George Sipp Rutledge, Sr., have as an illiterate laborer who grew up in the South? Our family's oral history casts him as a man of rugged body and gentle disposition, but on May 24, 1967, fired by the Bradenton Department of Public Works and with no recourse, he collapsed, struck his head on the corner of the kitchen counter, fell into a coma, and was gone. His death was a suspicious mystery—some thought a murder. Beginning with his external examination, the medical examiner transformed my grandfather's wholeness ("The body is a well developed negro male appearing somewhat older than the stated age of 49 years") into a clinical autopsy of disparate parts, of biological objects: a 475-gram heart, two 600-gram lungs, a liver (2,200 grams), spleen (80 grams), kidneys (180 grams), and a brain (1,350 grams). "Massive intracerebral hemorrhage" is the autopsy diagnosis according to the medical examiner. But the *other* cause of death, which the black Bradenton community did *not* need an M.D. (or even literacy) to know well, appears earlier in one of the most straightforward, understated sentences in the entire report: "The cerebellum and brain stem appear grossly normal save for pressure defects" (Foley 1967).

Pressure defects.

Cultural pressure—and eventually physical defects—killed him. It didn't need guns, bullets, ropes, bats, poisons, or anything tangible—just ubiquitous, smothering, unrelenting, and sometimes smiling-in-your-face racism.

Paul Laurence Dunbar sounded a sublime truth when he lyricized "We Wear the Mask" (1895); racism relies upon a "masterful duplicity" full of its own sights, sounds, silences, and smiles. Frederick Douglass famously articulated how a slave named Sandy betrayed escape plans to the slave owners. It is as true now as it was in 1830s Maryland and 1960s Florida: there are too many Sandys, male and female, black and white.

The only things more scanty than the meager stories we have of my grandfather (because of times too painful to remember and talk about) are the photographs. There are none—of this American, a native son. He died months before I was born. A near Total Blackout.

Since the revolutionary fervor of the 1960s, and the death of my grandfather, the black community has seen some remarkable gains—a sizeable middle class has formed and Senator Barack H. Obama became President Obama in November 2008—although along with massive incarceration rates, community decay, and outrageous electoral disenfranchisement that mainstream America accepts as normal, making much of the black community a Third World lurking within the First.

And to think that African Americans—dating back to the writers of the nineteenth-century *fin de siècle* who were most attuned to the cultural performance—equated American/European epic performance and racial mythology. Sadly, only a small percentage of even well-educated African Americans know this. Words patently fail to capture this *über* contradictory and elusive reality, hence the risks I have assumed—with my method, perspective, and even tone—to make my analysis *perform*.

On a personal level, if I had not undertaken these risks, none of this would I have ever known. Although I hope my success is a failure, either way it is a worthy cause for those—like my grandfather—who have suffered from "pressure defects."

Acknowledgements

Shout-Outs

to the beloved "60 million and more" victims, native sons and daughters, past and present, each with their own chestnut held tightly in a fist struggling against the marrow of tradition

As the story of my grandfather indicates, this book would not exist if I had not been an inseparable part of the lives and legacy of my family. They are the first contributors to the insights I obtain and articulate.

Likewise, there are many people whose help made the successful completion of this book possible. They include Keith Cartwright, who wrote the book I wish I could have written and provided continuous support for my project; Sandra Adell, Michael Thornton, Brenda Gayle Plummer, and William Van Deburg of the Afro-American Studies Department of the University of Wisconsin-Madison for starting me on the cultural studies path that I consider so integral to what I do; Tejumola Olaniyan who kept faith in me and supported my efforts and fledgling career when others doubted; Nellie Y. McKay, Craig Werner, and Jeffrey Steele, who guided me through my M.A. thesis and dissertation; the gentlemen-scholars of Harambee Afrikan Cultural Organization, of the Nebraska State Penitentiary, whose dedication to Mother Africa and critical cultural knowledge inspires me to keep going; Susan Stanford Friedman, for encouragement and advice that seem inexhaustible; Kim Blockett, for being a friend and reader of this project during my tenure years; Gretchen Michlitsch, who brought Keith Cartwright's book to my attention (she gave me her copy); the late Oyekan Owomoyela, a gentleman-scholar whose work enriched my own; the late Nick Spencer, who sought to combine theory and class issues in his approach to literary studies; Thomas Sienkewicz, whose encouragement and Sunjata-Greek comparative work was extremely helpful; Dae-Ho Cho, for scholarly encouragement and support from the other side of the world; David Izzo Garrett, who valued my work with Charles W. Chesnutt; Hong-Kyu Song, my Seoul-brother supporter; Stephen Belcher, who kindly entertained too many of my African epic–related queries; Tom Gannon for several key eco-criticism references that I used in my Richard Wright chapter; Matthew Grady, a graduate student whose interest in epic, tragedy, and drama enriched this study; UW-Madison reference librarian Richard

West for general support and help with my Tolkien query; University of Nebraska-Lincoln reference librarian Charlene Maxey-Harris for critical research support as I started to overhaul my dissertation; Smithsonian reference librarian Janet L. Stanley, who worked magic several times in an instant; Barry Hecht, for graciously agreeing to let me use his Ijo image; Joyce Ann Joyce, George Wolf, and Ruth Nisse, former UNL professors who provided, and still provide in most cases, wonderful encouragement for my work; Wai Chee Dimock, for enriching my Toni Morrison chapter as a reader and a researcher whose own work paved the way for some of my key arguments throughout the manuscript; Jerry Ward, for helping me to the finish line; Elizabeth Schultz, who kindly provided an offprint of her eco-critical article on Odysseus; Carrie Walker, who kept me hopping with epic and hip hop–related suggestions; Paul Olson, Kwame Dawes, and Fran Kaye, whose amazing support deserves emphatic note; and the graduate research assistants who provided critical leg and eye work to help me wade through reams and bytes of data—Jaclyn Cruikshank, Erica Rogers, Eduardo Blanco, Joel Puchalla, and Aubrey Streit Krug.

To you all (and any one I missed), my deepest thanks.

And, of course, a *special thanks* to my mother and sister, Carolyn E. Rutledge and Stephanie A. Rutledge, who provided essential and continuous moral support during some of my most difficult times; Sung-Mook Cho and Boum-Woon Lee, my mother- and father-in-law, respectively, whose constant prayers and emotional and financial support make our family's professional success as much theirs as it is ours; and Dr. Jong-Im Lee, my wife, best friend, colleague, harshest critic, greatest supporter, and *in-yeon* co-author.

1 Introduction

Then King Lion called the rabbit. The timid little creature stood before him, one trembling paw drawn up uncertainly.

"Rabbit," cried the king, "why did you break a law of nature and go running, running, running, in the daytime?"

—*Why Mosquitoes Buzz in People's Ears: A West African Tale* (1975), retold by Verna Aardema

We now find that mythology also conceals an ethical system, but one which, unfortunately, is far more remote from our ethic than its logic is from our logic.

—Claude Lévi-Strauss (1978)

The hero is but welcome on troubled days.

—Malian Proverb

In a West African folktale famously retold by Verna Aardema in *Why Mosquitoes Buzz in People's Ears: A West African Tale* (1975),[1] King Lion, symbol of rulership, courage, and epic heroes, among other things, has convened a tribunal and called before it rabbit, a symbol of speed, soft frailty, and trickiness, among other things. "Rabbit," cried the king, "why did you break a law of nature and go running, running, running, in the daytime?" (15). Seeking the ultimate cause for why Mother Owl has refused to call upon the sun to rise—a shading of the world bearing apocalyptic implications—King Lion does not punish rabbit, who was responding to a chain of events initiated by mosquito's lie to iguana. That fact that the topic of the lie was mosquito-sized yams, which set in motion a series of events concatenating discord between iguana-python-rabbit and causing Mother Owl not to raise the sun, and the fact that this Sunless state threatened the entire world suggest four cardinal principles that characterize my study of the heroic epic performance.

First, all life is interconnected, from the smallest insects to the strongest animals. It is no accident that the story begins with mosquito, the carrier of disease, distorting the truth about yams, a staple crop. Iguana and python, water spirits who symbolize hydration, then become nonresponsive and wayward, directly endangering domestic stability. Even the tiniest fissures in the foundation of a healthy body and community can eventually threaten all of reality. Second, running in the daytime is a transgression of the laws of nature. It can be done for legitimate reasons, which the rabbit's testimony reveals, but King Lion's concern perhaps needs to be rearticulated: rabbit has been continuously "running, running, running, in the daytime," and thus the world has been shaded. Rabbit's exceptional behavior, which King Lion fears, has become normative and upset the balance. Third, King Lion and rabbit—archetypal symbols of heroic exceptionalism and fleet trickiness, respectively—are themselves engulfed by this threat. Fourth and finally, the cultural performance that informs the archetypes is the most important element in determining what roles they will play. In this tale, mosquito is the Trickster and rabbit a figure of domesticity who relies upon King Lion's stable governance.

Unfortunately, the archetypes Lion and Rabbit, Epic Hero and Trickster, not the cultural performances that inform them, dominate our understanding. Teleological approaches limit our imaginations regarding these archetypes, for our tendency is to think of the abilities that define their purposes. Epic heroes are heroic and tricksters are tricky by this classic logic. Moreover, racial stereotypes join the archetypes such that Epic Hero in white Europe and Trickster in black Africa have become synonymous verities. Achilles and Odysseus are European heroes, adventurers, and builders, whereas Hare is an African trickster, a witty wordsmith who stands against custom and oppressive structure. But what if we concern ourselves with the early, pre-heroic part of epic cycles and mine them for universal principles and cultural particulars? Because the underdog position of the protagonist in the early portions of the epic narrative is akin to the trickster's and the trickster often ends up occupying the place of Lion (or some other strong predator), the archetypes merge. But in spite of scholarly recognition of the trickster as the *trickster-hero* or *culture-hero* and the advent of performance-based scholarship on traditional African epics, both occurring in the 1970s, an absolutist regard for the divide prevails.

Surely, with the African-American renaissance of the 1960s and 1970s, one expected it to be challenged. Many black scholars believed America's Homeric performance to be the correlative—if not cause—of white supremacy just at the time traditional African epics were first being published and studies of the well-known African trickster were soon underway. In light of their understanding of the relationship between Homeric performance and the African trickster, Old Massa being outwitted by the slave, these scholars' awareness of the movement of African culture—including traditional epics—across the Atlantic into New World slavery raises a question that impinges on the absolute purity of archetypal thinking: would not the cultural agency represented by traditional African epics have been reduced to the position of a trickster in a New World in which Homer's epics defined much of the Western ontological sense and ensuing cultural performance?

The answer seems to suggest the existence of an *epic trickster*, the possibility that within the human condition's giving rise to genres of heroic epic possibility lies the trickster type considered its antithesis. In other words, along with the African trickster-proper, some of whose tales crossed with slavery and survived verbatim, a corresponding aesthetic and figure within the traditional African epic performance—what I call the epic trickster—may have made a similar journey. But its berth in the New World, as its name implies, is the quintessence of paradox: African epic potentiality is the last ideology slaveholders would have embraced, and yet the substantial role the Homeric epics played in modern Western culture worked to make epic potentiality mainstream for these New World natives.

The possibility of the epic trickster raises another question: if the epic hero learned the *modus operandi* of the trickster, can the trickster-proper be subversive enough to deconstruct epic potentiality borne of the trickster's guile and wit and the heroic epic protagonist's unsurpassed physical abilities? Also, once such a trickster-savvy epic figure is unleashed, is there anything that can stop him/her/it? To face such questions in mythology is one thing, but the existence of an actual, real-world belief in heroic epic mythology is another, one that infuses a potentially apocalyptic urgency into them. Live Homeric performances can no longer speak to us, but living epic performances represent traditional wisdom about such.

If the dearth of Americanist—including African-Americanist—scholarship treating the traditional African heroic epic performance is statement by omission, the question such omission begs is clear enough: why focus on the traditional African heroic epic performance? Why, indeed, when, as Catherine Morley indicates in *The Quest for Epic in Contemporary American Fiction* (2009), a transnational, James Joyce–inspired study of European epic influences on John Updike, Philip Roth, and Don DeLillo, "epic is critically regarded as a predominantly masculine genre" and "has long been considered the exclusive domain of the male literary genius, an incarnation of patriarchal values"? Morley's subsequent statements defend her exclusive focus on white male authors, a noteworthy corpus if one realizes that addressing the problems of epic-centrism in Western (literary) history requires soul-searching within the majority community as well as work from minority artist-activists.

Still, Morley's justification and literary genealogy provide answers to our original "why" question. Instead of a transnational focus and comparative methodology, she focuses on the "literary epic" as her source-text and holds that the epic is "originally a European genre" (3, 6). There are obvious problems associated with this Eurocentric positioning when one considers that the epics attributed to Homer[2] were originally oral performances; the absence of any definitive proof means that even *The Epic of Gilgamesh* cannot be claimed as the first epic, and the recent work on oral epic *performance* traditions situates Homer's epics within a world genre and establishes them as frozen, limited versions without the participatory vitality of the original performances forever lost to us.

The literary epic is part of an epic narrative tradition itself originating, almost absolutely, in a storytelling performance tradition whose genesis truly existed at a time and place absolutely lost to us. But the epic's folk roots, however literary it has become, still shape us and our cultural performance because we vigorously participate in the mythmaking endeavor tapped and amplified by contemporary novelists, film-makers, celebrities, musicians, video game creators, fashion leaders, advertising agencies, and, of course, politicians, just to name a few. Contemporary Western textuality must be understood as a performance in an intertextual, or contextual, environment: "Any print text is a product not just of an individual author's mind, but also of the oral and published statements that the author has encountered" (W. Belcher 214).

The *Iliad*, as Martin Hammond believes, may be the "cornerstone of Western civilisation" (7), but historian James McLachlan suggests a vital aspect of the American neoclassical performance: the "Ciceronian Toga" was so central to Revolutionary War–era American iconography that it could be worn by a speaker who made "virtually no references to the classics" in a 1775 address and yet invoke in the "conscious and subconscious minds of his audience what might be called the 'cultural code'" or "classical code" (82–84). Such a "cornerstone" is not only a "classical code" but also a "root metaphor," a term used by anthropologists like Victor Turner and Sandra Barnes to describe how the concept behind a word may serve as the etymological underpinning for a broad range of cultural performances. Though tension between the ancients/Old Europe and the New World creates complications and forces us to recalibrate this model to account for its performative adaptability, Homer, like the toga, performs along a spectrum running from the conscious to the subconscious: from explicit references (e.g., Achilles and his heel, Odysseus' odyssey), to explicit and implicit "utterances" from material symbols like togas and recreations of the Trojan Horse (e.g., the Trojan Horse Internet viruses and countless Trojan Horse reproductions) to the metaphors of the collective unconscious, a genetic commonality shared by all humans and generalized as epic or epical, but rooted in Homer as part of the West's social contract.[3]

Perhaps because Homeric aesthetics and race, sex/gender, and class problems in America are so obvious, few scholars have bothered to approach Homer as a performance in which narrative is just one of numerous elements in the storytelling we may better apprehend by studying epic performance instead of making assumptions about myth from the *Iliad* and *Odyssey* narratives or archetypes. Indeed, what need for study of other epics if, as Aristotle first indicated in *Poetics* and literary theorists like Mikhail Bakhtin and Northrop Frye accepted, "Homer was the first to use all of the [epic's formal] elements in a completely satisfactory way" (Bakhtin, "Epic" 39)?[4]

Fortunately, recent transnational theories and work on traditional African epics disprove this Aristotelian fallacy. The modern, narrative-based Homeric archetype may be too obvious and unambiguous, but the epic performance and its relationship to the novel and society are not. If Homer and the European literary tradition, which have been too transnational as far as West Africa is concerned since the mid-fifteenth century, are the foundational paradigms for Western literature and much of its civilization, imagine the monkey-wrench thrown into this ages-old universal if, out of the heart of darkness, the Congo, there comes an epic performance not associated with conquest? What if another, performed in present-day Nigeria, hails from a matrilineal society featuring a supreme Goddess? And what, finally, if there exists a third extant epic performance tradition in Senegambia, one whose imperialistic past has itself long fallen to the capriciousness of Fate to become an epic of ethnic unity in this conquered, colonized, and then post-colonial region?

Such are the *Mwindo Epic*, *Ozidi Saga*, and *Sunjata Epic* traditions, none of which is imperialistic now; the *Ozidi Saga* never belonged to an empire, and the Banyanga have never been conquest-oriented, though their *Mwindo*, in many respects, is more epical and mythological than the others and is realistic enough to recognize the potentiality—salutary and cataclysmic—of epic within humanity. Simultaneously full of epic potency and yet toothless, the binaries represented by these epics collapse in a number of ways helpful to us. They provide actual examples of how epic mythology is performed, the role of the individual body and the body-politic, the place of mind and body, a perspective on gender not obfuscated by the rise of nation-states and bourgeois hyper-individualism, and, perhaps most instructively, lessons beyond the "epics are bad because you do bad things to 'other' people" paradigm. Beyond battlefield endeavors of the Heroic Age scholars easily dismiss, these epics speak to and perform the *self*-victimization of the individual in full Trojan War mode and, more importantly, in an ontological frame in which the martial has become civic norm.

In short, these epics have bad-ass protagonists and antagonists, males and females, but no existing empire—or even past will-to-empire in some cases. What is the common element, if any, that these performances can convey to us in the Homer-centric literary tradition that, in fact, is all too full of performative folkness, though most classics scholars could/would never admit it? The answer to this performance-related question, I argue, is the transnational frame, useful, especially for those of West/Central African descent in the Americas, as a form of *New Epic Studies* that has as its object of study the *epic performance in the diaspora*. Thinking broadly about epic and novel and "planetary modernisms," as Wai Chee Dimock's work encourages us to do, and the absolute distance of Homeric *narrative* from Homeric *performance* Gregory Nagy has brilliantly excavated, puts Homer in the diasporic New World space just as surely as the Mwindic-Ozidic-Sunjatic ("MOS") tradition is part of the African Diaspora.

The MOS-epic speaking-performance here is not top-down, greatness trickling green vitality down to the mouth-open and head-empty *demos*, or even the call-and-response staple of Africana studies, but a tricky call-and-be-called-out. "On with the story, man!" and "Tell it on, man!" the aged

Okabou Ojobolo, storyteller *par excellence*, is repeatedly *called-out* to do by his jocular auditor-participants.[5] It's enough stress to make a strong man, not to mention a seventy-something-old fellow like Ojobolo, hard pressed to hold his water. His sweating is a rather nominal part of his performance, which includes, not surprisingly, rather frequent sprints to the Old Bard's room.

The revolutionary, nonmilitaristic comeuppance of this jocular episode is lost if literariness, Europeanness, and Homeric epic are established as given universals. The leakiness is not just a personal weakness and response, but allusion to a greater threat seldom addressed: the ecological, green dimension of myth that speaks not only for us but to and against us.

The methodological urgency guiding this study of epic performance should be all too clear: "Everything," Walter Benjamin notes in seeking to define allegory, is relevant when it comes to comprehending the epic performance in a given society (233). The challenge for would-be traditional African epic performance experts who believe, like myself, that epic heroics can be positive and spiritually salutary, is extreme; it requires one to balance artistry with structure/function and resist an apolitical insistence on epic artistry, with an attendant sense of supremacy, and the reduction or dismissal of African artistry, creativity, and higher thinking faculties to fit into an anthropologist's typology of ritual.

For an African Americanist studying the epic performance, where the social epic of slavery and racism is real and now, everything is valuable. I see in the notion of *nyama*—a soul force of West African epic creativity, of the land of sol, and beyond—an organic precursor to Benjamin's notion of "philosophical allegory," the everything needed to reconcile the contradictions and dangers inherent in the heroic epic. The luxury of being closely associated with one's African roots, as Okpewho is,[6] or a scholar who has the luxury of her or his culture to study another, is simply not possible for the African American activist-scholar, whose nation saddles him or her, as W.E.B. Du Bois famously observed, with

> two-ness,—an American, a Negro; two souls, two thoughts, two unreconciled strivings; two warring ideals in one dark body, whose dogged strength alone keeps it from being torn asunder. The history of the American Negro is the history of this strife,—this longing to attain self-conscious manhood, to merge his double self into a better and truer self. In this merging he wishes neither of the older selves to be lost. He would not Africanize America, for America has too much to teach the world and Africa. He would not bleach his Negro soul in a flood of white Americanism, for he knows that Negro blood has a message for the world. . . .
>
> This, then, is the end of his striving: to be a co-worker in the kingdom of culture, to escape both death and isolation, to husband and use his best powers and his latent genius. (Du Bois, *Souls* 11)

Implicit in his conceit of "double-consciousness" articulated above, is the answer to my dilemma as an African American. Humanity comprises "co-workers" who offer unique cultural insights—Negro and American—for the "kingdom of culture." Here, the man merges into the (artistic) text and (sociopolitical) context to impart important methodological essentials: lyricism, which created a sublime statement making *Souls* an instant classic that emotionally stirred numerous African-American writers and poets; social scientific insight, borne of Du Bois' quantitative work as a sociologist documenting the black condition as well as qualitative fieldwork into the Black Belt; and what Robert B. Stepto called its "pregeneric" and "extrageneric" character, which "assembled" autobiography, sociology, history, political science, spirituals, and fiction. The overall result, Stepto maintains, is that *Souls* is orchestrated, not just assembled, and more transcendental (metaphorical and archetypical) than technical ("edited, prosaic, documentary"). Du Bois' methodology moves from classical Western *technê* to a soulful fusion of art and technique (*From behind* 52–53).

Du Bois' insistence that "all Art is propaganda" ("Criteria" 782) makes the right "sounds," as Houston Baker understands them to signify (*Modernism* xv). Setting aside the possibility of a Utopic Nowhere where nonoppression abides, function and form are synergistic: liminal and transgressive figures, tricksters and epic heroes, all occupy the creative space needed to thwart oppressive order and make possible its consequence, re-ordering. In essence, everything falls into this dynamic.

Indeed, the "Setting" for this dynamic performance, as the late August Wilson saw and wrote it, is "an ancient two-story brick house set back off a small alley in a big-city neighborhood" (xv). One half of this "ancient two-story" follows middle-aged Troy Maxson, a sanitation worker and former Negro Leagues homer-hitter who has always been hemmed in by, and is thus still swinging for, the fences. His life is a "ritual of talk and drink" (1) borne of racism, epical social forces, and blue(s) collar existence: risqué storytelling and hyperbole, sexual innuendo, bullying of his sons, and a love affair that threatens to destroy all the good he has built, brick by brick. So reads the ironic surface of *Fences* (1986), Wilson's *Cosby Show*–era drama. Taking middle-class readers' stereotypes of strong black males as part of genesis, Wilson stages conflict between Troy's Old World common-sense and the New World class-consciousness of his wife Rose's desire for white picket "fences" and his sons' wishes for the material ease of racial "progress." Herein lies the real tragedy: not only is being "twice as good" (34) insufficient to live the American Dream, but any local, gradual success by blacks under this epic ontology almost ensures a spectacular collapse in the future.

Notwithstanding the sharp irony that Wilson uses to structure Troy's dark side, the other half of the "two-story," a more "ancient" performance of the Trojan (American) diaspora, is far darker and deadlier. After all, if an angry, trash-talkin' Achilles could call Agamemnon "dog-face" (Homer/Hammond, *Iliad* 54), then it should be no surprise that a postbellum, white-trash performance of white supremacy betrays hip hop, bling-bling aesthetics. In this regard, consider Charles W. Chesnutt's 1901 description of a white supremacist: "Captain McBane wore a frock coat and a slouch hat; several buttons of his vest were unbuttoned, and his solitaire diamond blazed in his soiled shirt-front like the headlight of a locomotive" (*Marrow* 53). This Scottish-American "bane" to all African Americans is nevertheless a native son who betrays urbane badness decades before the birth of rap and, significantly, represents generations of many Americans to come.

Against all the canon-based logic and intuitive judgments, I argue that one solution to this performance of white supremacy and self-inflicted agony is a turn *toward* the traditional heroic epics of West and West Central Africa. For African American scholars such as myself, and writers like Toni Morrison, I argue, the existence of traditional African heroic epic performances has particular, not-so-obvious meaning. Though the epic or grand narrative has received considerable attention, much of the examination has been too metaphorical, tangential, modern, and literary. For example, Eugene Redmond's "The Black American Epic: Its Roots, Its Writers" (1971), Nathan Huggins' *The Black Odyssey: The Afro-American Ordeal in Slavery* (1977), and Kimberly Benston's idea that "Afro-American literature may be seen as one vast genealogical poem" (Gates, *Signifying* 123)[7] all point to the same problem. But missing, as ironic and uncanny as it may sound, is the real body: not individual bodies, racialized and gendered, though these are *sine qua non*, but the performing, epical body, which is a collective body-politic blacked-out in narrative considerations. Perhaps it is the modern (I mean this broadly and inclusively, including postmodern criticism) bent: we moderns do not perform; only the Other performs. What does it really mean to perform the master narrative?

Keith Cartwright, speaking of the epicality immanent in Du Bois' *Souls*, foregrounds the "singing tree"—Mother Africa—as Du Bois' eco-centric trope for the recovery of a lost African self (*Reading Africa* 11–13). Mother Africa, widely acknowledged by biblical and scientific scholars to be our roots, frames everything for me, just as Benjamin said the "idea" of anything "has its roots in the extreme. Just as a mother is seen to begin to live in the fullness of her power only when the circle of her children, inspired by the feeling of her proximity, closes around her, so do ideas come to life only when extremes are assembled around them" (Benjamin 35). The epic potential we all possess demands a motherly embrace because together they encapsulate the horrendous costs to Others and the Self associated with performing epic myths outside of organic, ecological context.

We are, all of us, and everything, within this "circle." The only real question for this project—as distinguished from Africanist imperatives represented by the aforementioned scholars—is not Why? (do you use this method), but for Whom?

The answer: for all of US . . .

EXORDIUM: *SUNDIATA* AND *OZIDI* AS EPIC PHENOMENA

The history and modern performances of two epics, one Malian and the other Nigerian, demonstrate both the antiquity and the totality of these phenomena. Thus, as early as the fourteenth century A.D., Ibn Battuta heard griots praising a Malian king by invoking Sunjata's[8] genealogy. The griotic invocation, a continuing tradition spanning centuries, occurs septennially between late March and early May. At this time, before the rainy season of the Western Sudan begins, after ten kola nuts arrive at Kangaba (considered the birthplace of numerous West African ethnic groups), and following two full moons, the cycle begins anew. At the center of this cycle is the Kamabolon ceremony, which marks the return of Sunjata. More than a performance or a reenactment, although these, too, the five-day Kamabolon ceremony symbolizes the re-creation of history and life itself, which the Kamabolon sanctuary embodies. On the fourth day of the ceremony, thousands of travelers and pilgrims hear the genealogy of Sunjata, considered by many to be the founder of the Mande (or Manding) culture and the ancient Malian empire as well as the heart of the Republic of Mali. The Kamabolon ceremony is specifically designed to reconstitute society in much the way that a blacksmith forges and molds metal. From eleven villages it draws upon the Keita, Sunjata's descendants, and from Kela, home of the Diabate griots, those wordsmiths who use language to forge and re-create a new society. During those five days, a new age group, or *kare*, is integrated into the old society.[9] The *kare* builds a wooden hedge around the old Kamabolon sanctuary, creating a "dancing place" called the *bara*, removes the old roof, and, armed with long reeds, protects the sacred space thus created. The *bara*'s task is very important, for Kamabolons bear the significance of other sanctuaries *qua* "gatehouses" located throughout West Africa. They occupy a significant symbolic role for the structure of Mande society itself. The interior walls of the Kamabolon bear ritualistic markings relevant to the ceremony.

Since Mande society is precariously exposed and anarchy prevails in this "hot" (i.e., transitory) state, which the roofless Kamabolon sanctuary represents, the "heat" created or embodied by other things or activities is forbidden. The *kare* has the critical role of protecting this space until Friday afternoon, at which time the local youths directly descended from Sunjata reinstall the roof, the event which will "cool" and stabilize society. The new/old order established, travelers and pilgrims are now free to approach and touch the new roof of the restored Kamabolon, and then take their blessings back home with them.

But none of this would be possible if not for the *Mansa Jigin*, the "gathering of the kings," which begins on Thursday afternoon and lasts virtually all night long as a nocturnal incantation. It is the witnessing of this event—held on the last two days of the Kamabolon ceremony—for which the throng gathers. They amass to see the Diabate griots of Kela, who officially enter the Kamabolon hot space on Thursday afternoon. In solemn progression with thousands of eyes upon them,[10] the *jeliw*, or griots, have walked from Kela along the "old road" in simple but appropriate adornments and light brown cotton hats as dictated by tradition.

Led by the *kumatigi*, "the master of words," they swear to uphold the taboo of silence with any outsider until Friday, and are prepared to perform for hours without respite. Soon, the Diabate begin the *Mansa Jigin*, the defining moment of the Kamabolon ritual, for their incantations empower the Keita youth to lift the roof and restore society. Once the Diabate enter the darkened interior of the Kamabolon sanctuary, which obstructs vision and retards nearly all sound, music begins, perhaps the *Sunjata fasa* ("praise song for Sunjata"), for thirty minutes.

After dinner, and at other times during the late night, the Diabate exit, make their ritualistic journey around, and then reenter the Kamabolon. Starting before dinner and lasting about four hours, then ranging from 9 p.m. until 6 a.m. the next morning and briefly the next afternoon as the *kumatigi* recites praise lines during the installation of the new roof, the *Mansa Jigin* performance consists of one unifying element: the recitation of the Sunjata epic to cool society down before the roof is affixed.[11]

The unique Kamabolon ceremony is not the only one of this genre in West Africa. If one travels farther south, a similar event of more recent pedigree but still indeterminate age unfolds in the recesses of the Niger delta. Despite lacking the intense and sometimes violent secrecy attendant with the *Mansa Jigin*, and situating ownership in the public domain as opposed to the Diabate griots, its ritualistic significance is perhaps no less. Consequently, this cultural performance is not told in the sacrosanct space of a sanctuary, but draws upon a narrator, actor-performers, a chorus, and spectators in a public artistic orchestration featuring narrative, dance, music, mime, and ritual. Set in Orua, the ancestral home of the Ijo, a seven-day festival begins when seven virgins are directed to the home of a storyteller. After the virgins pay homage to him and his personal gods, the white-clad storyteller, the *Amananaowei* ("the town-owner"), and the town elders begin an august singing procession in which the virgins are led "to the stream washing the feet of every Ijo village." In obeisance to the water spirit whose blessings are required for the successful issue of the festival, the procession makes a sacrifice to ensure fecundity in both art and life. Seven pots are filled with water so that the spirit of the stream may be in attendance.

The worship officially over, the procession takes up a lively pace of song and dance as it shadows the stream until reaching the public square of the marketplace. Here, the ozi master-drum awaits them, along with the *okoin*, *kainga*, and *ekere* drums as accompaniment. Soon the *ogele* dance begins, women following the men, more and more people joining by voice, step, and hands all the way to the market. Meanwhile, three sides of the public square fill with rows of children and adults, the remaining side left open for the stream, forest on the far bank, and skies. Adolescents scramble into mango and coconut trees, stand atop canoes being carved near the stream, and climb onto rooftops to improve their view.

Each day for seven days the festival begins this way as the spectators await the storyteller, who is both the narrator and the epic-protagonist, accompanied by a troupe of actors, a chorus of male dancers, a group of women to provide rhythmic hand-clapping, and the musicians. Even in the absence of props both natural and artificial, for the public square is otherwise bare, the stage is now set: when the narrator-protagonist waves his fan for the audience, directing the blade of his sword to the far bank of the river, Orua, an ancient city-state of broad highways transversing swamps and streams, comes to life. In the collective consciousness of the Ijo people, Orua, or Oruabou, the realm providing the foundation to their own cosmology, exists in an heroic age of gods loose among humankind.[12] It does so largely on the tongue of the narrator whose masterful repertoire of artistry and ritual includes verse, peroration, metaphor, simile, imagery, hyperbole, and onomatopoeia.

In the midst of all of this, a story is told of a hero's quest to avenge his father's death. This is no simple matter of honor restored, for if the son does not succeed the father's soul cannot join the ancestors because it will be forever entrapped in an evil grove. The consequences could be dire, for the Ijo believe that the ancestors provide integral assistance to the living by guiding and blessing them. Fortunately, the story ends happily: the hero defeats his enemies and becomes the ruler of a land purged of evil, living with his grandmother and mother in their *fatu*, or "final womb," which is his (grand)mother's ancestral home. All of this and more, unfolding over four hours each day for seven nights, is the festival and epic of the same name: *The Ozidi Saga*.

These grand ceremonies, though useful because they delimit the scale of some of the performances, are also misleading. They are staged but not scripted events and, more importantly, are often much less resplendent. Like Ozidi, Sunjata, and epic heroes in West/Central Africa and elsewhere, Mwindo is himself capable of the sublime, a "producer of wonder (*mpunda*) as common people are not." His birth is a variation on *in media res*, fingered by Aristotle in *Poetics* as evidence of Homer's greatness, for he literally emerges from Nyamwindo's middle finger. However, contra the *Ozidi Saga* and Sunjatic performances narrated above, the *Mwindo Epic* unfolds informally before villagers or the "hunting camp," where there are "no large crowds and no diverse musical instruments for big dances; there is no reason for major celebrations, initiations, or rituals." Close ties and friends constitute the milieu, and men, women, and Pygmies may be part of the audience. The "percussion stick," also used in circumcision rituals, provides accompaniment to the narrative and song (Aristotle 38–39; Biebuyck, *Hero* 17–18, 91–93). Similarly, Sunjata performances may be equally nondescript, familial, personal, and local. Spanning the highly formal and informal, the occasions include, among other things, high-tech production studios and "local family events" such as weddings, family reunions, banquets, birthdays, births, and graduations (Conrad, "Introduction" 5; Newton 322–25).

As compelling as the epic protagonist and this description of the performance may be, together they constitute but a masquerade calculated to provide sights and sounds for easy consumption. This masquerade, or mask, may seem to be little more than a sublime carnival of glory for "great" people, especially since it is easy enough to apprehend epic grandeur in the context of the good/bad dichotomy represented, Hegel opined, by "troubled days" or a "world-situation" in which one group stands at the "bar of history" (*Aesthetics* 1051, 1061). However, studies of epic performance dynamics reveal the complex reality beneath the mask of glory, a complexity involving all the parts and, of course, their greater sum. Epic narrative, Homeric narrative, and literary epics are the parts; to truly understand epic, narrative needs to be situated in a generic performance not folded into modernity and the nation-state, which then become the lenses by which epic performance is understood. Instead, modernity and the nation-state must be understood, in substantial ways, as expressions of ongoing epic performance of planetary, ages-old dimensions.

The Epic Trickster is calibrated for this particular dynamic, for it situates epic performance—nuanced for the role of the trickster genre ascribed to the hegemony's Other—as its generic focus. Consequently, this study, consistent with my attempt to avoid unduly theoretical jargon that stifles activists and the policy potential of such studies by making them inaccessible to lay readers, includes everything between the epic and the trickster, except for the proverbial kitchen sink.

It is fitting, then, that the next chapter of *The Epic Trickster* subverts the millennia-old, Homer-based ideas about the heroic epic first articulated in Aristotle's *Poetics*. It introduces the traditional West/Central African epic performance with its common essence, the African epic trickster, and its encounter with the West. Central to my goal of fleshing out its dynamism, I concentrate on its own unique form of allegory, the insights nonteleological and nonarchetypal approaches to the epic protagonist reveal, and the cautionary aesthetic native to the performance of traditional West/Central African heroic epic performances.

Contra the canonical approach of establishing European/American culture as the timeless universal, and in accord with scholars who recognize the "deep time" contained in genres and their cultural spaces, Chapter 3 frames the East/West, African/European encounter as an *epic performance diaspora*. With neither native to North America, both African and European cultures are essentially simultaneous incursions into American Indian cultural spaces; both are part of a diaspora. Of course, the African and European influences did not enter as coequals: the Homeric performance arrived under a logic of conquest later authorized and rationalized by the U.S. Supreme Court in *Johnson v. M'Intosh* (1823), a case about property rights in Illinois, while MOS-epics arrived in the cramped holds of slave ships that forcibly brought millions of Africans into such spaces as cargo.

Thus, Chapter 3 represents my movement to an African/American frame in which I attempt to construct an epic performance context. Though shared by the enslaved Africans and the mainstream American community, this space was and is mediated—indeed, policed—by racial divides arising out of the epical imaginary. In this chapter, I foreground American Homeric iconography as a way of delineating the contents of the modern American performance of Homer. Homer, a root metaphor and cornerstone of creative Selfhood, is a constant performance in the New World and new nation. With the rise and constitution of America as a new nation, *La Quarelle des Anciens et Modernes*—the centuries-old debate in Western Europe about the greatness of the ancients compared to the moderns—entered a new, intensified phase.

This new phase, which coincides with slavery, establishes the foundation for the African-American epic trickster aesthetic that emerges in the 1870s, the postbellum period known as the "Nadir." Starting with the Nadir and using forty-year increments equivalent to the Hebrews' time in the wilderness, an Old Testament form of "bad lands," I foreground the work of three preeminent African-American novelists as a way of tracing the evolution of the epic trickster figure and aesthetic in African-American culture, storytelling, and literature.

In Chapter 4, I engage in a literary and critical race theory reading of Charles W. Chesnutt's *The Marrow of Tradition* (1901), a novel situated in the epically charged environment of (Homer) *Plessy v. Ferguson* (1896) and violent white supremacy. It is also one of the earliest appropriations of the African-American epic trickster folk figure, which Chesnutt uses as he constructs his own form of literary jurisprudence. Hinging on a cautionary ethos associating racism, the social disease of Wellington, and Homeric performance, *Marrow* offers a complex allegory. This strategy, based on the specific excavation of people, events, and places from North Carolina, New Orleans, and the British Empire, allows Chesnutt to render his own judgment: because the "marrow of tradition" is also a "heart of darkness," the prognosis for the American body-politic is dire.

The epical cautionary ethos Chesnutt taps for his medico-juridical rhetoric and judgment is also portable to other dimensions of the Homeric diaspora in America. One of those involves the ecological crises intellectual writers and activists have been addressing since the early decades of the twentieth century. Chapter 5, inspired by Richard Wright's call in "Blueprint for Negro Writing" (1937), responds with an eco-critical reading of Wright's *Native Son* (1940) and *Black Boy* (1945). Featuring the bad man or bad nigger ('bigger") type as a protagonist, these works, I argue, warrant a reading alongside the eco-critical elements of West/Central African epics, the urbanized epic trickster, and eco-epical crises, *viz.*, the 1930s Dust Bowl, Hurricane Katrina, and now global warming. Specifically, I seek to add Wright's *Native Son* to the canon of Dust Bowl literature exemplified by John Steinbeck's *The Grapes of Wrath* (1939). By excavating Wright's attention to eco-critical concerns, I hope to broaden and nuance understanding of the bad man aesthetic and reveal how Wright's "protest literature," *greened* by the ecological knowledge indigenous to African epic performance traditions, blossoms into a cautionary aesthetic that recognizes the catalytic potential residing within the deformed (racially, socioeconomically, etc.). The agency within the black community, insofar as it is an American hunger for equal rights, equal access, and middle-class consumption, is a double-edged sword representing bigger eco-critical problems.

My final close reading chapter is an attempt to use the common/sense aesthetic of the African-American community as the heuristic for understanding individual performances of excellence in an American society whose social contract is based, in significant part, on Homeric performance. No post–Civil Rights author appreciates Africa's participatory aesthetics more than Toni Morrison; few novels, if any, achieve the sublimity of her neo-slave epic, *Beloved* (1987). While Morrison's Africanist aesthetic is well known, no scholar has fully used the African epic performance as a critical lens to excavate meaning in her literature. Indeed, Morrison is the apotheosis of the epic trickster aesthetic as an African-American bearing its *common/sense* from her storytelling ancestors, and as a writer who makes strategic literary appropriations, among them, I argue, West/Central African epic performances. Reading *Beloved* as the culmination of the epic trickster aesthetic embodied in a *common/sense*, participatory dynamic, I pair post-1960s black proverbial wisdom with the Africa-influenced artistry of the community Morrison taps to comment upon epical, excellent efforts to overcome race-ism. As Morrison would have it, the premodern and postmodern divides are collapsed in this manner.

The Epic Trickster, of course, seeks the old and ancient within the new. My conclusion and seventh chapter, then, gestures toward film, hip hop, Afro-Orientalism, and Afro-futurism as domains very much in need of the African/American epic trickster's second sight. Hence, OH READER, if the so(u)lful existence of a traditional African heroic epic storytelling performance, and its rapping cogitations, muscular "cool," trickster quick-step, and Heroic Age sci-fi, disrupts your notion of Epic-as-Homeric paradigm, read no further! You are likely to get hurt a *dozens*-times. But you are not faint of heart, and if cool your epic body is and stodgy it ain't, then *this* "Odyssey" is for you . . .

US-AGE LEGEND

A few brief words about my terms and tone. It should be amply clear that the term *epic* used herein is about cultural performance. Older than Homer's narrative, or the anonymous *Epic of Gilgamesh* narrative, the epic performance is one of the oldest catalogs and metrics of greatness (actual and apparent) humans have.

Hence, my style often flows between grounded theory, as criticism for scholars and those invested in literature and performance aesthetics, and creative nonfiction, for the people: the *people* are African-and-all-of-US-Americans, hence my hip (hop), folksy usage. Several key, hip (hop) terms are important in this regard.

- Allegorye/Allegorycal: the performance- and context-driven allegorye is an aesthetic mode far more universal and ancient than typography- and narrative-based allegory/allegorical.
- US denotes "us" and the United States of America, of course, but it also represents all of us, as in Mother-of-US-all-Africa.
- West/Central Africa(n) denotes West and West Central Africa.
- MOS-epic references the three West/Central African traditional epic performance traditions collectively; when I reference a specific traditional African epic tradition, I will refer to the Sunjata (Sunjatic), Mwindo (Mwindic), or Ozidi (Ozidic) performances.

My sincere hope, of course, is that my method inspires other work in New Epic Studies to better understand the Diaspora and this modern world of US-all-Americans.

2 Introduction to West/Central African Epic

> All of you, open your ears and listen to me. I am not talking any more, the story I didn't start is finished.
>
> —Okabou Ojobolo, "Night Two," *The Ozidi Saga* (60)

> The presently known heroic epics occur in societies that exhibit a wide range of social structures, political and religious systems, and historical backgrounds. . . . Of these observations, the most fascinating is probably that great heroic epic traditions do also occur among people who have no traditions of conquest or a centralized political system.
>
> —Daniel P. Biebuyck, "The African Heroic Epic" (337–38)

The phenomenon of the African epic, the story no one starts, finishes, or even talks, was deeply integrated into traditional African culture. For hundreds, maybe thousands of years, the African epic has been much more than an art form. Indeed, to characterize these traditional epics as long oral poems narrating the heroic exploits of individuals who are facing national threats to their communities diminishes the real vitality they embody. Against the canonical definition privileging the individual, heroic ethos operating in the service of great nations or empires, African epics emerge from a variety of sociopolitical contexts, some having nothing at all to do with idealistic notions of an Heroic Age of antiquity. At its most glorious, the African epic has enthralled royalty in the capitols of great empires, large masses at magnificent ceremonies, and awestruck youths awaiting their rites of passage. In its less bombastic moments, it has passed time for seasoned veterans wandering far from home in savannah or tropical forest. Its totality, its phenomenology, arises from an epic habitus encompassing all those things African. It can be found wherever there is the simple pluck of the ngoni, hodda, and mvet lutes, the strumming of a kora, a calabash guitar, the living beat of drums such as the jembe, or the ozi master-drum and its kainga-drum accompaniment, and the call of the bugle. At its center is life and death, belief and practice, love and violence, harmony and war, all of which are immanent in the human voice and the perorations, metaphors, allusions, and tropes of the griots and bebom-mvetts, those "vessels of speech . . . which harbour secrets many centuries old" and for whom the "art of eloquence has no secrets" (Niane, *Sundiata* 1). Along with the people and cultures they represent, and as part of countless ceremonies and gatherings, the epics these wordsmiths perform even today are part of a larger economy of signification that links the epic habitus to the body bio-logic and body-politic. Moreover, they are also symptoms in two competing and yet complementary senses: as rich cultural signifiers deeply embedded in the psyche, en-fleshed through the body, and evoked as a sociopolitical externality, but also as symptoms of trauma operating at the same levels in response thereto. These epics, in short, as artistic cultural performances, collectively embody the ancient phenomenology of African culture.

Performance dynamics, uniting art, culture, and politics into one vibrant, ever-shifting space organically attuned to the surrounding world, move tra-ditional West and Central African epics far beyond the sublimity of the individual hero(ine) and great civilization, and far beyond the literary—and sedentary—narrative all too often elevated as its universal essence.

The protagonists of *The Ozidi Saga*, *The Epic of Mwindo*, and *Sunjata* do not, in fact, begin, sustain, or end their careers as epic heroes. This is true even as Ojobolo of Sama characterizes his hero, who carries a seven-pronged sword, as one whose terrible and mighty battle affirmation is the "sound of hornbill, sound of kingfisher, oh Ozidi the grove! oh Ozidi the grove! sound of monkey—I am, I am, I am!" (Clark, *Ozidi Saga* 63; subse-quent citations noted as *OS*). Mwindo, according to Shé-kárisi Rureke, was "born with a conga-scepter, holding it in his right hand," "born with an adze, holding it in his left hand," and "born with a little bag of the spirit of Kahombo, wearing it slung across his back on the left side; in that little bag there was a long rope (within it)" (Biebuyck and Mateene, *Mwindo Epic* 57; subsequent citations noted as *ME*). And Sunjata, according to Mamou-dou Kouyaté, is "the son of the Buffalo, the son of the Lion," the "hero of many names," and seventh and "last conqueror on earth" who followed but was greater than Alexander the Great (Niane, *Sundiata* 2, 83). Notwith-standing such honorific epithets, they have consanguinity with tricksters in one or more manners, a point implicitly recognized by John William John-son as he speaks of the evolution of Sunjata: "Beginning as a cripple, the limping hero goes through several transformations, each gaining him more power than the last, until finally he is the most powerful hero to have ever lived" ("Yes, Virginia" 318). Sunjata's physical deformity is matched by his cognitive impairment as a slow, moody child. Although Mwindo and Ozidi do not share these deformities, except to the extent they are too young and inexperienced at first, both of them share three other deformities or dis-abilities in their early careers: social/political, maternal, and geospatial.

All three, Sunjata, Ozidi, and Mwindo, are politically and socially deformed. Thus, Daniel Kunene makes the salient observation that one of the decisive occurrences that sends the epic hero on the journey is a deformation in which the community denies the hero his rightful share of patrimony or inheritance (213). Indeed, though, one must extend this logic further, for the denial of an heir among several heirs of coequal vestment would hardly be cause for initiating an epic journey.[1] Thus, it is not just the rejection of an heir, but the specific denial of his predestined entitlement as a future leader—be it political, ethical, militaristic, or all three—who is vital to the well-being of the society itself which deserves materiality.

But this reading of the epic protagonist's centrality depends on classical, teleological, and unduly flat assumptions about great leaders and civilizations. The epic artistry, combined with a broad range of cultural perspectives on heroic epic protagonists, also offers statements about morality, being, and the salutary and deleterious potential of epic performance. Again, the morality here is not reducible to goodness/badness, for West/Central Africans traditionally associated the endeavors of the living, the ancestors, and the natural ecology represented by the cosmology of the spirit world. The MOS-epics should not be interpreted anthropocentrically, based on a contest of wills, or any odyssey about mythical and natural challenges surmounted.

The heroic exploits, transgressive and otherwise, which are performed on an epic scale cannot be overlooked, for as symptoms they are also markers of the uniqueness of the hero-to-be. But a qualitative difference steeped in irony characterizes the early narratives of these epics, which together serve as a pivot which establishes these protagonists as trickster-types and epic figures. They are not tricksters *proper*, but ironic/epic tricksters with epic potential soon to be manifest. As the narratives of Mwindo, Sunjata, and Ozidi attest, only when this formative—not formal, or proper—trickster period has passed will these heroes mature into their epical character. Thus, Nyamwindo, Mwindo's mother, the seventh and favorite wife who is "the preferred one" (*ME* 54), is deformed because Shemwindo has issued an edict forbidding his wives to give birth to any males. While the other six wives promptly and properly give birth, Nyamwindo suffers an extended pregnancy that makes her the *bête noire* of the other wives and the community. When she does give birth, to a boy, Shemwindo immediately levels the powers of the state against him and "Nyamwindo [who has been] turned into the despised one" (60). Already isolated and orphaned because his mother cannot help him, Mwindo engages in an assortment of measures, including back- and double-talk, directed against the injustices of his father. Nevertheless, Shemwindo succeeds, with the help of the townsfolk of Tubondo, in shipping the infant Mwindo off in a sealed drum to float down the river to meet his doom. Here, Mwindo has to also outwit Mkuti, a water spirit who would do him harm. Defiled by his own father and community, Mwindo sings of his impending death which he—through his quick, ironic tongue—twists and turns into a song against his tormentors and would-be killers:

I am saying farewell to Shemwindo;
I shall die, oh Bira!
The counselors abandoned Shemwindo.

Scribe, move on!
The counselors will turn into dried leaves.
What will die and what will be safe
Are going to encounter Iyangura. (64)

Only by using various wiles to reach his paternal aunt, Iyangura, can Mwindo then acquire the necessary tools—symbolized by the connection to his aunt, a metaphor for the absence of paternal justice—to engage in direct physical combat with his nemesis, Shemwindo, in an effort to purge the land of corruption.

Sunjata, even in Niane's westernized novelization, is likewise situated. Prophesied to be a great empire builder, he is nevertheless born to a physically deformed mother. His mother, one of the most unattractive maidens in her native land of Du/Do,[2] is called, in Niane's text, Sogolon Kedjou (or Sogolon Kondouto) because she is a woman with a humped back. In accordance with prophecy, the Malian king marries Sogolon and consummates the union, leading to the birth of a son, Sunjata. His ugliness and physical deformity delight the king's first wife, Sassouma (or Saman), whose son is the handsome, adventurous, and ambitious firstborn. Sunjata has a large head, large eyes, and yet weak legs. Not only is he still crawling at the age of three, but also when he is seven. Moreover, he is melancholy, slow of tongue, and dangerous to other children because of his strong arms, while Sassouma's son is healthy and successful, by comparison. The king loses faith in the prophecy at one point and banishes Sogolon from his household. His faith is later restored, but he dies and Sassouma uses sorcery and collusion to deny the king's will and install her own son as regent, which imposes even more misery on Sogolon until she loses faith and strikes her son. He is now an early adolescent, between seven and nine years old. As soon as he is hit, Sunjata finally emerges as the prophesied one: he walks, bends a heavy iron bar into a bow, and uproots a tree. Immediately he becomes the people's beloved, but Sassouma's power over the state is too much of a threat to his family. Sunjata and his mother, along with their siblings, are forced to leave until such time as Sunjata has grown and become ready to return as a young warrior.

Finally, Ozidi, conceived as the result of the magical insemination of his mother, Orea, after his father is assassinated, also begins his life under the taboo of the city of Ado, state of Orua. Although he is the city's hero, his father is hated so much by Ado's other defenders that they scheme to murder him shortly after the crown legitimately passes to his ward. That ward, the last to receive the crown, is the most barren of the seven wards of the city, probably because of the city's spite against its own hero. After the generals murder his father, he is left defenseless with his mother and half-crazy uncle, Tegumegede. Fortunately, Ozidi is taken under the wings, quite literally, of his maternal grandmother,

Oreame. Both a remarkable sorceress and warrior, Oreame whisks her daughter and grandson off to her home far away so that she can begin schooling Ozidi in the ways of warfare in anticipation of his return to Ado. His challenge is no less formidable than those of his epic colleagues, for the younger Ozidi is just an adolescent when he confronts an array of fantastic foes: the Olotu (generals) from Orua such as Ofe the Short, Azezabife the Skeleton Man, Agbogidi of the Naked Parts, and Ogueren "of twenty hands, twenty feet" (*OS* 65); champions engage Ozidi in battle as his reputation spreads, like Tebesonoma of the Seven Crowns; and finally, once he has defeated the corrupt Olotu and many champions and regained his proper seat, he must fight against Anglese, the Smallpox King, and his invaders who arrive by boat wielding guns.

From this perspective on the early careers of Mwindo, Sunjata, and Ozidi, the evolution of the African epic hero *vis-à-vis* the community and the larger conflict comes into clearer focus. The African epic hero is not simply given this status as a "blackened hero," as Dean A. Miller observes, speaking of the relationship between tricksters and epic heroes (272–74, 364–66), but undergoes a complex process by which such a condition is meticulously worsened. The material condition of the epic hero, then, is often far from the teleological luminance customarily associated with the epic hero. This situation, in part, has already by identified by Joseph Mbele in his study of the African epic hero, "The Hero in the African Epic" (1986). To avoid the unitarian dilemma of oversimplifying the epic hero and to debunk the monological valorization of the epic hero, Mbele decenters and culturally contextualizes the African epic, the context of cultural conflict simultaneously rendering the hero relative and transgressive. Hence, Mbele argues for a reading of the epic hero, contra Hegel's idealism, that would see the trickster's liminality as "an integral part of the hero" (197). Mbele further states that the "Mande say that the hero is welcome on troubled days. Yet, it is these dreadful qualities that enable the hero to accomplish his mission. The hero embodies what in Mande philosophy is called *fadenya*, the force that impels the individual to 'work against the stabilizing and conservative forces of his society,' as Bird and Kendall put it" (198).

According to Mbele, then, the epic hero is fundamentally a transgressive entity who violates taboos, which makes him a liminal figure in much the same way as the trickster. The isomorphism between them is the centerpiece of the epic trickster model, which departs from Mbele's insight by recognizing the immanence of the trickster in the epic, the agency of the community, and the evolution of the epic hero's career irrespective of intercultural or international conflict. In other words, whereas Mbele's liminal/transgressive epic hero-trickster is dependent upon sociohistorical matters external to the epic, the epic trickster also recognizes a strictly internal dynamic. This internal essence runs a high risk of overheating, as the next section reveals.

THE EPIC PERFORMANCE: HIP "HOT" AND COOL

Like West and West Central African performances generally, epic performance is not just a narrative event, but is hip, hot, and cool. For example,
dance is traditionally regarded by numerous West African ethnic groups as
a form of power, inseparable from music, from narrative, and thus from
belief. Indeed, for some dancing is one of the most important elements of
African performance; for others it is drumming,[3] while music, spirituality,
and storytelling no doubt lay just claims to centrality, too. This quality
reinforces Henry Drewal's preference for a heterarchical model in lieu of
hierarchical taxonomies that rank the performative elements and thus miss
the point: African performance is best understood as "not just multimedia
events, but multisensorial ones" that require the perspective of multiple
performers, cultural insiders and outsiders (212). The "multisensorial"
African performance, including the traditional African epic performances
centered here, can rightly be understood as *common/sense*, an embodied
and organic form of wisdom-knowledge. This should not to be confused
with, and limited by, Western notions of common sense as a marker of
ordinary, reasonable, and prudent intelligence. West/Central African performance and dance traditions imported into slavery embody an aesthetics of vitality and equilibrium, angularity and asymmetry, composure and
balance, healing and purification, all in connection with the earth, a performance aesthetic which Robert Farris Thompson calls the "Cool" ("An
Aesthetic" 88–90).[4]

Indeed, not only do multiple forms of expression envelop the senses, but
even time and space are warped at the site of the communal performance.
The artistic and cultural strength of West African oral epics might very well
be their multiform fluidity, which simultaneously allows them to achieve a
sublime poetics through the interaction of narrative, performative virtuosity, and temporal flows. This is because "past and present coexist happily
in African mythology" and the bardic performers recognize "no rigid time
boundaries" (Biebuyck, *Hero* 3, 75–92; Okpewho, *African Oral* 50–51, and
Myth 72, 104–05). Not surprisingly, the epic performance for societies existing in organic association with their traditions, unlike modern nation-states,
is not separated by an "absolute" time and distance. The Mande's Sunjata
performance is a "rarefied space in which past and present merge" to link
family, community, and nation. The *Mwindo Epics* unfold in a time and place
"remote, but undetermined," and ultimately rooted in "timelessness" (Biebuyck, *Hero* 3). Ojobolo's performance might put "stress . . . on Orua, on
Oruabou, that is, the city seen as a state set in some remote time and place"
(Clark-Bekederemo, "Introductory" xxxvii) filled with impossible beings and
feats and the resurrection of the slain Ozidi the younger multiple times by
his sorceress grandmother, Oreame, but Ojobolo's "remote" past is peppered
with futuristic anachronisms. English-language expressions and idiom, along
with iconographic references—e.g., "Futbol" (football), "railway station,"

"electric pole," and Ozidi's "polo" shirt—simultaneously collapse time and distance and engage in post-colonial critique by associating such figures with the West (*OS* 107, 181, 263–64, 331).

The four temporal zones—the performance present, and the epic protagonist's past, present, and future (S. Belcher 111)—are complemented by an assumed futurity for the ethnic group. As an ancient form of time and space travel, the performance is both "intervention" and "reinvention": first, it is an "intervention" into a preexisting "complex of social interactions" and an epic narrative already fully developed. But it is far from mere rote, for stock epic performance elements, in accordance with the performers' abilities, allow for an artful "reinvention which breathes the life of shared cultural traditions into the circumstances of the present, and vice versa" (Newton 314–15).

The temporal multiplicity is significant, for the absolute distance of the ancient setting is deeply informed by present circumstances. This diachronic aesthetic, combined with performances attuned to *present* sociopolitical realities and the wide range of cultural differences of African groups, demands reconsideration of the automatic association of heroic epics with greatness *cum* empire. Indeed, these heroic epic performances may be a form of heteroglossia stripped of will-to-empire, for even the Sunjatic tradition, arising out of a "pluralistic world" of Old Mali (Austen, "Criminals" 388), now functions in a modern, post-colonial Mali as the common mythology "in a shifting landscape in which diverse systems and their institutions—Bamana or Maninka (and those of other regional language groups), Islamic, French, Malian state, or those of the international development community—are mixed and matched in the daily struggle to obtain resources and maintain the health and well-being of the extended family and community" (Newton 315). The Ozidi tradition incorporates into its Ijo-based performance Ibgo, British English, and cultural referents showing the influence of the Benin empire, albeit a nominal one (Okpewho, *Once* 19–20, 23). In the *Mwindo Epic* Biebuyck foregrounds for readers, heteroglossia also takes pre- and post-colonial form: Nyanga, the primary narrative language, sometimes transitions into Hunde, and "Nyanganized loanwords from French and Swahili" punctuate the narrative. Even this small forest-dwelling group has "complexity" engendered by "differing traditions"—Nyanga, Pygmies, immigrants from East Africa—that have "thoroughly amalgamated." In contrast to the monoglossia Bakhtin centers as an autocratic feature of traditional epics, the linguistic heteroglossia of the *Mwindo Epic*, contributing to its "international character," turns the Bakhtinian paradigm on its head. For the Nyanga, "Traditions of conquest and large-scale warfare are nonexistent." In fact, the Nyanga find the qualities that characterize epic protagonists—"[r]ashness, impetuosity, verbosity, arrogance, intemperance, ruthlessness, thoughtlessness, hardheartedness"— "amusing because of the unreality of the hero" and the hero's unethical behavior. Consonant with their peaceful, egalitarian values, the Nyanga consider its heroic epics as nonproprietary, light-hearted "*kakoro* (things of daytime), that is, as usually devoid of danger. They are not the sacred or esoteric texts that belong only to an exclusive group of people; they can be heard, enjoyed, and understood by all" (Biebuyck, *Hero* 5, 6).

Indeed, the hipness of Ozidi is a rich, ambiguous signifier, for hipness is a form of badness connoting total cool. It is a mask of power (the black leather jackets and gloves and dark shades of the Black Panthers and the Fonz), but also the literal and open laughter at Ozidi and all of the epic's figures, and the comic marginality bespeaking the trickster's presence, such laughter forming the Ijo *communitas* (Babcock-Abrahams 153; Clark-Bekederemo, "Introductory" xlviii; Okpewho, "Critical Introduction" xvii–xix). The trickster analog here is no mistake or mere coincidence, but a defining feature of the epic trickster aesthetic developed herein. The "teleological" and "monological" interpretations" that reduce the ambiguity and paradox of the epic protagonist are, not surprisingly, most directly challenged by the "coincidence of a trickster and a culture-hero." The temporal and spatial configurations considered unique to the trickster—"marketplaces, crossroads, and other open spaces which are 'betwixt and between' clearly defined social statuses and spaces" (Babcock-Abrahams 155, 157–65)—are essential to the ideal culture hero relevant to this study, the African epic hero. For example, the journey motif leads "away from home" into the "fluid spaces" and "exile" of Old Mali's wilderness (Kunene 207, 215), or the river that carries Mwindo "upstream . . . to the river's source, at Kinkunduri's," and "downstream" away from Tubondo (*ME* 65). With regard to this "exile," what Keith Cartwright calls the Malian "diaspora," the marketplace episode figures prominently because, as Cartwright observes, it serves as a critical moment in which "imperial motherwit" initiates Sunjata's return ("Reading" 35).

As these crossroads/crossing episodes demonstrate, the epic protagonist may be physically remarkable, but this hard epical body is nevertheless limited in its efficacy. In other words, and in contrast to Niane's *Sundiata* and to the westernized notion of the great mind and body, the hypermasculine epical body is leaky, so the maternal strength of patience and charity is needed to pass the important crossroads and crossings in life. Whereas hardness often represents precious strength needed for these crossings, rashness and selfishness makes this hardness a liability. Gold and silver are critical from the outset, for Fa-Digi Sisòkò notes that "'Wealth' is the 'Voice of Transgression'" (Johnson, *Epic* 81–82), and political greed and gold are often associated, while Sunjata is often associated with various forms of deformity, wilderness, and ruin—the leaky body.

HEGEL'S PROPHECY: *AESTHETIK*, RACE, AND MODERN HOMERIC PERFORMANCE

Homer occupies a mythical place in the Western imaginary in much the way that the mind disappears into the body through the creation of the nation-state. Homer exists at an absolute time and distance, as Bakhtin notes of the epic *vis-à-vis* the novel, but instead of being a detraction or caution sign, the Homeric residue serves to reinforce the primordial origins of Western civilization. Western philosophers imagined whole historical and aesthetic genealogies from these Homeric ruins. The epic poet, Georg Wilhelm Friedrich Hegel explains in *Vorlesungen über die Aesthetik*, or *Lectures on Aesthetics*, is close to the "entire world-outlook and objective manifestation of a national spirit" of the early "heroic" age (*Aesthetics* 1044, 1053) in which the epic protagonists are "whole men" whose strength is "self-disclosure" unfettered by the weakening bonds of "moral pedants" (1067). The epic poet writes in the "turning-point in world history," a revolutionary period in which the poet, no longer inclined to admire and be dominated by great model nations, can act with "free boldness of creation." "Only when the poet, with freedom of spirit, flings off such a yoke, can the period of epic proper dawn" (1046–48). Epics are essential to Hegelian thought, for they are memorials, "epic bibles" for "every great and important people" (1045).

Of course, Hegel is not only concerned with the epic aesthetics of Homer, the epic *Zeitgeist* par excellence, but the perfectly robust, racialized, gendered thinking-bodies of Achilles and Odysseus, who both precede Homer and succeed him by bequeathing their *Zeitgeist* to the Western body-politic. Important to note is that Hegel, writing in the early antebellum period of America, apparently reads its Revolutionary War victory against Britain and Europe in epical terms. America's rapid rise against the Old World is a decisive turn for Hegel, who imagines that any epics "that may perhaps be composed in the future" may "describe . . . the victory, some day or other, of living American rationality over imprisonment in particulars and measurements prolonged to infinity. For in Europe nowadays each nation is bounded by another and may not of itself begin a war against another European nation; if we now want to look beyond Europe, we can only turn our eyes to America" (1062).

A work steeped in epic ontology, Hegel's *Aesthetics* ventures beyond objective description toward a prescriptive subjectivity as he collapses the divide between art and politics, ancient past and the modern present. His study of aesthetics, which is a form of epic performance insofar as it notes the proper past and future conditions, becomes *prophecy*. Though he theorizes the "world-situation" (1053) appropriate for Homer, his exemplar for all epic bards (1051), Hegel's description establishes—prescribes, to be precise—Homer as the medium through which modern "noble savages" can reclaim their epicality. After all, the political economy of modernity is characterized by a morass of legalities, politics, and prosaic egoism until the world is "diametrically opposed in its plastic organization to the requirements we found irremissible for genuine epic" (1045–47, 1109). Hegel's Germany, charged with an epic performance that brought the British Empire to its dusk, would dismiss those European boundaries not once, but twice. Hegel's prophecy anticipates not just the rise of Hitler; America would demonstrate a sum of epic performance at least equal to that of Germany, and probably greater, based on the outcome of two Great Wars and the American Holocausts—*viz.*, American Indian history, slavery, racism, Jim Crow, and the threat of global warming.

As might be expected, in the climate in which Hegel valorized the ancients over the moderns and America over Europe in an antebellum era charged with racial implications, he defends Homer against the "barbaric idea," voiced by some scholars, that his "individual" poetic efforts "lack unity and are a mere juxtaposition of different sections composed in the same key" (1050–51). This would, of course, suggest that Homer belongs to a collaborative folk tradition and was not a "whole man" as idealized by Western scholars. In other words, Homer's mind and body, like neoclassical alabaster sculpture—and unlike traditional epic performances—must be a unified "whole" that has no significant flaws, fissures, or leaks.

Epic storytelling is not just a call to perfect, transcendent poetic narrative, as Aristotle, Hegel, and numerous others have suggested of Homeric narrative, or even a call-and-response performance, but a polyphonic participation in which the bard calls and may be called out. Aristotle's epic and dramatic "unity" and Hegel's "whole men" paradigms are roughed up considerably when the narrative and reader are exposed to the "world-situation" of the epic performance tradition far older than the *Iliad* and *Odyssey*. For example, Shekarisi Rureke interjects, "Substitute, replace me now!" (*ME* 14) in his narrative and during the Mwindic *rori*, loosely equivalent to epic digression; Nyanga bards "meditate," "rest," express "fatigue," and try to relocate the *iyanira*, the "thread of the story" (Biebuyck, *Hero* 25). Ojobolo is told, "No stuttering!" as he gets tongue-tied and finds himself mercilessly heckled by Owayei, a female auditor who is, he says, "forever at my back" (*OS* 336, 339). Though Mande epic performances are comparatively "static" compared to West/Central African performances (S. Belcher 29), with the *jeliw* being narrators accompanied by a *naamu*-sayer and limited musical accompaniment, the call-and-response, *jeli*-and-*naamu* dynamic moves toward a call and be called-out *intermezzo*. The participatory aesthetics may not be equivalent to the interjections of auditor-participants in the Mwindic and Ozidic performances,[5] but call and be called out has its place in the Manden, too. Sisòkò forgets narrative, repeats himself, and confuses characters, especially as the narrative matures and his fatigue increases.[6]

At any rate, the Western merger of Homer into Achilles and Odysseus as exemplification of the perfect mind-body-politic can hardly be gainsaid. Indeed, swift-footed Achilles, by virtue of his epithet, may metaphorize the importance of long-distance running, certain body features some scientists theorize as critical to human evolution, and presumably, the rise of physically superior runners.[7] In this regard, extending the metaphorical significance of feet is useful, for in some ancient Eastern cultures the foot is a stand-in for the body. From this purchase, Achilles' epithet, opposed to the shuffle-footed sloth of the enslaved, projects excellence not from blonde-head to swift-toe, literally construed as white racial superiority sacralized by the natural law, but metaphorically in the obverse. Achilles' body—perfect, godly tendon, long-and-swift feet and legs, broad chest and shoulders, and blue eyes crowned by fair hair—is a foot-to-head contrast with Hector's slower feet, inferior body, and dark hair. Hector's flight from Achilles around Troy works doubly, then, circumscribing the fate of all those within its doomed walls and, more specifically, establishing a measure and action—a perfect, swift foot—that allegorizes the Trojans' physical inferiority by paces. The subsequent funeral games Achilles organizes in Patroklos' honor, ritually marked by Achilles' repetitive dragging of Hector by his pierced heels, extends this performance-trope to all the assembled Greeks.

Hence, the actions of feet determine how to read universal, timeless truths through the short narratives of Hector's death and the long narrative chronicling the outcome of epic conflict, but the cautionary tale of excess is unmistakably transparent: Achilles' feet bring his own head to dust, as a shade, just as he had drug Hector by the heels—and dusted his head—in ritual desecration. Achilles' treatment of Hector is an archetypal Bronze Age performance appropriated and mimicked by modernity without due regard for the cautionary sense: as antebellum-era removal of the Achilles tendons of slaves captured after abortive flight (Price 3) and, more horrifically, American lynching performances often resulting in graphic images circulated as postcards or remains of lynched bodies displayed as keepsakes.

How ironic, then, to turn back toward Africa—found by Immanuel Kant and Hegel to be wanting in beauty and history, respectively—to unveil this agonic merger too seamlessly symbolized by narrative flow. The results are profoundly instructive, for the perfect bardic body, as much a maestro as a ranconteur, reveals itself to be leaky, forgetful, aged, fatigued, and tongue-tied—in other words, perfectly human.

GENDER AND THE EPIC

Much of the heroic epic, Stephen Belcher notes, is founded upon the "uniform notion of personhood" that foregrounds "individual development." The masculine premise runs counter to the "social construction of the individual in Africa" and to the realization that gender relations, including those in African epics, is not one of female support of males, but an "essential" role in which the male/female "pair forms an indivisible unit." This "indivisible unit," Belcher adds, recognizes male and female agency within a complex dynamic: "isolating the (male) hero disregards an essential dynamic of the stories. While the male hero may possess tremendous powers, he does not always control them and he certainly does not work alone. . . . He furthers a larger social dynamic that begins with parents" (49). Derivative of this dynamic is the African precept that women are not merely supporters, or agents, but also principals—epic heroines and empire builders in their own rights who exercise imperial mother-wit. Drawing significantly upon the scholarship of Sarah C. Brett-Smith[8] to inform his study of women's roles in the Mande, David C. Conrad notes that in the Mande an "essential truth" is that "men derive their power from their mothers and that human existence and survival depends on the strength of women." This strength is not the exclusive domain of the exceptional, that which exists "entirely beyond *musoya* (womanhood) of daily life," or separate from gender relations. For example, cloth, particularly the red cloth that, in Bamana society, is "central to girls' rites of passage, including excision ritual and marriage," is inseparable from women's sexual power and the unknown dangers associated with it. To tear or remove a woman's clothing exposes the male transgressor to a "danger signal, serving notice that men are straying over the boundary, approaching an area of female nyama." Thus, women—especially Du Kamisa as well as Sogolon Wunde and Sogolon Kolonkan, Sunjata's mother and sister, respectively—are essential elements to the "establishment of the Mali empire." The shape-shifting Du Kamisa, Conrad argues, is a "reproductive decision maker" archetype: as a post-menopausal women, she is one of the "female elders" who have earned equal social stature among male elders, and who, like grandmothers, are matrons protective of their female progenies' fertility ("Mooning" 190, 197–98, 200–02, 209–15).[9]

The economy linking creation myth, animal spirits, and gender that Keith Cartwright distinguishes from the Islamic narrative "patrimony and patronymics" (*Reading* 26, 62–63, 70) is central, too, in other West/Central African epic traditions. Among the Ijo ethnic group of the *Ozidi Saga*, most Ijo diviners are women, engaging in divination activities akin to war as they confront bush spirits, "serve shrines," and "prescribe herbal remedies and rituals." Ijo lore maintains that Queen, the most famous of them all, was dragged underwater for seven days and had "nine powers" (three is a sacred number) revealed to her to fight evil spirits. It is significant that Queen lived in the Tarakiri clan village of Anyama in 1963, considering her far-reaching reputation for being the "most powerful" and "intrepid" Ijo diviner (Anderson, "Bulletproof" 112, 114, 117). Queen offers a real-life parallel of Oreame, for among the Ijo, the feminine essence exists at the center of a matrilineal social structure, incarnated as supreme goddess and situated as a core feature of its language. Ironically, a feminine parallel to the epic excess motif associated with the strong man anticipates the epic trickster aesthetic.

Okpewho reads significant parallels between an Ijo creation myth and the *Ozidi Saga* (Okpewho, *Myth* 137–51), which means the trickster aesthetic informs this Ijo epic in multiple ways that speak to female potency, the need to situate such figures within the cultural performance, and the multifaceted character of epic protagonists. Given the power the Ijo associate with femininity, which is also the source of maternal sensibility, Okpewho notes that one Ijo narrator is hard-pressed to reconcile the two oppositions. He achieves this by conflating the cosmogenic mythology of creation and the trickster tale: "We may therefore see this tale as an attempt by our narrator to match the usable ingredients of the [Tortoise] trickster tradition with his society's anxiety to affirm the feminine virtues against the oppressive claims of a feministic or matrilineal culture. The result—a plea for social sanity through subdued self-awareness." In other words, against the excesses of female creative power and in the recognition of maternal virtue, the Tortoise trickster's aesthetic and social function as a marginalized, disempowered "misfit" is deployed by the narrator to fuse together the powerful to the weak and thus achieve moral balance. Clearly, beyond his focus on the narrator's "selective use of the trickster tradition" and artistic "deliberateness" (*Myth* 152), Okpewho's gendered close reading points toward a brilliant isomorphism here, one refusing the male/female, divine/vulgar, and epic/trickster binaries and creating more artistic possibility because of ontological and generic ambiguities.

A form of Oreame's tutelage of Ozidi can be seen in Nyanga culture and symbolized in the *Mwindo Epic*. Although Mwindo's mother, Nyamwindo, is sidelined in Rureke's version, like the "suffering woman" motif Biebuyck finds common to the epics, paternal aunts are critical to the Nyanga. The "ritual wives," who bear those who would become chief, may be selected from the existing chief's half sisters, which means the children produced from this union have a mother and a paternal aunt. Paternal aunts, aside from being mothers, have special relations with their nephews, who may be breastfed by them in the mother's absence, and instructed in moral concerns. Mwindo's close relationship with Iyangura, whose name relates to the Banyangan verb "to arbitrate," establishes the feminine as an essential character trait of Mwindo (Biebuyck, *Hero* 51, 53–54; *ME* 41, fn.3).

HOT AND COOL/DRY AND WET: THE NEGRO SPEAKS OF RIVERS, HUSTLES, AND FLOWS

Since the body in the African epic performance is radically different from the Homer-centric imagining of the Western Self, it stands to reason that identity construction for the individual and community significantly departs from Western ideals. These differences are not simply a matter of artistic disparity and individual or cultural ability, but have broad geopolitical implications that make the inherent question of greatness moot. Much depends on what might be identified as a culture's *epic ontology*, namely the foundational relationship of Being/Self to the epic, the Other, and the world.

In "The Negro Speaks of Rivers" (1921) Langston Hughes' voice migrated from Southern shadows into what he called the great Harlem "vogue," but considered in the West/Central African epic performance context, his title takes on surprising meaning. In the MOS-epics, the storytelling performs, through hustles and flows, openings that are at once flashbacks, "in the beginning," and *in media res* unions of time, physicality, and culture. Just as Hughes' poem starts in somber voice, reaching back into a riverine genesis, and then pauses to let modern biology ("human blood in human veins") move over for the spiritual ("My soul") flows—

> I've known rivers:
> I've known rivers ancient as the world and older than the
>   flow of human blood in human veins.
>
> My soul has grown deep like the rivers. (1–3)

—the epics stage intertwined movements of hot and cold, earth and water, hustle and flow. In short, the macro-scale heating or cooling of epic spirit also plays a role in the micro-scale performance moment. One way of understanding identity formation as the past and present meet is through thermometrics: readings of the spirit as evidenced by the metaphorical role of water and forging in the performances. This metaphor reveals much about the flows and firmness of identity essential to understanding epic ontology.

The Sunjatic performance, like other traditional epic performances, is saturated with the hot/cold, forging/water metaphor. Recall that the Sunjatic ceremony in Kangaba reaches its peak intensity in the fluid, hot state when the roof is removed from the ceremonial Kamabolon and society is forged anew. Parallel to this are Sunjatic storytelling performances, where power flows into the *jeliw*, the "*faasa* singers fire us up for the battle," while the "maana ["epic narration"] tellers calm the body and soothe the soul after it is over" (Bird 278, 281; brackets mine, translation Bird).[10] Rureke saturates the precis of his narrative with hustle and flow even before the musicians, tuning and scaling, can get into the rhythmic groove. Under the cool guise of Banyangan marital customs and the seemingly blissful betrothal of Iyangura—Shemwindo's sister and Mwindo's paternal aunt—to *Mukiti*, Rureke provides a watery, love-you-back story that is, plain and simple, an old-fashioned hustle. Shemwindo is the Tubondo big man who moves his sister's just presence out so that he can be the topdog. The game here is not three-card monte on the streets of Suzan-Lori Park's *Topdog/Underdog* (2001), but a game of seven in which Shemwindo seeks to reinforce the Troy-like impregnability of Tubondo's seven gates. The underdogs in this are justice, properly sent "down the river" as far as Shemwindo is concerned; as far as Mwindo is concerned, the law against his birth Shemwindo has decreed makes him the ultimate underdog and sets him singing, literally, the equivalent of sorrow songs: "I've known rivers . . ."

Though he is the underdog, symbol for the quintessence of hustle and flow, hot and cold, earth and water, wit and fluid ass-kicking like a crouching tiger, hidden dragon, it is relevant to note that Banyanga wisdom makes Theodor Adorno's well-reasoned *caveat*—"In the end, glorification of splendid underdogs is nothing other than the glorification of the splendid system that makes them so" (28)—a no-brainer embodied in real, traditional common/sense. Mwindo's "heart is high," full of "pathos" and "reckless ambition" that mark him as an unseasoned hot head; the chief's "heart is low" and he respects and is "awed" by people because he has "purified himself from excess and proven his wisdom." The widespread presence of rivers, brooks, and pools in Nyangaland are significant: even before Mwindo begins his odyssey "upstream" and "downstream" by river away from Tubondo to the river's source, the opening narrative tells the back story. The real genesis of this epic begins with the marriage negotiations and ceremony of his paternal aunt, Iyangura, to Master *Mukiti*, a water spirit in serpent form "said to live in deep pools"—he is the "master of the pools"—that the Nyanga associated with "mystery." As one might expect, the pools, some with "deep, somber waters" or "gigantic whirlpools," exist as "places of mystery and awe near which enthronement rites for chiefs are sometimes held" (Biebuyck, *Hero* 4, 37; *ME* 43–53, 82, 88–92, fn.11). Hence, well before the epic proper begins, the story has already been situated within the life-flows of water that are essential to Mwindo's cooling.

Ijo society feautures similar flows within its culture and instances of epic performance: its warriors visited shrines to "splash herbal concoctions" on themselves both before battle and "to cool down afterward," and the seven nights of the *Ozidi Saga*, an epic performance far more violent than either Sunjata or Mwindo epic performances, begin with daily ablution rituals at the river (Anderson, "Bulletproof" 96). Ojobolo masterfully brings his performance to a close with Anglese, the Smallpox King, setting out to cool Ozidi, who was, he heard, "so powerful that he has executed everybody in town . . . [and] completely laid waste what was once a proud capital city." Anglese, a Rambo-like figure whose name and epidemiological association lend themselves to post-colonial reading, comes by "war boat" with his henchmen to the wasteland where Ozidi lives alone with his mother and the warlike Oreame. The ensuing attack results in Ozidi's smallpox infection, and threatens to finally destroy him as Oreame's magic falls short. But his mother, Orea, unstained by violence, saves him by identifying the disease that had befuddled Oreame, who then secures and prepares the proper herbs. He is cured once she "poured," "splash[ed]," and "dashed" the herbal waters on him, allowing him, at the very end of Night Seven of Ojobolo's performance, to defeat the Smallpox King, sink his boat, and swear, "I shall never seek another fight" (*OS* 375–88).

The epic performance, then, is the medium from which the constitution of the contemporary epic community is re-contracted. The ancient mythology of the epic hero sublimates the contemporary community, ennobling and empowering it. In the hot moment of the epic performance, the contemporary community itself becomes epical or superhuman. This is transparent social construction seen as a temporary condition that must be cool and cooled down—one must be level-headed when the heat is on, as people injured in past Kamabolon ceremonies can testify, and soft-hearted when it has been extinguished. Excesses, and empire, ensue when the social construction continues beyond necessity, and social contingency becomes mistook for human ontology and the ensuing US/ Them code.

The epic protagonist's command of forces of Creation and Destruction, just like the epic storyteller's construction and deconstruction of the narrative according to artistic temperament and social context, are metaphorized by flows of hot metal and cool water. The West/Central African epic hero and the epic bards who perform their stories are wielder/bearers of *ironyc* transgressiveness; that is, swords are needed, but irony—iron and irony—immerses the violence in the ironyc. Epic performances contain a multifaceted allegorical spirit in which simple, ideal archetypes regarding epic bodies and actions are paired with transgression and the potential for excess. From this African perspective, and once we unveil the epic performance masked by Western modernity, the epic mythology informing the Western body-politic replants Cartesian dualism in an organic context too complex for simple binaries. The association of two of Mwindo's praise names—"Master-of-strength, Smart-One"—is critical, as Mwindo's "rough," epical body eventually gives way to the coolness of the mature, thoughtful chief (Biebuyck, *Hero* 95).

In sum, using archetypal patterns may very well be, as Belcher argues, "valuable as an interpretive tool [for] those elements of the story that show most signs of narrative streamlining, that makes the hero almost generic." One has to balance this paradigm with sociohistorical contingency that adds the new dimensions the story incorporates and the particularities of the culture owing to language, beliefs, idiosyncrasies, and customs. Thus, against the simpler "truth" of the epic hero ideal, figures like Sunjata emerge as "trouble, for they represent disruption, change, and the drive for self-fulfillment," and operate, along with their antagonists, in an environment that defies a "simplified moral allegory of right and wrong" (*Epic Traditions* 111–12).

The complex allegory—not simple, one-to-one "moral allegory"—of the West/Central African epic performance starts with the word (narrative), but then expands to include the totality of the specific performance in which all the elements do not equal the sum of its parts. What is important here is that for some eminent intellectuals writing against Western hegemony, the shift away from the song and orality of complex folk allegory into the "simplified moral allegory" arising with modern print culture is inseparable from good/bad, white/black binaries informing the West's epic performance.

FORM AND EPIC PERFORMANCE: *NYAMA-ATAMBGA* AS THE ORIGINAL, ALLEGORYCAL, BAS-LINE AND MIXER

Against classical Western epic ontology and the literary allegory arising from it, in which the ultimate binary claims Homeric/epic *literature* is great and its absence bad, Walter Benjamin's approach to allegory is insightful. In his departure from and challenge to conventional literary allegory, Benjamin excavates *Trauerspiel*, a performance-based allegorical form he foregrounds as a genre that redefines understanding of the epic and society. Indeed, it bridges West/Central African cultural and Western/European traditions as the complex allegory Benjamin articulates in *The Origin of German Tragic Drama* [*Ursprung des deutschen Trauerspiels*] (1928), for it explains his embrace of Bertolt Brecht's "epic theatre" and performance genres, predilection for proverbial and aphoristic expression, and the philosophical method he espouses for knowing everything about a genre. The clear parallels between ancient West/Central African allegorical essences relevant to epic performances, such as *nyama* and *Atambga*, make an examination of Benjamin's thought most useful.[11]

Against what he calls "popular" or "common linguistic" denotations of allegory used by Western European artists and historians since the Middle Ages, Benjamin offers a "philosophical understanding of allegory" that escapes the problem of modern Western allegory, which arose from misreadings of Egyptian hieroglyphics and classical culture. Western allegory—a parallel between "an illustrative image and its abstract meaning" (39, 162, 189)—arises out of theological distrust of the "common" people's ability to confront the "earliest rude world," which was considered "crude," "uncivilized," and full of a "chaotic mass of metaphor." Since this uncensored chaos could overwhelm the people's understanding, religious leaders believed, the attendant solution was allegory-making based on the theologian's expertise with the eternal truth of perfect symbols and their ability to correctly quantify objects and symbolize correspondences in much the way engraved coins teach history. For this reason, moral lessons and knowledge of God were allegorized (hidden and beautified) in simple things the "common people" could grasp and appreciate, such as rhymes and fables (168–74).

Benjamin's philosophical and theological solution to this in German art is the *Trauerspiel* form of tragic drama. *Trauerspiel* is the "allegorical" perspective in which all of the historical and phenomenal data associated with a specific "idea" are considered the "representation of truth" (28).[12] The sublime symbol or image is nothing more than a "fragment," or "ruin," that is the last vestige of antiquity out of which the modern world creates sacred "artificiality." Moderns are alchemists who have constructed out of the ruin the "perfect vision" for the purposes of leaving something that will "endure" and be "eternal" (176, 178, 181).[13] Lost in the violence of this arbitrary process, in which "[r]eading was obligatory" and "educational," and "vast libraries" function as the ultimate "monument" to the "power of knowledge," are the "ordinary every day affairs" (181, 184). In other words, particularly in view of the "free, spontaneous utterance of the creature" (i.e, "spoken language") and the cultural practice Benjamin values against the way "written language of allegory enslaves" (202),[14] honest and objective openness is obligatory.

Instead of allegory, representing superficial "judgment" grasping for the eternal but creating a simple surface that, in fact and performance, closes off truth, one might profitably call Benjamin's concept *allegorye*, or the *allegorycal*. Here, the *y* denotes openness, liminality, and contradiction (vowel and/or consonant), and, perhaps most importantly, the irrefutable logic of orality.[15] For Benjamin, allegory arises out of Western subjectivity located in "historical codification" and "extreme foreshortening of the historical perspective" (27, 202–03), inductive and deductive knowledge as "possession" (29, 42–43), art, and Christianity, for intentionality is seen as the mechanism for achieving the eternal in a world full of "transience" and "variety" interpenetrated by the Greco-Roman pantheon so much that Christianity is inseparable from it (38, 220–26).[16] Allegory, then, brought to Westerners imagined Order and Truth by investing in the discrete "individual phenomena" (30) of eternal appearances: perfect symbols, emblems, and typography, the antithesis of spoken language and its freedom. For example, Hegel's genealogical history is idealism that sacrifices "authentic" evidence, *viz.*, the "most singular and eccentric of phenomena" (46). Allegorye, by contrast, is not a "metaphysical" exercise in knowledge that is "found within, but should appear in action, like the blood coursing through the body" (39). Thus, when Benjamin says, "The idea is a monad," he is speaking about unified essence and infinitude. Allegorye, as the real-world, artistic corollary of the idea, is a monad that reveals ultimate unity when one has "absorbed"—note the passive, receptive tense—"all the history" of a given "phenomenon" (47). Benjamin's allegorycal holism, in which the "corpse as life" erases Cartesian dualism and gives vitality to life (216),[17] ultimately reconciles everything—African and European, pre-modern and modern—in the true "Christian origin of the allegorical outlook" (220): "And God saw *everything* that he had made, and, behold, it was very good" (Genesis 1:31, quoted by Benjamin at 233; italics mine).[18]

Just as "everything" is God-given here, the deepest spirituality, so is *nyama*, fittingly, the soulfulness of everything.[19] As Biebuyck's Africanist outlook informs us that "great heroic epic traditions" occur among African peoples who are not imperialistic ("African Heroic" 337–38), the "allegorical outlook" demands that we leave behind conventional, allegorical understanding of Homeric epic and seek the allegorycal epic. We are ready, in other words, for the spirit of West/Central African epics— *nyama* and *Atambga*—to help foster a better understanding of Western epic performance.

Senegambian and Banyangan *nyama* and *Atambga* of the Niger Delta's Ijo, constitutive and deconstitutive incantations of "ancient speech" and "unknown language" that are also performances, represent the spirit of allegorye giving the possibilities of life and light, rhythm and blues—*sol* and *soul*—to the epic performance. It is the original Word, allegorycal bas-line, a drum-beat strengthening community and a maker/mixer allowing US to dance to our own unique hip hop and, literally, talk trash.

Instead of "griots," a term resulting from colonial violence[20] and simple allegory, *nyama* is a mathematical sublime in its own right, for it is a multifactorial signifying whose formal denotation, according to David C. Conrad and Barbara E. Frank, *"does not equal the sum of its parts."* Contra colonial taxonomies that flattened and thus distorted Mande *nyamaka-laya*, the professional collectives of artists and artisans, *nyama* likewise comprises complex and shifting forms of "contradiction and ambiguity" (Conrad and Frank 1, 7–10, 13). While Mande *nyama* denotes what can variably be described as a "natural force," "soul," or "energy of action," the specific type of force can be "(a) evil or satanic; (b) morally neutral; (c) dangerous; (d) polluting; (e) energizing or animating; (f) necessary for action; or (g) indicative of imperfect control." If one considers that *nyama(m)*, for some Mande speakers, doubles in meaning as "garbage" or "refuse," the multiple denotations of *kala*, which leads to a proliferation of meanings of *nyamakala*, and that regional and individual denotations and the Mande nobles' (*horon[w]*) perspectives amplify this exponentially,[21] *nyamakala* quickly subverts colonial taxonomies. In this regard, *nyamakala* itself is a post-colonial critique that goes from a confusing Bakhtinian carnival (*nyaga*, in the Mandekakan dialect in western Mande, is a "celebration, festival") to a trash-talkin' allegorycal performance and all out revolution and riot of meaning (Bird, "The Production" 283–84; Bird, Kendall, and Tera 28–31; Bird, Keita, and Soumaouro vii; Hoffman 39).[22]

And the trouble of formal definition is only the start, for the "Mande believe that in concentrations, especially when they are massive and uncontrolled, this force is potentially dangerous, even deadly" (Hoffman 39, citing Patrick McNaughton). If, then, to Obi Wan Kenobi's spiritual injunction that he "use the force," Luke Skywalker had rightfully asked, "But which one? And how much?" *Star Wars IV: A New Hope* would have had to be re-subtitled "A Really, Really, *Really* Thoughtful—and On-Time— Response, We Hope . . ." And if the Jedi—*jeli?*—master had said, simply, *"you* follow your bliss" (91; italics mine), as Joseph Campbell enjoined US in *The Power of Myth* (1988),[23] would not this counsel, in the logic of *nyama*-excess and the movie, create a Dark Knight-Jedi, a second, sorcerous Darth Vader?

Of course, in simple terms that are pre-/post-slavery and pre-/post-colonial, *nyama* is also natural, holistic, and balance-minded—and in a place that is neither *terra incognito* nor *tabula rasa*; it is the forest. The forest is a place about which the Ijo in central and western Niger Delta proverbially admonish one another, *viz.*, "Beware of the bush, the bush is a difficult place," because of its natural and "supernatural dangers" (Anderson,

"Bulletproof" 105). The rain forest, the "world" of the Nyanga, is a place where "there are many customs" and "strange ways." *Nyama* takes on different but related meaning here. For the Nyanga, *nyama* designates the bulk of forest mammals, but the primacy of hunting and the forest for the Nyanga does not encompass the hero-chief. The hero (*murai*), the future chief, has a "mystic bond or alliance" with "certain animals," and the chief's symbolic embodiment of "Nyamurairi, chief of the divinities" (Biebuyck, *Hero* 26–27, 62, 98–99), serves to transport *nyama* from the mundane and toward the animals of the forest in a manner that folds them into everything spiritual. The forest is full of "dangerous beings" and "deceivers," but it is also the location of life and death and spirituality. In Nyanga circumcision rituals, held in the forest away from the village, the epitome of this dynamic is *nya-masangwa*, "one-dressed-in-many-things." The *nyamasangwa* is associated with turtle, iguana, and many birds, especially the hornbill, which symbolically represents female and male elements ("intelligence [nesting care] and aggression [when his young are attacked]"). Nevertheless, it finds truest representation in the forest's *kirímu-dragon*, "a big animal with black hide, seven heads, teeth like a dog, huge belly, and tail of an eagle" (Biebuyck, "Nyanga Circumcision" 89, 90). The importance of *Kirimu*, as metonym for *nyamasangwa*, seems to be borne in the fact that he is "prominent" in the Nyanga corpus of epics and heroic tales (Biebuyck, *Hero* 27, 67).

Correlative to the many-thing-ness of *nyamasangwa* created out of Rureke's word-picture performance, a natural and supernatural African sublime meant to overwhelm one's sense of comprehension, is the Sunjata performance. In these moments, the *faasa* (personal praises) contained in the *jelikan* "power language" is a context-specific performance of *nyama* whose very syntactic structure transforms the simple into empowering obscurity.

Contra the common tendency of equating the sublime, epical surface with substance, traditional African masking practices epitomize the danger of epic performance. As Charles Bird observed of griot training, particularly regarding experts in *faasa*, "all believed that there was something lying underneath the words, and that it was something dangerous" ("The Production" 280). Thus, though Bakhtin famously refers to folk performances as "carnival," a designation that scholars have used to undermine the binary between Europe and Africa, a more useful—and less celebratory—designation for the West African epic performance is the masquerade (and mask). While Bakhtin sees medieval Europe's carnival as "a second world and second life outside officialdom," his emphasis is still on the discrete festival event and "[c]lowns and fools" in "everyday life out of carnival season" (*Rabelais* 197–98). The masquerade obscures reality and thus cautions individuals against seeking powers of the spiritual world and, when culturally uninformed, from misconstruing the mask. It is not an object masquerading as a simple pre-modern celebration accurately defined by an objective gaze and symbolized by our knowledge.

Although the masquerade may be celebratory, in its daily existence it is an object folded into much greater signification owing to its shifting symbolic role in cultural performance.[24] The masquerade is irony embodied, the surface of a static object all eyes see and read the same, and a shifting figure whose depth of meaning is impossible to contain. In the traditional epic performance context, those who take the mask's sublime surface too literally not only mistake the complex tropes the masquerade performs, but may be scorched by irony or subjected to the allegorycal danger of a total reversal. For example, though the Mwindo epic performances constitute *kakoro* ("things of daytime") entertainment, its "strong didactic and moralizing undertone" parallels Nyanga cosmology: "Rashness, impetuosity, verbosity, arrogance, intemperance, ruthlessness, thoughtlessness, hardheartedness—all are implicitly criticized" (Biebuyck, *Hero* 5). Moreover, the masquerade figure includes an essential gender dynamic. In the Mande men might be the "instruments of conquest and destruction," but women are those who can bestow life as the "*sabuw* (sources, providers) of all that these men accomplish." This "miraculous" potency is traditionally understood as a form of "sorcery"[25] that helped to co-found the Malian empire (Conrad, "Mooning" 191, 194).

Taking her cues, in part, from Mande's Komo masks and the Mande proverb *Nyama bè kuma la* ("There is *nyama* in speech"), Barbara G. Hoffman analogizes its aesthetic of power to that of bardic language at its best: "elaborate speech obscures it, hides all or part of its referential content, renders its meaning ambiguous, and thus dangerous." Thus, she says of the transformation of a Komo mask *vis-à-vis* other non-Komo masks, it is unique because of

> the matter that is added to it over time, the multiplying of horns and quills, the layering of clay and blood, and the quantities of dangerous force (*nyama*) that these materials bring with them.[26] The more obscure the original becomes, the more hidden it is, the more powerful an object the mask becomes.
>
> Griot language (*jelikan*) . . . derives power from a simple syntactic structure whose meaning is made obscure.

The syntactic structure is comprised of "conjoined noun phrases, not complete sentences," that are "uttered very rapidly, . . . like gunfire, bombarding the noble with more sound than can be assimilated, causing confusion." In this powerful rap, where staccato chants fly like bullets and sensible referentiality is *know*-where to be found, Hoffman suggests that meaningful "predication is performed not with verbs and objects but through the interaction of the griot and noble in the performance context" (Hoffman 39–42).[27]

Thus, the *faasa*—or "personal mottoes" or praises—of *jelikan* evidence, for Hoffman, the genre "most laden with dangerous force (*nyama*)."

For Christian Seydou, speaking of the identity-shaping potency of such praises, these mottos act as a "sublime" catalyst (Hoffman 41; Seydou 313–14). Though the self-referentiality is absent from West African pan-egyrics, compared to the South and Southeastern regions in Africa, the structural mechanism is essentially the same (S. Belcher 19–21). These bards, getting a bad rap from the *horon(w)* even though these nobles greatly admire, and fear, their power at the same time, exemplify their allegorycal rap in ways all too reminiscent of complaints about gang-sta rappers, and tricksters: "They dabble in the occult. They lie. They act shamelessly. They comport themselves without constraint or control. They plead weakness. They beg. They manifest sexuality in public places. They dance with wild gestures. They raise their voices. They shout and yell in public. The *nyamakala* are utterly alien: they are 'The Other'" (Bird, Kendall, and Tera 31).[28]

Even if this perspective is quasi tongue-in-cheek, as Hoffman suggests, the upshot and shout-out centers the *jeliw*, and their performances, as obscure, transgressive allegorysts and allegoryes in which "meaning is not the sum of its parts" (Hoffman 41). This notion of obscurity, that it is dangerous and should be held in secret, is the peroration that frames and regularly punctuates Okabou Ojobolo's performance of *The Ozidi Saga* on several of the nights. These perorations are, in true allegorycal mode, both openings and closings, beginnings and endings. One of Ojobolo's best perorations, if not the best, occurs at the start of his Night Seven performance:

Now I'm going to take it up from there.

When I have narrated it as
far as I know it, I am too
well aware of tradition to
go any farther.

I do not come from the seat
of the gods.

Therefore I cannot properly
finish the story for you.

Yes, but I'll tell you as much
as I know it, I won't speak
more, indeed I didn't open
it, now the matter is ended. (326)

In the absence of the proper context, Ojobolo's remarks would appear merely as "inelegant nonsense" (Okpewho, *Myth* 59), jibber-jabber, or nonsensical rapping.[29] But Ojobolo's performance betrays the craft of a master allegoryst, one who knows not just narrative artistry, but complexity and "tradition," that only the "gods"—the Creator/Destroyers and Makers/Mixers—can "finish the story." Of course Ojobolo can tell and finish a story, as his performance over seven consecutive days amply demonstrates, but his statement weds the heights of artistry to the firmament of the unknown. Thus, Ojobolo says, inscribing his limits within the infinite limits of allegorye, it is a story he "didn't open," and, in purest allegorycal inversion, he notes that "the matter is ended."[30]

Atambga, the Ijo equivalent of *nyama*, is a "body of magical knowledge" mastered by the "most successful warriors." Specifically, it is through *aunbibi* ("unknown language") that the Ijo warrior-sorcerers acquire their power. "Command of this language," which is "unintelligible to ordinary Ijo" according to Martha G. Anderson, "enabled them to accomplish miraculous feats simply by uttering a few words" ("Bulletproof" 96). The *Mwindo Epic* offers a contrast since its bards, even the highly skilled ones capable of deploying all the poetic devices, avoid "archaisms and secret and cryptic formulas" in favor of "ordinary Nyanga spoken and understood by the people." However, just as the bard is a master of speech, so, too, is Mwindo, for reasons parallel to those elucidated for Sunjatic and Ozidic performances:

> He has the power of speech and possesses the magic of the word. His word has a compelling force, commanding the father's spears not to cause injury and lightning not to strike him. His *verbal magic* is enhanced throughout the epics, in his invocations, his blessings, his commands, his wishes, his boastful threats, and most of all in the dazzling effect of his songs. (Biebuyck, *Hero* 102; italics mine)

Together *nyama* and *Atambga* allegoryze the "obscure" and "unintelligible," at once establishing knowledge as a powerful magic and as a mask behind which power takes forms no-body, no matter how epical he or she is, can or should take for granted.[31]

But at the same time, the double meaning of *nyama* as "garbage," "refuse," or "straw" enjoins us to, indeed, take it for granted! The pairing of the sublimity of epic protagonists and "garbage" enables a reversal that suggests the limitations of our heroes. They may be great, perhaps even epical, but they are "refuse" like us, too. Thus, as Charles Bird deduces, the "semantic ambiguity" of *nyama* makes possible the following:

Nyama, nyama, nyama	Garbage! Garbage! Garbage!
Everything hides under nyama	Everything hides under nyama
And nyama under nothing.	And garbage under nothing.
	Everything hides under garbage
	But not fire.
	("The Production" 283–84)

Again, the inclination might be to dismiss this as nonsense, but the significance of *nyama* and epic warn against such, or against ascribing one meaning or value to *nyama*: Is *nyama* mere hypermasculine braggadocio? Is all human reality, situated in *nyama*, ultimately "garbage"? Or is *nyama* the human spirit? Though unintelligible in the abstract, this reading seems to recognize the transgressive nature of the epic, and the fundamental paradox about human relations and time.

The temporality is perhaps most evident when we consider the death of Sugulun Konde, Sunjata's mother, in Fa-Digi Sisòkò's the *Epic of Son-Jara*. This occurs not only far from their native Mali and years into their exile, but after Sunjata had served the Prince of Mema well as a military leader. When the Prince of Mema issues a "decree" refusing Sunjata's request to use a plot of land for Sugulun's burial, "Unless he were to pay its price," Sunjata's immediate response is to offer him, by all accounts, garbage:

[Sunjata] took feathers of Guinea fowl and partridge,	(Indeed)
And took some leaves of arrow-shaft plant,	(Indeed)
And took some leaves of wild grass reed,	(Indeed)
And took some red fanda-vines,	(Indeed)
And took one measure of shot,	(Indeed)
And took a haftless knife,	(Indeed)
And added a cornerstone fetish to that,	(Indeed)
And put it all in a leather pouch,	(Indeed)
Saying go give it to Prince Birama,	(Indeed)
Saying it was the price of his land.	(Indeed, ha, Fa-Digi)
	(Johnson, *Epic* 86)

Though the heroic epic often centers male potency as the ideal founder, Sunjata's relationship to his mother and to the non-ideal is significant. The conflict between Sunjata and Prince Birama of Mema is based on the multiple meanings of "ruin" relative to his mother's honor, the symbolic artifacts Sunjata offers him, and the fate of Mema. In many respects, one might say that Sunjata's life had been a series of events that, taken together, amount to a pile of "ruins." He had been forced to leave his homeland. The first nine years of his life were characterized by physical disability. His mother, Sugulun Kòndè, was also severely disabled as a hunchback dwarf. Now, in his adulthood, his mother dies in exile and Prince Birama, the king of Mema, refuses Sunjata's request for "a grant of land, / In order to bury his mother in Mema" (86).

Although unspecified in the narrative, presumably the plot would be very small, so Prince Birama's ruling that Sunjata must pay for the land, even when Sunjata was his close associate, suggests impropriety. One might consider this situation to, indeed, be ruinous, for the implication here is that Sunjata may not have had the resources. After all, he was a long-time exile and had no means of earning income. However, Sisòkò's use of the All-Saying-Sage to describe the things of "ruins" (87) is in keeping with what we know of the logic of this epic performance, namely the significance of the deformed, small, old, and ostracized on the one hand, and, on the other, the centrality of *badenya*, or female energy, in the epic. Sugulun is the source of Malian ethnic identity; her imperial mother-wit is essential for the restoration of Sunjata's own Malian identity. Given this importance, Prince Birama's demand "ruins" Sugulun. In other words, akin to traditional notions of virginity, Sugulun's Malian purity is directly assaulted at a time—death—all human societies recognize as significant. Sugulun, as the mother of Sunjata, is the mother of the Malian empire he founds, and thus this insult assaults the very legitimacy of Sunjata's Malian inheritance.

Sunjata's response makes the consequences of this quite clear. Since Sugulun represents imperial mother-wit, the Founding Mother for the Old Malian empire, one might expect Sunjata to make every effort to offer a payment sum considerably better than the items Sisòkò enumerates: "some leaves of arrow-shaft plant," "wild grass reed," "red fanda-vines," "one measure of shot," "a haftless knife," and a "cornerstone fetish," all placed in a "leather pouch." This motley assortment of worthless items thrown into a cheap pouch would be trash, or some discarded ruins one might find at a temporary campsite, or in a heap of garbage. But this interpretation, devoid of the second sight so crucial to West African heroic epics, would be misleading, a point the *naamu*-sayer's response—"Indeed, ha, Fa-Digi"—accentuates. Indeed, great civilizations rise and fall, and rising up out of seeming garbage, often through warfare and the fire that razes and replaces them, is another. This is even more true here where a Sorcerer such as Sunjata commands *nyama*.

Again, archetypal readings focused on great civilizations and men mistake the mask for the essence. The importance of *badenya* magic here, and regard for women, as balance of and complement to *fadenya*, speaks to the overlooked role of gender in epic performance. Unlike the Prince of Du, Magan Jata Kòndè, who exiled and "slashed off" the breast of Kamisa Kòndè, the aunt who reared him, or Sumamuru, who also "slashed off [his mother's] breast" (Johnson, *Epic* 32, 92), the male figures who respect women and the deformed acquire more occult power. Sunjata emerges as the most maternal figure in this regard. Contrast him, for example, with the first heroes of *Son-Jara*, the brothers Dan Mansa Wulundin and Wulanba. These hunters, from the heartland of Mali, responded to the destruction Kamisa Kòndè had brought to the land as the raging Ginda ("Buffalo") of Du. The Ginda is a fabulous creature, its very appearance—"horns," "ears," "tail," and "hooves" all of gold and silver—bespeaking the "Wealth" and "Transgression" apparently motivating her nephew.

Every day this giant Ginda killed a man in each of the "seven quarters of Du." Describing themselves as Taraweres, an ethnic identifier Johnson associates with a mystical creature bearing second sight,"[32] they offer "leftover rice, / . . . to the old woman" (33, 35), an act of kindness which prompts her to tell them how to subdue the Ginda. Instead of guns and arrows, masculine implements of modern technology, the Ginda is brought low by the Taraweres' command of artifacts, again resembling garbage, the most significant of these being the woman's "spindle" with which they shoot and kill the Ginda. The two hunters, who show son-like kindness and follow her instructions to boil "[m]any eggs," some of which they toss down—they "become a great wilderness," "great lake," and "great forest" (35–37)—stop her rampage. The fertility *topos* here is clear: the prince's transgressions made Du a symbolically barren wasteland and the Ginda's "almost radioactive *nyama*" made it excessive, thus the need for an extended fertility ritual. In this regard, the lameness Sunjata overcomes to begin his "empowerment," Cartwright notes, is linked by *djeli* to a "Mande trope of power, the tree" ("Reading" 34) out of eco-logical necessity: *nyama* is a veritable nuclear reaction of Creation/Destruction whose excessive, radioactive potential can scorch the sky and leave everything beneath a charred wasteland.

Dan Mansa Wulundin and Wulanba succeed where the men of Du and other hunters had failed because of, as Cartwright points out, their second sight, which is the same "bifocal, syncretic powers" Sunjata inherited from his father's *barakha* (Islamic "grace") and his mother's *badenya* ("Reading" 32–33). Hence, beyond second sight, a genetic inheritance borne of their connection to the Manden, founded by Sunjata's father, one might even say that Du Kamisa's occult tutorial offers them something even greater than bifocalism. Their deployment of second sight is enhanced when Kamisa reveals to the elder brother the power of invisibility: "Dan Mansa Wulanba, / On the charcoal chunk should step. / Thus will he become a shade!" (37). The Tarawere brothers, as Manden hunters, represent both bifocal semiotics, a second sight into things behind things, while simultaneously having the shadowed or shaded being which disrupts the second sight of even the most powerful, such as the Buffalo of Du.[33]

This episode brings together allegorye, transgressiveness, and female power in an episode that epitomizes the essence of Sunjatic potency. So why are they not the epic heroes, especially when Sisòkò gives attention to their praise names? The Tarawere brothers' behavior following their epic success over the Buffalo of Du may explain why. Their effort to sleep with Sogolon, knowing she is fated for another and greater destiny, evidences what Walter Benjamin, thinking of Shakespeare, calls the "allegorical cloak of invisibility" (191). Even good characters behave in spontaneous, transgressive ways.

The moral lessons here are critical to the second sight and common/sense the traditional African epic performs and requires. Epic transgression can easily become epic excess for quantitative and qualitative reasons: too much power, held for too long, or some combination of both, is to be avoided. The lesson is a universal one, for those who would take advantage of the weak and deformed *and*, apparently, those deformed individuals who rise up to prominence and leadership. Just as garbage is *nyama* (epic spirit), and *nyama* is, or can become, garbage, epic transgressiveness is a spirit's breath away from epic excess and apocalypse, the ultimate garbage-maker.

TRANSGRESSIVE/IDEAL TO EXCESSIVE/CAUTIONARY

Contra classical Western, Homer-centered notions of the ideal epic hero,[34] the West African epic hero is an ideal/transgressive persona, a "transcendent" figure "whose heroic qualities are never perceived without some taint of deviance" (Austen, "Criminals" 385).[35] This transgressive aspect closes the Western, imagined divide between epic hero and trickster-proper and creates the possibility of a deformed, hybrid, context-dependent figure, the epic/trickster. Deformation as masked or unrecognized power, in epic narratives, resonates with the spirit, if not form, of trickster tales across a range and combination of markers including, but not limited to, sociopolitical, spatial, filial, maternal, age-related, and physical factors.[36]

Deformity and sublimity are the twin components of traditional African epic protagonists. Such thinking, in accordance with African ontology and cosmology, does not isolate good and bad into an epic protagonist and antagonist, respectively, but sees both as an organic flow of hot and cold in which magic, spirituality, and human subjectivity all operate to shape the world. Instead of simple linearity, as the weak throws off the yoke of an oppressor to become good and great, the understanding is that the forces making this creativity possible also deform character in a quantum equal to the sublimating aspect. Epic and Trickster are not two generic archetypes opposed to one another in various ways, but epic and trickster, representing universal capacities in each of US, are genetically related by the ennobling and corrupting power of deformity.

Though not indexed to trickster aesthetics, the deformity that motivates the behavior of African epic protagonists, of course, is well understood. While coded as "hardships and tests," Biebuyck's assessment of Mwindo's sociopolitical deformation speaks to epic protagonists and their families more broadly. Biebuyck's catalog of Mwindo's challenges—"Born against his father's will, the son of a wife who has no ritual status, threatened at birth, rejected, abandoned, confronted with many enemies" (*Hero* 104)—may seem a mere listing, but an insightful reading into the material and psychological conditions the challenges imply is revealing. Over a widening chasm of time and space, they open up the identity question into one that impinges on the ontological: it is an existential question Daniel Kunene articulates as "Who am I?" (205).

"Who am I?" is a question of identity in Kunene's formulation, but the *sine qua non* of the existential is dignity (humanity) and life (existence)—in short, a fully whole and healthy body. The survival of the hero, and the tribe, relates to a question of the well-formed body. Biebuyck's catalog, then, provides a definition for deformity as an existential question relating to matters of hardship. The idea, implicit in Biebuyck's catalog, is that each subsequent hardship deforms the protagonist's body. The deformed body, quite frankly, means survival itself is at stake. Next to this, humanity and then identity need to be vindicated. Biebuyck's thoughts on Mwindo's "ability to reverse destiny" warrant a critical revision, for Mwindo's destiny is not to simply consecrate his epic ontology, but to escape it with equal urgency. He may be an epic hero, but as a necessary evil Mwindo is one the Nyanga are far from imagining as a celebrity-hero to be emulated. Mwindo, in other words, exemplifies the African epic performance's ideal/transgressive dynamic.

Though Biebuyck notes the "contradictions" of Mwindo, because he privileges the individual hero of destiny as the future chief,[37] he flattens out the Nyanga's cosmology, flattens the people/folk ("comitatus"), and dematerializes the epic corpus represented by the deformation. Here, even as he recognizes in Mwindo a figure, like Sunjata, in whom "fighting skills" and "great battle scenes" are deemphasized in favor of "trickery and magic" (*Hero* 42–43), Biebuyck commits the error common for those concerned with epic heroics: the classical heroic template is normalized, as the allegory focuses overwhelming narrative weight on what Homer scholar Mark Buchan calls the "comfort . . . of teleological readings" (17). In other words, "Destiny" overshadows everything because of the luminescence of The Epic Hero. Though noting Mwindo's apparent lack of fighting prowess, and his magical fortitude, Biebuyck still references the resplendent abilities making his body "strong and invulnerable" (*Hero* 101). In this manner, we implicitly follow the traditional allegorical script.

But allegorye calls for an alternate reading strategy. Instead of reading the specific moments of epic action with knowledge of the outcome, we should forget destiny and what we know of the story, for it is full of stock assumptions about success. If we approach Mwindo in this regard, then his destined success against the impossible and metamorphosis into chief could be considered a mere *dénouement* to what is most important: the specific values the culture foregrounds, including warnings, not only the glory of a destined apotheosis for the great individual and tribe whose dawn has just begun.

The African epic's allegorycal outlook helps to illumine deformity as a central feature of the epic's folk semantics that are too often obscured and shadowed by epic/special effects. Against the antiseptic orientation of the West toward cleanliness, classical beauty, greatness, and epic/perfection associated with Homeric epics, African culture associated with traditional epic ontology is more organic and complex in its reading of the mask. For example, lest we too easily praise Sunjata, the Sorcerer, for his surpassing greatness, it should be noted that male and female sorcerers who are "practitioners of the most dangerous sorcery are distinguished by physical anomalies that they either acquire or are born with." They will specifically avoid "cleaning themselves, lest they weaken their powers" (Conrad, "Mooning" 196).

Throughout Sisòkò's telling, Sunjata is in close association with, or the narrative privileges, those who also have such "physical anomalies." These figures, who are always more than what they seem, frequent the story from beginning to end. For example, deformed women are critical: Du Kamisa, an exile with a slashed breast, is also described as an "old woman" when she receives rice from the brothers—the Tarawares—who are hunting the giant buffalo-wraith, Ginda, she transforms herself into to ravage a land dry of justice; likewise, a "snuff-dipping little old woman" informs Magan Jata Kòndè of the Ginda's demise (Johnson, *Epic* 35, 42). In addition, the Taraweres receive instruction, next to the "rubbish heap," from an "old male dog . . . / With a [black] cat beside him" (43–44).[38] Indeed, in the beginning of the narrative, which includes a genealogy and listing of the thirty-three "noble clans," the last clan consisted of "pariahs." At this very point in Sisòkò's performance, the *naamu*-sayer's response cadence goes from his steady baseline rhythm—"Indeed"—to a jazzy riff—"That's true, Eh, Fa-Digi, true" (27)—that calls attention to itself, and for second sight and hearing, with good reason: "Deformed people, or those with epilepsy, are considered by many to be possessed of special occult power (nyama). Presumably such a person would be of benefit because of his/her power" (Johnson, "Annotations" 113). These "deformed" vessels of power foreshadow the *leitmotif*, and epic irony, of the narrative.

All of this prepares us for the most masked source of power, the humpbacked Sugulun Kòndè, Sunjata's mother. Sugulun is ostracized by "six young maidens" who "all moved away and stood apart" from her because of her appearance, which an old dog described to the brothers: "Warts and pustules cover her. / They call her Sugulun-of-the-Warts!" (Johnson, *Epic* 44–45). As discussed in more detail later, Sugulun's deformities, particularly the humped back that marks her as a human Ginda, are iconic traits. These liminal character markers signify a unity between tricksters and epic heroes or heroines that is nominally recognized, but not pursued, by African epic scholars.[39] Perhaps this oversight exists because the trickster-hero has critical salience and function among African Americans and other diasporic Africans because of slavery, or because the Epic Hero and Trickster archetypes, even when the latter is widely considered a divine culture-hero, are so dissimilar: animals/humans, ideal superhumans/grotesque animals, regents/bush-dwellers. "One fundamental difference must be stressed between trickster tales and the general run of heroic lore," Okpewho notes, getting to the quick of the divide: "Trickster tales are mock-heroic in character and are seen as a perversion of true heroic values and ideals" (*Myth* 280, n.67). Likewise, Ralph Austen recognizes Sunjata as a "gluttonous thief," but says the epic hero is "another, very opposed, type" ("Criminals" 366, 388). Moreover, from a proprietary perspective, the "common" ownership of tales told by anyone versus the epics, which generally belong to "specialists" (S. Belcher 7), contributes to the apparent divide. The epic/trickster intersection merits far more attention, for in it lies an heuristic for

reducing to proper proportions divides between pre-modern and mod-
ern/post-modern, black/African and white/European, male/female, and
beautiful/ugly.

This last dyad, beauty and ugliness, is critical since Enlightenment notions
of beauty, race, and epic performance, influenced by ancient Greco-Roman
ideals, define Western modernity and ontology.[40] Race, beauty, and presumed
competence have been in lockstep for centuries in the West, with whiteness/
Europeanness and blackness/Africanness existing as oppositions.[41] "[B]ecause
the hermeneutic machine of the West has long relied on Africa's otherness to
stage its grandest and most exclusive theatres of the self," theorist and cultural
studies critic Sandra Nuttall writes in *Beautiful/Ugly: African and Diaspora
Aesthetics* (2006), there is a sore need for the "emergence of a properly global
epistemology of beauty and ugliness."[42] Motivated by the need to locate an
aesthetics of ugliness in regard to beauty because of Africa's past and ongoing
encounter with the West, Nuttall advances an intimate, paradoxical, and synergistic relationship between the two poles. Instead of an oppositional binary,
though, Nuttall holds "that beauty always stands in intimate relation to ugliness, both in Africa and elsewhere, though this configuration of the beautiful and the ugly has often been suppressed in Western-based philosophies of
aesthetics." Some critical scholarship on African masks, she notes, advances
an "aesthetics of the ugly" predicated on the idea that truest epistemology
depends on an ability to read the world, including beautiful masks, ironically.
Hence, "nothing becomes visible for the one who does not know how to rec-
ognise disguised power" (Nuttall 8, 21).[43]

Beauty, then, may mask deformity, just as surely as deformity may bespeak
a truer beauty. What's more, instead of an either/or configuration, and/both
offers an extraordinarily more complex reading of the self and African folkloric
figures. Turning back to the beauty/ugly paradox of African epics/tricksters,
we find that tricksters and epic protagonists are genetically related through
deformity. The deformity is not just a happenstance, but an essential element
that motivates—indeed, empowers—tricksters and epic protagonists.[44]

Consequently, the humpback transforms a relationship that may seem
merely rhetorical, if not gratuitous, into a substantive feature that sutures
together epic and trickster and our three epics. David C. Conrad earlier
charted the same course as he meditated on the physical appearance of Sunjata's mother: "Sogolon's ugliness and physical deformities are both blessing
and curse. They signal the secret presence of occult powers qualifying her
to become mother of Sunjata. The physical faults also cause her to languish
unwed long after her age-mates have gone to their husbands." Focusing on
the power that identifies Sogolon as the female icon of allegorye, he adds,

> Sogolon is as complex and ambiguous a figure as exists in the Mande
> (or any other) literary world. On the one hand, as she endures the ritual
> entry into marriage, she cuts a pathetic though undaunted figure with
> her humped back, bald head, and crooked feet, raising clouds of dust as

she is dragged along. . . . At the same time Sogolon is fierce as a lioness, a potentially deadly, animal-like presence with a distinctly masculine side that is normally associated with elderly women like Do Kamissa.

Like Du Kamisa, though much younger, Sugulun/Sogolon has the experience and qualities of a "reproductive decision maker" who is a fusion of *fadenya/badenya*—"a woman with a powerful or masculine physique" who is as "strong as a man" ("Mooning" 198, 201–02).

The humpback defines Sugulun of Du, the Buffalo, but if her humpback and short stature are disaggregated from the buffalo, the epic/trickster unity takes quick form. For example, the tortoise trickster is common in West Africa, where he functions as a "'misfit in organized society because he is ever at pains to upset, by the sheer force of his over-active wit, the contracts and constraints that society establishes in the interests of stability" (Okpewho, *Myth* 151). This "misfit" is known as Ewiri among the western and central Ijo, and Ikaki among eastern Ijos. Ikaki, a divine culture hero and liminal figure, is an amphibian—primarily *oru*, or "village hero," but also considered *biniyou, bini orumo*, or *owu*, "water people" or "water spirits." At the same time, to the Ijo *owu* also means "mask, masquerader, and masquerade dance. . . . Interestingly," Martha Anderson observes, "the masks neither conform to the stereotype of the beautiful, light-skinned mermaid nor capitalize on import symbolism, suggesting that they may represent an older conception, as well as distinct category, of water spirits" (Anderson, "From River" 148; Drewal 195).

Not surprisingly, the allegorycal emerges from the twining of deformity and power, as does the Modernist and Afro-Modernist aesthetic affiliated with these masks.[45] A case in point is Ikaki who, like other *oru*, according to Lisa Aronson, is associated with "superhuman" power, although it is also a typical "short [and] stocky" African trickster engaged in "antisocial" and often "paradoxical behavior." This "superman" figure is eminently defined and empowered by its deformity. One of the tortoise species most familiar to the Eastern Ijo, the *Kinixys belliana* (a.k.a. Bell's Hinge-back), is known to be "exceedingly slow, awkward, and voiceless," with a "slow lumbering gait" and skin having a "dry, wrinkled, and scaly appearance" (See Figure 2.1). Chief among Ikaki's traits, making it a liminal, "powerful spirit and a trickster par excellence," is its shell. The tortoise's *genigeni* ("variegated" or "multicolored") exterior design parallels the mythical potency it incarnates, according to Aronson:

> The shell is clearly a source of the tortoise's dangerous powers. The . . . shell is a kind of container of secretive and potentially harmful things, if not a source of Ikaki's power, trickery, and deceit. . . . It is worth noting that the Kalabari, and other Eastern Ijo groups, regard hunchbacks with a similar degree of fear and trepidation because of the mysterious mound on their backs and the perception that they exhibit an evil, sour temper. (Aronson 252–55)

Figure 2.1   Male adult tortoise (*Kinixys belliana nogueyi*, a.k.a. Bell's Hinge-back).

Ikaki's carapace recalls the Banyangan *nyamasangwa*, for its "variegated" and "multicolored," "secretive," and "mysterious" qualities suggest the very essence of sorcery and epic potential: "many-things," that unknowable unknown.

   Add to this Ikaki's short stature, along with the Ijo belief that "short people are strong-minded" (Anderson, "Bulletproof" 110), and humpbacked deformity emerges as the essential unity between animal tricksters and epic protagonists. Sunjata's name, following the Maninka's "practice of linking the offspring's name with the mother" (Conrad, "Mooning" 190), is a matronym that anticipates his deformity and epical, ironyc potency. Hence, Sunjata, as crippled child, is defined by his bent back, awkward gait, and shortness. Mwindo, the very essence of *l'enfant terrible*, is the shortest of them all, and arguably the rudest, too. Though rare to the collected transcripts of Mwindic performances, Turtle, a trickster figure in the Nyanga cosmology, does associate and travel with Mwindo as a "blood" friend; as one who "separates the water with a whip" to let them all to pass a lake, Turtle also carries the "magical bag" with which Mwindo "revivifies his people" killed in a confrontation with "Kabaraka, Lightning's brother" (Biebuyck, *Hero* 33, 280). Ozidi the Younger is short symbolically, as an adolescent, and literally in comparison to many of his antagonists, such as Tebesonoma of the Seven Crowns whose entrance is a cacophonous, polyphonic eyesore of gigantic proportions:

SONG AND DRUM

Solo:

Oh, oh, Tebesonoma

Oh, oh, Tebesonoma

Morning, it's Tebesonoma

Evening, it's Tebesonoma

Of Tebesonoma's fighting fame we've heard a lot!

Chorus: (*Ditto*)

Caller: O TOWN!

Group: YES!

When "Tebesonoma burst in there singing his song," a rapping to be sure, on his head is an allegorycal theater and veritable house-party: "ululating daemons," some of them dancing, two pairs of heads dialoguing, some others cooking and drinking, with "noise . . . like a market." Tebesonoma had seven heads, his head itself, Ojobolo apparently suggests through gestures, "spread as wide as this house." His appendages are normal in number, but Tebesonoma himself "was so tall that he almost disappeared in the air, like a tree he stood. And a cockerel stood at the crown of his head calling 'Kokoroko!'" (*OS* 236–37). The cacophonous, allegorycal image Ojobolo and the Ozidi troupe performs is not only fabulous, but a form of epical realism. Hence, Ijo sculptors portray bush spirits as warriors with no physical deformities, except multiple heads, to signify, according to Martha G. Anderson, "clairvoyance, vigilance, and superhuman powers rather than anomalies" (see Figures 2.2 and 2.3).

But the simple gaze is belied by the critical ambivalence the warlike Ijo have toward these figures, who are occasionally represented, Anderson indicates, "as uncouth misfits, so independent and diffident that they transgress Ijo ideals." Such ambivalence is reflected in proverbs such as "Beware of the bush, the bush is a difficult place," and "The bush holds many grudges; the bush is a different town (or world)" (Anderson, "Bulletproof" 106–07).

In the Ozidi performance context, epic idealism itself shows many faces over a progressive spectrum that ultimately folds back onto itself, necessitating some ritualized form of closure Ojobolo artfully manages. His revenge-quest just initiated following the primer in epic potentiality he receives from Oreame, the youthful Ozidi is still very much a deformed social pariah whose success is not a teleological given. Since Ozidi wears an allegorycal cloak that marks him as a species of trickster, it is less surprising that Trickster appears in the narrative on his behalf. At the end of Night One, just after Ozidi the Younger has dispatched Ofe's and Azeza's wives,[46] the "man-who-owned-the-town, that's / Ewiri Mr Tortoise himself, known also / as Abamelakpa, because in all the town / he was the fabulist," explains to the Olotu the rise and success of Ozidi. Fittingly, Ewiri Mr. Tortoise speaks the common/sense, the proverb and his sharp reminder

Figure 2.2   Shrine figure or bush spirit with seven heads. This multiheaded bush figure may represent Tebesonoma, a figure in *The Ozidi Saga*. 20th century, Nigeria, Cross River, Ijo people. Wood, glass eyes, paint 68.5 × 14.5 × 18 in. (The Fine Arts Museums of San Francisco, museum purchase, gift of Phyllis C. Wattis and the Phyllis C. Wattis Fund for Major Accessions, 2004.93).

Figure 2.3   Shrine figure or bush spirit with seven heads. 20th century, Nigeria, Cross River, Ijo people. Wood. (Private collection of Barry Hecht/used with permission of the owner/photograph by Gregory R. Staley).

associated when he says that "A man wronged will often bear a strong / son, didn't I tell you so?" (*OS* 57). This is an important cameo, for the Ijo's "cunning idler" is here aligned with the purpose and function—the weak, "wronged," deformed challenging the Authority—of the epic hero.

Just as epic is allegorycal (in Benjamin's sense), the epic hero is a figure—magic bearing and wielding—of ironyc signifying; like Gates' Signifyin(g) Monkey, a trickster-proper cousin of Ozidi, Sunjata, and Mwindo, the epic trickster disrupts the ideal, symbolic understanding because s/he is always already transgressive. The difference between the short narrative of the trickster-proper and the long-performance of the epic trickster may come down to a magical, sorcerous brew of *nyama-atambga*. Whereas epic requires a narrative and spatial imagery long, wide, and deep enough to contain the occult, the spare trickster[47] tale is too quick to the witty, subversive point, and the Trickster too unreliable to bear witness and wield magic. To find allegorycal extension in the terse figurative corpus of trickster tales requires one to perform a narrative—or narrate a performance—out of its lean, deconstructive neck bones.

But the epic performance is a spatial, full-bodied, and embodied aesthetic and cultural catalog into which one pours shifting figures (including tricksters) and forms a multisensorial mumbo-jumbo of narrative, dance, music, history, politics, theology, and sol/soul. Yes, sol/soul, or so(u)l, for the constitutive dynamic is not a Spirit, an overarching, simply ideal and benign *Zeitgeist* metonymically imagined by Hegel as a Napoleon Bonaparte, but a violent magic, *nyama*, that is itself an allegorycal trope. It is as true of the *urban* forest as it is of the West/Central African forest, *viz.*, "Beware of the bush, the bush is a difficult place." The forest, in Nyangaland, is a place where "there are many customs and ways" and is "full of strange ways." Full of "dangerous beings" and "deceivers," the Nyanga's epitome of this is *nyamasangwa*, "one-dressed-in-many-things." The *nyamasangwa*, associated with turtle, iguana, and many birds, especially the hornbill, symbolically represents female and male elements ("intelligence [nesting care] and aggression [when his young are attacked]"). *Nyamasangwa* finds truest representation in the forest's *kirímu-dragon*, "a big animal with black hide, seven heads, teeth like a dog, huge belly, and tail of an eagle."[48]

It is this performative figure—a magical and multiplex dragon—that embodies excess, and which defines the nature of the occult and the uncertainty that lies at the core of epical allegorye. Dragons, in Western mythology, are slain by epical dragon-slayers, but this allegorycal reading suggests that this is because they are themselves dragon-like. Names, particularly epic epithets, are telling in this regard. Yes, Sunjata is identified early as the "Spear-of-Access, Spear-of-Service!" and associated with other similar epithets, but these ideals follow far more ambivalent and terrible epithets that Sisòkò used at the outset: "Sorcerer-Seizing-Sorcerer!," "Stump-in-the-Dark-of-Night!," "Granary-Guard-Dog," and "Adversity's-True-Place!" (Johnson, *Epic* 21–24). By their very essence, these epithets mark Sunjata as transgressive, if not excessive. Likewise, one of Mwindo's praise names is "He-is-not-a-man-to-provoke" (Biebuyck, *Hero* 95). Though Ojobolo's Ozidi does not bear names, transgressiveness is equally applicable to him as an epical, multiplicative factor, for the "copycats" that materialize to test his mettle and infamous celebrity sport names—e.g., Odogu the Ugly, the Scrotum King, Tebesonoma the seven-headed ogre, and Tebekawene, "He who walks on the head" (*OS* 324, n.16)—at once terrible, lurid, and profane. Ojobolo makes no explicit statement regarding this phenomenon, but Rureke, chiding Mwindo's equivalent excesses, does: "Even if a man becomes a hero (so as) to surpass the others, he will not fail one day to encounter some one else who could crush him, who could turn against him what he was looking for" (*ME* 144).

The Smallpox King seems to be just such a one. To some extent, one may dismiss these copycats as a necessary evil for which the epic protagonist bears no blame, but the epics are clear to dismiss such evasions. A "power-drunk Ozidi," Okpewho notes in speaking of a repeated theme that he finds characteristic of the close of Ozidi's *tête-à-tête*, "rages all over the places, bragging about his invincibility" (*African* 76). Though Okpewho's "power-drunk" metaphor is provocative and suggestive of excess, Clark-Bekederemo's language ranges beyond "places" of domesticity to confront the full face of the total destruction immanent in the epic's artistry. Hence, Ozidi and Oreame "conquered the world and are now terrorizing everybody," and Ozidi "executed everybody in town" and "completely laid waste" to Ado/Orua, Tebekawene (*OS* 321), and the Smallpox King report, respectively.

Ojobolo's Oreame transcends the empowerment of the female recognized by Mbele, who notes that certain epic heroes could, on rare occasion, have female names (160), or Cartwright, who credits Sunjata's sister with taking active measures to reach toward and save him in his "moment of greatest need" (*Reading Africa* 33). The *Ozidi Saga* presents a grand-maternal figure who nurtures the hero and teaches him the art of warfare in his father's absence. Consequently, on several occasions, Ozidi not only calls upon Oreame for magical help, but when her magics fail and Ozidi is ineffective or fatally wounded, Oreame shows her willingness to use his sword (*OS* 113, 122, 123, 166, 175, 224, 283). Oreame herself becomes transgressive and excessive. Although she sometimes pursues her aims by disguising herself as a beautiful woman, at other times she engages in unremitting violence. In one instance, as Ozidi battled a challenger, her "body became as steel"; in another, she pushes the envelope of violence until, as one spectator remarked, she became "Quite a war-monger!" whose "body just brittles (sic) all over for battle" (*OS* 106, 182). In contrast, young Ozidi washes the violence from his face, has a peaceful appearance, and shows an inclination to mercy lacking in Oreame (*OS* 142, 159, 169, 252–56)—before the end of the epic, that is, when he has matured into a battled-honed warrior whose attack on Anglese, despite Oreame's advice, brings him closest to a death even Oreame is hard-pressed to prevent.[49]

Perhaps most significantly, the epic performers pair the transgressive/ excessive dynamic with an eco-critical cautionary element that stems from the close association—often genetic—of the epic protagonists to the deities associated with the sublime power of nature. In the beginning of the epic cycle, "The advent of the hero is an astounding phenomenon which is sometimes connected with cosmic turmoil (rain and thunder) or with unusual social and physical situations" (Biebuyck, *Hero* 93).[50] As a pre-modern epic myth out of Africa, the dark continent, one might easily dismiss this as prehistorical superstition, but as epical realism that comments upon the role of epic grandeur, our post-modern world of global warming cannot help but take note. Again, the epic protagonists' names and epithets are revealing. Mwindo moonlights as "Mr. Excess"—a figure the Banyanga identify with the hornbill (Biebuyck, "Nyanga Circumcision" 89)—because he serves as the metonym for a transgressive world-shatterer represented by the hornbill's powerful, prodigious bill, one equally suited for a blast of destructive hot wind (boasting) and the knocking on, and down, of trees.

In this regard, the *nyama* of the *Mwindo Epic* performance Rureke invokes, as artist and Banyangan, establishes an eco-logical core embodied in the opening and essence of the narrative, and by its protagonist. This explains the etymological affinity of Mwindo with *indo*, the Nyanga verb meaning "to fell trees" (he is also praised as Kakiria, "the little one who makes the trees fall in the forest"), and the interconnection between the hero-chief and Nyanga divinities. This situates Mwindo as a possible apocalyptic force in the rain forest, as well as a spiritual transcendence that protects the very (animal) life it harbors. The "magico-religious atmosphere" of the Mwindo *epos* is created, then, by the presence of the protagonist and the chief Nyanga deities, Ongo-Nyamurairi, who are together the emblems of "life and death." The etymological parallels Biebuyck offers—Mwindo : *indo* and Nyamurairi : *murai* (Banyangan for "hero")—makes possible the linkage of epic performance, a "supreme," divine code of ethics, and the eco-sphere (Biebuyck, *Hero* 61–62, 64, 68, 93–94).[51]

What the West/Central African epic performances make clear through cautionary elements is that epic aggression itself is not meant to become a cultural mainstay. Ozidi begins his epic career not only on a worthy and sanctified "mission," but in the green, for the Ijo understand his very wellbeing to be jeopardized by the murder of his father. Since the ancestors preside over their living descendants' spiritual and material prosperity, questions of justice and survival are inseparable. Thus, as Clark-Bekederemo indicates, "In the epic proper, the worthiness and sanctity of the hero's mission clearly is self-evident in that he has to find ultimate rest for his father" ("Introductory" liii). However, even after he has succeeded, Ozidi's violence continues. Now, the violence literally becomes domesticated as Ozidi, like *l'enfant terrible*, repeatedly leaves the safety of home to go out and "play." His play, of course, is that of a tree-leveling, forest-destroying epic figure whose excesses now issue from the home itself, bringing homelessness, famine, and a host of dangers: to those oblivious to, fleeing from, and ultimately consumed by his desire for sport, as well as, eventually, his own comeuppance in the form of a fatal disease.

Likewise, Mwindo's epic cycle closes with the capture of his father and the tribunal that brings him to justice. Mwindo, himself the new regent, continues to play as well, and eventually makes sport of Kirimu (Dragon) by killing him. Not only has Mwindo made sport of an animal, but he has killed the very emblem of allegorye, one symbolizing the eco-diversity of the rainforest. Perhaps recognizing this, three spectators tell Mwindo such, after which "he killed them on the spot." It is MOS-fitting, then, that Nkuba, the god of lightning whose thunderstorms replenish the pools so vital to the rainforest animals and humans, sweeps the hot-headed Mwindo off his throne in Tubondo and into a nomadic state of being subject to a year-long celestial journey. This odyssey is an eco-mythological one—beginning with the realm of Rain, which drenched him with a rain that "fell upon Mwindo seven and seven times more," and then Hail, Moon, Sun, and Star—that finally cools him down. Wizened, Mwindo passes laws to prevent such excesses on his part and others (*ME* 132–33, 138).

Hence, against the Western tendency to read heroes through the "physiognomic features of the morality-play allegory," the MOS-epic figures move about in an allegorycal "cloak of invisibility" which reveal that morality proper is not just superficial and simplistic (W. Benjamin 191), but dangerous. Instead of a cycle exposing the self-destructiveness of unchecked and normalized epic potential to others, self, and the land, too much of modern, Western culture, founded on a cornerstone situated in epic ontology, performs a more limited understanding of the heroic epic genre because its visible, physiognomic symbols prevail. The result makes the evolutionary basis of natural selection and survival of the fittest, the foundational assumption underlying discussions about modern hegemonies, truly contextualized by performance: "Welcome to the desert of the real," spoken by Morpheus (Laurence Fishburn) to Neo in *The Matrix* (2001) and appropriated by Slavoj Žižek after 9/11,[52] becomes another, post-modern Marxist way of declaring, "Born in a mighty bad land," a phrase which Jerry H. Bryant appropriately recognizes as African-American longstanding common/sense about the epic of slavery and racism.

EPICAL AGONY: EPIC PERFORMANCE AND SELF-DESTRUCTION

Why have a cautionary tale that is coextensive with the epic heroics in the first place? Because, as these West/Central African epic traditions suggest, cultures must not romanticize epic figures, even if their epic potentiality and transgression may be "welcome on troubled days." Once this Pandora's box has been opened, even if to defuse "troubled days," there is no guarantee the epic protagonist will exercise self-restraint, though the mythological Sunjata does so. Nor, of course, can the Trickster cycle answer it, for its reversal aesthetic, the weak-overcoming-the-powerful morphology which the epic narrative parallels, marks the end of these short narratives. Since the epic protagonist is a former epic trickster who knows the Trickster's indirection, wit, and signifyin(g), it is no surprise that these epic tyrants are not thwarted by weaker opponents. In fact, not even strong human opponents can defeat them, for the tyrants are also epic figures who have, usually, bested them already. Hence, the hotness of this epic potentiality, a sure threat to over-whelm anyone—including the epic protagonist—who channels it, needs to be literally cooled with water, and figuratively cooled through the act of reading the context and exercising self-restraint. Besides, though *nyama* is everything, maybe world-shaking badness, it might also be garbage, or hot air, that is equally effective if one knows how to manage appearances.

At any rate, its *modus operandi* is agonistic, and its airing is explosive on a domestic and urban level in the public sphere. The cooling agent is the greatest paradox, for it is as small as common water, which Trickster tales even take for granted, and yet as powerful as the spirits associated with it, those who are the sources for the elemental magic the epic figure wields. Thus, in a quintessentially symbolic unity, the epic storytellers rely upon an ablution ceremony to close the epics: Sunjata's ceremony to the "jinn of the water, Master of the Moghoya-Dji, master of the magic water," at which time he drinks "three times" before "he washed his face," simultane-ously marks the formal end of the march into the civic sphere and Sunjata's transfiguration (Niane, *Sundiata* 71–72); Ozidi is washed by herbs, the "pharmaceutic virtues of the natural environment" (Okpewho, "Critical Introduction" xiii), to cure a bad case of the (self-inflicted) "yaws"; and, Mwindo is taken on a celestial journey.

Immersion in and emergence from the waters is essential in the narra-tive and the actual performance because epical agony is a double-jointed problem defined by the "scorching irony" Frederick Douglass located at the very core of American performances of freedom and identity ("What to the Slave" 470). It goes without saying, of course, that the victims suffer epical agony, a totalizing enlightenment of the worst sort. Here agony, from the victims' perspective, erupts into a mathematical sublime in which the conju-gation of *agon*, agony, is knotted together with Enlightenment epistemology, race, class, and exceptionalism in a fierce debate—one that too often dis-misses the folk's agonistic sense. Most of these debates, to be addressed later, turn into attacks against what many scholars call the aesthetics or politics of victimization—Richard Wright's sociological fiction (black Naturalism) and the protest novel mode in general; Toni Morrison's victims; the need for black men, according to Bill Cosby and Alvin Pouissaint, M.D., in their co-authored book, *Come On People* (2008), to "Just do it" and go from being "victims to victors." But what is often overlooked by characterizing the "Problem" of race as a denial of equal access to a "seat at the Nation's feast," or entry into the "promised land" (Du Bois, *Souls* 12), is the impact on those who channel, and normalize, the transgressiveness of epic potential. According to the folk sense associated with heroic epic performance, hunting, and warfare, if one's face is not washed of violence, the transgression of entering the domain of the gods by taking lives of humans or animals, then this transgressive mask potentially becomes an excessive one with implications for the self, household, and community.

For example, among Ògún followers in Benin, according to Robert G. Armstrong, *ògwú* is a "key concept" in Idoma male society. When a man has killed an animal or another warrior, he has to undergo the *èōgwóōnà*, a ceremony for "washing *ògwú* from the face," which is held as a high honor. Armstrong is clear to delineate an honor associated with ritual and a deep, nuanced sense of human nature when he says, "From a sociological point of view, *èōgwóōnà* may be regarded as the resocialization of a dangerous hero, the acclamation of his brave deed, accompanied by the cleansing of the spirit of the dead animal or man from his face." Usually the blacksmith is the one who "washes the killing from the face" of the hunter or the warrior. He does it with medicinal leaves that have been dipped into the wooden trough of water, in the forge, which is used to cool red-hot iron or steel implements. Likewise, a similar ceremony occurs among Ògún hunter-warriors of Yorubaland, where blacksmiths wash the hunter and warrior to strengthen them and protect them from the spirits of animals and other warriors they have killed. Without this washing, the transgressor could be "crazed" by the killing (31–32, 34).

This purification ritual is not new or unique, for rituals to resocialize warriors can be found among the Navajo and the ancient Greeks. In these cases, as with the MOS-epics, the threat to the domestic sphere is quite clear. Among the *Diné* (Navajo), it has long been known that the *Anaa' jí ndáá'* ("Enemy Way") ceremony[53] is a community-wide ritual, deeply rooted in tradition, meant to purge the "effects of actual warfare" suffered by warriors (Haile 24–25). Its symbolic and social significance are deeply central to Navajo practices as they have evolved over the centuries, from the origin myth of the *Naayé'ii* ("Monster Way") legend to the anti-colonization struggles against European Americans, and to the legacy of such battles adapted for contemporary struggles.

The Monster Way legend narrates the Emergence from the four underworlds, an act necessitated because widespread immorality had made the existing race of humans begin to produce monsters. When First-man emerged, he used his medicinal "bundle" to create, among other things, Changing Woman, who gave birth to *Naayéé' Neezghání* ("Monster Slayer") and his brother, "Born for Water." With Born for Water as his assistant, Monster Slayer engages in an epical campaign that ultimately results in the defeat of the monsters. However, the monsters' "ghosts" remain and threaten both them and the world. There is no unanimity on this account,[54] but a line of traditional thought links Monster Slayer's warfare and his contamination. The Enemy Way ceremony targets these "jealous and angry" ghosts, which are associated with the introduction of illness, disharmony, and *hocho* ("disorder") in Navajo cosmology, which relies upon collective ontology and hózhó (literally "beauty" or "beautiful conditions"), the holistic approach to "health and harmony." With this ceremony, reproductive, vegetal wholeness is restored and the world is now safe for Changing Woman to create the four original clans of the Diné (Haile 12, 14–19; Witherspoon and Peterson 7–32).

In the contemporary Enemy Way ceremony, its male "patients" have their name publicly announced, and the patient, his wife, and her possessions are "blackened" with "charcoal to symbolize the dark flint clothes of Monster Slayer." The Enemy Way prayer, Sam D. Gill argues, is fully interconnected with the blackening: it establishes identification with Monster Slayer, provides for defeat of the spiritual impurity, and ends with restoration of health and balance. The actual blackening, which follows this prayer, works in similar vein, the blackening corresponding to Monster Slayer's "powers of destruction" and, equally vital, his "acquisition" of the creative powers of "health and life" (Gill 113–15; Haile 20, 23–26; Schwarz 310–11, 317–20).

Although the Navajo and American majority represent the colonized and colonizer, respectively, American psychiatrist and Homerphile, Jonathan Shay, M.D., Ph.D., articulates a principle—in *Achilles in Vietnam* (1994) and *Odysseus in America* (2002)—corresponding to the resocialization concept motivating the *eōgwóōnà* and Enemy Way ceremonies. According to Shay, the ritualization and "communalization of grief" for the reintegration of veterans is a defining feature of ancient Ionian culture, reflected in the *Iliad* and *Odyssey*. Taking direct aim at modern simplifications and idealization of the Homeric heroes, Shay says, "To the ancient Greeks," by comparison to contemporary people familiar with Odysseus,

> Odysseus' name *meant* "man of hate" or "he who sows trouble." . . .
>
> Odysseus, like Achilles, is remembered as a *hero* of Greek myth. Today we see our heroes as unmixed blessings, almost as though pure beneficence is part of the definition. . . . However, the ancient Greek idea of the hero was deeply mixed. As I just noted, Odysseus' name means "man of hate." Achilles' name means "he whose host of fighting men have grief"—referring to his own Greek heroes were men of pain who were both needed by their people and *dangerous* to them. (*Odysseus* 2)

While the general reputation Shay notes for Odysseus is very much in keeping with the trickster's attributes,[55] compared to Achilles' more noble persona, these war veterans present to civilians the inseparable paradox of *thumos* and *gastēr*: "When we are in fear of the enemy, nothing is too much or too good for the 'greathearted spirit' (*thumos*) of our fighting men; when they return as veterans we see their needs as greedy, demanding, uncultivated belly (*gastēr*)" (*Odysseus* 13). The war veterans, modern analogs to Achilles and Odysseus, suffer an injury to *thumos*, the *"universal and normal"* form of "character" associated with honor, recognition and ambition. Perhaps because the ancient Greeks had an organic relationship to *thumos*, which could "develop [into] dangerous excesses, deficiencies, or deformities," Athenians used public ritual in the form of "sacred," tragic theater to convert veterans into citizens. "The ancient Athenians had a distinctive therapy of purification," Shay reveals, "healing, and reintegration of returning soldiers that was undertaken as a whole political community" (*Odysseus* 152–61; italics in original). American war veterans, because of military efficiency in removing the dead and the disconnect between civilians and veterans, are deprived of the "communalization of combat traumas" they most need. This ritual involves, Shay argues, discussion of the trauma, open exchange and expression of "emotions" related to it, and the interpersonal connections of those "who will not let one go through it alone" (*Achilles* 55).

In spite of these insights, Shay limits his communalization paradigm to veterans, rendering his insight both revolutionary insofar as he sees ages-old, universal principles at work, but also myopic. Shay leaves untreated the most important clinical question: if community ritual is necessary to heal and cope with war veterans' trauma and grief, what ritual can heal the community's self-victimization and epic agony when its ontology, and hence social compact, is epic-oriented? Since Achilles may be "'already dead' before he begins his bezerk frenzy," as Shay observes (*Achilles* 49–50), it stands to reason that his soul has also suffered a death. This notion of soul death, paired with its fraternal twin, soul murder, sounds the deeper trauma of epic performance.

Historian Nell Irvin Painter, writing from the objectivity of feminism, American slavery, Marxism, and psychoanalysis, implicitly recognizes the ancient folk concept pertaining to the full costs of violence. Painter offers a complex understanding of what happens to victims of traumatic violence when she speaks of "soul murder" in the context of slavery, particularly its impact on enslaved women and children:

> child abuse, sexual abuse, sexual harassment, rape, battering. Psychologists aggregate the effects of these all-too-familiar practices in the phrase *soul murder*, which may be summed up as depression, lowered self-esteem, and anger.
>
> Soul murder has a long genealogy, going back to folk beliefs in Europe and Africa about the possibility of stealing or killing another person's soul.

Painter avoids the victimization paradox by steering a middle course in which she situates "soul murder" as victimization, resistance to it through religion and community, and self-victimization that slavery imposes on those who consider themselves part of the master race (127, 130–31, 139). Painter parallels, using critical methodology, a folk common/sense located in the West/Central African epic performance, one which speaks with equal authority about the double-edged sword of slavery.

Although Painter centers slavery, and this study considers slavery a mere outcome of an older performance causality, the double-sided danger of soul murder is a bedrock to the slave and abolitionist communities, judging by slave autobiographies. Consider Frederick Douglass' perspective on the soul-stealing impact of slavery.[56] Douglass famously remarks upon the impact the ownership of slaves had on the delicate Sophia Auld: "Slavery proved as injurious to her as it did to me. When I went there [Baltimore], she was a pious, warm, and tender-hearted woman. . . . Slavery soon proved its ability to divest her of these heavenly qualities. Under its influence, the tender heart became stone, and the lamblike disposition gave way to one of tiger-like fierceness" (*Narrative* 31). Even Douglass' second sight underperforms the real, allegorycal import immanent here. Instead of saying that racism gets into and transforms Sophia Auld, it is more appropriate to recognize the established place of the epic inscribed in the American body-politic. Indeed, William Blake's "Tyger" (1794)—"Tyger! Tyger! burning bright"—is always already in her body-biologic, and just waiting for the right spark to trigger her "fearful symmetry," "dread hand" and "feet" (1, 4, 12), and agonized howl of pain.

Hence, beyond the traditional epic performative context, where vicarious association is made between the epic protagonist and the auditor-participants, this cautionary lesson is also for them/US, the epically charged scions of Mwindo, Ozidi, Sunjata, Helen, Odysseus, and Achilles. This makes perfect sense, for epic potentiality is such that it is not enough to merely warn auditor-participants; the cautionary dimension must equal or eclipse the ideal/transgressive dimension. Mwindo's end narrative is a celestial journey, a sci-fi trip, and symbolic *soul*ar eclipse that strips Mwindo of his boastful pluck and returns to him his common/sense. Ozidi's transgressiveness, long turned into an excessiveness lying somewhere on the epic highway situated between killing innocent villagers, a new mother, his own uncle, and leveling entire forests with gleeful abandon, finally brings him face-to-face with an epic antagonist he, even with Oreame's aid, cannot best. Hence, the Smallpox King's arrival on a "war boat" bedecked with "all manner of fearsome guns" (*OS* 376). The Smallpox King fells Ozidi with a deadly case of the yaws (*yangaba, yangaba*, or "rough" or "twisted body"), a body-deforming malady which is associated with excessive behavior beyond the transgressive warrior ethos the Ijos admire (Anderson, "Bulletproof" 105–10; Clark-Bekederemo, "Introductory" xl–xli, xlii; cf. Okpewho, *Myth* 138, 164).

THE MOS-EPIC UNDER WESTERN EYES: A HISTORY OF TRANSLATION

The preceding discussion of excessiveness and the problem of symbolic violence highlights the allegorycal complexity of the performance, one that cannot even be captured by modern technologies of reproduction, not to mention the allegories of the grand narrative and neoclassical reconstructions predicated on such allegories. Sunjata expert Charles S. Bird, speaking of the production of Sunjatic transcripts out of performances even less dynamic than Clark-Bekederemo's *Ozidi Saga* transcript, highlights the problem best when he says, "If transcription is a journey across the Sea of Despondency, translation is the Wallow of Despair." Notwith the aid of two tape recorders, because of the "comfortable indeterminacy . . . incompatible with our objective and formal concerns" in which a "letter has to be either this or that, either *t* or *d*," the final transcripts are "full of holes at the most fundamental levels" ("The Production" 282–83). Robert Newton echoes this in his description of modern transformation and dissemination of Malian Sunjata, for he finds that the less local the performance and auditor, the more generic is the end result. The commodified performance as "epic cassette" disrupts the control of the *jeliw*, becomes

> fixed, repeatable, transportable. It does not make the same kind of adjustments to circumstances as might be made by a live performer in front of a live audience. . . . For this reason, locally recorded performances dubbed on the spot for potential customers exhibit a greater specificity in the use of names of people, places, and things. Those which have been recorded for nationwide broadcast or distribution and are reproduced through studio technology tend to make broader references, use fewer local names, and emphasize more general narrative passages and songs which serve to encapsulate a series of events.

Once the Sunjatic epic performance becomes an international epic cassette, the "long narrative" gives way to forms "more musical and more danceable, highlighting the vocal virtuosity of the lead singer and the dynamic playing of the lead guitarists" (Newton 323, 325–26).[57] Likewise, Nyanga epics may provide an "extensive inventory of Nyanga material culture," but they are "poetic" syntheses that are "selective[,] . . . limited, incomplete, and imprecise" (Biebuyck, *Hero* 34–35, 47–48). As Newton and Conrad indicate for the Sunjatic tradition, a truism appropriate for the Ozidi Saga festival performances, too, no epic performance can exhaustively represent Banyangan cultural breadth and intricacy; the bards' artistry shapes structure and content significantly, and the common cultural milieu obviates explanatory detail. Context, Okpewho repeatedly notes in his discussion of the synergistic dialogic between bard and audience, is indispensable to a full appreciation of bardic artistry (*African* 42–69; *Myth* 76–91).

In this sense—an embodied, context-rich common/sense for sure—and considering the modern American/Western European perspective, Marcel Detienne is correct when he implies, in an ironic critique of Greek classics scholars, that the "Greeks are like the others," too. That is to say, whether one speaks of modern reconstructions that mimic the ancient

Greeks, or a modern deconstruction that dehumanizes Africa and the Other, both proceed from a fundamental mistake and impossibility: as challenging as it is to know the spirit of one's own culture, the difficulty of competently knowing cultures significantly different and far older, if not ancient, is impossible. Knowledge concretized out of past cultures into symbolic narrative is more imaginative—and hence distorted—than it is materially objective.

To the extent classical American/Western European understanding of the Homeric epics allegorizes the erasure of the above-mentioned impossibilities, this peculiar performance of the American Homer and its peculiar institutions merit further consideration. Just as allegorye becomes allegory through an iron-driven violence, the modern processes of epic performance miss the cautionary tale that is a latent, late-narrative warning about the danger acquiring such epic potential entails. This Western European phenomenon, predating trans-Atlantic slavery by centuries, anticipated Hegelian and Kantian racism and shows how white sublimity was created out of a simple, supposedly perfect, binary opposition to dark/blackness. The historical evidence and scholarship focuses on two forms of violence that dismissed the African epic sublime.

Misinterpretation

Closely related to the evolution of Western European thought and culture, particularly its enlightenment, is the misinterpretation of Africa's orality and holistic orientation as absence of culture. However, far from being an empty *tabula rasa* space, the "Dark Continent" was full of cultural *nyama* and material culture too varied and ancient to be reduced to Western typology. In this regard, misinterpretation amounts to a colonial misfeasance, for the mechanisms of colonial administration moved too swiftly to even begin to approach the cultures' illimitable complexity. Generally, Europeans treated oral performance like Sunjata as "history" to be separated from "legendary and supernatural details" (S. Belcher 107). This general misinterpretation of Sunjata had specific aspects. In the Mande, "French colonial practice, which was to rotate officers from post to post and from one cultural region to another, worked against the development of language skills. Aside from this difficulty, in the age before tape-recording even a linguistically competent scribe would have found it impossible to keep up with the performance of a jeli." Complicating this even more was the colonial administrators' assumed superiority; they cavalierly discarded details "considered 'far too puerile and childish' or episodes 'too long and tedious,'" substituted their own "modern judgment of the hero," and prematurely dismissed "praise singers" secured as "informants"—in the absence of sufficient time, their "tirades" obviously could add nothing (Bulman 237). Such changes can have disastrous consequences for both communities. While the Nyanga epic performances dwell upon "strife and endless quests accompanied by violence, deception, and destruction," and have a "richly nuanced vocabulary to express dying, destroying, killing, fighting, cutting, attacking, smashing, beating, etc.," the allegorycal perspective is the sharpest point: not only do the Nyanga "not extol warlike traits," but they consider such as antitheses to their moral code (Biebuyck, *Hero* 68).

(Re)Ordering

Essential to Western notions of mathematical precision, and the misinterpretation of African complexity as chaos stemming from it, is the project of enlightening—by ordering, or re-ordering—the Other. The ensuing *misfeasance* is understandable because an imperialistic malfeasance, borne of European epicality, was the motivating agent. The efficiency of conquest amounted to a colonial policy that emphasized "mastering local languages," using folklore as heuristics, and inquiring into the "historical background of local cultures." This followed the principle articulated by François-Victor Equilbecq, a French colonial administrator in West Africa (1902–1932) and publisher of a three-volume set of West African folk tales: "it is necessary to know those whom one wishes to dominate" (Bulman 236, 238).[58]

This (re)ordering was not simply a matter of establishing an hierarchy, but was a fundamental process in which radical complexity, allegorye, was reimagined as simple matter, both *res* (things, or chattel-objects) and Other. Walter Benjamin articulates this process as part of his genealogy of allegory, one in which "spoken language" is the extreme antithesis of the typographical; allegorists saw writing as sacred, but for him it is "cold, facile technique" that strips the "dignity" away from "spoken language" in favor of writing, which "tends toward the visual" and the limits of "strict codification" (175–76). Benjamin and West African epic scholars speak to one another in this regard. For instance, Okpewho's recognition of and insistence on the performative artistry of heroic epics, which offers "useful ways of looking at Homer" and other epic traditions, is understandable and obligatory. His mission has been a struggle against past and present reductionism by literate European readers, hence the role of performance aesthetics in his comparative approach to African, ancient Greek, and European epics:

> In examining the art of composition in the oral epic, we must be constantly in mind the moment of performance—with music, histrionic resources, emotional relationship between singer and audience—which makes this tradition of art different from the literate variety. Each performance is the product of one specific moment or context and, in a creative tradition of the oral epic, is never exactly repeated. Though there are some fixed structural laws which the narrative will obey by

the very nature of its oral medium, the results of any performance depend mainly on the particular audience, mood, and atmosphere.

Clearly, there can be no fixed pattern to the context in which a song is performed, and some of the peculiar features of a performance are due to a variety of circumstances. (*The Epic* 30–31, 135)

Like the performativity of epic myth that Okpewho suggests operates in all societies with such traditions, even the literate ones, oral artistry betrays the deeply human. This contextual basis for artistic production is obscured by the mask of civilization/literacy that hides the elements lying at the fount of a given culture's social contract.

Concern with the facile gaze of literate readers echoes among African epic scholars. "Against a background of common thematic and stylistic elements," Biebuyck notes of four Nyanga *karisi* (epics) he compared, the "epics develop many antithetical viewpoints and motifs. The examination of these oppositions should have a sobering effect on those who, on the basis of limited information, relish in facile generalizations." This takes on more authority when he adds, in his comparative analysis of those four versions of the *Mwindo Epic*, that the "differences far outweigh the similarities," and that the historicity contained in these epics "requires considerable insight into the broader cultural and historical continuum of related and intermingled populations in eastern Zaire, of which the average Nyanga listener is fully aware" (*Hero* 8, 46, 86).[59] In their description of how European explorers repeatedly misconstrued *nyamakalaya* and then, after trans-Atlantic slavery, "codified" the "Mande caste system" in a manner that ran roughshod over, and simplified, that (*nyama*) which could and should never, in fact, be classified, David C. Conrad and Barbara E. Frank's summative metaphor performs their objection to these processes: "The cumulative effect of their efforts to classify the artisans and bards of the Western Sudan suggests wanderers in a hall of mirrors, determined to locate within a plethora of images social patterns derived from their own experience with which they could be comfortable" (2–10).

When considering the various media and senses wielded by the epic performers as part of this "cultural performance," each performance functioning "like a hall of mirrors—magic mirrors, each interpreting as well as reflecting the images beamed to it, and flashed from one to the others" (Turner, "Images" 23–24), one quickly understands the far-reaching implications of the colonial intervention. The violent process was calculated to deny the same (or greater) complexity of non-Western, nonwhite peoples, and strip away all the high-performance potential to make the African Other simple and static, natives in a land of no "movement" (Hegel, *Philosophy* 99), while claiming all the complexity and dynamism as their *a priori*, ontological given. For Malians, for example, this deconstruction of *nyama* and colonial construction of a Mande case in its place is the equivalent of falling into the vast Black Atlantic abyss, framed by West

Africa's allegorye-rich epic performances on one side, and a totally simple understanding of it from the distant, Enlightened, other side. Just as black (*negro*) became synonymous with *necro* (death), and necromancer is the practitioner of dark arts, *jeliw*, *funew*, and other Senegambian epic bards became griots. The griot is a catch-all that, in its deformation of complex African forms, represents the violence of misinterpretation and containment, and the demonizing of African spirituality as un-Christian conjure, roots, juju, hoo doo, and voodoo.

Traditional West/Central African epic performances suffered by virtue of European colonialism. Under the *ancien régime*, British Empire, and the like, the MOS-epic tricksters cease to be Banyangan, Ijo, and Malian to become African and, more perjoratively, colored in their own native land. The MOS-epic protagonist's subjectivity is foreshortened, attenuated, deformed, and ultimately disregarded in and of itself as a species of epic folk performance to which the Homeric narratives are indexed. The generic masquerade that overlaid the epic for early and far too many European studies, becoming the norm for American and now African-American studies, is the African trickster. The massive corpus of trickster studies accurately reveals that this figure is pervasive throughout Africa, including West and Central Africa. Serving both as a secular and a religious figure, the trickster links the profane, the anti-social, the treacherous, and selfish—the liminality to which the trickster is often associated—with an opposition situated in creativity, human spirit, and, ultimately, the sacrosanct. As such a figure, the trickster is the master of irony through the constant interpolation of contradiction that is life itself.

The importance of the trickster tales have received widespread scholarly attention, much of it deserved, but the exclusion of other genres is problematic insofar as creativity and agency are associated with narrative length and performance complexity. Indeed, the overemphasis on traditional African tricksters, often fox, rabbit, and others, led African literary scholar S.A. Babalola to produce a text on another generic corpus, the *ijala* poetic chants recited by the hunter-followers of Ògún, just to debunk the "false impression created by numerous existing European language translations of African myths, legends, and fables—that African literature consists of nothing but prose narratives in which tales about Tortoise and Spider loom large" (*Content and Form* v). Although American—especially African-American—scholars have accorded much more attention to African literature since the mid-1960s, when Babalola made his observation, the traditional African epic performance, despite its fundamental relevance for understanding the performance of epic mythology and race in America, remains largely unknown.

Though immense, these challenges confronting African epics are less daunting by comparison to the problems related to its diasporic continuity. The epic performance was suppressed or undermined by colonial forces (Seydou 322; Johnson, "Introduction" 5; Biebuyck, "Nyanga

Circumcision" 20), but West/Central Africans still occupied the African cultural and topographical space of the ancestors, a connection allowing for retreat and regeneration. In the story proper, Sunjata may have been forced into a diaspora away from Mali, but it was a diaspora *within* West Africa, present-day Senegambia, that made his deformity and sociopolitical blackening—a symbolic death—a temporary condition.

Even though the post-colonial Malian leaders sought to retain the boundaries created by France, Sunjata remained vital, Robert Newton argues, for the "cultural heritage of precolonial empires has always maintained a living presence. Thus, the [Rassemblement Democratique Africain's] program of establishing and spreading a new national identity has had less to do with reclaiming lost cultural forms and social relations which might be suppressed by the overlay of assimilation policies of the colonial French than with redefining existing structures that had continually resisted such efforts" (319).

A case in point is that of D.T. [Djabril Tamsir] Niane's *Sundiata* (1965), a transcription and publication of Mamadou Kouyaté's performance, which was nearly three times longer than any previous version and is, today, the best-known version of African epics among Western audiences. The complexity Niane's epic narrative permitted, albeit muted and sanitized to conform to Western epical conventions, coincided with the African post-colonial movement and yet was, as an African epic in literary prose, an ideal intermediary for Western audiences familiar with Western epics. Ostensibly, djeli Kouyaté is the sole authority, but this is little more than a very effective rhetorical mask wielded by Niane to entice Anglophone readers with the exotic, ancient wisdom and artistry of *a* native genius. However, Niane actually composed *Sundiata* by creating a seamless prose narrative out of several different performances, probably in a manner similar to the creation of the *Iliad* and *Odyssey* out of the centuries-old performance culture which predated Homer's codification. According to historian Stephen Bulman, "*Soundiata* marks a stylistic break with most earlier literary accounts" created by Europeans, for though magic remains an element, Niane's text "does not emphasize the excesses of the characters or revel in the 'chaotic' nature of some themes." Eurocentric considerations of "African soul and African culture," Bulman argues, are missing in his "direct and (perhaps disingenuously) simple style" (242). In other words, though Niane's work is an important break from the Eurocentric gaze, missing from the literary *Sundiata* are the performative elements essential for understanding heroic archetypes in a given culture.

In the end, and notwithstanding the *Sundiata* novelization for French- and then English-reading audiences, the traditional Sunjatic essence remained among the folk. *Nyama* could be tapped to re-create identity, for it was a living tradition that worked before, against, and after colonization.

To understand the implications the discussion of European intervention in the West/Central African epic habitus has for its trans-Atlantic diaspora, a nonteleological, allegorycal reading of traditional African epic figures is necessary. One must approach the problem of traditional West/Central African epic continuity and discontinuity through the question of deformity, for the various forms of deformation lend themselves to allegorye and the trickster-like figures whose survivability mirrors and foreshadows the deeply human will to overcome obstacles that manifests itself in the epic cycle. The yin-yang relationship of trickster-epic owes its dynamism to deformity. Although the traditional approach of privileging a valorized epic heroic is critical to understanding its continuity, the African epic is not, contrary to expectations, a monological celebration of masculinity and warfare. As demonstrated earlier, the hero and the community contribute to the epic cycle. Because of a conflict, both the epic hero and the epic community undergo an evolution that often separates them and puts them on an antagonistic path. The initial phase of the cycle creates an antithetical relationship in which the epic community swells in strength while the protagonist—far from being a realized epic hero—endures castigation, ostracism, life threats, and eventually exile to prevent further damage to himself and his family. Because of the agency of a wayward community, the drama and suspense builds in the early careers of these figures, who are forced into indirection, signifying, chicanery, and physical retreat. They resort to these and other artifices of the trickster proper until they have developed, through various rites of passage, the personal qualities and skills necessary for their emergence as epic heroes who can return and confront their antagonists. Hence, out of this state of deformity, the epic trickster is born.

Or reborn, for the epic trickster is not just a structural feature of the long heroic narrative known as the traditional African epic, but a deep structure of the West African habitus whose counterpart is the short, heroic narrative: the trickster tale.

3 Epic Performance in the American Epic Diaspora

Within the West/Central African epic habitus, the strength that comes from deformity motivates the narrative performance and simultaneously defines a genetic feature shared by all of humanity. But is this so for the African Diaspora? Owing to the deformation from slavery, the colonization of Africa, and the evolution of race in the eighteenth and nineteenth centuries, the MOS-epic trickster, starting with Banyanga, Ijo, and Mandingo, Bamana, and other related ethnic groups in the Mande, became "African" and then negro ("black"). In short, once extracted from the recuperative space of Africa, and re-located in Western modernity, the indigenous trickster figure was e-raced, "blackened," and deformed by the epistemological and other historical forces that marred its entrance into a New World. Hence, Hegel's rhetorical move, in the "Introduction" to *The Philosophy of History*, to

> leave Africa, not to mention it again. For it is no historical part of the World; it has no movement or development to exhibit. Historical movements in it—that is in its northern part—belong to the Asiatic or European World. . . . What we properly understand by Africa, is the Unhistorical, Undeveloped Spirit, still involved in the conditions of mere nature, and which had to be presented here only as on the threshold of the World's History. (99)

This erasure is a bleak gaze at African culture, and a total black-out for the African Diaspora in the "European World." Fortunately, West/Central African epic performances were greater than the sum of their parts, just as allegorye is not containable by modern European philosophy and history.

Though not referencing West/Central African epic performances, or even epic performance explicitly, Houston Baker's insightful and influential concepts, in *Modernism and the Harlem Renaissance* (1989), operate at the site of race, cultural production, African folklore, and Modernity/Modernism in ways relevant to the epic trickster as an Afro-modern aesthetic. Specifically, Baker's invocation of the "mastery of form" and "deformation of mastery" heuristic establishes useful parallels that translate the epic trickster across the Black Atlantic and into Western modernity. "Deformation" is the linchpin of his thought:

> The mastery of form conceals, disguises, floats like a trickster butterfly in order to sting like a bee. The deformation of mastery, by contrast, is Morris Day singing "Jungle Love," advertising, with certainty, his unabashed *badness*—which is not always conjoined with violence. *Deformation* is a go(uer)rilla action in the face of acknowledged adversaries. It produces sounds radically different from those of, say, Sade, whose almost mumbled initial exposition gives way to subdued (but scandalously signifying) lyrics in "Smooth Operator."
>
> The deformation of mastery is fully at work in "gorilla" display. Man—the master of "civilization"—enters forests and triggers a response. (50)

Baker goes on to elaborate, establishing "mastery of form" as the trickster's indirection and "deformation of mastery" as the heroic "response" (51). As an insightful species of the African-American trickster-hero aesthetic, Baker's deformation is response- and protest-oriented: how African-Americans responded to and protested against the problem of slavery and race, through various cultural productions. However, because Baker's deformation is not informed by traditional African epic performance aesthetics that speak to the de-forming of the *white* body, he reifies the teleological, archetypal divide between trickster and hero and thus simplifies the complexity of the epic-charged "master of civilization." In other words, the "Man" might appear to be straight and classical in his musical taste, and inclined toward Hector Berlioz's *Les Troyens* (1858) or Aaron Copland's *Fanfare for the Common Man* (1942), but whole musical careers, and even Hollywood celebrity, have been built on economies of disguise and mainstream American mastery of black performance forms.

Still, Baker's focus on performance aesthetics inclusive of the "trickster butterfly" and "go(uer)rilla action" brilliantly frames Western ontology, too. It also offers a lyrical companionship to the genealogy of scholarship ranging from the large corpus of Africa-to-America trickster texts to the emergent scholarship on African epic influences on African/American culture. Although very few studies have seized upon the canonization of the African epic to read it into American literature, those studies have provided a critical component for its epic trickster foundation. The other component, of much longer pedigree, is the literary anthropology which traces the African trickster across the Atlantic.

Since the nineteenth century, it has been known that the African-American trickster tales had an African origin, although it was not until the early decades of the twentieth century that a deeper appreciation of the African antecedents began to generate significant scholarly interest beyond Joel Chandler Harris' Uncle Remus and Br'er Rabbit tales. However, because of

Homer-based Eurocentrism, a lack of knowledge of African influences not really addressed until the mid-1950s, and a rejection of heroic epic by many minority scholars and writers because it was associated with patriarchy, it is no overstatement to say that treatment of Africa-based trickster and epic aesthetics has been defined by an archetypal divide. Consequently, these genres are not only seen as mutually exclusive, but antagonistic.

Naturally, the scholarship which has created this divide has also been unwilling to explore the deeper mutuality they share. The conspicuous dearth of African epic–informed studies among African Americanists, in light of the African epic performance renaissance of the late 1970s, is in many respects an epic-sized methodological gap. Hence, what is needed is not a general Africa-to-America cultural genealogy, which solidly supports the transatlantic continuity of MOS-epic performance culture. Nor is the equally well-explored trickster inheritance sufficient, or even the rise of African-American epic performance scholarship out of both, though this work is itself singular and the foundation-stone without which this study would be impossible. Instead, a most useful inquiry would focus on an epic trickster performance genealogy, for it would not only enrich the corpus on African retentions, but act as something of a unified theory with parts of all the other African retention and genealogical studies and yet more because it does account for African/Trickster and European/ Hero oppositions.

Over the decades, the epic/trickster unity has flashed in the work of folklorists and writers. As a folklore pioneer, it is fitting—and most ironic considering her feminism, nationalism, and individualism—that Zora Neale Hurston provides the first epic trickster figure in her World War II–inspired essay, "High John de Conquer" (1943). Though Hurston may have fabricated High John de Conquer from knowledge of folklore and Afro-folk pharmacopeia,[1] and may have lent it for the dubious enterprise of supporting one epic-motivated and white supremacist regime (America) against another (Germany), "High John" is a remarkable watershed. Hurston fuses together epic and trickster in a hybrid form—a "literary and esthetic" quality folklorist Alan Dundes celebrates (*Mother Wit* 542)—that was matched only by the sociopolitical possibilities represented by High John: a hypermasculine figure of epical pedigree who was combined with the trickster and imperial "mother-wit."

Hence, High John de Conquer, a pun on the root of the same name, is the folkloric emblem of the epic trickster: a "mighty man" who was "touristing around the plantation as the laugh-provoking Brer Rabbit. . . . And all the time, there was High John de Conquer playing his tricks of making a way out of now-way. Hitting a straight lick with a crooked stick." It should come as no surprise that he is a two-faced allegorycal figure: to some a big and epical "man like John Henry," and a returning-king figure like King Arthur; to others, he is small and deformed, "a little hammered-down, low-built man like the Devil's doll-baby" (542–44).

The African provenance is anthropologically sound, but because her epic trickster is meant primarily for white readers, Hurston liberally weds minstrel politics and aesthetics to black-male militarism. She negotiates this dangerous space by deracinating High John de Conquer's potency and rooting his agency in idealized laughter, but also expropriation. "Even if your hair comes yellow, and your eyes are blue," she states in this vein, "John de Conquer will be working for you just the same. From his secret place, he is working for all America now. We are all his kinfolks. . . . White America, take a laugh out of our black mouths, and win! We give you High John de Conquer" (548). Although confronting a world crisis of unimagined proportions, Hurston's infusion of more epic potency into America helps to set the stage for postwar imperialism.

In the existential climate left by the remnants of World War II and the ongoing Korean War, Ralph Ellison, novelist and literary critic, offered another fleeting glimpse of the epic trickster in his 1958 essay "Change the Joke and Slip the Yoke." Ellison, passionately critiquing Stanley Edgar Hyman's understanding of the relationship between black tricksters and literature, also assaults the archetypal divide. "Hyman's favorite archetypal figure is the trickster," he says, "but I see a danger here. From a proper distance *all* archetypes would appear to be tricksters and confidence men; part-God, part-man, no one seems to know he-she-its true name, because he-she-it is protean with changes of pace, location and identity" (46; italics in original).

A modern man and quintessence of the classically enlightened intellect who states in the essay that "ours is no archaic society (although its archaic elements exert far more influence in our lives than we care to admit)," Ellison implies that folkloric categories are messy, imprecise constructs, useful to literature, although the archetype exposes its inadequacy "before the realism implicit in the form of the novel" (51–52). Given his pro-modern, pro-novel stance, Ellison's shifts into autobiographical mode to proclaim the following is perhaps to be expected:

> I knew the trickster Ulysses just as early as I knew the wily rabbit of Negro American lore, and I could easily imagine myself a pint-sized Ulysses but hardly a rabbit, no matter how human and resourceful or Negro. . . .
>   My point is that the Negro American writer is also an heir of the human experience which is literature, and this might well be more important to him than his living folk tradition. (58)

Ellison does not provide evidence here for his observation, but this much is clear: the "trickster Ulysses" is an epic trickster, and this aesthetic guided his best-known fiction. Hence, *Invisible Man* (1940), Ellison's *magnum opus*, exemplifies this perspective by brilliantly mapping out the sheer potency of a space in which trickster and epic hero transgressiveness shape modernity. An epic the guise of a racial protest novel, and a racial protest novel framed by the narrator's equivalence to a "trickster Ulysses" who lives most brightly in the underworld, *Invisible Man* tracks its exceptional, enlightened protagonist's odyssey through the bright lights and bowels of New York City. Ellison, in his epic/novel, fills this representative American space with what he sees as the archaic, emotional culture of black America full of tricksters and epic figures, the racism and archaic trickster/epic behavior underlying white society, and his protagonist's effort to emerge from the invisibility caused by these external forces and his own socialization in them.

The epic/trickster paradigm Hurston and Ellison articulated did not itself become a subject of study, but scholarship over the next several decades framed this unity. The watershed folklore studies of Roger D. Abrahams in the 1950 and 1960s, particularly his study of urban toasts in *Deep Down in the Jungle: Negro Narrative Folklore from the Streets of Philadelphia* (1970), provide a critical foundation for subsequent scholarly and creative work. Abrahams' examination of black lore—inclusive of trickster tales, toasts, signifying, and the dozens—may have been problematic because it emerged out of a scholarly climate of rampant racism and stereotypes, but the urban locale of his fieldwork (the Camingerly neighborhood of Philadelphia from 1958 to 1959) foregrounded the racism-based contest-hero dynamic informing black culture. Critical to his methodology, which required participatory observation in the performative space, was real engagement with the myths carried and shaped by men like Bobby Lewis, his closest confidant, great talkers like John H. "Kid" Mike and Charley Williams, and scores of children. At its best, Abrahams' *Deep Down* centers the performing body, a raced, urbanized figure but nevertheless a dynamic "talker-performer [who] may strongly influence our attitudes" by commanding a vast repertoire of stories and "linguistic (or paralinguistic)" performance skills. The storyteller uses "subtle words," as an actor, orator, and narrator in the task of outperforming other verbal jousters and, like many African-American narrators extending back into slavery, "creating a world wholly his own" (*Deep Down* 16–19, 21–22, 29–30, 36–39, 58–59).

Abrahams' most important contribution is his serious treatment of urbanized black folklore as a complex font of creativity worthy of study. His oral/aural appreciation of a black storytelling culture in which the valorization of the "talker-performer" contrasted with the typographical/chirographic culture of white Americans, challenges the most simplistic notions about black literacy.

Because *Deep Down* and Abrahams' articles, like "Some Varieties of Heroes in America" (1966), foreground race as an agonistic performance, his genealogy of and remarks upon the trickster from rural South to urban North establishes a lens making possible, decades later, a scholarly conception of the epic trickster.[2] Abrahams' "trickster hero" is inclusive of the slave-era animal-trickster incarnation, an anthropomorphized figure who became John in slavery, figures like the Signifying Monkey, reflecting the violent conditions urban black Americans often encountered, and the much more popular, overtly epical figures like John Henry and bad men like Stagolee and Railroad Bill. In particular, his excavation of the toast, the epic-like "long narrative poem constructed with the highest wit and performed only by the best talkers" anticipates the emergence of rap, an urbanized instance of epically real performance embraced by the mainstream (*Deep Down* 59, 62–70; "Some Varieties" 344–47).[3]

One of the most important texts that benefits from folkloric studies and collections is Lawrence W. Levine's encyclopedic survey of black folklore, *Black Culture and Black Consciousness: Afro-American Folk Thought from Slavery to Freedom* (1977). *Black Culture* is a watershed because of its unprecedented encyclopedic range, which enables Levine to advance a paradigm for the transmission of culture and syncretic continuities between African and African-American vernacular culture. Even when the original generic forms of the African lyrics were forgotten, Levine suggests, the West African connections remained evident, as the polyrhythmic beat, call-and-response style, and social function in slave spirituals indicate. Here, the body and its movements are critical, for they "intimately" relate to African dance, vivify the art of storytelling, and even manifest themselves through the subversive behavior of actual slaves who foiled their owners' wishes in much the way tricksters would.[4]

More importantly for this study of the epic trickster, Levine complicated the trickster stereotype. Against the given "slave-as-trickster, trickster-as-slave thesis," Levine related the African-American trickster to European/American behavior and raised the possibility that the "ubiquitous" amoral trickster could also represent the master class. Thus, he argues, opening up a Pandora's box he leaves mostly unexamined, the animal trickster tale parodies the racial, patriarchal, and hierarchical orders underlying chattel slavery:

> The animals were frequently almost perfect replicas of whites as slaves saw them. . . . Though they might possess great power, they did not always wield it openly and directly but often with guile and indirection. *This last point especially has been neglected; the strong and not merely the weak could function as trickster.* . . . Former slaves recalled numerous examples of the master as trickster. . . .
>   Slaves tales are filled with instances of the strong acting as tricksters. (118–19; italics mine)

Since trickster tales are ages-old studies of human nature and the natural world, and the master class was part of a Homeric tradition, Levine's epiphany here is another flash of lightning grounded in empirical studies of the lore.[5]

Levine's connection of the trickster and epic hero, Africa and America, meets a dead-end, however. Although Levine specifically drew upon

Abrahams' scholarship, and even saw the epic potential in the folk heroic,[6] his work reiterates the African trickster/European hero binary, with the African culture hero's origins being limited to the trickster figure who "continued the African patterns of manipulating the strong" and the West populated with epic-capable figures "who grew in proportion to the problems they faced" (400–01). Even as the African-based animal tricksters fell into disfavor and African-American slave trickster tales featured "direct confrontation" between slaves and the masters, Levine argues, the heroic potential for such stemmed from the antebellum slaves' Old Testament heroes (370–97). Although he does recognize the "intricate genealogies and historical narratives common in the African oral tradition" as a cultural tradition informing the slaves' genealogical tales,[7] Levine's assessment is borne out by the total exclusion of Sunjata, Mwindo, and Ozidi, not to mention the Zulu's Shaka,[8] from *Black Culture*.

Although Levine could not countenance the African epic performance, subsequent scholars could not ignore the traditional African epic even though they confronted the same ideological and methodological quandaries that may have silenced Levine: how does one find empirical evidence for the crossing of the traditional African epic performance, and what form—or disparate forms—would its continuity take in the Americas?

This problem is greater than the ones generally confronting African retention scholarship, for while languages, names, and cultures of the enslaved were suppressed as a matter of general policy, the African epic performance itself lay at a panoptic site of cultural surveillance and suppression because of its catalytic, revolutionary nature. Although African epic scholarship does not indicate the existence of any material symbols specifically designated for and limited to the MOS-African epic performances,[9] nonmaterial, epic-specific artifacts offer a few possibilities. For example, and largely thanks to Lorenzo Dow Turner's *Africanisms in the Gullah Dialect* (1949), scholars have often turned to occurrences of African names as direct evidence of retention, particularly since the naming of children bore deep cultural significance for Africans (Baird and Twining 25; Joyner 217). The documented existence of one or more slaves named Sunjata, Ozidi, Mwindo,[10] or one of their variants would offer strong, perhaps irrefutable, evidence of some degree of cultural retention. However, while no small number of American slaves bore classical and even Homeric names— Roman as well as names from Greek and Homeric mythology, such as Hercules, Scilla, Penelope, Calypso, and Telemachus, with rare or extremely rare occurrences of Hector, Ulysses, and Achilles[11]—examination of slave name records on the American mainland and names of slave contraband seized by authorities from cargo ships breaking international laws against transatlantic slave trafficking reveal no instances of a Sunjata, Mwindo, Ozidi, or one of their orthographic equivalents.[12] Among those already seasoned it is no surprise that their "day names," often given by their masters but not infrequently selected by slaves themselves under the auspices of slavery, would not be so audacious. It is much more likely that the African epic protagonists would be reflected among the "basket names," the names chosen, and kept in secret, by the enslaved. Beyond the limited records, it is reasonable to assume that discovering such information would be virtually impossible for researchers because of the danger inherent in disclosing epic-charged names.

In spite of these dead ends, there is empirical evidence associated with epical names. There may be no Sunjatas, Mwindos, or Ozidis, but the names of secondary or tertiary MOS-epic figures might be useful. Traces of Senegambian country marks receive more support if we reconsider the names of individuals outside the possibility of patent MOS-epic reference, particularly the basket names often held in private against the masking name. Names of figures that are secondary (e.g., Sos[s]o Bal[l]a, Bala Fas[s]eke) and tertiary (e.g., Sos[s]o kingdom, Tumu Maniya)[13] might be more useful. The results here are interesting, for though there are no Sugulun(g)/Sogolons, Oreames, or Oreas, there are slaves named Bala and Soso.[14] Are these figures cultural signifiers for Sunjata's second *djeli*, Bala Faseke, or Sunjata's archnemesis, Soumamoro, the King of Sosso? More research is needed here, but one could surmise that since these names do not personify the epic protagonist, being his attendant and his defeated opponent, respectively, Westerners might have concluded that such names were innocuous.

Perhaps the most convincing evidence relates to the role of Islam in the Mande. Sunjata is unique in that it is both an oral tradition and a literary one situated in the Arabic language, each part of a former empire whose sociopolitical strength spans centuries and oceans. Strong evidence suggests that the Sunjatic legacy did cross into and influence the Diaspora and mainstream (European) cultures: the broad role of Islam throughout the Mande, the cultural homogeneity of the Mande associated with the Old Malian empire, the extensive incursion of the slave trade into the Senegambia, Robert Farris Thompson's seminal documentation of Mande-derived "cone-on-cylinder" Kamabolon huts and textile art in the New World (*Flash* 193–223), and the documented evidence of enslaved Africans—including princes like Abdl Rahman Ibrahima Sori (see Figure 3.1)—who were highly literate in Arabic. Cartwright's observation[15] that "the Sunjata was almost certainly told throughout the American colonies in the early days of the slave trade" by Muslims is supported by older scholarship on the Manden/Mali diaspora in the New World, such as Thompson's, and equally recent historiography on Afro-Muslim continuities. Thus, as Michael Gomez asserts, very likely "thousands" of them were enslaved. Their insistence on practicing their religion, the legacy of "cultural phenomena" traceable to Afro-Islamic influence, and their anti-"Negro" exceptionalism (a form of intraracial "social stratification") profoundly shaped African-American identity (Cartwright, "Reading Roots" 36–40; Gomez 59–87).

Figure 3.1   Abdu-l-Rahman Ibrahim Ibn Sori (a.k.a. Abdul-Rahman).

But the type of deformation slavery creates is paradoxical: at the same time that it dehumanizes, it catalyzes the epic immanence that is humanity's genetic and generic inheritance. The nonretention of discrete traces of immaterial and material culture may reinforce the epic/trickster unity which, in its occult essence, participates in and extends from the spiritual, cosmological, and theological base that scholars foreground as the primary West African cultural retention. The syncretism of West/Central African cultures, then, means Sunjatic specificity tended toward a new "black" racial identity in the reconfigured African-American epic habitus.

Hence, one might make a generalization, in the form of a question, that shifts the evidentiary burden to naysayers: the question is not *if* it survived, but *how* and in *what form*? Resting on the pro-Africa paradigm shift of the 1960s and 1970s, work by Henry Louis Gates, Jr., John W. Roberts, and Keith Cartwright represent the evolution of the epic trickster toward a fully realized aesthetic.

Hurston's anthropology and her "speakerly texts," the orality of African trickster tales, the theological and larger cultural phenomenology of which they were signifiers, and issues of race, gender, and class were definitively linked to African-American written literature by Gates' *Signifying Monkey*, which advanced a literary anthropology based upon the centrality of Esu-Elegbara, the Yoruba trickster deity and god of interpretation. This Nigerian deity, Gates argues, is the most significant member of the Yoruba pantheon, for he mediates the communicative, hermeneutical space between the gods and the humans supplicating them (*Signifying* 6–31).

In particular, the trickster tales, like the exchanges between slaves and their masters, and other verbal expressions such as spirituals, were highly charged with ironic wit based on a two-way communication system: direct communication between slaves and enslavers, and the indirection of the slaves' *signifying*, which was the extra, subversive meaning attached to words which re-figured or even reversed the semantic content of a word, phrase, or sentence (*Signifying* 44–54). Hence, Gates traces into modern literature the Signifying Monkey, a figure whose "signifyin(g)" he calls "the black trope of tropes" (51–52), from the pre-modern African trickster tales, across the Atlantic, and into a post-modern and post-structuralist analytic suitable for interpreting the complexities of metaphor and irony in African-American written literature. This is understandable, for Gates uses Derridean linguistic theory, what he believes to be a recent articulation of its older Esu-Elegbara counterpart, to disrupt the racial and gendered hierarchical orders and binaries Western Enlightenment epistemology constructed. Consequently, Gates argues, the Signifying Monkey is neither male nor female, neither black nor white, but a "trinary" source of disorder unto and for itself, which could be a force for solidarity one moment and, in the next, indeterminate and paradoxical (*Signifying* 28–35, 55).

Gates does not reference the epic—or African-American toasts,[16] an epic genre often featuring the Signifying Monkey—although it is immanent in his model. The obvious appeal is Esu-Elegbara, a trickster-creator god who aligns both with trickster liminality and state-making potential without the ideological baggage of the epic. But if, as this study argues, the heroic epic already anticipates trickster immanence and stratagems—Zeus, after all, is grandsire of Achilles, and a veritable zoomorphia of swans, golden rain, and so on—then the trickster's revolutionary potency, the alterity of being/ becoming, is already a co-opted signifyin(g).

Following the lead of Abrahams and having the benefit of the canonization of the African epic, other scholars have attempted to link African epic literature and the African-American folk heroic. The result is a genealogy and explication of a specific trickster figure, the trickster hero, in John W. Roberts' *From Trickster to Badman*. In this study,[17] Roberts constructs a heroic genealogy from the African-American slave trickster to the black "bad men" of the 1890s, and finds much common ground with his predecessors, Abrahams and Levine, in this general endeavor. The black folk heroic, he argues, represents the continuity of an African culture-building process which must be understood relative to the European/American heroic.

In addition to devoting significant attention to the conjurer-hero and heroic tradition of spirituals, Roberts centers African heroic culture more to excavate the isomorphic features and utility it shares with African-American heroic culture (*From Trickster* 1–14). Although he does not theorize a place for epic narrative continuity, Roberts seeks to establish the cultural and aesthetic economy linking the African epic hero and the African-American spiritual tradition, which he routes through and roots in the religious and heroic expression of African oral epics *vis-à-vis* "the mythic traditions or the Euro-American religious song tradition" (121). True to his critical methodology as a folklorist, Roberts interpolates the African epic habitus into his study to synopsize a full cross-section of its phenomenology, from the most mundane material aspects to the cosmological ones. Thus, he discusses the role of the African bard in the normalizing, valorizing, and transmission of culture, along with the multigeneric qualities of the epic performance, the militaristic and ecclesiastical significance of the African epic, the role of *nyama*, and the question of the emulative and transgressive characteristics of the hero in his relationship to the community, among other things. The actuating force which reinforced the sublime ideology, he argues, continued in America. Although ambivalent regarding whether a former epic tradition led slaves in isolated instances to characterize some maroons as epic-like Christian warriors, Roberts believes Christianity and its epic stories and figures provided an analogous sublimating power (121–66).

As an instance of recovery of the African epic and articulation of the relationship between the African epic heroic and the African-American folk heroic, Roberts' study may be the first to provide a critical paradigm necessary for filling in the cultural-aesthetic space between them. Much of this stems from his identification of both African tricksters and epic heroes as heroic figures. However, *From Trickster to Badman* can only inaugurate or complement—not complete—a study purporting to follow the African epic from slavery to the African-American written heroic. Although his extensive discussion of the trickster and folk heroes includes the African epic heroic, Roberts does not start with the epic heroic as a primary text and context of study and follow its evolution from slavery to freedom.

Still, *From Trickster* signaled a critical sea change as a few scholars began to interpolate the traditional African epic into their analyses of diasporic literature, some of it African-American.[18] Hence, Roberts' work reveals the foundation that existed for Keith Cartwright's *Reading Africa into American Literature: Epics, Fables, and Gothic Tales* (2002), the only book-length study to center a traditional West African epic performance (Sunjata) and address its continuity in the United States.

In *Reading Africa*, Cartwright reads Senegambian folklore, especially the epic of Sunjata, from West Africa into America's creolized spaces (Louisiana and the Sea Islands) and national (literary) culture. In his genealogy, he excavates and traces the originary epic culture and "the age-old paradigms," a critical methodology which he believes is necessary to delineate the African provenance of orality informing American literature (2–3).

Thus, Cartwright identifies the "epic impulse" of the African epic, based on the Muslim/Koran-influenced Sunjata epic from the Senegambia region, and then foregrounds its *nyama* ("energy in action"). *Nyama* constitutes the roots of soul whose aetiology he finds not in a phallocentric or logocentric (scriptural) heroic narrative of *fadenya*, or "father-child-ness," but in the quest for *badenya*, "mother-child-ness," which is the most indispensable aspect of this epic. The quest for *badenya*, he argues, is troped in the unitary figure of the tree of knowledge and life, a recurrent image of Africa as the cultural and biological root source immanent whenever slaves and their descendants sang of trees (8–13).

Following the dialogic of *badenya*, Cartwright displaces the traditional monologic that valorizes the epic hero. In lieu of centering Sunjata's militarism, he re-reads the Senegambian epic habitus as one which foregrounds the *nyama* of African women, especially Sunjata's mother and sister, Sugulung and Sugulun Kulunkan, who both act "as [his] supporting sorceress and 'Answerer-of-Needs'" (32). As such, they wield their *badenya*-inspired occult insight and cultural practices in ways which enable Sugulung to initiate Sunjata's epic talent and nurture him in exile, and Sugulun Kulunkan to literally reach out to him across many miles and re-establish kinship and community. Sugulun Kulunkan's intuitive understanding of the associative power of food, Cartwright argues, is the mediator which defies the diasporic distance, geographical and filial, between her rootedness in their Malian homeland and Sunjata's disconnectedness in remote Mema.

> It is through Sunjata's sister's use of a few Mande food items that the epic orchestrates its crucial recognition scene in a reversal of the action from *fadenya* dislocation to location in bonds of imperial mother-child-ness. . . . Sugulun Kulunkan's powers enable her to organize a group to search for Sunjata "With fresh okra, / And flour of eggplant leaf." . . . In the Mema market [where Sunjata is found and recruited to return], okra and leaf thickener are veiled signs of *badenya* intended to spark recognition, solidarity, and the reintegration of a Mande diaspora. (32)

Cartwright finds the constitutive power food holds to be pivotal, for the "reversal" denotes more than a plot change, but a significant transformation of the locus of epic energy; "Sugulun Kulunkan's powers" are not those of a passive helpmate. Consequently, he says of the Sunjata epic, "despite its celebration of transgressive heroic actions," it "is an epic of imperial mother wit, ideologically feminizing much that is locally or nationally Mande, mediating realms of *fadenya* and *badenya*, Islam and non-Islam, Arabic and Mande language use, collisions and readjustments of worldview" (32, 33).

In addition to a paradigm situated in *nyama*, *fadenya*, and especially those tropes signifying *badenya*, Cartwright's critical vocabulary in *Reading Africa* links American literary identity with the African epic impulse. He explicates the epic of Sunjata within the contours of its epic habitus of Mali and excavates its constitutive cultural economy (26–34). The cultural resiliency he posits enables him to reach a critical insight:

> Although the Sunjata was almost certainly told throughout the American colonies in the early days of the slave trade, only a trace of its imperial memory and a stronger vein of the folktales, worldview, and Mande/Senegambian semiotics at work in it seem to have survived the transformations of American acculturation. . . . Through the horrible dislocations of North American slavery, what was successfully adapted from Sunjata's cultural storehouse was (along with narrative motifs and modes of performance . . .) a deep matrix of cultural reenactments, a semiotics that shaped patterns of language, music, worship, cookery, and spiritual traditions such as divination and second sight. (34)

Moreover, Cartwright adds, the pluralism immanent in the parataxis of "string instruments, body, and voice," which substituted for traditional performed polyrhythms of West African drums, continued the cultural viability of *nyama* (35). Hence the significance of the sorrow songs for Cartwright, who begins the literary recuperation of the African epic with the "epic impulse" of what he considers the founding and sounding text—the "bible"—of the African-American condition, Du Bois' *Souls* (42–47).

Reading Africa represents the final critical piece needed to answer the question of whether the epic trickster continued into American culture. His close reading of the narrative and context, which foregrounds *nyama* and *badenya*, contributes a critical dialogic to the female and communal epic heroic. Significantly, Cartwright recognizes the epic trickster paradox in Hurston's "High John de Conquer" (57–60) and identifies, if only in passing, the common face of transgression bringing epic and trickster together:

> Kin to Leuk-the-Hare and Bouki-the-Hyena of Wolof takes, Brer Rabbit and Brer Fox (Bouki in Louisiana tales) animated African memory in America. Their tales imparted an understanding of the *nya* or "means" so important to Sunjata and even more important to Africans enslaved in America. . . . This brand of briar patch mother wit, shared by John de Conquer and the means-finding Sunjata the Conqueror,

offers the energy of action that . . . Ellison's narrator would seek in his basement struggles with Monopolated Light & Power. John de Conquer (as a trinity of hoodoo root/John the folk hero/Brer Rabbit) stands as Hurston's foundational "soul" ancestor. (59)

The "trinity," or trinary, which could be simplified as epic/trickster/root, represents the final and most recent glimpse of the epic trickster.

The recovery work of Roberts and Cartwright, essential to understanding epic performance and American culture, offers instances of an African agency operating along with European agency to construct the Western sense of ontology and the cultures arising therefrom. Against the continuous tendency to undermine African cultures' agency in their encounter with the West, Wendy Laura Belcher argues for a more fully realized "*reciprocal enculturation* model of encounter, in which both cultures are understood as actively engaging and changing the other." Her concern with the colonized extends to the commodified slaves and scholars' treatment of them and their African cultural heritage: "Africans, for instance, were not just consumed objects but consuming subjects, not just an ingredient of European identities but themselves alchemists." Belcher is right to identify Cartwright's *Reading Roots* as a "wonderful example" of this realization (220–21, 224). Still, to focus on African epic performance traditions in America implicitly reconstructs the hegemony of African folk operating within the modernized West. This divide, if uninterrogated and unaddressed by a proper methodology, posits an incommensurability which forecloses real investigation into the ancient folk-based performance of Western identities masked by modernity. To fully understand the place of the traditional African epic performance aesthetic in the Diaspora of Western modernity, to unveil its epic-past, modern-present *two-ness*, one needs to reckon with the Homeric performance dynamic informing the European/American social contract, for therein lies the deformity of Other, Self, and the Land performed as racism.

INTRODUCTION TO AMERICAN HOMER

How can you relate the West/Central African epic performance, a so-called pre-modern form, to the sophistication of American modernity? Marcel Detienne's argument in his essay "The Greeks Aren't Like the Others" (*Dionysos Slain* 1977) is a significant start. Detienne assails the "Hellenists" for privileging Greco-Roman mythology as fundamentally different from, say, "African or Polynesian myths," enshrining Greek history as exceptional when it, too, betrays the mythmaking process, and continuing to promote the myth of the "elect" status of the Greeks (1–6, 16–19).[19]

Establishing that the Greeks and Romans are, indeed, like the Others, is a necessary step, but our two epic-related questions still remain. Classics scholar Seth L. Schein does not attend to these specific questions, but his

"Cultural Studies and Classics: Contrasts and Opportunities" essay does imply an answer. Noting its potential for redefining "culture" and bestowing critical thinking, "Cultural Studies," Schein argues, "has broken with both the high cultural and the anthropological approaches to 'culture.' . . . [I]t deprivileges texts and other high cultural artifacts, treating them like all institutions and other phenomena to be studied. In so doing, it places them on a continuum with, say, the products of 'mass' or 'popular' culture." In this regard, he favors debunking the "self-evident" status classics texts enjoy and the dynamic that associates them with "bestness" (286–96).[20]

Page DuBois, a classics and comparative literature scholar, deploys these methods and the feminist critique elucidated in Schein's article. Indeed, in *Trojan Horses: Saving the Classics from Conservatives* (2001), DuBois asks the essential methodological question upon which a cultural studies and comparative literature treatment of the classics rests:

> Is it necessary to "think like Greeks" in order to study and teach classical civilization, as if teaching and scholarship on historical subjects required identification with the objects of that scholarship? . . . Historical study need not, probably ought not to, imply overt and conscious exhortations to return to the past, especially to a slave-owning, militarist, imperialist, often xenophobic, patriarchal culture like that of ancient Athens. (25–27, 38–39)

Employing this perspective in *Slaves and Other Objects* (2003), DuBois deftly examines ancient slavery through feminist and cultural studies lenses and classical erudition. Mindful of classics experts, literary scholars, and museum curators of antiquities, DuBois extensively excavates ancient slavery to demonstrate how classic scholarship overlooks slavery and provides the foundation for the lesson she articulates: "it is time to come to terms with the ways in which American slavery and its aftermath have formed and deformed all our knowledge, including that of the ancient world, producing blind spots, suppression of certain kinds of bodies and presence, and even an unconscious acceptance and replication of the strategies of distinction in ancient texts." Though falling short of the epical agony associated with epic performance, the "deformed" knowledge DuBois attributes to the American classicist's "problem of historiography" with ancient and American slavery results in psychoanalytical difficulties—"cathexes, fetishization, defenses, and disavowals" as well as "projection" (112–13, 117–19).

Given that such methodologies are suitable, that Latin and Greek are not necessary, the last remaining course is to find the frame for situating Homeric Americana in comparative dialogue with traditional African epic performances. Treating the classics—especially Homer—as Americanized artifacts, stripped of their ancient sheen, is critical. It is insufficient to critique classical culture performed among the American elites based

on trickle-down theory; instead, an anthropological, participatory performance perspective in which the cultural logic is seen as the ultimate
challenge is essential. Indeed, even the original European-American elites,
the founders, were not elite by the cultured standards of the day. Measured by their noncontribution to "Classical scholarship," Meyer Reinhold
argues, they were far less capable of understanding Greco-Roman intricacies than even their British forebears (*Classick* 1). Identifying the artifacts
and subjecting them to qualitative and quantitative analysis makes more
transparent the cultural logic of the epic performance, its dangers among
the traditional, original elites of the memorial past, *and* their would-be
replacements of the present, from classics adherents who may have no such
elite pedigree to minorities.

Such work is hardly new. Certainly, long before Schein's call and the
brilliant work of Detienne, DuBois, and other contemporary classics scholars, David Walker's 1829 *Appeal* foregrounded Greco-Roman Americana
as an artifact. The absence of methodological closure here between African
and American epic performances—when scholars have compared African
and Homeric epics (Okpewho, Sienkewicz), highlighted the suppression
of African epics by European colonizers (Bulman, Conrad, Newton, Seydou), traced African epics into America (Cartwright, Roberts), pointed
out divides between imperialism and African epics (Biebuyck), and shown
parallel behavior between aggressive epic-performing African societies
of recent centuries and contemporary Americans (Anderson)—is another
tragic injustice in the long history of African subjugation. The obvious fear
here—traditional African epic performance spaces might teach, even correct, US—is as palpable as it is evident.

Though racialized and gendered, *inter alia*, the epic performance centers
space and the magical possibilities it unleashes. The three West/Central
African epics suggest that mythology is a *sine qua non* of the social contract giving rise to the body-politic and its codified laws and institutions.
Not surprisingly, the very "flexibility" and "adaptability" Robert Newton[21] finds for the Sunjatic tradition foregrounds the place of the traditional
epic performance within a (post)modern nation-state. In his watershed
study of the impact of modern music technologies on the "once and future
nature of the [Malian] epic," Newton asks, "What has occurred within the
performance of these [Sunjatic] epics to maintain their ability not only to
survive but to thrive in the postcolonial era?" (315). For him, the "multiple
histories . . . at play in any given performance portraying a moving picture
of practice viewed from multiple points of reference" clearly anticipates
modern technologies. Focusing on 1970s audiocassette technology that created home library editions, and noting the massive changes to post-colonial
Mali, Newton highlights the Sunjatic epic's "adaptability to transformed
technological conditions and social relations" as the essence of its ability to
weather changes and serve, for Malians, as a part of the "ongoing negotiations between the performers and the changing world" (316–26).[22]

Consequently, Sunjata defines a core aspect of Mande identity whether one considers the French-inspired socialist democracy of Mali or the Soviet-influenced culture of a post-colonial Guinea that rebuffed its former colonizer (Conrad, "Introduction" 3, 9). The Manden has been and remains a place of multiple, indigenous oralities, and multiple, colonizing literacies (Arabic and French). Moreover, over the last several centuries it has been the site of a world religion, Islam, which is understood by many to be inconsistent with an indigenous—read "pagan"—heroic epic tradition. While each has its own distinct semiotics and hermeneutics, and tension persists along a male/female axis, they coexist and are even, now, mutually reinforcing (Conrad, "Mooning" 223).[23]

Clearly, the Sunjatic tradition is one in which resilience—pragmatism?—is part of its adaptability and flexibility. To a lesser but significant degree, Homeric performance has shown similar adaptability and flexibility in America. Lesser is relative, for even though the Sunjatic performance may be distinct from a Western/European tradition of nineteenth-century "national epics" because of its role in creating consensus out of "cultural heterogeneity" and "substantial geographical distances" (S. Belcher 111–13), the similar function of Homer in the European/American West begs for deeper consideration. European/American Christianity, like Islam, advances a spiritual narrative seemingly antagonistic to the paganism of Homeric influence. But spirituality motivates these epics and these religions, oftentimes in ways that mutually reinforce one another, as Sacvan Bercovitch and Meyer Reinhold argued of Virgilian influence on the Puritan Americans, Cotton Mather's *Magnalia Christi Americana* in particular (Bercovitch 1966; Reinhold, *Classick* 129–30).

HOMERIC MIMICRY

The critical difference here is the Mande's relationship to Sunjata compared to America's relationship to the Homeric tradition. The Mande's Sunjatic history is organically related to, and shapes the identity of, its present residents. Homeric organicity was lacking for Old World Europe and, to an even greater extent, for America as a New World space. Walter Benjamin's excavation of the "extreme foreshortening of historical perspective" at work in sixteenth-century Germany reveals how, despite vast historical discontinuities, European regimes constructed a Greco-Roman heritage for themselves. For example, Benjamin notes how the German language was seen as "first place among the 'major languages'" and as descended from Hebrew or, more radically, as the origin for Hebrew, Greek, and Latin (202–03).

The assemblage of fragments, shards, and debris into monuments Benjamin problematizes is an idea shared and extended by Gregory Nagy, a Homer and oral epic scholar. While Nagy deems it absolutely necessary for understanding Homer to go well beyond the text and reconstruct the Homeric performance in Athens around the sixth century B.C., he clearly delineates the limitations of the enterprise. A live performance transcript is an "impossibility," Nagy reasons, and material from Plato's writings, though useful, are still "relatively meager"; at best, the evidence allows for "synchronic cross-sections or even 'snapshots'" of the performance ("Homer" 124–28).[24]

American Homer, a cultural performance matching and perhaps exceeding Germany's Homeric interests after the American Civil War, presents another instance of the "rarefied atmosphere" Benjamin foregrounds. Instead of the "slavish imitation" classics scholars reject as behavior applicable to the American founders, a theory of classical mimicry—Homeric or simply epic mimicry, in particular—is appropriate. Relying upon studies of eighteenth-century theory and performance studies, Joseph Roach argues that America, like other circum-Atlantic rim societies, is one of the *Cities of the Dead*. "The key," Roach maintains,

> is to understand how circum-Atlantic societies, confronted with revolutionary circumstances for which few precedents existed, have invented themselves by performing their pasts in the presence of others. They could not perform themselves, however, unless they also performed what and who they thought they were not. By defining themselves in opposition to others, they produced mutual representations from encomiums to caricatures, sometimes in each another's presence, at other times behind each other's backs. (5)

In Roach's estimation, both Eric Lott's work on blackface minstrelsy and Homi K. Bhaba's "mimicry" present a paradox: empowerment through appropriation and, simultaneously, disempowerment by virtue of the human commonality that makes possible the appropriation and copying by the "other" (6). When slavish imitation was neither desirable nor possible, because of the paradoxical objective of transcending the old for the sake of one's own greatness, built upon the civilized foundation of forerunners, then some form of "mimicry" offers an optimum model.

In light of this, Newton's perspective concerning the necessity of context for the Sunjatic text is even more applicable here: Homer's performance tract was already "out of print" well before its post-printing press proliferation. If we confront the allegory of the Homeric epic in the West, not the allegorycal structure of other epic performance traditions, then the belief in the absolute divides of time, distance, and culture are most correct. The soul is missing from the mythology. Benjamin's critic of the baroque period's relationship to "ancient mythology" is significant in consideration of American Homer *vis-á-vis* the West/Central African epic habitus:

> The baroque vulgarizes ancient mythology in order to see everything in terms of figures (not souls): this is the ultimate stage of externalization after the hieratic religious content had been aestheticized by Ovid and

secularized by neo-Latin writers. There is not the faintest glimmer of any spiritualization of the physical. The whole of nature is personalized, not so as to be made more inward, but, on the contrary—so as to be deprived of soul. (187)

The implication for early American culture, what Meyer Reinhold called "Classica Americana" and the "cult of antiquity," is critical. "Early Americans," Reinhold states, "lived in the afterglow of the Renaissance. Despite the distance from the great centers of humanistic learning," he continues,

> Classical learning was swiftly naturalized on American soil, and in consequence a fair number of colonial and revolutionary Americans was nurtured and moulded by the humanistic tradition. . . . But while adding nothing to the fund of Classical learning, they plundered the Classics liberally for the advantage of their own lives and the national good. . . . They knew far less about the ancient world than we do today, but the learning they acquired, circumscribed though it was, affected their thought and action far more. (*Classick* 1–2)

Whether one concentrates on the exceptionalism the Latin etymology of "classics" denotes or the much older performance of epic folk potentiality Homer symbolizes, the fault lines portending excess are transparent. On the one hand, compared to contemporary culture and especially classics scholars, ancient Greco-Roman cultures were little known to the founders' generation. At the same time, Americans were the most literate of the modern nation-states, leading Reinhold to venture that "is it nevertheless probable that never since antiquity were the Classics . . . read by a greater proportion of a population." On the other hand, despite frequent uses of Homeric and Virgilian references, allusions, comparatives, parodies, and material icons, "critical analyses and understanding of [Homer and] Vergil as poet[s] and thinker[s] rarely emerge." The combination of this dynamic and certain features of this performance—the limits of authentic "literary works [that] serve us [even today] as inaccessible norms and models" because they have "traveled to us over too many centuries, through too many vicissitudes of performance," along with liberal translation aesthetics that shelved "slavish imitation,"[25] poor textbooks and translations, and the new-nation pragmatism privileging "useful knowledge" (Detienne 18; DuBois, *Slaves* 144; McLachlan 82–84; Reinhold, *Classica* 222, 225–26, 231, and *Classick* 1–2, 8–16)—create a powerful paradox: even as the cultural distance becomes more "absolute," its usable, material symbols bear more *modern* import in direct proportion. While this antithesis is a form of cultural schizophrenia, it does not negate the fact that the split consciousness, which can be catalytic, is supportable by the most ancient of human cultural forms, the ritual.

Anthropologist Victor Turner's thoughts on ritual, performance, and liminality, concretized by his fieldwork in central Africa, help to reconcile ritual, epic performance, and modernity. Turner debunks hegemonic thinking—civilized/modern versus uncivilized/pre-modern—by locating a deep ritual and performative commonality as the very essence of self and society. Central to this is his *Homo performans* underpinning, the notion that "[i]f man is a sapient animal, a toolmaking animal, a self-making animal, a symbol-using animal, he is, no less, a performing animal." Foregrounding *Homo performans* as the source of senses-rich "cumulative wisdom" more profound than any constructs of knowledge, Turner embraces postmodern thought because it eschews the perfect, symbolic masks of the (neo)Platonic ideal. Truer understanding lies not in the idealized typographical event, he maintains, but in a human dynamism borne of the "very flaws, hesitations, personal factors, incomplete, elliptical, context-dependent, situational components of performance." However, the divide between the daily demands of life and the reflexive escape of art produces a tension on the "self," which is "split up the middle." The very pervasiveness of "workaday social processes (including economic, political, jural, domestic, etc.)" forces the self to violence: this violence assaults the mainstream, serious, "commonsense" norms and laws so that the sacred, mysterious, ambiguous, and indeterminate may return.

Turner's liminal, "split" self is a universal and salutary form of what we might call double-consciousness. Whether it is the Puritanism Turner describes[26] or the epic turn Bakhtin articulates, Western double-consciousness presents a clear crisis for the emergent Western ontology, the Other, and Nature. The foreshortening of the senses into the privileging of "vision" that characterizes modernity fits nicely with Turner's understanding of how crisis moments, what he calls "social dramas," create shifts in genres of cultural performance. The collective memory of the crisis bears determinative force, especially since the "formal characteristics of collective ceremony or 'ritual' are clearly transferrable to other genres" ("Anthropology" 73, 76–77, 81–82, 84, 93–97; "Images" 23–25).

A quandary emerges here, for while African-American double-consciousness originates in the "social drama" associated with European/American enslavement of Africans, there is no equivalent historical trauma for Western Europe. In contrast, if we are to fathom the role of Homeric performance as European social drama, we must excavate the role of the ancients as an external force and the source of European/American double-consciousness.

THE WHITE ATLANTIC: "WHITE" MODERNITY AND DOUBLE-CONSCIOUSNESS

Though a brilliant application to the "two-ness" in African-American psychosocial formations, a species of Du Bois' American/Negro double-consciousness is equally applicable to Europeans and European-Americans.

Indeed, the roots for a European/American double-consciousness began centuries before the transatlantic slave trade started, well before race came to denote European whiteness in contrast to African blackness.

Medievalist Lee Patterson maps out twelfth-century Western Europe's historical consciousness in a useful manner. Patterson notes that this consciousness, informed by Virgilian historicity and based on the *Aeneid*, pivots between "a final exorcism of discredited Homeric values or a fully achieved appropriation of Homeric heroism."[27] The ambivalence in the literature played a large role in disseminating Virgilian socio-aesthetics as secular history. "It was, after all," Patterson states, "by means of the Virgilian model, transmitted through the topoi of Trojan foundation and *translatio imperii*, that the notion of a secular, purposive, linear historicity was made available to the Middle Ages." Certainly, Christianity attenuated total adoption of such a model, but the result is double-consciousness. Whereas Christianity assumed a modern currency against the pagan, that pagan past is nevertheless a "monumentalized past" while the present, by measure, had a "corresponding impotence." Patterson continues:

> Put simply the tension that at once animates and inhibits the *Aeneid* is a struggle between, on the one hand, a linear purposiveness that sees the past as moment of failure to be redeemed by a magnificent future and, on the other, a commemorative idealism that sees it as instead a heroic origin to be emulated, a period of gigantic achievement that a belated future can never hope to replicate. Thus the past is endowed with a *double, contradictory* value: it is at once a guilty if potent origin to be suppressed and forgotten, and a heroic precedent to be reinvoked and reenacted. And so too the medieval rewriting of Virgil becomes itself—as we shall see—a site of both emulation and exorcism, of slavish imitation coupled with decisive rejection. (160–62; italics mine)

The "double, contradictory value," which Patterson alternatively calls a "double perspective" in his examination of the *Roman d'Eneas* and Chrétien de Troyes' *Erec et Enide*, two twelfth-century texts, establishes a larger temporal and imaginary frame for Western double-consciousness. In *Eneas*, Patterson holds, the "double perspective" shows itself in the poet's strategy of "suppressing an apparently too-powerful past" while foregrounding the "ascending future" predicated on the purity of lineage. His discussion of *Erec* reveals that Chrétien saw this dynamic as

> that of the dwarfs of the present astride the giants of the past. . . . The ancients are awesome in their magnitude but impaired by their very gigantism: they are titanic overreachers, figures of earth whose size mirrors an overweening and finally hapless ambition. But the moderns

are in their turn dwarfs, canny yet parasitic, alert but stunted, and it is typical of their elliptical, even elvish, wit to express itself in such a figure. (171, 174, 184–85)

Though interesting, this twelfth-century debate—which continued well into the *eighteenth* century and then into the decades of early nineteenth-century America as the Battle of the Books ("La Quarelle des Anciens et Modernes") (Aldridge 99–118; Reinhold, *Classica* 235–38)—is beside the point when a zero-sum world view motivates Western-European consciousness. Conservative/liberal differences amount to nothing in the afterglow of Homeric luminance,[28] for the problem of this double-consciousness, oriented as it is toward greatness in the past or present, performs a fundamental misconception of the human self and society. But the self-apotheosis and orientation toward perfection that serve as the mask of Western Modernity are the real problem, not questions of racial purity and white supremacy situated in an ontology of white epical individuality, or in hybrid, syncretic demurs.

But double-consciousness is the violent mask and performance of epic-centric ontology: civilized on the one hand, but capable of epical, Homeric savagery on the Other, and on the Self. Modern/ity is the present, logical and technological, but ancient ritual centers it by referencing a pure, epical, Greco-Roman whiteness that makes the present, and all things, possible. In this dynamic, all time collapses into the European imaginary.

Though potentially revolutionary, the critical lens and methodology offered above is sketchy and abstract. Just as the West/Central African and African-American epic performance habituses require one to fully see, hear, and imagine their epic spirits, so, too, is the same gesture needed to construct the modern European/American epic habitus and the double-consciousness it creates.

No doubt detractors—progress idealogues, patent Eurocentrists, latent racists, elitists, and well-intentioned, ethical individuals who believe that modernity is fundamentally different and incommensurate with pre-modern cultures, among others—rightly point to the problem of scale and data set. After all, the modern Western totality of Homeric references, allusions, re-creations, wooden toys, techno-upgrades, hypermediated Trojan viruses, digital samples, Hollywood-inspired rec-reations, and the like is not only too immense for one scholar—or super computer—to tabulate, but is not wholly apprehensible because so much of it is unavailable for various reasons. What do you do, for example, with all the names of persons, places, and things, such as Union general and eighteenth U.S. president Ulysses S. Grant, and the stamps, photographs, references about him, or General Hector, Troy State, USC Trojans, Trojan Horse, Achilles Heel, Troy Lake, Kirk Douglas' *Ulysses* (1954), Arthur C. Clarke/Stanley Kubrick's *2001: A Space Odyssey* (1968, film and book), Brad Pitt's *Troy* (2004), Homer Simpson, and so on (see Figures 3.2 to 3.5)?

Figure 3.2   Five-cent (1894) and eight-cent (1923) Ulysses S.
Grant stamps.

Figure 3.3 Movie poster of *Helen of Troy*; (bottom) Rossana
Podesta and Podesta with Jacques Sernas (1956, © Warner Brothers).

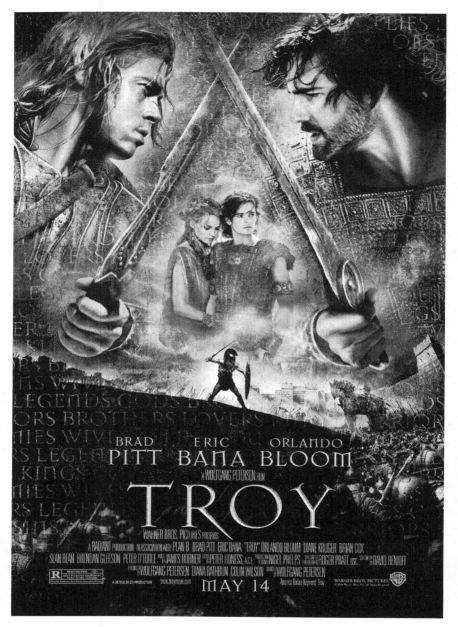

Figure 3.4 Movie poster of *Troy*, featuring Brad Pitt, Diane Kruger, Orlando Bloom, Eric Bana (2004, © Warner Brothers/courtesy Everett Collection).

Figure 3.5   Ulysses, with Kirk Douglas as the Greek epic hero and king of Ithaca (1955, ©1954 UGC).

Remember that Hollywood cast Sydney Poitier as a wandering ex-soldier named *Homer* Smith, in *Lilies of the Field,* a film released in 1963 at the height of the Civil Rights and Black Power movements? How does this "Negro" Homer character relate to another Poitier performance, *In the Heat of the Night* (1967) in which he was *Virgil* Tibbs, a Philadelphia detective helping to solve a murder mystery in *Sparta,* Mississippi?

Though ideal, it is unnecessary to have before us all the data if the essence—*Zeitgeist*—is known, for apprehending the performable essence of the social contract allows insight into the broader whole. If we extrapolate from Pierre Bourdieu's argument, in *The Logic of Practice,* that in the habitus everything reflects everything else, which makes possible metaphor, metonym, and synecdoche, then an epic habitus suggests that epic spirit waters the roots metaphor for the social contract for pre-modern and modern societies.

AMERICAN SOCIAL CONTRACT, EPICAL BODY-POLITIC

Hegel's observation that no country showed more epic potential than the United States and Alexis de Tocqueville's 1830 statement that "Americans show a sort of heroism in their manner of trading"[29] both document America's epic performance and, to a lesser degree, suggests its origin in deformity. The deformity of Americans, the New World Europeans who were the hinterland of the modern European World, betrayed a deep truth often lying at the core of the epic—greatest power, creativity, and mobility rests among those who are deformed in relationship to others. Indeed, the rebellious "natural man" hero-ethos was "fashionable during the early days of the United States," Roger D. Abrahams argues, because of a deformed sense of identity. Thus, he continues,

> there was much in the early national experience of the United States which was conducive to thinking and acting in such heroic terms. The newness and vastness of the land, plus the problems of wrestling the land from the Indians and life from the soil, breathed the spirit of solitary adventure into American life. . . . Further, our history is in a sense one of adolescent search for national identity. Our revolutionary past, our reaction to the authoritative restrictions of Great Britain, emphasized this fact and has allowed American history to be seen by many as a purposive movement, a vast Utopian plan. ("Some Variety" 353)

The very founding of America, understood in these terms, goes well beyond the common historical gesture of simply detailing the heroic rugged individualism of a destined people; this history is coextensive with the plight of those who were religious exiles.

Indeed, Christian demons and epical mythmaking are synergistic, contra what one might expect from Puritanical anti-literature and anti-pagan fervor. Consistent with the Hebraic-Hellenistic duality scholars locate at the center of the American cultural performance, they are synergistic elements that mutually define the American social contract.

In an award-winning study, Theophus H. Smith reveals the continuity of a centuries-old European double-consciousness among Puritans. The Puritans manifested their European pedigree in their "errors of inversion," what Smith equates to a form of "incantatory impulse, comparable in effect (however unconscious) to magical performances in the operation of spells or solemn invocations." These errors, Smith argues, amounted to a form of conjure deployed by the Puritans to rewrite the Bible and make the New World—and displace the Old as—God's foreordained. The obvious danger in this, Smith states, is that "[i]t may be existentially impossible for a collective to become an authentic biblical exemplar, an unambiguous example for faith." The contradiction being as obvious as it was, a form of double-consciousness resulted in which the Puritans' hyperorthodoxy and "ostensible biblicism . . . functioned as a mask which veiled or disguised their 'inversion' of the traditional relationship between Scripture and experience" (Smith, *Conjuring* 70–75).

Cotton Mather is paradigmatic in this regard, for his paternity placed him at the very center of Puritan orthodoxy. Nevertheless, he drew upon Virgilian aesthetics to enflesh his hagiographic depiction of Puritan "saints" in *Magnalia Christi Americana* and even counseled his son that it would be unwise to "be wholly *unpoetical*. . . . I wish you may so understand an *Epic* poem, that the Beauties of an *Homer* and a *Virgil* may be discerned within you" (Bercovitch 1966; Reinhold, *Classica* 230; italics Mather's). The genesis of the Puritans' biblical mask parallels the ancients versus the moderns debate Patterson found in twelfth-century Europe, the greatness implicit in colonial America's study of Homer and Virgil even when belles-lettres were censored (Reinhold, *Classica* 129–30, and *Classick* 5), and documents the European form of double-consciousness discussed earlier as an essential cultural foundation for American democracy.

AMERICAN HOMER: AMERICAN ILIAD AND ODYSSEY

Two years after the ratification of the United States Constitution officially created a new nation-state the Meddler, an anonymous contributor to the January 1791 edition of the *New Haven Gazette*, had this to say: "Under a similarity of circumstances, America has at length become the seat of science, and the great mirror of freedom and politics. Her Attica has produced a Homer, who leads the way; a Virgil, who was the pupil of that great master, and a Horace, who resides at the seat of Augustus." Timothy Dwight, author of *The Conquest of Canaan* (1785) biblical epic, may have been properly designated the "American Homer" (Aldridge 99)[30] among the Federalist poets of his generation, but far more important is the "American Homer" socio-aesthetic performance context, a veritable looking-glass into the centuries-old European quarrel concerning the greatness of the ancients/pagans *vis-à-vis* the moderns/Christians, which the Federalist poets and American founders joined.[31]

For the founders and the elite-educated white males of their generation, American Homer was a founding cultural resource, being part of the symbolic code of classical culture performed through a complex process of mimicry peculiar to eighteenth- and early nineteenth-century America. The code consisted of "badges of class, taste, wisdom, and virtue," from togas to pseudonyms to neoclassical architecture, and, most importantly, a performative sum greater than these parts and measurable only in the intangible depths of the psyche and social associations (McLachlan 81–84; Richard 39–52). Some scholars argue that the classic culture derived from Europe quickly lost influence because of the break from Britain, concretized in 1789 with the ratification of the Constitution, and the beginning, in theory, of a radically new and modern enterprise. Historian Carl Richard, focusing on the role of the classics among the founders, categorically disagrees with this:

> The classics supplied mixed government theory, the principal basis for the U.S. Constitution. The classics contributed a great deal to the founders' conception of human nature, their understanding of the nature and purpose of virtue, and their appreciation of society's essential role in its production. . . . The classics provided the founders with a sense of identity and purpose, assuring them that their exertions were part of a grand universal scheme. The struggles of the Revolutionary and Constitutional periods gave the founders a sense of kinship with the ancients, a thrill of excitement at the opportunity to match their classical heroes' struggles against tyranny and their sage construction of durable republics.

More than serving as textual authorities, Richard argues that this generation, seeing their history through Britain and in direct lineage from antiquity, treated classical authors as "ancestors in a common struggle" (7–8, 12). Not surprisingly, Homer was among the classical figures who were "commonly read" in the 1790s (Reinhold, *Classick* 6).

Doubtless, most of the tangible and intangible icons of Homeric performance are forever lost, while others await the excavation of enterprising scholars. Nevertheless, the available documentary evidence from transcription collections (known as "commonplace books"), personal diaries, and letters demonstrates how the founders performed and took inspiration from Homer and antiquity. True to the epic mimicry guiding them, it constituted part of a *translatio* dynamic of American epic performance in which "beneficial Greco-Roman ideas were considered to be always improved or brought to perfection in the West" (Aldridge 104–05).

The life of George Washington embodies the *translatio* principle more than that of any other American figure except, perhaps, "Honest Abe" Lincoln, the savior-figure attributed with preserving the Union. As the evidence introduced below strongly indicates, Washington's career and life loom large as a type of Sunjatic performance that exists synergistically with America's constitutional performance.

Washington's life may have been, ultimately, more classical and mythologically significant than his peers' (Richard 69–72), but his lack of a classical and collegiate education, considered alone, puts him at a disadvantage compared to men like Thomas Jefferson and John Adams. Since most of the founders, including Jefferson and Patrick Henry, were the first to attend college, they were not introduced to Homer and the classics by fathers. Instead, in both northern and southern colonies, they had to wait until their matriculation in grammar school, at age eight. Grammar schools were drilling academies whose educational mission—teaching Latin, Greek, Hebrew, and the mechanics of reading by repetition and rod—eschewed the goal of trying to understand the authors (Richard 15–19) in favor of their sole purpose: providing entrance into the few elite colleges in which that same classical subject matter and pedagogy constituted the curriculum.[32]

In terms of classical erudition, few could compare to Jefferson's preparation and interest in Homer. A classical overachiever as drafter of the Declaration of Independence, founder of the University of Virginia, delegate to the Constitutional Conventions, scientist, inventor, ambassador to France, and then the third president of the United States, Jefferson is noteworthy for having *two* commonplace books, the literary one rich in classical transcriptions. Favoring Homer above all other poets, including Alexander Pope,[33] whose *Iliad* he quoted, along with Homer, twenty-nine times, Jefferson also held Greek as the nearest language to perfection ever produced. Though he read the newspaper to keep current, the distraction away from the classics gave him some distemper: "I read one or two newspapers a week, but with reluctance give even that time from Tacitus and Homer and so much agreeable reading." Jefferson was so devoted to Greek and could use it with such facility that even the learned John Adams, upon receiving one of his personal letters, could lament, "Lord! Lord! What can I do with so much Greek?" (Richard 27).

Jefferson's devotion to ancient Greek notwithstanding, the two-tiered classics education of Harvard, Yale, and other institutions made classical habits central to the American cultural performance. The college entrance exam and curriculum in Greek and Latin may have set the curriculum for grammar school, but the colleges' extracurricular "secret literary societies" were equally critical, if not more so. These societies, according to James McLachlan, were "colleges within colleges." They dominated collegiate life from 1760 to 1860, and student members "underwent an intense internalization and identification with the classical tradition." Their hazing-type initiation rituals constituted a "symbolic transformation" in which one learned the tribal mythology and "deeds of the Supernatural Beings" ("perfect Models of Antiquity"), and were even given their names.

The oftentimes compelling subject matter, the classics-based curriculum of formal education, the harsh disciplinarity of grammar schools, the colleges' mission of instilling virtue based on "worthy Characters, with the noble Sentiments, and perfect Models of Antiquity,"[34] the hazing-type severity of secret societies, and the cultural capital associated with classical erudition together provided, for the founders and their peers, an adulthood which "rested on youthful internalizations of the classical tradition." The love of the classics, despite the often unpleasant education of the masters who introduced most of the founders to them, actually intensified with age. Or it and the classics aged well, as Jefferson indicated in his "Thoughts on Prosody" essay: "When young any composition pleases which unites a little sense, some imagination, and some rhythm, in doses however small. But as we advance in life these things fall off one by one, and I suspect that we are left at last with only Homer and Virgil, and perhaps with Homer alone" (McLachlan 84–90, 94–95; Reinhold, *Classica* 232; Richard 12–13, 18, 19, 21, 23–28, 30, 35, 51–52).

America's public libraries,[35] unparalleled literacy rates, and Homeric interests brought together the founders' political wit to such a degree that, in colonial and post-Revolutionary War America, the ancients versus moderns debate spoke doubly—to all moderns versus the ancients and, significantly, to Americans versus the traditions and culture of Europe. While Christians like Timothy Dwight (American Homer) and Joel Barlow (American Virgil) used classical forms but favored modern culture over the paganism of the ancients, the founders, perhaps because they were the "fathers" of the nation, were ambivalent. The founders believed they had to prove themselves to their "social superiors by surpassing them in classical knowledge. Even while repudiating European corruption, American leaders longed for European respect. Like the Puritan ministers before them, these leaders defined America in European terms, emphasizing the national mission to save the mother continent by acting as a political 'city on a hill.'" Both John Adams and Jefferson, especially, evidenced this by entering into the Janus-space of the ancients versus the moderns debate in support of the ancients and the Americans. Adams preferred Homer and Virgil to Milton's *Paradise Lost*. When Frederick the Great reputedly dreamed that Homer and Virgil returned to earth and, because of Voltaire's writing, burned their works, Adams bristled: "His adulation of Voltaire is babyish. He knew nothing of Homer or Virgil. He was totally ignorant of the languages of both." A year later, in 1813, Jefferson defended Americans against the charges leveled by Edinburgh reviewers that English would fare poorly under their usage. Athenian dialects, he responded, reflected the vitality of a language and "made the Grecian Homer the first of poets, as he must ever remain, until a language equally ductile and copious shall again be spoken." Some twenty-six years earlier, in 1787 and in the heady days of constitutional drafting following the Revolutionary War, Jefferson was even more paternalistic and caustic in defending the still-unincorporated nation. The provocation occurred with the publication of a report in a Parisian journal that a British farmer had read Homer and forthwith developed an ingenious method for taking a wheel's circumference. No, it was a New Jersey farmer, Jefferson famously retorted, adding, "Ours are the only farmers who can read Homer." In short, these statements and their socio-political import together form an incredible syllogism. If we take Jefferson's and Adams' logic to its conclusion, namely that America produced founding leaders who were greater even than the ancients, in light of historian Carl Richard's argument that "the founders viewed America as the only land in which classical ideals could be translated into reality," then the result of this classically oriented syllogism is as contradictory as it is definitive. The ancient "ancestors" were better than the European moderns and the Americans in terms of aesthetics, but the Americans, ultimately, were superior to both because of their political ingenuity, the country's great men, and the promise it held to fulfill that which the ancient civilizations could not (Richard 28, 30, 51–52, 82).

As the founders matured, the classics were often an inspiration to them that they hoped to pass along to their children and loved ones; moreover, as final, parting gestures, the classics, even Homer, gave shape to grief when loved ones died. In 1781, John Adams, obviously concerned with the classical preparation of his oldest son, John Quincy, indicated that he could learn Greek from Homer and Latin from Virgil, and eventually concluded with an unmistakable admonition: "If there is no other Way, I will take you home and teach you Demosthenes and Homer myself." When John Quincy started Harvard in 1785, Adams could write to another and boast of his son's classical prowess as a translator of texts, such as Virgil's *Aeneid*, and reader of "several books in Homer's Iliad." Given that Adams' idea of femininity led him to prefer knowledgeable women who could have interest in asking, "What do you think of Helen? What do you think of Hector and c.?" it is hardly surprising that Homer inspired his love for family. In 1778 in Paris, Adams was so struck by *Adieus of Hector and Andromache*[36] (see Figure 3.6), "a painting depicting the famous parting of the *Iliad*'s Trojan hero from his wife and child," that he captured the moment in his diary: "With Feelings too exquisite to produce tears or Words, I gazed in silence at every Line, at every light and shade of this Picture, and could scarcely forgive Homer for introducing the Gleam of the Helmet and its Effect upon Astyanax [Hector's infant son], or any circumstance which could excite a Smile and diminish the Pathetic of the Interview." What is surprising is the approach of Abigail Adams, John's wife, to the classics. An opponent of "classical education," like other opponents of classical education *in Greek and Latin*, most notably Thomas Paine, Benjamin Franklin, and Dr. Benjamin Rush, Abigail Adams frequently used classical metaphor, simile, and allegory.[37] Thus, in 1782 she wrote to John Adams, then in Holland negotiating an alliance for the United States, "Eight years have already past since you could call yourself an Inhabitant of this State. I shall assume the Signature of Penelope, for my dear Ulysses [Odysseus] has already been a wanderer from me near half the term of years that Hero was encountering Neptune, Calipso, the Circes and Sirens." Love of Homer took sculptural form in the household of James Madison, who had busts of Homer and Socrates next to ones of himself, his wife, and Thomas Jefferson. Perhaps the Homeric expression of love most touching, and timeless, belongs to none other than Jefferson. Following the death of his wife Martha in 1782, Jefferson selected Achilles' lament, a pathos-rich utterance made after Patroklos' death, for her epitaph: "If in Hades the dying forget, / Yet even there I will remember my dear companion" (Richard 30, 32–33, 48–50, 67, 99, 196–223).

Figure 3.6   Hector Taking Leave of Andromache, by Angelica Kauffman (1741–1807), exhibited at the Royal Academy in 1769 at Saltram, Devon (© National Trust Images/John Hammond).

Richard's assessment of the paradigmatic effect of the ancients on the Americans, namely that the "mythological heroes in the works of Homer, Hesiod, Virgil, and Ovid," and various Roman statesmen, were "important, if *imprecise*" models, also explains the epic mimicry giving rise to the George Washington mythology (Richard 53, 57–67).

FROM *CONOTOCAURIOUS* TO COMMANDER-IN-CHIEF: GEORGE WASHINGTON'S EPICAL BODY

Just as a culture's habitus reinforces itself through great ceremony or in innocuous-seeming, playful verse for children, an epic habitus does the same. Washington's death, according to historian François Furstenberg, served as an event that inspired both grand and juvenile performances. Though Furstenberg holds that the U.S. "was grounded not on an ideology of divine right or ancient tradition, but rather on the consent of the living" (50), his analysis of "civic texts," an ephemeral performance genre, directly parallels the traditional African epic—and presumably ancient, pre-Homeric—performances. Only, instead of Sunjata, Mwindo, or Ozidi, or even Achilles or Odysseus, Washington's death concretized his new status as the epic hero for the new nation. Through his own efforts and that of others, Washington, like Lincoln later, ceased to be a mere man and became the center of an American epic performance whose modern components consisted of words, constitutional performance, and a numismatic dimension represented by coins and dollar bills.[38]

Of course, the epic mimicry—as opposed to slavish imitation—of greatness is best epitomized by Homer, associated with Washington and his father by Parson Mason Locke Weems, in *The Life of Washington*, the most significant civic text with respect to the construction of the Washington mythology. Epic mimicry may be America's bellwether of greatness, but this form of mimicry, in accordance with its nature, does not depend exclusively on Homer. As Furstenberg's analysis of civic texts indicates, Washington is an ideal icon of epic mimicry because he lacked aristocratic or royal heritage and formal classics education. He was not primogeniture or the seventh son, but a common second son born of a second marriage. Still, the civic texts, especially Weems' mythology, did two things: they channeled the epic spirit of the nation in a performance that rendered Washington at once common and aristocratic, and anticipated the democratic ethos of translation and epic mimicry that carried greatness toward the distant future.

The "apotheosis" of Washington occurred at a fluid, uncertain time: the nation was just ten years old, partisan Federalist-Antifederalist bickering was at its height, and Washington's sudden death on December 14, 1799, Furstenberg implies, put the integrity of the constitutional performance in jeopardy. The near-total national mourning and praising, "instant and overwhelming," shuttered businesses and led to countless events Furstenberg calls "rituals": eulogies, sermons, and speeches; special editions of newspapers, many with engravings; impromptu group meetings held by countless societies and "funeral parades" in towns; and, mourning and memorial attire in the form of black ribbons, armbands, pendants, and rings. In this moment of national mourning and crisis, the "spoken, printed, and engraved" civic texts constituted a national, epical performance that used the memory of Washington and the "eternal future" and "aura of permanence" of the republic to ensure the future. Akin to the effect of the call-and-response epic mottos of Sunjatic performance, where radical individualism folded back into the potency of proto-state cohesion, the civic texts "were calls to action. Audiences were not to be passive recipients of the nationalist message being transmitted; they were to respond with active remembrance and emulation" (25–28). After all, whether one addresses the MOS-African oral performance texts or these early Republican civic texts, a truism unites them in spite of the many cultural differences: "all individuals are engaged in producing representations in particular discursive milieus" (W. Belcher 214).

The remarks of Robert Liston, the British ambassador and resident of Philadelphia, cited by Furstenberg to document the "purpose" and "effect" of the civic texts, are most germane because of their similarity to the participant-observer dynamic of the MOS-epics:

> The leading men in the United States appear to be of the opinion that these ceremonies tend to elevate the spirit of the people, and contribute to the formation of a *national character*, which they consider as much wanting in this country. . . . The hyperbolical amplifications, the Pene-gyricks in question have an evident effect especially among the younger part of the community, in fomenting the growth of that vanity, which to the feelings of a stranger has already arrived at a sufficient height.

Furstenberg elides consideration of the Hellenistic and Homeric influences, but the "emulation of Washington" that "were coaxing audiences into becoming not just better people, but better Americans," highlights the paradoxical resilience and adaptability of performances of epic mythology. In his estimation, the runaway success of Weems' *Life of Washington* and the fabricated anecdotes contained therein, noted by twentieth-century scholars as blatant mythologizing, stems from a rich performance dynamic. In this regard, text and context merge into a reciprocal accord. *Life of* Washington is less popular, ephemeral success than a sounding of the lowest frequencies because it is the "complex back-and-forth [dynamic] between Weems and his reading public," its use of fables to appeal to children, the narration of an idealized history devoid of political rancor and slavery, and, ultimately, the resonance of these myths as an Ür civic text and context replicated many times over in religious tracts, prints, cartoons, and schoolbooks (25–28, 32–46, 107, 123–29).[39]

Civic texts, then, were equal parts theatrical and patriotic contexts, understood as a form of speaking by colonial Americans. Though the confluence of text and oral performance in a significant way parallels the speakerly texts Gates locates as the essence of the trickster-influenced African-American literary vernacular, the epic-trickster performance is perhaps most analogous. As Jason Shaffer argues, tapping oral performance theory, the revolution-era Americans saw themselves, because of theatrical culture, as heroic characters in the "*theatrum mundi*, or world stage" of the American Revolution, even as they deployed folk (American Indian culture and guerilla) military strategies. Washington, an avid theater aficionado for decades before 1776, Shaffer notes, became the patriotic epitome, a "patriot king" or "ruler," by virtue of his attendance, colonial mythmaking processes, and Washington's own acceptance and use of such heroic performances (1–3, 10–13, 26–29).

Washington's ultimate performance, a postmortem martyrdom encouraged by his own sense of self and political need, was as intense as it was paradoxical and transformative in intent. Washington became a father to the American children targeted by the civic texts, and father to all of the U.S., thus bridging public and private domains, past and present time, and ancient/

universal and modern/American fertility myths. Consequently, future generations could vicariously give their "consent to the nation" and its founding compacts and leaders. Moreover, like the participants in MOS-epic performances, they could reconcile revolutionary potential and futuricity with the centripetal forces that homogenized Western European differences.

Jefferson's adoration for all things Homeric, including statuary and the neoclassical architectural design he used for Monticello and the University of Virginia, and celebrated in the national capitol completed in 1812 (Richard 43–49), suggests the critical role of the Homeric space we inhabit. But just as scholars, James McLachlan shows, sought to undermine Cultural Studies approaches by arguing that the classics provided mere "débris" and "purely decorative phrases, tags, and allusions" (81–82), the existence of Homeric cartography, places named after Homer, have been similarly overlooked or dismissed. Chief among the numerous examples is the classical renaming of portions of New York state, first site of the federal capital, land of the Iroquois until 1789 when yet another treaty dispute terminated indigenous claims, and site of a military tract to pay Revolutionary War soldiers land in accordance with a 1776 act of the Continental Congress. Thus, when New York Surveyor General Simeon DeWitt surveyed the military tract and the Land Board approved his action in July 1790,

> The old towns in the Hudson and Mohawk River valleys were marked with English and Dutch names. These new American settlements required something different. It is widely believed that Secretary Robert Harpur, as a former professor and librarian, was responsible for the litany of classical names. There was Homer and Tully; Brutus, Marcellus and Cicero; Camillus, Manlius, Cincinnatus and Romulus, to name a few. *Over the years, despite occasional laughter over those sturdy farming villages with such pompous names, folks have learned to live with what may have been Robert's greatest legacy in central New York!* (Herbert 70; italics mine).

Historian Charles Maar investigated the origin of the Greco-Roman names and reported his findings at the New York State Historical Association meeting in Syracuse, New York, on October 3, 1925. Maar corroborated the claim that "merriment" and "amusement" have been associated with the names, but also revealed that their ultimate *raison d'etre* is no jocular matter. Maar noted that "the real situation was correctly described some years ago by a newspaper writer":

> When the military tract was surveyed, it became necessary to designate the township by name. There was then no very pleasant feeling toward the Indians or English, against which the colonists had recently fought. At the same time the prevailing classical education had made the history of Greece and Rome familiar and their achievements admired.

Indeed, it was the period, not so long brought to a close, when no ora-
tion was complete without its classical allusions and no literary effort
complete without its classical motto or quotation. (155, 156, 163)

Maar does not elaborate upon this, perhaps because the subject matter was
sensitive to historians and New Yorkers, many of whom must have had classical pedigrees, but it brings together revolution, conquest, and the classics
in a way most fitting for the role New York played in colonial America.

The renaming of Coreorgonel and other settlements, land first used by
the Cayuga Nation of the Iroquois Confederation, as Ulysses, then Ithaca,
establishes an allegorical instance of capital economies: a supreme land grab
opportunity folded into the Empire State of New York, the nation's first
capital, by virtue of epical performance. Indeed, General George Washington concretized his epic pedigree by ordering the 1779 expedition to eradicate the Iroquois, an act leading them to (re)name him *Conotocaurious*,
an epithet meaning "Town Destroyer."[40] In the compressed world of 1779,
this must have loomed large in the mythological cartography then being
explored, pioneered, colonized, and finally folded into the constitutional
performance of the new nation. The final act in this remapping process, of
course, is allegorical: the Native-world flattened and charted as institution-
alized, civilized, converted, modern, and reproducible knowledge.

Maar's assessment of post–Revolutionary War circumstances, combined
with the acquisition of huge tracts of Iroquois land, anticipates William R.
Farrell's *Classical Place Names in New York State* (2002), which provides
a "classical cartography" of New York's Greco-Roman, biblical, and other
classical names. Belonging first to the Algonquins and Iroquois, the latter
called the "Romans of the West" by some sixteenth-century writers because
its League or Confederacy suggested aspects of European-style civilization, New York, by historical reckoning, is the very capital of mythology,
democracy, conquest, and empire. The sobriquet of New York, the Empire
State, Farrell recounts, may stem from a 1785 speech given by General
Washington in New York City: "I pray that Heaven may bestow its choicest
blessing on your city . . . and that your state, at the present seat of (empire),
may set such examples of wisdom and liberality as shall have a tendency to
strengthen and give permanency to the Union" (Farrell xvii).

The unprecedented growth of New York beginning in the latter half of the
eighteenth century made its temporary status as capital understandable. The
presence of Washington, himself well on his way to becoming a democratic,
constitutionally supported embodiment of epical mythology, and the subsequent work of Harpur, gave the Empire State an infusion of classical and epical names into its body-politic. In this regard, the anti-British/Ancients versus
Modern/Americans climate frames Farrell's observation that "[t]hese names
. . . offended a number of people. They were foreign and had their origin in the
Old World. Many felt that they should be changed," but the existence of such
names, the "spirit of neoclassical revivalism," and events like the naming of
Troy, New York, in 1789, also support his assessment of New York as a "the

cradle of classical naming." Central, and maybe eastern New York State, that is, established a classical "cradle" used by the state for the next several decades into the mid-century (1–2). Indeed, Farrell describes his work as "toponymy," whose standard and archaic meaning[41] literally adds to revolution, conquest, and the classics an anatomical dimension that births the imaginary cartography of the body-politic. Various hamlets, towns, and cities of central New York—Homer, Ulysses, Ilion, Helena, Ithaca, Troy, Hector, and Penelope for sure, and maybe Paris, Greece, Sparta and West Sparta—embody Homeric cartography in the core fabric of the everyday. "To most central New Yorkers," Farrell states, "classical names like Plato, Homer, Aristotle and Euclid are commonplace. They are taken for granted. And why not? These communities have been around for a long time, many since shortly after the Revolutionary War" (3). Though common and unobtrusive now, the deep structure of the social contract guiding New York and the nation is itself immersed in ancient Mediterranean mythology, including Homeric performances. Hence, Farrell concludes, "To the trained ear, such appellations are deeply rooted in western civilization" (3). The "deeply rooted" classics culture, scholar Donald H. Mills writes in support of Farrell's work, "had, and continues to have, important influences on the modern world," and Farrell's "maps and illustrations will provide the means to visualize the breadth and depth of our classical toponymy" (xi).

Again, in New York as elsewhere in the colonies and new nation, this was no slavish imitation. Instead, it evidences a form of mimicry that simultaneously adulates the Ancient Greats and brushes them aside as the New World battled for its place as a great, modern body-politic that had its own distinct cultural traditions. Part of this tradition, ironically, was the noble savage sentiment, now combined with the desire for a national literature separate from the Old World, as reflected in a 1819 satirical poem, "An Ode to Simeon DeWitt, Esquire." Though the poem mistakenly identifies DeWitt as the source of the names, it is nevertheless valid, and remarkable, as a witty critique of the naming strategies used by their New York ancestors. It is significant that the poem begins with modern Americans' quest for "Fame" and asks, against the "bright record" of the ancients:

> What place remains for thee?
> Who, neither warrior, bard, nor sage,
> Hast pour'd on this benighted age,
> The blended light of all three.
>
> God-father of the christen'd West!
> Thy wonder-working power
> Has call'd from their eternal rest
> The poets and the chiefs who blest
> Old Europe in their happier hour:
> Thou givest, to the buried great,
> A citizen's certificate,

And, aliens now no more,
The children of each classic town
Shall emulate their sire's renown
In science, wisdom, or in war.

The bard who treads on Homer's earth
    Shall mount to epic throne,
And pour like breezes of the north,
Such spirit-stirring stanzas forth
    As Paulding wold not blush to own!
And he, who casts around his eyes
Where *Hampden's* bright stone-fences rise,
    Shall swear with thrilling joint,
(As German did), "We yet are free,
And this accursed tax should be
    Resisted at the bayonet's point."

. . .

Lo! Galen sends her Doctors round
    Proficients in their trade;
Historians are in Livy found,
Ulysses, from her teeming ground,
    Pours Politicians, ready made;
Fresh *Orators* in Tully rise,
Nestor, our Counsellors supplies,
    Wise, vigilant, and close;
Gracchus, or tavern-statesmen rears,
And *Milton* finds us pamphleteers,
    As well as poets by the groce. (Maar 157–58)

In this ode, signed by "Croaker & Co.,"[42] one sees all the elements of the "Battel" recast in a critical period, the War of 1812 (to 1815), in which anti-British nationalism surged once again, assuming here a muted form of "self-reliance" and more conspicuous Christian orthodoxy. Clearly, Croaker & Co. found wanting an "Old Europe" ethos in which a "God-father of the christen'd West" would, indeed, reanimate the ancient, pagan worthies, beginning with Homer, give them citizenship in the New Republic and, finally, endow them with the power to procreate classical greatness in accordance with the names of New York towns. Though the Croaker's satire is merry and amusing on its face, and nationalist against the Old World threat to the new country and the Ancient Greats who belonged to it, the poem betrays the desire for a distinct American greatness comparable to the "Old" forms it simultaneously repudiates.

For someone like Harriet Jacobs, a fugitive slave writing under the pen name Linda Brent forty years later, the merriment behind this epic whiteness would have been darkly ironic. Though seldom if ever remarked upon, Jacobs' *Incidents in the Life of a Slave Girl* (1861) recounts a short episode involving a common carrier, segregation, and protest that, in the antebellum era, has little apparent relevance. On a superficial level, the episode itself identifies the dynamic of legal strategies culminating with the selection of Rosa Parks to spark the Montgomery, Alabama, Civil Rights efforts of the 1950s. The symbolic, performative essence of this episode is far more complex than its formal legal genealogy. Recall that Jacobs, living in New York City as a fugitive slave and working as a nursemaid for Mrs. Bruce, an affluent woman, traveled with her by the steamboat *Knickerbocker* through Troy, New York. This is the aforementioned Troy, New York, named and incorporated in the same year the Constitution was adopted, existing in the state where the first federal capital was located, and a mecca for the cultured—artists, writers, and affluent—from the nineteenth century into the early decades of the twentieth. In Troy, Jacobs follows the course of her slave-narrative forerunners by unveiling the North's racism. The incident occurs when Jacobs takes a seat with Mrs. Bruce in spite of, and after expressing, her fear of "being insulted" because of Jim Crow:

> "O no, not if you are with *me*," [Mrs. Bruce] said. I saw several white nurses go with their ladies, and I ventured to do the same. We were at the extreme end of the table. I was no sooner seated, than a gruff voice said, "Get up! You know you are not allowed to sit here." I looked up, and, to my astonishment and indignation, saw the speaker was a colored man. If his office required him to enforce the by-laws of the boat, he might, at least, have done it politely. I replied, "I shall not get up, unless the captain comes and takes me up." No cup of tea was offered me, but Mrs. Bruce handed me hers and called for another. I looked to see whether the other nurses were treated in similar manner. They were all properly waited on. (136)

Nothing happens in Troy, except more apprehension settled by the landlord's generosity, and Jacobs passes on to Saratoga with *no* explicit comment. However, this incident, situated within Troy and its racial performance, closely parallels African Americans' legal and literary challenges to the color-line predating and succeeding it. Jacobs, perhaps under the influence of Lydia Maria Child, her editor, clearly suggests that she is in the right and the black man in the wrong. Race, gender, and breeding are deployed here to protest the Jim Crow laws and the black man's enforcement in ways central to civil rights groups' protest efforts. Equally important, this event shares in the Homeric toponymy underlying the landmark U.S. Supreme Court case (Homer) *Plessy v. Ferguson* (1896), which has been repeatedly and more recently restaged in criminal cases like that of Troy Anthony Davis[43] (see Figure 3.7) and the racial incident that occurred in Homer, Louisiana. Here, ironically, the mask of Trojan whiteness Jacobs' incident implicates is worn by an unnamed black man who polices her presence.

Figure 3.7   Troy Anthony Davis in a booking photo-
graph (Georgia Department of Corrections).

Though connected only by Homeric toponymy and race, *Incidents* is
noteworthy here for its top-down strategy of racial protest, which relies
upon exceptional, talented-tenth blacks. These black people's racial loyalty
will make them natural, dedicated spokespersons for and against women
and men like this, the narrative suggests, who are unlettered and unex-
ceptional blue-collar black laborers and race traitors, if not Uncle Toms.
Consider that Jacobs begins her narrative by establishing her exceptional
pedigree through her father, a gifted carpenter, and her grandmother, a
gifted cook. Moreover, Jacobs constantly references the whiteness and brilliance of her relatives, including the manly fighting spirit of her Uncle Benjamin; Jacobs' dialogic representations of her own speech show her to be
superbly articulate in comparison to typical users of slave dialect.

From this perspective, and in keeping with the exceptionalist pedigree
Incidents establishes early, Jacobs' narrative—and performance to the
extent this accurately details a real event—betrays her own complicity
in upholding American Homer even as she challenges racial segregation.
However, both Jacobs and this fellow perform their respective roles within

the parameters of space literally mapped out by American Homer and with respect to their proximity to the epicality of the social contract defining the American body-politic. Truly, the common/sense perspective requires analysis to go beyond the truths of the literate narrator to reckon with the performance totality.

Consequently, one might conclude that Jacobs was right (or wrong), as was the black *Knickerbocker* server who accosted her to more or less the same degree, because the performative space itself made rightness and wrongness, politeness and "gruff[ness]," impossible to disentangle from the sum of New York's cultural parts. She rightfully sought refuge and human dignity; he, quite possibly, rightfully sought to keep a job and avoid censure, physical abuse, and maybe even a blacklisting that would have stripped him of his economic dignity. Whose subjectivity deserves more attention? Can she, a mere colored invitee—albeit a beautiful, exotic, and cultured mulatta from an exceptional southern family of slaves who defied Dr. Flint—trump his position, demanding and deserving his racial solidarity, courteous service, and manly chivalry when his very livelihood demanded the opposite treatment and maybe even a conspicuous display of racial policing? Ultimate rightness or wrongness, based on the brief facts narrated to us in the text, is inaccessible; what is more important, anyway, is the conclusion that it is *not* impossible for both of them to be right. Here, the disjunctive either/or, equivalent to Manichean (white/black, good/bad) thinking, becomes a conjunctive and/both needed to fully understand the moment in all of its common/sense totality. After all, *Incidents* itself participates in the performance context demanding that we know all the details—everything, including the "spoken language" of the "creature," as Benjamin suggests—to reach an allegorycal truth not limited by the facile truths of allegorical possibility. Though far from the high mythology of the *Iliad* or *Odyssey*, it is still *Troy*, New York, and situated in the mythological firmament enveloping the people—especially southern and fugitive slaves, and free black laborers—and the land. Oppositions may occur in such a place, or in any Homer-inspired American locale, because epic mythology, although existing as a modern form of epical realism, ultimately defies reason and ethics by claiming that "impossible is nothing." It matters not that it is 1850s New York, or a steamer, as opposed to an Adidas slogan amplified by twenty-first-century sports phenoms and the virtual technologies promoting their epicality; indeed, the steamer's technology may owe its very existence to the American spirit of inventiveness equally impossible to disentangle from the cultural performance of race.

This particular Trojan episode is a far cry from Homer's *Iliad*, but symbolically it establishes an American Iliad that intensifies in (Homer) *Plessy v. Ferguson* and the African-American literary jurisprudence that demurred to its landmark precedent.[44] It continues today, in various nondescript disguises: the aforementioned *State v. [Troy] Davis* criminal case, the racial strife of Homer, Louisiana,[45] and in countless stories of people living their lives and struggling in places where Homeric myth seeps deeply into the earth, like the red clay and dark soil of the Deep South. Hence, even in the flat, two-dimensional space of blackletter newsprint, the Homeric mythology has a three-dimensional vitality begging for excavation. In "Ex-Husker Dixon trying to run with second chance at Troy," a sports article published by the *Lincoln Journal Star* (see Figure 3.8), epical realism vivifies the entire story. Though literally about Kevin Dixon, a defrocked Husker footballer from Sebring, Florida, Troy functions as a trope that seamlessly sutures together numerous proofs—for example, experiential, metaphorical, territorial, juridical, academic, and, of course, athletic—deployed to meet the evidentiary standards of AP-style objectivity and human interest subjectivity. In the article, by journalist Drew Champlin of *The Dothan (Ala.) Eagle*, Troy is a he/she/it trinary: an imagined male confidante for the first third of the story—

> **Dixon:**   "'The first couple of days I was down on myself for not doing what I was supposed to do, but after a couple of days Troy called, so I took it and ran with it'"
>
> **Champlin** *(narrative):* "Troy had been on Dixon since he was a star in high school . . . , but couldn't sign him in 2007 as he chose Nebraska"
>
> **Dixon:**   "'Troy had always been loyal to me since high school'" (Champlin D2)

—an imagined, incorporated place that is part of the motherland (Troy, Alabama), an imagined university thing (Troy University), and everything that links them into a dynamic, ever-shifting cultural performance comprised of living and nonliving parts. Indeed, some of these parts, such as the past names of Troy, unfurl like a blossoming flower: Deer Stand Hill, former Creek hunting land which unofficially became Troy by virtue of a deed recorded on October 9, 1838 before becoming Zebulon and then Centerville, was officially incorporated as the municipality of Troy on February 4, 1843.[46] Of course, countless students, alumni, faculty, administrators, and players perform on behalf of the Trojan mascots representing their schools. The only unique thing, in such a matrix, is the banality Homeric myth possesses for far too many Americans.

This particular performance of epical realism in newsprint is powerful, but far from unique in America and the West.[47] When the FAO Schwarz toy store opened in Las Vegas in late October 2004, the Trojan Horse literally performed for visitors. Its forty-eight-foot-tall mane equaling the three-story height of the store, this animatronic replica greeted visitors and harbored them, like Odysseus and his gang, in its epical womb, which launched or berthed them onto a second-floor balcony overlooking the store (Del Franco 2005).

Ex-Husker Dixon trying to run with second chance at Troy

BY DREW CHAMPLIN
The Dothan (Ala.) Eagle

TROY, Ala. — Last year, Kevin Dixon had high hopes.

He was supposed to start at Nebraska under new head coach Bo Pelini, hoping to help start the Huskers back to national prominence.

That changed when he was dismissed from the team for rules violations before camp started. For a couple of days, the defensive tackle thought it was all over.

"The first couple of days I was down on myself for not doing what I was supposed to do, but after a couple of days Troy called, so I took it and ran with it," Dixon said.

Troy had been on Dixon since he was a star in high school in Sebring, Fla., and even through junior college, but couldn't sign him in 2007 as he chose Nebraska.

He started four games in 2007, but was cited for public urination and marijuana possession, according to the Daily Nebraskan, before being dismissed.

Dixon caught on with Troy later, sat out last year as a transfer, and is set to begin his one and only season with the Trojans as a starting defensive tackle.

'I want to give back to the community and work with troubled youth, teaching kids the right things to do and what not. Having to transfer, having to sit out, that was the biggest moment in my life. That's a thing that when I do help with young guys, I'll be able to tell them stuff I went through so they won't make the same mistakes I did.'
— Kevin Dixon

He's also eager to put the past behind him.

"Troy had always been loyal to me since high school," Dixon said. "In a nutshell, it was some issues within myself, not taking care of the things I needed to take care of. Now that's in the past so I've moved on."

Troy coaches felt comfortable enough for Dixon to come to Troy. When he first got there, he joined the scout team and gave the first-team offensive line fits.

"I remember very well seeing somebody

so big that looked so athletic, it was surprising seeing that person on the scout team," Troy center Danny Franks said. "I had to ask around and found out he transferred from Nebraska. To go up against him and not give your best effort and have him beat you, it's shellshocking.

"Thank God we had him on the scout team, because he made our O-line a lot better."

Sitting out of football for the first time since he started playing, Dixon said he was humbled and got closer to finishing his degree requirements. He'll graduate in the spring with a degree in social sciences and minor in recreation.

"I want to give back to the community and work with troubled youth, teaching kids the right things to do and what not," Dixon said.

"Having to transfer, having to sit out, that was the biggest moment in my life. That's a thing that when I do help with young guys, I'll be able to tell them stuff I went through so they won't make the same mistakes I did."

This year, the only mistakes he hopes to take advantage of are ones by opposing offensive lines.

"He's a really good kid with a great personality that has worked hard," defensive coordinator Jeremy Rowell said. "He can have a big year for us."

Figure 3.8   "Ex-Husker Dixon Trying to Run with Second Chance at Troy" (*Lincoln Journal Star*, 21 Aug. 2009, D2).

The epic size of this modern-day Trojan Horse is unique, but its scale is actually dwarfed by the countless reincarnations of toys fashioned to meet the appetites of everyone, not just toy-loving boys and girls and their Vegas-bound families. In 1999, Donn Keofsky's L.A.R.K. toy store contained a Trojan Horse, this one "3-feet tall, made of balsa, and pulled by hundreds of handpainted horses. The Greeks were all fighting around it with catapults and horses. 'Took me 2,000 hours to build,'" said Keofsky, a master toymaker (Hart 1999). Susan Hoover, who constructed a Trojan Horse out of LEGO blocks, disclaimed any affiliation with the Lego Group or "malicious computer programs" (a Trojan Horse),[48] the irony being that the currency and potency of the fear regarding the Trojan Horse virus is indirect publicity that supports her effort. "This is an original design," Hoover states, thus echoing concerns historians establish as central to the founders' generation. Her (dis)claim has immediate legal ramification, of course, but just as importantly it engages in a centuries-old rebuff to charges of slavish imitation (of the Lego Group) by authenticating her "original" creation. Hoover's description of her LEGO Trojan Horse—

The inside of the horse is hollow. There are two guys climbing down the ladder from the hole in the belly.

I tried to keep the armor and weapons authentic for the Trojan period. Thus, only spears and broadswords, except for the one guy who has figured out how to use a bow and arrow. Just pretend it's not a longbow.

The Greeks were a cheery lot, as you can see by the smiles on their faces as they go off to war. (Hoover 2006)

—invites further analysis, particularly of the warring Greeks' smiling cheerfulness. Apparently, as a toy, its epical agony must be sanitized, modernized, LEGO-ized, and masked to meet the discriminating, epic-oriented taste of contemporary consumer-parents.

As a species of epical realism, the attractiveness of Trojan Horse replicas as child-friendly toys is not only unoriginal, but quite ancient. Along with nursery rhymes in Greek and Latin, ancient Greek and Roman children could count material representations of the Trojan War cycle among their possessions. "Not surprisingly for 'born warriors,'" Marc Wellens writes, "the Romans also had miniature soldiers. Toy soldiers were unearthed at Pompei, but also marionettes and money boxes. The money boxes, often still containing some coins, were pear-shaped. *A curiosity that Roman and Greek children often received as a gift was a miniature 'Trojan Horse', made of clay or wood, with a cavity for miniature soldiers*" (2006; italics mine).

Obviously, the influence of Homeric mimicry on the founders, which they inherited from the Old World, continues today in modernized forms of epical realism. At the same time, MOS-epicality has informed the founding figures—the masses of culture-bearing slaves—brought from an even Older, African World. Linking the two worlds is an epic performance culture closely associated with racism and creativity, one that has continuously fed into an African-American epic trickster aesthetic. The epic trickster not only underlies African-American culture and its storytelling tradition, including the most contemporary literature and post-soul/racial aesthetics, but has also boomeranged back into mainstream American culture in ways heretofore unexamined. The phenomenon, which speaks to MOS-epic artistic agency insofar as it influences literature and culture, a Mali-to-America exchange well-documented by Keith Cartwright, ultimately offers up philosophical commentary on human ontology through such epic aesthetics.

INTRODUCTION TO AFRICAN-*AMERICAN* EPIC TRICKSTER

Evidence abounds for an American cult of antiquity during the eighteenth century, particularly during the second half: the ubiquitous classical quotations and tags; the common use of Classical pseudonyms; the revival of Classical place names; the constant adducing of Classical parallels; even the frequent use of Classical names for slaves in the southern states.

—Meyer Reinhold, *The Classick Pages* (2)

Reverend Ephraim Peabody's characterization of slavery as a "whole Iliad of woes" and a "modern Odyssey" gets the moral sentiment right, but its

Homeric Eurocentrism betrays the customary fault of white liberalism: even when generally correct on the specific issue pertaining to race/ethnicity, and the *social* epic of slavery Peabody's review of Frederick Douglass' *Narrative* unveils, the larger problem of Homeric Eurocentrism that informs the culture (minds- and bodies-politic) remains or is reified. William Andrews' understanding of the latent racism Peabody bore toward African Americans in the form of an assumption of greater subjectivity for European Americans (*To Tell* 109) evidences itself in the abolitionist-created-and-controlled slave narrative genre. Epical performance defines most of these slave autobiographies from beginning to end, the slave authors betraying—but never examining—the exceptionalism giving rise to slavery and the culture. They never ask, in other words, what the cost of that exceptionalism—whether of whites or talented slaves—presents to the person and dominant culture as well as the victim.

As partial corrective to this oversight, Cartwright appropriated Du Bois' *Souls* as a necessary step toward an epic performance model that can provide a Sunjatic account for African-American exceptionalism and the potency of its influence on American aesthetics. Though race, gender, and class are immanent in his work, Cartwright's emphasis on performance aesthetics does not engage the art/politics intersection immanent in Peabody's Eurocentrism and thus cannot answer the question of how the Homeric performance, which suppresses African sublimity, reads Sunjatic potency. Just as Du Bois uses a generic formulation inclusive of Sunjatic performance—the souls of black folk—en route to a pan-Africanism equally aesthetic as it is political, I would like to expand its *nyama* beyond the Senegambian domain to account for American Homer, tricksters, and MOS-epic tricksters. Du Bois' work, as it existed in the Nadir, is a critical start, for the *nyama* of his *Souls* is charged with allegorycal potential: political bible, multigeneric, folks and Talented Tenth, African and European American, African and European, pre-modern and modern. The harmonizing spirituals, or sorrow songs, straining toward the transcendental and American, follow in the tracts of medieval allegory immanent in European/American culture.

The spirituals and much subsequent "authentic" black expression, as Paul Gilroy argued in the *Black Atlantic*, are born of a process of "authentication" that transformed African-American men and women into "lamp-blacked Anglo-Saxon[s]," though not in the manner suggested by George S. Schuyler (1222): the "prominence and popularity of minstrelsy" that fed into an intensifying theatricality of "hateful antics of Zip Coon, Jim Crow, and their odious supporting cast" led the Fisk Jubilee Singers to successfully fashion an "aura of seriousness around their activities," Gilroy argues. Their travels lent themselves to "allegory" operating on multiple registers, from European/American spiritual transcendence to the "development of black political culture":

It is clear that for their liberal patrons the music and song of the Fisk Jubilee Singers offered an opportunity to feel closer to God and to

redemption while the memory of slavery recovered by their performances entrenched the feelings of moral rectitude that flowed from
the commitment to political reform for which the imagery of elevation
from slavery was emblematic long after emancipation.

Gilroy locates the birth of Du Bois' "polyphonic montage technique" in the
milieu created during his stay at Fisk University, where he was immersed
in jubilee performance and the multitextual culture that arose from their
many publications.

The sorrow songs cannot contain the allegorye, although they are an
essential timbre voicing one aspect—classicized and exceptional—of the
response to slavery and Jim Crow. However, they miss, Gilroy reads Zora
Neale Hurston to argue against Du Bois, the "vital, untrained, angular spirit
of the rural folk." After all, many among the masses of black folk valued the
culture, creativity, and catharsis in the "crooked legged" rhythms. Indeed,
the black community, too, had its own politics, far deeper in time than U.S.
constitutional performances inaugurated in 1789 and—in its epical, allegorycal extension—great enough to validate Hurston's artistry and sharply
rebuff her apolitical stance. Hurston also advanced an "essentially invariant,
anti-historical notion of black particularity," too, Gilroy argues (87–92).

Though richly insightful, Gilroy's "Black Atlantic" construct itself fits
into a larger and deeper spiritual flow. While Gilroy advances water as
the defining trope, Cartwright foregrounds the spirit, *nyama*, as a Sunjatic
trope inclusive of woman, man, bush and water spirits—everything. Well
before the formation of the Black Atlantic with the start of the transatlantic
slave trade in 1453, there existed an Homeric Atlantic that flowed equally
on land and water, its folk spirituality statically individualist (anti-essentialist) and radically nativist. One of the lessons the traditional African epic
performance offers is the timeliness of "essentializing" when a threat—
particularly an epical one—is imminent. In regard to the duration of *this*
essentializing, Wai Chee Dimock puts it into perspective: the past should
not be measured by "thin slices of time" as documented by Western "standard national histories, organized by dates and periodized by decades, if
not by years," but one situated within "'centuries this time: the history of
the long, even of the very long time span'" (*Through Other* 4).[49] Any anti-
essentialist theorizing needs to be measured against the deep time. It goes
without saying, though many black Americans have pointed it out in recent
decades, that anti-essentialist rhetoric and policies, among them opposition
to affirmative action programs, are dangerously *un*timely, if not a reification of the racist hegemony under the guise of a color-blind society.

Souls appeared at a time, the Nadir, when the souls of black folks were
literally valued less than rotten fruit swinging on a tree. True enough,
contained in the "darky" figure is the deformed trickster, and contained
within it is not only an African-American epic trickster aesthetic and
political will, but an hermeneutic for understanding the Homeric folk

essence—hero and trickster—masked by American modernity. In an epic Atlantic in which epic individualism and epical race wore a white face and a canon of African Studies did not exist, Du Bois' *Souls* is, indeed, a prophetic, insightful, and second-sighted expansion of black souls out of "darky" lore, minstrelsy, and an assumed ontology of inferiority. But without an expansive second sight calibrated for European/American Homeric performance, Du Bois could not plumb the deep time lying beneath the veneer of European/American modernism, and the soul-murder immanent in its exceptionalism. Neither "immersion" nor "ascent" into the culture of the American South and North (Stepto 67) offered him a way of "articulating," sounding, and correcting the racial problem caused by the Homeric folk performance. The canonical Du Bois-Washington, North-South frame misleads and fails us, for the untutored, common African folk sense foregrounded by writers like Charles Chesnutt and Pauline Hopkins cannot compete. In the high-stakes contest of racial politics, Washington's uplift model, which sacrificed classical and higher education to industrial education, and Du Bois' enlightenment model *both* reduce the African common/sense to caricature.

For example, Mark Twain's *Adventures of Huckleberry Finn*, flowing with epic performance though masked by a boy's adventures, could not be appreciated under a classical enlightenment model of racial uplift. Those dependent on such would find themselves incapable of reading beyond the many uses of "nigger" which have occasioned bans on the novel, some of them instigated by contemporary black parents. But what is the trash talkin(g) of Bob and the Child of Calamity but Twain's Americanization of the epic performance dynamic, Child of Calamity being mythical, ancient, and Bob a typical figure needed to invoke and channel the epicality into present culture? A more nuanced version of the same is the episode involving the undertaker and the minister at Peter Wilks' funeral, a complex and irreverently humorous moment farce that quickens as the minister begins the eulogy and a dog in the cellar launches into the "most outrageous row . . . a body ever heard." Preceded by the King's repeated malapropisms (he confuses "funeral orgies" for "funeral obsequies") and Huck's "outrageous" behavior in stashing a "money-bag" containing $6,000 in gold coins into the coffin with Wilks' body, the "row" during the funeral reaches a level of hilarity sufficient unto itself. But this incident parallels *La Quarelle des Anciens et Modernes*, for the undertaker, like (s)Hades of death, is working on behalf of a modern Christian minister as he "glided" down into the "cellar" underworld. There he fetched the barking dog a terrific "whack," after which the "dog finished up with a most amazing howl or two, and then everything was dead still, and the parson begun his solemn talk where he left off." Huckleberry Finn, Twain's objectively reliable narrator of fact who is naïve to underlying cultural performances, provides critical language as he describes the closure of this episode. The undertaker, Huck writes, "glided, and glided, around three sides of the room, and then rose up, and shaded his mouth" to whisper to the minister: "*He had a rat!*" (220–21, 229, 231). This episode is curious, even undecipherable, unless one considers the dog to symbolize Cerberus, the three-headed, dragon-tailed dog who allowed Greek shades into the Underworld, but denied their exit. The modern Judeo-Christian undertaker not only enters and exits, but "whacks" the dog into silence, maybe even death, thus symbolically putting the ancients, and Odysseus, in their place.

Twain knows the South, from "white trash" Huckleberry Finns to the aristocracy, and North. Showing keen awareness of the formation of the Homeric diaspora, its adaptability and the self-parody and self-caricature informing it, Twain uses important mythological cartography and allegorye as, in the novel, North becomes Old England, the precursor to the New England locus of high culture. But whereas *Huck Finn* symbolically folds the contemporary performance of exceptionalism—the King, the Duke, and Shakespeare—into a larger farce, Du Bois and Washington embrace the North as more enlightened. But the folk performance is there as well, and older and deeper, requiring even more excavation. Hence, because Du Bois was learned in the classics and valorized high culture as modern progress, he could not properly decode the parody and mimicry. Failing to see Jim—ironically established as the most astute member of Twain's entire cast—as more than caricature may not be problematic.[50] But Du Bois' failure to grasp parody and mimicry made him the easy pawn of Washington's (the man's and nation-state's) tricks and an actor in a real-life racial burlesque made all the more intense, ironically, in direct proportion to his embrace of (neo)classical enlightenment. Would he have known that the "burlesque [of] a Greek Epic," held at the Milwaukee Normal State School in 1898 (see Figure 3.9), simultaneously encouraged the classics by reference to the ancients and "whack[ed]" them into an off-stage position that reinforced modern/American superiority, racial *and* non-racial?

After all, Du Bois, young and optimistic, envisioned a utopian modernity free of racism, one where American and "Negro" can exchange racial wisdom; he has no patience for the "wild" pleas and warnings of David Walker or the prophetic wisdom of black Christianity. Consequently, Du Bois' *Souls* enters American cultural performance as another African-American variation on *La Quarelle*. *Souls* excavates the greatness of African Americans and situates Du Bois as the Harvard- and Berlin-educated challenger of Washington, each man jockeying to position himself as the successor to Frederick Douglass.

On account of this orientation toward greatness, Du Bois' sorrow songs strategy overlooks the vibrant, exuberant, even "static" folklore and music that had given birth to John Henry and Staggolee at a time and place (late 1860s to early 1870s American South) when Du Bois himself was born in Connecticut (1868). In other words, upon publication of *Souls* in 1903, Du

MILWAUKEE YOUNG PEOPLE BURLESQUE A GREEK EPIC.

The seniors of the state normal school presented one of the most cleverly executed pieces of amateur stage work to a large audience at Pabst theater last evening. That Milwaukee citizens have seen in the city. The play was The Story of the Siege of Troy modernized and localized in a laughable and clever manner. There was considerable of what in old carnival days was called "impersonation of local celebrities," some of which were extremely funny. That the gods and goddesses of the story wore garments of the latest style and rode bicycles, while the Grecian and Trojan maidens were garbed in bloomer suits and played basket ball; that Paris and Menelaus settled their dispute over that daughter of the Gods, "divinely tall and most divinely fair," with boxing gloves a la Marquis Queensbury; that the Greek company which marched upon Troy was "fearfully and wonderfully made," as motley as the group which followed the Pied Piper of Hamelin, or more so, only added to the popular estimate of the production which was heightened to extravagant mirth when Paris and Helen, with all the hand luggage of the modern traveler, eloped on a tandem and were pursued by the army of the Greeks, who received their first call to arms by telephone.

The dances and tableaux were well executed and well conceived, so much so that Miss Marion Jean Craig, whose skill had made the success of the piece assured, was called to the curtain, and there presented with a beautiful bouquet of roses.

Figure 3.9 "Milwaukee Young People Burlesque a Greek Epic" (*The Milwaukee Journal*, 1898).

Bois veils the bad or hard wo/man, jazz and the blues—the epic trickster—even as he theorizes the "Veil" of the "color-line."

Of course, though *Souls* is charged with epic and Du Bois wrote his Ph.D. thesis on the Atlantic slave trade, as a Connecticut-born man whose exposure to African trickster lore was limited or nonexistent, there is virtually no chance that he knew of Sunjata, Mwindo, and Ozidi. Even if he did, and if he had encountered one or more of them, there was no mechanism for him to study the performance of epic mythology and its implications for responding to racism, including full appreciation of the most deformed among the "ten thousand thousand" black Americans he sought to uplift. Indeed, the MOS-epic mythology has its own enlightened truism: the "second sight" of the Talented Tenth Du Bois taps to heal the "double self" and effect the "merging . . . of the older selves" is nothing without the epic potency and nonclassical, irregular folk sense of the *Bottom* Tenth.

The Bottom Tenth's "message for the world," reaching back millennia before the "dawning of the Twentieth Century" Du Bois uses as his "Forethought" (*Souls* 5), is MOS-deep: blacks don't only possess second sight or just "wear the mask," but in a place where agon(y) abides, they are (*is* if you hip) MOS-epic sHades wielding an allegorycal *nyama*.

In sum, and contra Gilroy and Du Bois, the epic soul is classical sounding and equally jazzy, only deep time capable of telling when Africa is classical and Europe jazzy, and vice versa. This soul flows with spirituals essential for racial equilibrium, and computes with its own irregular mathematical sublime: second sight plus invisibility equals out-of-this-world possibility and a cautionary threat to the *eco*-librium of the entire planet.

PLANETARY SHADES: HOMERIC MIMICRY/PARODY, BLACKFACE MINSTRELSY, AND EPIC MIMICRY

The African-American epic trickster, then, is an allegorycal figure, parts Du Bois and Hurston, epic hero and trickster, yin and yang, cool and hot, dragon and in-drag, toe-jam and yams, Alpha(s) and Omega(z), rhyme and reason, hip and hop, bad and *ba-ad*. The convergence between epic and trickster, via deformity, begs the question, what is the critical difference between the oppressor and the oppressed? For the oppressors, belief in epic ontology makes them more conscious of their great distance from the trickster. This is surely yet another matter of epic agony because the continued epic performance creates an aporia and contradiction that is, by all means and measures, excessive. For the oppressed Other, the excesses of the oppressor's epical realism force the two ontologies much closer, making the individuals in these communities doubly transgressive and actuated by a hip hop soulfulness simultaneously feared and fetishized in the oppressor's imaginary. The black criminal, rapist or jezebel, has long been a defining racial trope, but the heroic, exceptional black is the very ontology of fear conquered and controlled by blackface minstrelsy.

Taking measure of the phenomena of Homeric mimicry and epic minstrelsy requires examination, of course, of the interracial, class, and gender dynamics of blackface minstrelsy. Minstrelsy peaked in the mid-nineteenth century (1846–1854), Eric Lott argues in *Love and Theft: Blackface Minstrelsy and the American Working Class* (1995), as an ambivalent way for working-class Americans to address the overwhelming presence of black slaves and, later, their threat to white culture because of emancipation. Blackface minstrelsy satisfies erotic fascination and simultaneously commutes these anxieties by using the caricature, a theatrical, audiovisual form of the diminutive, to maintain a communal, white lens capable of assuring whiteness as a secure and privileged identity and culture. "The black mask offered a way," Lott argues, to play with collective fears of a degraded and threatening—and male—Other while at the same time maintaining some symbolic control over them. Yet the intensified American fears of succumbing to a racialized image of Otherness were everywhere operative in minstrelsy, continually exceeding the controls and accounting, paradoxically, for the minstrel show's power, insofar as its "blackness" was unceasingly fascinating to performers and audiences alike. This combined fear of and fascination with the black male cast a strange dread of miscegenation over the minstrel show, but evidently did not preclude a continual return to minstrel miming. (6–9, 25)

On the mythic level beneath racial affects and effects, this minstrelsy allows the performers and audience to use blackness, Otherness, as a proxy for Death in and Rebirth from the Underworld that defines the ultimate Homeric hero, Odysseus. He travels to Hades—symbolically assuming a mask of Death, his own *sHades*, if you will—to tour the realm of the Dead, consult with the dead Greeks, and, then cheat Death by leaving with a new second sight borne by the living and the dead. Blackness establishes Death as the ultimate epical Otherness, for it is the foil of Life itself; no feat could be more epical than defying mortality and orchestrating one's own rebirth.

In the logic of America's minstrel performance, African Americans' and Africans' "black" skin marks their Otherness and proximity to the power of darkness, but it is not a personal trait enabling them to reach the higher echelons of epic ontology. Instead, even this blackness is commodified, appropriated, and redeployed through a socio-aesthetic economy associating Self, epic, whiteness, and nation: it forms the consideration upon which the American social contract negotiates identity, and is used to simultaneously perform epical anxiety and conquest for "white" sense and sensibility in the nineteenth century. Thus, speaking of the distorted Greco-Roman and Christian cultural underpinnings of Western Europe, Walter Benjamin notes that the "present age" is not creative, but mimics "past or distant spiritual worlds in order to take possession of them and unfeelingly incorporate them into its own self-absorbed fantasizing" (53).

EPICAL REALISM: ABRAHAMS, MARX, AND MASS PRODUCTION OF COOL *BLACKNESS*

Whereas magical realism is a mode in which celebrated authors like Gabriel García Márquez locate and narrate the magical strangeness of the everyday, *epical* realism attributes this strangeness to an ongoing heroic epic performance in which authors extract artistry from the epical mythology saturating reality. Although both have objective existence that can be sensed, apprehended, believed, appropriated, and refashioned by everyone, epical realism is less diffuse and innocuous. Indeed, the vicarious, participatory dynamic of the MOS-epic performance makes this patently clear. The gap between epic/myth and realism, while an opposition in the modern objective mind, is a healthy space for pre-modern society because of the porosity of time and the body. The distance between the remote ancestors and the present is mediated by a fluid common/sense of juxtaposition. In the most organic sense imaginable, what happened then among the ancestors (in the place of epic/myth) happens again in the storytelling-performance reality of the present descendants, *who gratefully receive such instruction and (re) connection.* Epical realism, just as its reading here is a linguistic flow from left to right, is the flow—of time, culture, spirit, and life-giving waters— from the imagined and real past into the real imaginations and material conditions of the present performance context. This flow is both disrupted and augmented in an ancients/ancestors vs. moderns environment where the fundamental, ontological sameness of this context (*con-*) is shorn into con/text and reduced to a privileged text devoid of the broader commonality that makes it whole. Although disrupted, the context is not destroyed because it is the essence of being human. However, the site of the return of this repressed, the modern collective unconscious, is caustic and catalytic; it is an unacknowledged place of tension that augments creativity since modernity must work so hard to deny the whole return of its own organic otherness and yet deploy the epic lore that flows from it.

In the text-based Homeric performance diaspora of the West, this dynamic has been the deep superstructure—dating back, arguably, centuries—of the Western European social contract. Through historical contingency, it has expanded and risen to the surface to such an extent that reality itself is often understood in these terms and no other. Ontology itself is seen as coextensive with epic whiteness—white supremacy, in other words— and if one cannot produce an epic, Hegel notes, then one is insignificant. In America, the farthest, wildest West deemed most epical by Hegel and brilliantly satirized as such by Twain, however, the truism has been manifested in a violent process of epical realism in which epic/myth has been increasingly converted to realism through the classical alchemy of useful knowledge. The common terrain "necro" and "negro" share lies at the very core of this process.

Karl Marx identified a significant part of this aspect of capitalism in the nineteenth century. Indeed, his analysis amounts to an unmasking, as his earlier engagement with modern practices of "reification" and "commodification" starts with a modern form of forgetting; however, in his later work, this process evolves backward into the necromancy at work in capitalism. Christopher May makes a pertinent point in this regard:

> In notebook VI of the *Grundrisse*, Marx argued that 'The crude materialism of the economists who regard as the *natural properties* of things what are social relations of production amongst people, and qualities which things obtain because they are subsumed under these relations

. . . imputes social relations to things as *inherent characteristics*, and thus mystifies them.' . . .

Earlier in the notebooks, Marx had noted that the 'economists' put considerable effort into this 'forgetting': the wilful depiction of socially-contrived relations as if they were natural occurrences. . . . Indeed, the aim of such depictions was to present production 'as encased in eternal natural laws independent of history, at which opportunity *bourgeois* relations are then quietly smuggled in as the inviolable natural laws on which society in the abstract is founded.' . . . Reification, then, is the abstracting of a particular set of relations into an ahistorical, naturalised (and hence non-political) set of occurrences.

Marx moved on from regarding this process as merely 'forgetting' in his subsequent writing: in *Capital*, reification and fetishisation had become 'magic and necromancy.' (May 39–40)

Thus, beyond a modern "forgetting" of the nonrelationship between commodities, value, and labor, Marx's "magic and necromancy" speaks to ancient magic and the universal human drive that transforms ideas into reality. In the West, the generic form and cultural performance through which much of this human drive expresses itself is the heroic epic. Homeric performance has been the normative ontological mode and its epical realism—inclusive of and older than the "magic and necromancy" Marx references—the aesthetic that is simultaneously at the center of, and coextensive with, the boundary of the social contract. That boundary far eclipses the territorial boundaries of the nation-state, for epical possibility by definition defies limits.

However, Homer-based epical realism is a dialectical two-step, one in which the launch toward greater epical ontology and possibility occurs in direct proportion to the "magic and necromancy" of reducing everything and everyone else to an Object-Other one acquires to support one's odyssey. This Homeric performance of the social contract establishes an epical realism rooted in super-normativity: these are, after all, "eternal" and "inviolable natural laws." Epical realism, then, is thesis, antithesis, and synthesis: an established aesthetic (e.g., bourgeoisie novel and *Homo performans*) as well as the underlying capitalistic labor of transmuting the impossibilities of (epic) mythology into reproducible, commodified, and realized materiality, the resistance of the Others thereto, and all of the shades of difference in between.

Considering the West/Central African epic performance, the African-American continuity and discontinuity, and the everyday performance of American Homer, Marxist necromancy invites discussion of "negro." Is *negro* (black) and *necro* (death) mere coincidence? The ultimate disillusionment many African-American intellectuals reached with Marxism speaks to their awareness of deep-seated, centuries-old processes. Those historical processes, they realized, shaped the racial consciousness of the *lumpenproletariat and* Marx, and set in motion an essential epistemological frame as Greek *necro* becomes medieval necromancy and African blackness; to wit, from the root-word

> **nec·ro-** [< Gr. *nekros*, dead body], *a combining form meaning* death, corpse, dead tissue

springs

> **nec·ro·man·cy** [ME. *nigromancie* < OFr. *nigromance* < ML. *nigromantia* (altered by association with L. *niger*, black)] 1. the practice of claiming to foretell the future by alleged communication with the dead 2. black magic; sorcery

and

> **Ne·gro** [Sp. & Port. *negro*, black, black person < L. *niger*, black] 1. a member of the dominant group of mankind in Africa, living chiefly south of the Sahara, and characterized generally by a dark skin.[51]

Though blackness is racialized as a static object (i.e., whiteness is dynamic, blackness its antithesis in the Western imaginary), *negro* and necromancy are performative conduits in which occult powers of death are sought, conquered, channeled, and, in the capitalist democratic state, commodified and reproduced. In the early sixteenth century, satirist Ishmael Reed writes in *Mumbo Jumbo* (1972), the Faust "legend" epitomized this. From a "wandering conjurer and medical quack" who used bad Greek and made-up titles, his salesman's "Hocus-pocus," he gets lucky with something that works. He "repeats this performance," is seen as "supernatural," and he becomes a wealthy man who has a castle. Whispers start that a "Black man, a very bearded devil himself visits him," and after Faust disappears, supposedly dead, "The village whispers that the Black men have collected. That is the nagging notion of Western man" (90–91).

The *Odyssey* is an ancient variant on this Faustian legend. Odysseus achieves the ultimate second sight—one that is both a "culturally constituted parallax effect" and "an extra-sensory ability to discern the workings of spirits and power(s)" (Cartwright, "Reading Roots" 33)—and invisibility when he travels to, abides in, and then returns from Hades, the Greek underworld and domain of the dead. By virtue of his patron goddess Athena, he regularly benefits from second sightings of her no other Greek shares, but his second sight merges into a symbolic invisibility—restaged upon his return from "death" to the chagrin of the suitors—by virtue of his odyssey into Hades. The Islam/Maninka bicultural "parallax" behind Sunjata's second sight, what Cartwright associates with bifocals (and Benjamin Franklin's American insight), can be retrofitted onto Odysseus, too:

he, an Ithacan hero and chief who embodies the knowledge of the Greek confederation, also acquires the ultimate spiritual knowledge of the land of the living. Achilles may be the greatest in the *Iliad*, but he dies and in the *Odyssey* is bound to Hades, whereas Odysseus conquers death (*necro*) and the ultimate blackness (*negro*) symbolically representing it. Out of darkness, Odysseus returns from death cloaked in sHades, secures *his* Helen (Penelope, Queen of Ithaca), routs the army of suitor-competitors in a bloody orgy, and thus protects his wealth and future prosperity.

The end of the *Odyssey*, then, narrates the epical realism operative throughout the Homeric epics and much of Western history. Out of darkness, death, and nothingness (remember, Africa is the Dark Continent) comes its imagined opposite: whiteness as the (epic) heroic, modern, and civilized capital/capitol enterprise. This enterprise, democratized and disseminated, eventually leaves the domain of epic mythology embodied in singular figures like Odysseus, Achilles, and Beowulf, and assumes a normative place. The *Odyssey* merges into the corporate body as American Dream, represented by a home "castle" and the wealth one collects, and as quotidian careers and professions of modern capitalism.

The irony, of course, is that the "negro" is recognized—even if subconsciously—as a fount containing essential epicality; consequently, America's racialized epic performance is a two-step of racist (most often white supremacist) harangue, harassment, and horror, on the one hand, and a form of epic mimicry, on the other. Blacks are simultaneously abhorred and, because of America's epic fetish, "loved" as the truest form of the "underdog," "dark horse," and "Cinderella story." Thus, under this "love and theft" formula and out of the post-60s fervor, Blackness became increasingly *ba-ad*, meaning cool and hip. Now, hip hop is consumed by seventy percent of white suburban teenagers, and shades—one is tempted to say sHades—and tinted windows are signature markers of the hip middle-class cool. The greatest irony in this, perhaps, is that the Honda Odyssey, the middle-class suburban van of choice that defines "soccer moms," the post-9/11 cohort prominently featured in and recognized since the 2004 presidential election, seems to travel our roads with at least seventy-five percent of them sporting tinted windows. "Truly," the West/Central African epic *necromancers* might say, "There goes epic, capitalistic excess, a veritable chariot of death, in the invisible garb of modern civility and the true *Japanese*-American values of mom, God, and apple pie."

SOULFUL HIPNESS, HOTNESS, AND COOLNESS:
SUN SHADES & HONDA ODYSSEY

Using Rinehart the minister, numbers runner, gambler, briber, and lover as inspiration for the protagonist of *Invisible Man*, Ellison taps the

Greek underworld to offer his unnamed, exceptional black protagonist the ultimate ancient defense, invisibility, to use against Ras the destroyer, Harlem's Garvey-like bad-man:

> I looked back. I felt that they were watching me from somewhere up the street but I couldn't see them. Why didn't a taxi come! Then three men in natty cream-colored summer suits came to stand near me at the curb, and something about them struck me like a hammer. They were all wearing dark glasses. I had seen it thousands of times, but suddenly what I had considered an empty imitation of a Hollywood fad was flooded with personal significance. Why not, I thought, why not, and shot across the street and into the air-conditioned chill of a drugstore.
>
> I saw them on a case strewn with sun visors, hair nets, rubber gloves, a card of false eyelashes, and seized the darkest lenses I could find. They were of a green glass so dark that it appeared black, and I put them on immediately, plunging into blackness and moving outside.
>
> I could barely see; it was almost dark now, and the streets swarmed in a green vagueness. (482–83)

In other words, and because of his exceptional literacy, which is in part earned through what John Stark calls his "Black Odyssey" (60),[52] Ellison's protagonist has the insight to see through the folk's garbage ("sun visors, hair nets, rubber gloves, a card of false eyelashes"), Hollywood celebrity, and the dark-green necromancy of capitalism underlying both. It is only a matter of time before he recognizes the potential of invisibility and second sight and shifts from defensive to offensive deployment. His logic unfolds neatly like a syllogism: I am "invisible" to whites and "even with" blacks, and Rinehart's "world was possibility and he knew it," therefore I should embrace invisibility ("I'd make invisibility felt if not seen") (Ellison, *Invisible* 498, 506–07, 509). As he signifies against Wright's folk-call, Ellison echoes Sutton E. Griggs' statements that the black working class was passive—"toiling, unthinking masses"—while the "educated class" was potentially revolutionary, and "barbarism" needed to be purged (51, 75).

Ellison, however, fails to wholly realize that "barbarism" is relative, existing beneath American modernity and enlightened epistemology, and that the folk knowledge of invisibility also stemmed from a West African epic power source representing the "barbaric" knowledge Mamadou Kouyate would keep out of books, for good reason. The broader West/Central African cosmology provides the necessary context for enlivening and limiting the narrative essence of the MOS-epic performance. Indeed, "Before / l o n g before" Islam, slavery, Christianity, and the rise of Asia, Wopashitwe Mondo Eyen we Langa, a Black Panther wrongly incarcerated since 1972, writes in "Kandles of Kwanzaa" from the Nebraska State Penitentiary,

> we knew of something greater
> than any of us
> greater than anything we could see or hear
> or feel or touch
> we knew
> of a Mother and Father supreme
> of a Love Supreme
> adorned in the limitless garments of
> invisibility. (84)

"Before / l o n g before" Rinehart the Afro-urbane trickster, African epic tricksters, forerunners to Ras who very likely antedated ancient Greek epic heroes and Gilgamesh, also knew the ways of invisibility *per force*. This knowledge challenges *Invisible Man* with the real unasked question, one requiring a performative context for an answer, while Ellison's modernist technique only offers a rich narrative portrait of Ras that provides a semblance of organic, participatory consciousness. It is not the superficial question, whether Ras or anyone is an unenlightened, hypermasculine militant, but the much more difficult, context-dependent problem of whether his/her/their concept of the self—including mind and body—is organic, an African "Love Supreme," or merely heroic. But Ellison does not ask this question, opting instead for modernist insight that flattens and allegorizes all "militants." Hence, the Other context needed to add the West/Central African invisibility and second sight to its Homeric-American counterpart, and to apprehend the threat to Human/Nature, lies in a basement darker and deeper than the one that frames *Invisible Man*.

To the extent this is so, Ras, Ellison's two-dimensional narrative analog for Marcus Garvey, should be seen as a shaded epic trickster who opens up invisible, second-sighted possibility equal to or greater than the one Rinehart represents. The invisibility and second sight of the epic trickster, part of the West/Central African allegorycal cosmology and aesthetic that gave Picasso his modernist technique, had already been portrayed by Aaron Douglas. A native son from the American heartland (Nebraska, Kansas) whose epical paintings featured Afro-modernist shades, Douglas' oeuvre, in significant part, responded to Garvey's call to look east, "back to Africa" (Earle, "Harlem" 24, 34). His Harlem and Chicago Renaissance paintings and murals, such as *I Needs a Dime for Beer* (1926), *Into Bondage* (1936), and *The Founding of Chicago* (1933–40), serve as iconography for the African-American epic habitus, the two-dimensional shades drawing upon their African origins to offer an allegorycal depth and potency influential on contemporary African-American painters (see Figure 3.10).[53]

Figure 3.10 Into Bondage, by Aaron Douglas (1936, © Heirs of Aaron Douglas/ licensed by VAGA, New York/image courtesy Corcoran Gallery).

Though inviting a classical allegorical reading as Judeo-Christian souls, Douglas' figures do not float like them or glide like Greek shades, but convey a West/Central African vitality sharpened by slitted eyes staring out of masks and heroic bodies often framed by a lush African landscape. Egyptian, ancient Minoan,[54] and Art Deco also influenced him, but Douglas consciously adopted essential aesthetics he found in West/Central African masks for his murals. For example, Nembe masks of the Niger Delta are known to have a Cubist style suggesting multiple angles, and slit-eye styles of the Dan and Mende people have been cited as Douglas' influences. However, beneath these masks, as his bush motif suggests, there flows the very potency of life. The slit-eyed West/Central African masks are less representations of actual eyes and "unmediated, lucid vision" than the veiling of eye-sight in favor of "spiritual insight." Likewise the "gradated concentric circles" motif emanating from objects in his murals, so distinctive to his work, "suggests some power or fourth dimension beyond the visible" (Ater 106; Drewal 201; Earle, "Harlem" 26; Kirschke 76–77; Powell 57–59). MOS-epic performances of multifaceted masquerades are hereby implicated. For example, among the Ijo *owu* doubles in meaning to reference spirits and "mask, masquerader, and masquerade dance"; these masks retain their indigenous "symbolism, suggesting that they may represent an older conception, as well as distinct category, of water spirits" (Anderson, "From River" 148, 150). Masks deform or shade the true reality, the unrepresentable flow of water/ spirits actuating MOS-epic invisibility and second sight.

Though black shades were given a larger-than-life association thanks to Douglas' murals, while blackness became *chic* when Coco Chanel unveiled the little black dress (previously reserved for mourning) as a fashion statement in 1926 and the first mass-produced sunglasses enjoyed a robust market when Sam Foster introduced them to Atlantic City, New Jersey, in 1929, shades did not become a vogue, really, until the Black Power era.[55] Then, under the New Black Aesthetic, "Black is Beautiful" mantra, and unprecedented potency of Black Panthers sporting aggressive Afros and black ensembles including berets, leather jackets, gloves, and, of course, shades, Black Power incarnated the *ba-ad* spirit of 1960s resistance. This reality was different from previous civil rights efforts, which lacked the Cold War–era negative publicity U.S. policymakers feared, and, equally important, the epic-in-a-"set" technology opening up soul-inspired, rock 'n' roll–oriented suburban kids to imaginary worlds far beyond their "Pleasantville"[56] reality. The Civil Rights movement, the epic-inspired shift in blackness as a signifier, and everything in between and beneath played out under the massive, near-instantaneous dissemination made possible—and given celebrity cool—by television.

Thus, Black Power and assertive black aesthetics became hip (hop), cool, and hot all at the same time the panopticon—epitomized by the FBI and J. Edgar Hoover's COINTELPRO, but a performance happening throughout the U.S.—geared up for a post-*Brown*, post-black policing of the new Negro-Black-African American. Thanks to celebrity, Douglas, and the counterculture of black militancy, shades crossed into the mainstreaming culture of television. Since the 1960s, black leather jackets, gloves, boots, berets, and shades have increasingly defined cool, bad, and hipness. Eventually, epic mimicry became the new blackface minstrelsy, and *vice versa*, as sHades no longer denoted the epical struggles of the scions of Ham, *les damnes de la terre*, but perfected bourgeois commodification and self-empowerment. The latest capitalism is one in which, in true American epic-capitalizing, Mom, God, and apple pie have been supplemented by the whitest, most perfect teeth ever seen in the world, bronzed-age*less* suntans perfected outdoors and in-*salons*, tinted windows perfect for all tastes, Honda Odysseys for all the perfect soccer moms, and sun shades—the perfect accessory— for all of US. The new black is . . . white, middle class, hip (hop), bronzed-age*less*, and, thanks to PoMo and pc-ness, US-multicultural.

But this is *cliché* (remember Vanilla Ice and hip hop, the Beach Boys, Elvis Presley, and rock 'n roll, and jazz before that?), *chic*, and boutique epic mimicry, something to be worn and exchanged while the controllers of the panopticon, especially in the post-Reagan 1980s and 1990s, propounded anti-tinting laws to combat the "War on Drugs."[57] In *that* Philadelphian society, "Just Say No" is the simple slogan; First Lady-like and grandmotherly, and supposedly a Truth-ful, nonallegorical witticism stripped of proverbial nuance, "Just Say No" is, in fact, the harsh hammer of epical realism. This American performance, ultimately, is about bodily perfection, white supremacy, right down to the optic white canines. The fundamental error here, committed by adherents—white and non-white—to this performance, is the failure to realize that optic whiteness is wholly a simplistic ideal. In contrast, and especially before modernity, the West/Central African allegorycal self recognized that the core within the ideal, perfect body as a State and stated norm is a twisted, deformed power—good and bad—that will out: come out of the closet, leak through the pores, "supersize" the gut, and melt down and bust walls, mains, streets, Wall Streets and main streets, or whatever. At any rate, to follow this recipe, like eating an ideal slice of apple pie, is to invite the couch on which one simply lies to eat it in perfect ease, and the ensuing diagnosis: epic agony.

Or, as Pauline Hopkins argues in *Of One Blood*, a back-to-Africa novel which critiques racial uplift based on embracing modern exceptionalism and repressing the whole "hidden self," the epic mythologies producing the tragic mulatto/a also result in multiple self-inflicted tragedies. The death of her antagonist, Aubrey Livingston, Jr., by suicide exemplifies the Judeo-Christian masquerade Hopkins uses to make this point: the positive law of criminal justice starts in American courts, but ends in ancient Ethiopian jurisprudence. Hopkins' shift from American to African, from positivist to magical or spiritual, excavates the ancient law at work beneath the modern. In other words, the cautionary lessons of the epic performance establish an-Other *corpus juris* revealed through consideration of African folk sensibility. The jural component of the epic performance, a form of folk or natural law, realizes the self-imposed dangers for any person or culture associated with epical performance. Thus, the ideal of modern epicality (Livingston's physical, superficial qualities—rich, smart, handsome) too easily obscures the transgressive qualities innately associated with it (he is, in fact, a villain who uses his ideal/classical appearance and position to ill ends) and the self-destructiveness owing to excessive consequences (his self-corruption and eventual suicide).

Understanding the laws of the American epic performance, then, is both classical and funky, chirographic and oral, earthly and metaphysical. As noted earlier, the intimate relationship of the American oligarchy to, and its folding into, the social contract—the mythical dimension of the body-politic—obviates actual exceptional performance of the physical body. It also deifies it, rendering it epiphenomenal, immortal, timeless, and supreme. Left is godstuff, the spiritual/cognitive presence overseeing all, a violent stripping away of uncertainty through omni-science/potence, leaving hard and fast "eternal" truths (symbols) of the blackletter Law and Narrative. Hence the heady "boast," by Sir Clifford De Vincent in Hannah Crafts' *The Bondwoman's Narrative*,[58] a novelized slave narrative believed to be quasi-autobiographical, that "his commands and decisions like the laws of the Medes and Persians were unalterable" (22). The nation-state, as sociopolitical concretization of the epic body-politic, allows and promulgates the flourishing of beautiful minds and the fetishization of classical culture. The modern birth of opera, that most rarefied of classic orchestration consumed by that most rarefied of tastes, is telling, and performing. Divorced from the rigorous, physical muscularity of the body-politic, opera nevertheless owes itself to epical orientation. As music no longer existing for and in organic relationship with its own essence, opera represents the evolution of the symbol into a linguistic excess whose abstract, rarefied songs function as the "primordial voice" of the noble savage: "'They could abandon themselves to the dream of having descended once more into the paradisiacal beginnings of mankind, where music also must have had that unsurpassed purity, power, and innocence. . . . The recitative was regarded as the rediscovered language of this primitive man; opera as the rediscovered country of this idyllically or heroically good creature, who simultaneously with every action follows a natural artistic impulse, who accomplishes his speech with a little singing'" (W. Benjamin 210–13).[59]

This leaves inner-city black Americans, native sons and daughters, to fend for themselves and get with it (the epical performance) as best they can, in a world far beneath the Olympian heights of the super-opera-class and with no means to challenge their ethereal bodies. Symbolically many sport, as do the whiteface-wearing Lincoln and his younger brother Booth of Suzan-Lori Park's *Topdog/Underdog* (2001), Trojan condoms to prove their manhood, and hustle with a three-card monte cant that mixes the (black and) blues with Da Troy-jams. Their hip hop carries the gangsta pomp and pop of fratricidal agony, Booth's closing act a repeat performance already played out in the real—and yet highly mythologized—history of Abraham Lincoln's assassination and, MOS-tragically, on today's streets where *brothas* shooting *brothas* is a real rerun.

To read this blues tragedy within the Manichean framework derided by many as outdated in a post-racial, post-soul climate, or redeemed from obsolescence by Pulitzer, misses the eco-critical point. Just as Hegel defined the epic as a "world-situation," the cautionary elements thrust into what Frederick Douglass dubs, in his "What to the Slave Is the Fourth of July?" address on July 5, 1852, "sacrilegious" and "scorching irony" (468, 470). Douglass' irony addresses racial myth and exposes its material timelessness as an horrific epical realism he sees beyond sight. His cautionary elements demonstrate the tragic paradox presented by global warming and global dimming, two hellish, pre-apocalyptic byproducts of the utopian, sci-fi impulse immanent in the perfect ideal of Western epicality.

In this regard, Douglass' use of "career" in his *Narrative* to describe his slave status is deeply ironic, maybe even anticipatory if not prophetic. The social epic made normal and masked within the black slave body collapses the slave's career into the tedium of slave labor. Douglass, of course, uses career to locate slavery within the place of an official employment scheme, a rhetorical move bearing massive implications for all American workers. Roger D. Abrahams fleshes out this dynamic in his Vietnam-era genealogical study of the variety of American folk heroes—from their mythical origin to the bad man in contemporary popular culture—in his discussion of the relationship of heroism to occupation. The "widespread" Anglo-American ballads of heroic workers demonstrates a late phase of epical realism. "The ballads of occupational groups," Abrahams states, "such as lumberjacks, cowboys, and railroaders tell stories in which a man emerges as a representative of the group and performs a difficult occupational detail valiantly, exhibiting strength and bravery, living a brief hero's life before dying an heroic death." The postbellum "occupational" heroics encompass European lore and John Henry, the "most ubiquitous and interesting of the [black] hard-man legendary heroes, and the one most acceptable to middle-class white audiences." Henry is "successful in the epic battle with the machine, but he dies in the throes of victory" as a "steel-driving man." The glory is not for the "occupational hero," but "his one representative act" which, he argues, arises from a "basically suicidal motivation" ("Some Varieties" 346–50).

Abrahams' focus on Henry and heroic workers like sheriff Matt Dillon of *Gunsmoke*, detectives Sam Spade and Mike Hammer, and superspy James Bond brings us back to Douglass' career and a "nostalgia" Abrahams suggests as a form of enslavement, and more: "American society, in its nostalgia for heroic manifestations of the past, sows the seeds of its own potential destruction" (360–61). His well-merited anti-imperialism, anti–Vietnam War sentiment exposes the patently martial form of an epical realism his interest in occupations brilliantly implicates. The transgressive, life-ending occupations of American culture serve as a template for contemporary careers and professions that are now excessive. Since the 1870s, the expectation associated with the heroic worker kept pace on the idealistic, unrealistic assumption of steel-driving laborers. This epical realism is epic myth transformed into the daily grind of the American Dream. The epical agony of individual Americans materializes in the workplace. Most American workers, many of whom are workaholics, live in environments, labor activist John de Graaf argues, according to activist and journalist Silja J.A. Talvi, of "overwork, over-scheduling and time-famine that now threatens our health, our families and relationships, our communities and our environment." The result in First-World nations is what Talvi translates from Japanese (*karoshi*) and Chinese (*guolaosi*) as "death-by-overwork." Literally, Talvi reports, people die at work or put themselves at high risk for "heart disease, obesity, insomnia and persistent fatigue," and, among women, a much greater risk of mental disease (2008).

Korean-American novelist Chang-rae Lee, situating *Native Speaker* (1995) and Korean-American private spy Henry Park in the epically realistic place of early 1990s New York City, fundamentally relies upon the South Korean parallel of "death-by-overwork," *gwarosa* (과로사).[60] Channeling Richard Wright's *Native Son* (1940) and the "Before / l o n g before" essence lying beneath the novel's Ellisonian voice, Lee foregrounds the Park family and the "classical immigrant story" of "heroic" self-sufficiency and, ultimately, tragedy. But the richest irony abides here, for the Park-family's realized success—the "heroic" myth made good—is tragic in direct proportion to that success. *Gwarosa* as overwork breathes life into the body of the Park family, allowing Lee to sound the cultural essence of the Big Apple and the immigrant politics that engendered fierce racial/ethnic conflicts, such as those between African Americans and Korean shopkeepers in New York and Los Angeles. Lee, through Henry Park, sums up the threat in terms medical and economic, personal (Mr. Park's ultimate demise) and political: "Massive global stroke" (47, 49–50).

The Afro-Korean politics of *Native Speaker*, beyond its reliance upon the profound racial and cultural insights of Wright and other African-American writers, shows Lee's indebtedness to the universal folk tradition that unites across ethnic divides. Indeed, the centuries-old career of blackness imposed on enslaved Africans and their descendants, within ongoing daily struggle, brings together epical realism in a way often addressed by African Americans and related among themselves by the full range of human expression. Their storytellers have been instrumental throughout this journey. With the epic trickster space already always coopted by Homeric performance (epical and tricky), and with the even greater apocalyptic threat of global destruction lurking behind the trauma of slavery and racism, perhaps no question is better put to the scholars of the African-American storytelling tradition than this one: how have our very best African-American writers, those who have been most attuned to epic performance by virtue of their senses, experience, and artistry, grappled with this double apocalypse?

Beginning with the Nadir, and then moving in roughly forty-year increments—across time, space, progress, and world warfare visiting Old Testament–like destruction upon humanity and Nature—I take up that question in the following three chapters.

4 All Green with Epic Potential

Chesnutt Goes to the *Marrow of Tradition* to Reconstruct America's Epic Body

> Joshua fit de battle of Jericho
> Jericho,
> Jericho
>
> Joshua fit de battle of Jericho
> and the walls come a-tumblin' down.
>
> —"Joshua Fit de Battle of Jericho,"
> African-American Spiritual[1]

> "There's no use talking, boys," responded the sheriff. "I'm a white
> man outside, but in this jail I'm sheriff; and if this nigger's to be hung
> in this county, I propose to do the hanging. So you fellows might as
> well right-about-face, and march back to Troy."
>
> —Colonel Campbell, "The Sheriff's Children" (79)

INTRODUCTION: THE DILEMMA OF MARROW

Charles W. Chesnutt, in crafting *The Marrow of Tradition*, had a grand
agenda before him: rewrite the official record of the Wilmington, North
Carolina, massacre of 1898, which the national press had mischaracterized
as a "racial riot." Before him lay a formidable task, one that Hegel could
have called a "bar of history" (*Aesthetics* 1061), for the white supremacy
of the South and North, past and present, contained within it hemispher-
ic—if not global—privilege. The "bar" personally threatened Chesnutt, a
licensed attorney and preeminent African-American novelist, because of
his strategy of staging an encyclopedic critique of this racial totality with
the Wilmington race riot as the focal point. His audience was overwhelmingly white, after all, and female. But Chesnutt had more personal incentive
because of his upbringing in North Carolina and his family's direct experience with the riot that, according to Ernestine William Pickens, "inspired
Chesnutt to write *The Marrow of Tradition*" (51).[2] Chesnutt, using his own
"bar sinister"[3]—the illegimate, interracial "ragged family tree" Chesnutt
deployed "in a most personal way" (Sundquist, "Introduction" x)—surely
knew the stakes. At the same time, his own literary ambition to produce a

"magnum opus" that equaled Harriet Beecher Stowe's *Uncle Tom's Cabin* (1851) probably presented too grand a challenge to resist (Andrews, *Literary Career* 126, 175).[4]

Thus, Chesnutt sought to write the next great American novel while simultaneously critiquing belief in the higher law with a meticulous attention to detail attuned to the encyclopedic range of possibilities he believed worked in concert to reify the body-politic. Though no drafts of *Marrow* exist to document the role Homer played in its formulation, Chesnutt nevertheless possessed an earlier, fictional template he deployed on a much larger scale to give shape and character to his plot: his short story "The Sheriff's Children," published in the *Independent* in November 1889.

As the "germ of much of Chesnutt's later fiction" (Andrews, "Introduction" xxv), insofar as it combined literary realism with an early form of sociology[5] to expose the color-line contradictions biracial individuals confronted, "The Sheriff's Children" is a critical break in Chesnutt's oeuvre. While Chesnutt's early fiction relied upon the African-American folkloric imaginary (conjure and trickster tales in dialect), the belief that he shifted to a mainstream literary modality—realism—obscures Chesnutt's journey into the epical lore underlying that realism. As his own journal reveals, this is especially true of the unbending ethos demonstrated in his fiction and his relationship to America's Homeric performance.

The journal he kept from 1874 to 1882 is critical, for between mid-October 1878 and his writing of "The Sheriff's Children," Chesnutt's relationship to Greco-Latin languages and the Homeric epic appears to mature from a strong desire to learn Greek (studied from 1881–1882) and Latin to a remarkable social critique he apparently felt too dangerous to make directly. In his journal entry for October 12, 1878, Chesnutt shifts from a statement that "I do not think that I will ever forget my Latin," because of the "labor" and "mental discipline" it required, to resentment at being denied "first class" tutoring in Latin, French, German, and music because he was a "nigger." Chesnutt resolves to go North, his journal here revealing his dedication to a racial exceptionalism that Du Bois later echoes, early in *Souls*, when a white girl "refused" his "visiting-card": "I will live down the prejudice, I will crush it out. I will show to the world that a man may spring from a race of slaves, and yet far excel many of the boasted ruling race. If I can exalt my race, if I can gain the applause of the good, and the approbation of God, the thoughts of the ignorant and prejudiced will not concern me" (Brodhead 92–93; Du Bois, *Souls* 10). Just as an adult Du Bois, writing in retrospect, said "this fine contempt began to fade" because "I longed for . . . all their dazzling opportunities" (*Souls* 10), Chesnutt's perspective on language, Latin, and Homer matures. But his Homeric antithesis is *not* predicated on the "power"-oriented racial uplift so central to Du Bois' *Souls*.[6] This development, unexplored by scholars, raises a crucial question his journal does not answer: how, when, and why does Chesnutt, a spurned Greco-Roman acolyte whose August 13, 1878, journal begins a forty-nine-page annotated summation of Books I through III of Alexander Pope's *Iliad*, mature into a writer who rejects this neoclassical form of exceptionalism, an understandable reaction to racism, and diagnose that racism as a symptom of the social problem, *viz.*, Homeric performance?

Although the only published version of Chesnutt's journal, Richard H. Brodhead's *The Journals of Charles W. Chesnutt* (1993), censors the vast bulk of Chesnutt's treatment of the *Iliad*, it contains several critical insights, beginning with Chesnutt's commentary on Book I. First, although Homer has been "criticised" by "so many great writers," Chesnutt still believes "there may still remain some reflections on his style, or some criticism on his heroes, some bright spot which has not been overflowed by those rivers of ink, or buried under those mountains of paper." Homer, in other words, is the writer and the cultural performance Chesnutt must divine if he is to achieve his own sublime lyricism. The ambivalence of Chesnutt's position—a writer needing Homer but a Christian who disdained paganism—is immediately apparent, as he observes that "the first book tells us the subject of the poem—'Achilles' wrath'—which by the will of Jove was the source of more misfortune to the Greeks than all their previous troubles combined." Whereas the *in media res* opening and the heroic archetypes strike many as points of emulation, Chesnutt affixes a cautionary hermeneutic to it. Not surprisingly, this expands to include a reading on the morality of the Greek pantheon and their "subject mortals": "The standard of Grecian morality was low, which could permit men to worship such corrupt and partial deitys. . . . The worship of the Greek was not that of a Christian . . . , but that of the slave who cringes obsequiously to a capricious and tyrannical master."

The problematization of Greek ethos directly relates to his own Judeo-Christian theology, but Chesnutt's subsequent comment on Book III, based on his study of the "ante-Homeric history of Troy as given in [Mary Ann] Dwight's Mythology,"[7] complicates this conclusion. Chesnutt's shift of the personal pronoun, from the studious "me" which opens his *Iliad* commentary to "we," indicates he is no longer an isolated male scholar, but part of a community of readers. Indeed, the community might have consisted of Chesnutt and his new wife, nineteen-year-old Susan W. Chesnutt (*née* Perry), whom he married in June. The parallels between these biblical stories and Greek, Indian, and Chinese myths, Chesnutt writes in the collective first person, "show us that all men come from a common stock." The moral corruption stems from geographic dispersion after Babel, the passage of time, "the ignorance of writing[,] and by the addition with which the imagination of different generations adorned them became the improbable legends which are preserved to us in classical literature."[8]

These comments shed light on the question of how Chesnutt's thought on Homeric performance shifts from that of a student of Latin and Greek to the critical perspective that would carry him beyond *Plessy* to *Marrow*. Though inconclusive since the "we" indicates a larger discursive context,

Brodhead's excerpt suggests that Chesnutt's anti-paganism sentiment is central. Though this reading has merit, the unpublished text debunks over-reliance on a Christian motif. In only a few instances does Chesnutt advert to Greek morality because of their pantheon. Instead, most of his summary and analysis treat Homer, "the poet,"[9] and his use of nature with unmistakable reverence. Indeed, the ancients versus the moderns debate rages within Chesnutt's journal, with the ancient Greeks' sense of beauty, love of nature, courageousness, and nonmaterialism trumping the moderns in all respects—except for Christianity and literacy: "We marvel at the strength of the machine which could reduce a beautiful figure to such small proportions, and wonder how the owner of it can breathe with her lungs so tightly pressed. The beauty of her magnificent hair fades in comparison with the skill which the artist has displayed in arranging it" ("Journal" 31).[10]

Though Chesnutt slants toward the Heroic Age, his critical consciousness remains intact as the occurrence of the Trojan War is an "if," not a given, and his admiration of Homer's portraits of the epic heroes is complicated by their greed and pride. In short, his perspective is part of a complex array of ideas in which Chesnutt combines sectarian tenets with a secular, cultural dimension as well. One of the principles is diasporic: culture evolves as it moves away—temporally, geographically, and culturally—from its genesis. A related principle, implied through his explicit reference to Indian and Chinese culture, is that Africa also shares in this process and made its own contributions. Chesnutt's belief in the commonness of humankind is itself a critical tenet which allows him to trace distinct traditions and simultaneously compare them. His dialogical "we" is participatory, and suggests that the only way of apprehending culture is through a discursive model at odds with individualism and racial, sexual, and socioeconomic dichotomies. The final underlying principle is also his first: the wrath of Achilles opens and frames the Homeric narrative. Significantly, Chesnutt's cautionary treatment of Achilles is not defined by an individual's personal excesses, or by the dictates of heroic archetypes, but the cultural performance that informs them both. The full expression of the interaction of these elements against the backdrop of America's Homeric performance requires an encyclopedic approach, one evident in *Marrow*. "The Sheriff's Children" represents the most direct implementation of these principles as the precursor to *Marrow*.

Through "The Sheriff's Children" Chesnutt asks a fundamental question of American society: how do you assess the laws governing a society, including its art, when a destructive mythology is coextensive with the highest forms of creativity? Sheriff Campbell, a Civil War hero also known as Colonel Campbell, "a man far above the average of the community in wealth, education, and social position," is Chesnutt's answer to this question. A student of arts and letters, traveler, and distinguished Civil War combatant who "was universally popular," Col. Campbell occupies the same place the more aged John Delamere, Esq., holds in *Marrow*:[11]

an honored member of a North Carolina community has been killed, a mulatto who claims innocence has been apprehended, a "coat" serves as damning evidence, and a lynch mob will exact its own justice unless Col. Campbell, who has a "high sense" of honor, can single-handedly prevent it (77). The prisoner needs the "tall, muscular" sheriff, because his appearance and demeanor, revealed through Col. Campbell's glance—"crouched in a corner, his yellow face, blanched with terror, looking ghastly in the semi-darkness of the [cell] room. A cold perspiration had gathered on his forehead, and his teeth were chattering with affright" (75, 80)—conveys the very essence of black southern stereotypes.

The story turns on Col. Campbell's *mis*perception of the prisoner, which Chesnutt later compels the reader to understand, in spite of all of the sheriff's heroic qualities, as fundamentally racist. Not only is the figure unmasked and revealed to be educated and heroic, but Chesnutt unfurls a critique of the racial regime not limited to the burden of the oppressed. Beyond the wounded affront to *noblesse oblige*, Chesnutt's plot gives Col. Campbell deeply personal and tangible stakes in the matter: the prisoner is Tom Campbell, the son he sold, along with his mother, down South to Alabama years earlier. Making the sheriff face the gun Tom took from him and literally see the stereotype through its barrel, Chesnutt reveals the eventual consequence of adhering to a deeply flawed epic mythology: "He saw in this mulatto what he himself might have become had not the safeguards of parental restraint and public opinion been thrown around him."

In *Marrow*, Chesnutt develops these perspectives more fully in the form of Tom Delamere, John Delamere's grandson, and Josh Green, two men whose unmasking reveals them to be dishonorable and honorable, respectively, but "The Sheriff's Children" shows that as early as 1889, Chesnutt saw an epical mimicry locking blood relatives—father and son, brother and sister—who exist just on either side of the color-line in a tragic, bloody embrace. The agonizing complication Col. Campbell confronts, of having to "struggle between his love of life and his sense of duty" (84–85), is left forever unresolved and unresolvable by Chesnutt. Col. Campbell's heroism exists, Chesnutt indicates, in direct proportion to his emotional and moral agony by virtue of the very normal reality that made him what he is. This dynamic, a self-inflicted form of soul murder, extends far into the future of the community by virtue of Col. Campbell and his daughter, Polly, a "comely young woman" (76) stained with the blood of her half-brother.

The "disquieting moral dilemma" that closes "The Sheriff's Children" (Andrews, "Introduction" xxv) signals a critical intertextuality between this short story and *Marrow*. Featuring Chesnutt's characteristic understatement, this interconnection provides the clearest insight into Chesnutt's understanding of "tradition"—post-Reconstruction plantation mythology is a product of the racial mythology evident in slavery which is, itself, a product of the Homeric imaginary. Significant in this regard is the backdrop for the short story, Troy, North Carolina. Chesnutt's approach here is significant, for he treats this highly symbolic and mythically rich setting in much the way he might treat any other sleepy southern hamlet or town. However, the point of emphasis lies, ironically, in de-emphasis: the realism of Chestnutt's pastoral details and brief socio-political frame, which makes Troy very *un*exceptional, reinforces the extent to which the Homeric mythology is so deeply embedded in the cultural imaginary that it is properly taken for granted *by the residents*. Chesnutt knows that such a setting is not mere rhetorical, neo-classical "debris" that is "purely decorative,"[12] or emblematic of the highly cultured creative mind, but the staging ground for deep-seated traditions of Homer-inspired exceptionalism that evolve in accordance with the changing American times. Just as the Troy, North Carolina, background of "The Sheriff 's Children," lends itself to analysis of its Homeric cartography, clearly a marrow of tradition, so, too, do the parallel plots between this short story and the novel: objective assessment of events in Troy and Wilmington—Wellington in *Marrow*—requires readers to construct an epical realism equal parts Homeric mythology and violent racial *politik*.

The Homeric mythology of *Marrow* is more muted than it is in Chesnutt's 1889 story, but reinforces its core assumption: "the marrow of tradition" is so deeply situated in the performance of Homeric mythology that it serves as the root metaphor informing all relationships, beliefs, and institutions in the South. The more silent and invisible is the Homeric antecedent—the more belief in it establishes a racial common sense considered ontological—the greater will be the distortions in natural laws and the danger to everyone.

This "disquieting moral dilemma," then, is the bond between Troy, a mythological and real jurisdiction[13] appropriated for a short story, and the subsequent, surreal events of Wilmington. As Chesnutt's Troy restages Homeric performance, the ancient sublimity of mythology, and the agony of epical (Civil War) defeat, his Wellington restages the events leading to the actual 1898 *coup d'etat*, situating two families—the white Carterets and black Millers—on center stage, both families interlocked by and yet confronting one another on the color-line. But *Marrow* does not stop here, for Chesnutt's novel is an artful narrative and careful sociological survey of the southern and national traditions as witnessed through the racial riots occurring throughout the South, particularly the 1898 Wilmington Riot and the New Orleans Race Riot of 1901.[14] The multitudinous and contradictory traditions of the marrow, a dynamic ripe for the complex allegorye Chesnutt attempts, are embodied by a panoply of allegorycal characters,[15] overdetermined racial tropes, numerous episodes exploring race- and gender-based codes of conduct, genealogical and nuptial politics, conflicts between old and new money, and ethics.

Believing Chesnutt attempted to put things in proper perspective in his final chapters, with the protagonist, Dr. William Miller, foiling the ostensibly militant Josh Green, scholars' oft-asked question has been, How do we read the ending (De Santis 92–93; Reilly 35–37; Wolkomir 252)? The disjunctive proposition presenting Miller *or* Green as the ideal, along with the artistic failings of Chesnutt's response to the racial problem, have been identified by scholars as a "dilemma" (Reilly 35–37), "unresolvable moral dilemma" (Delmar 269), "virtually unresolvable situation" (Hackenberry 197), and an "ambiguous ending" (Gleason 39–40). Despite the conclusion that Chesnutt failed as a novelist and visionary,[16] careful reconsideration of *Marrow*, in light of Green's and the Millers' coordinate significance to the African-American body-politic, rescues the novel from these open-ended charges.

Eric J. Sundquist roots the racial problem—and the Miller-Green dilemma—in the South's failed "white manliness," which resulted in the "Negro Domination" that white supremacy campaigns and the "plantation myth" sought to address ("Introduction" xxv–xxx). Dr. Miller is the European-trained physician, a genteel forerunner of Alain Locke's New Negro and epitome of Du Bois' Talented Tenth. Since their personal commonalities make Dr. Miller Chesnutt's presumptive favorite, "handsome" with "erect form, broad shoulders" (*Marrow* 49), Green's militancy seems to be an excessive response to the South's race- and gender-based manly ideals. But this reading fails on multiple levels: it elides the depth of Chesnutt's indignation about the Wilmington massacre and the national response, a failure prompting his authorship; moreover, it empties the narrative of Chesnutt's deployment of irony, which is studied, nuanced, and oftentimes vicious.

While the more obvious limitations of Dr. Miller's early ruminations ring hollow as a "philosopher['s]" (59), the militancy of Green makes his compromise understandable. However, Dr. Miller is the hero-protagonist more in form than substance because Chesnutt's nuanced irony erodes the solid foundation supporting him: notwithstanding his build and education, his self-conceit chafes at the arbitrariness of the color-line, which forces him to ride with a "noisy, loquacious, happy, dirty, and malodorous" horde of blacks; indeed, the "twilight" moments he spends with his white-looking "wife and child" (60, 63–64) position him—in fact, if not in law—on the white side of the color-line.

Chesnutt masks Dr. Miller's limitations, which align him with Col. Campbell of "The Sheriff's Children,"[17] because his hero-protagonist is the lens through which he conveys much of the racial dilemma. Significantly, Dr. Miller's decision not to join Josh Green in a suicidal act he considers "doomed," and that offers, he tells Green, "no glory and no reward" (*Marrow* 281–82), merits re-examination. Even this rationale loses the semblance of *noblesse oblige* as he, in pursuit of "wife and child" during the pogrom, profanes the Hippocratic oath by passing the injured and failing to even defend his own hospital where Green and his men make their last stand.[18] It is this Dr. Miller who shares the same first name (William) as the coachman for Aunt Polly Ochiltree; later, he is the coachman for Mr. Delamere, who repeatedly calls him "William," as they travel over the "sandy road" (200), an allusion to Delamere's retainer, Sandy Campbell. Chesnutt's thorough evacuation of Dr. Miller's professionalism and ethics, from the beginning to the *denounement*, leaves the shadow of a putative hero whose heroic, unmanly pedigree—as "William," a mere coachmen on the "sandy road"—cannot be resuscitated except by extraordinary means.

But why, if Dr. Miller is the talented solution to the problem by default, and especially by authorial choice, should Chesnutt eviscerate his manliness through ironic figures? It would seem unnecessary since, in light of white supremacy, Dr. Miller enjoys the moral high ground. The historical matrices of race in America, particularly the South's culture of manliness, meant his existence was already tragic and the ironic denunciation redundant.

Perhaps this dilemma begins with heuristics, with critics foregrounding *Marrow*'s literariness at the expense of the African/American folkloric aesthetic and episteme. This episteme is critical, for the presumptive humanity of Dr. Miller, an enlightened, modern man who ostensibly repudiates racial stigma, obfuscates the scale of the problem because of that promise. Indeed, in this capacity Dr. Miller functions as nostrum, presenting readers with a false antidote to manliness. Southern manliness fails to contain the scope of this dilemma, which rests not upon the denial of access to worthies like Dr. Miller, but the conception of the body implied by traditions that valorize epic and exceptionalism. Instead, it is more fruitful to approach *Marrow* from the lens of the epic performance, a genre that is greater than the sum of its multigeneric polyphonics. An epic-centric approach to *Marrow* helps to instantiate the necessary literary/cultural studies and cultural—not racial—performance as a centerpiece that resolves the so-called dilemma and, at the same time, elevates Chesnutt's crafting of *Marrow,* and African-American arts and letters before and after.

Hence, Chesnutt's allegorye channels the epic aesthetic as *Marrow* ranges episodically. Although not a formal divide, *Marrow* has two "books." Book I (Chapters 1 to 27) narrates the tension associated with Sandy Campbell's alleged murder-rape of Polly Ochiltree and allows Chesnutt to meditate on law, tradition, and lynchings. What appears to clearly be a dénouement actually opens Book II (Chapter 28 to the end), which resumes the underlying white supremacist political gerrymandering Chesnutt started at the beginning of the novel. Chesnutt's multitiered, interlocking allegorye consists of the literal plot of Wellington, which is thin allegory for the racial riots of Wilmington, and then multiple levels of history, time, and myth. This allegorycal structure, along with strategic asides, enables Chesnutt to judge the entirety of the southern types, racial dilemmas, and white supremacist stratagems.

A key component of this effort is his appropriation of Josh Green, one of the first "bad" men in fiction (Sundquist, "Introduction" xli). In real and figurative terms, Green performs the Africa-to-America trickster pedigree discussed in Chapter 2. The trickster (aesthetic)—for reasons detailed later—alone is insufficient for a fated encounter with the socio-aesthetics of white supremacy; thus Green is not a trickster proper, or even a "trickster hero" as Roger D. Abrahams ("Some Varieties" 341–42) meant. To sound

Green's role and the polyphonic, soulful force of his cultural provenance requires critics to deploy a unique performance—a poetics of scale—situated within folk aesthetics and ideology. Here, it is fitting to appropriate the second sight and seventh-son poetics of Cartwright's *Reading Africa into American Literature* (2002). Though Cartwright's mapping of Sunjatic poetics into American literature privileges the Senegambian/Mande epic influence, and elides its contested and complementary relationship to America's own Greco-Roman epic performance aesthetic, his point is well taken and necessary: the African epic performance informs American aesthetics (8).

Consequently, *Marrow* emerges from its status as a failed novel to become a stage in which Chesnutt recreates a battle between two antagonistic and mutually constitutive epic traditions. Chesnutt's understanding of this drama, much of which extends from his "fair knowledge of the classics" and "habit of studying character" (Brodhead 139), is evidenced by his Troy, North Carolina, antecedent. But the rural isolation and "primitive" backwardness Chesnutt attributes to the "white people" of Troy, a "social corpse" untouched by the "fresh blood of civilization" ("Sheriff's Children" 71–72), is proven false, for the urban racial riots of 1898 Wilmington and 1901 New Orleans reveal Troy to be a typical jurisdiction. Chesnutt's adherence to his belief that Homeric performance explains the marrow of the "social corpse" in Troy as well as locales such as Wilmington[19] and New Orleans, is borne out by his decision to re-use "The Sheriff's Children," a ten-year-old story. Did Chesnutt suspect, by 1900 if not earlier, the ultimate dilemma to be a color-line realized by Trojan North Carolinians who complemented epic sublimity with the trickster's "masterful duplicity,"[20] and thus threatened to fatally jar all of their bodies out of "their correct proportions and relations"?[21] Were professional experts in treating the body, like Dr. Miller, in need of an older training in folk pharmacopeia to enable them to see the problem and treat the body-politic?

Clearly Chesnutt was conversant in conjure and trickster lore and knew about Homer's epics, but his ability, by the time he wrote *Marrow*, to see the commons shared by tricksters and Homeric heroes deserves examination. To reconstruct the context making Troy Chesnutt's natural selection as the emblem of Homeric cartography and white supremacy in rural North Carolina, as well as the "cultural" or "classical codes" (McLachlan 82–84) underlying its urban centers, we need to reconstruct the imaginary cartography of the American Homeric performance.

AMERICAN HOMER: WHITENESS AND THE EPIC

If the sum total of the practices characterizing and reifying a given culture is what Pierre Bourdieu calls the "habitus," then Chesnutt's Troy-centered epic aesthetic reveals his reading of American performances through an hermeneutic that might be usefully coined an epic habitus: a society whose living tradition of classical codes has its root aesthetic in the Homeric epic performance. The elements in the habitus mirror one another, thus making possible metaphor. The body figures here as the enabling corpus between life and art, sociopolitics and performance, for "it is through the capacity for incorporation, which exploits the body's readiness to take seriously the performative magic of the social, that the king, the banker or the priest are hereditary monarchy, financial capitalism or the church made flesh." Naturally, and often supernaturally, the ultimate expression of the habitus is what Bourdieu calls "great collective ceremonies," which instantiate ideology by "re-placing" the body in evocative moments; likewise, even the most innocuous ephemera, such as "nursery rhymes," reify the habitus through an "implicit pedagogy which can instill a whole cosmology" through simple statements and manners, until one's "arms and legs are full of numb imperatives" (57, 69).

One might logically conclude that proper understanding of a Western or *American* epic habitus, whose Homeric aesthetic is too often associated with the literary classics, demands the methodological rigor of cultural and performance studies. Chesnutt foregrounds the body-politic as the center of the American Homeric epic habitus, a locus in the Homeric diaspora. To reconstruct and deconstruct such an epic habitus required Chesnutt to understand ancient mythology in its vegetal and heroic codes as precursors to North Carolinian founding and contemporary racial politics.[22] Chesnutt's reconstruction of the cultural flows that nourished the classical roots of the greater Cape Fear region (Wilmington) allowed him to follow the flowing myths and waterways, from the Ancients around the Atlantic rim and through the "Dark Continent," to New Orleans. He uses *Marrow* to superimpose a multilevel allegorye extending to colonial events in the Congo, likely making *The Marrow of Tradition* the first critique of Joseph Conrad's *The Heart of Darkness* (1902), which had been serialized as "The Heart of Darkness," in *Blackwood's Edinburgh Magazine*'s commemorative thousandth issue, published in February, March, and April 1899.[23]

The rhetorical maneuver of reading the place of race and slavery into America's Homeric performance is three centuries old. It occurred in 1711 with the publication of "Male Hypocrisy: The Story of Inkle and Yarico," in *The Spectator*, no. 11, a tragic story beginning with a young British merchant, Mr. Thomas Inkle, setting sail in 1647 on the *Achilles* for the West Indies but forced to land in America. There he falls in love with Yarico, a native American. After some months of her devotion, and concerned with his losses, he decides to sell her—though pregnant with his child—to a slaver bound for Barbados. As an allegorical statement of the Old-to-New World epic primarily addressing "male hypocrisy," and later as an anti-slavery tale popularized in Britain and beyond (Felsenstein 18) in print and on stage, "Inkle and Yarico" performs multiple transfers through mimicry, repetition, and dissemination.[24] The story's "hero," presented to the British reading public as a modern New World man nevertheless held up to moral censure, is Richard Steele's stand-in for Achilles as epic hero. Steele's act of Homeric appropriation translates the classical epic from verse into a short fictive parable meant for a modern British sensibility, and from an elite classicist to a broader readership and beyond. *The Spectator*'s mass popularity also contained a mutually reinforcing and conflicted dialogic. The specific, intended act of deploying epic irony and allegory to satirize betrayed the cultural context from which the critique issued. Unbecoming British masculinity, too Achilles- or Aeneas-like, is derided at the same time Steele, through inheritance, owned hundreds of slaves.[25]

Since Steele's satire re-performs itself through classical reference and mass broadcast and emulation, the New World epic performance should reveal its own materiality, albeit with a transatlantic colonial distance. After all, "there was much in the early national experience of the United States which was conducive to thinking and acting in such heroic terms," including the size of the land, the difficulties presented by Native Americans, and the authoritarianism of Great Britain (Abrahams, "Some Varieties" 353). In colonial Carolina, seventeenth-and eighteenth-century British explorers and noblemen, along with Scottish immigrants, provided a historical foundation for Chesnutt's investigation. Of most significance, perhaps, since the Carterets figure prominently in *Marrow*, is Lord John Carteret (1690–1763). Carteret was a statesman, Lord President of the Council from 1751 to 1763, and a major stockholder in the Carolinas. Chesnutt's interest in Lord Carteret very likely relates to his family's Norman origins, which implicate the ancient Francophone conquerors in *Marrow*, his aristocratic and intellectual disdain for commoners, and his lifelong love for the classics. On this last point, Jonathan Swift reportedly said of Carteret that "with a singularity scarce to be justified he carried away more Greek, Latin and philosophy than properly became a person of his rank." Moreover, Carteret, President of the Privy Council until his death, merges into heroic mythology. While listening, on his death bed, to the reading of the preliminaries of the Treaty of Paris (1763), he was so weak that the Under-Secretary, Robert Wood, author of *An Essay on the Original Genius and Writings of Homer* (1775), would have postponed the business. But Carteret allegedly said that it "could not prolong his life to neglect his duty," and quoted the speech of Sarpedon from the *Iliad*, Book xii, lines 322–328, repeating the last word "with a calm and determined resignation" (Ballantyne 16, 363–65).

Along with Chesnutt's interest in such British figures as Lord Carteret and William Hilton, who explored the Cape Fear River in the 1660s and who offers a historical precursor to Mr. Delamere, Hector McAlester, a Scottish immigrant, would be similarly significant. McAlester, who co-owned a North Carolina plantation with his younger brother Alexander, returned to Scotland for good after being banned from North Carolina in 1744. Beyond the ill-repute of McAlester, whose discharge from the wilds of colonial America suggests ruthlessness, and the obvious significance of "Hector," Chesnutt may have tapped the Homeric cartography of New Troy—as the McAlester brothers' plantation was called—as a parallel to Troy, North Carolina. New Troy was located in present-day Fayetteville, North Carolina, Chesnutt's home from childhood into his early writing career (1866–1883). Thus Fayetteville, springing from an Homeric body-politic, is the body-*biologic* that sutures together a mid-eighteenth-century locale (New Troy) and a separate late-nineteenth-century version (Troy, North Carolina): previously named *Campbelton*, Col. *Campbell* of "The Sheriff 's Children" symbolizes this merger.

Given North Carolina's Homeric performance in the period leading up to the Revolutionary War, the epic model loomed large as an aesthetic useful for constructing national identity. At the same time "Inkle and Yarico" broadened the Homer- and Virgil-based cultural performance, since "in eighteenth-century America there was a strong demand for 'sublime' and pathetic poetry." As late as 1785 John Adams thought Trumbull would yet write an epic; this was a colonial-American expectation, Alexander Cowie argues, "that was ultimately silenced by [Timothy] Dwight's *Conquest of Canaän* and [Joel] Barlow's *Columbiad*" (Cowie 294). Scholarly consensus has generally identified the American Revolution as a stern aesthetic break with poetic norms.[26] After "Revolutionary times," Roger D. Abrahams notes in his survey of American heroic types, the "concept of national epic broadened to that of a national literature under the proddings of many important literary figures from Emerson to Walt Whitman and beyond" ("Some Varieties" 353, n.16).[27] Similarly, critic Jeffrey Walker argues for and explores the transformation of the classical epic aesthetics, routed through Emersonian aesthetics and emerging, in Whitman, as something newer and greater yet, an American bardic ethos (13–33).[28]

Emerson's call is symptomatic of the potent adaptability of the epic genre. Emblematic is the epical portrait of George Washington in Mason L. Weems' *The Life of Washington* (1808),[29] which merges the Old and New World. Possessed of a broad-chested frame and standing over six feet tall, more than six inches above the average white male Virginian, Washington, the commander-in-chief of the Revolutionary army, framer, and first president, emerges from Mason's biographical monument capable of epic feats of both mind and body: to wit, "as great a scholar" as Mr. Williams, a famous scholar in "*reading, spelling, English grammar, arithmetic, surveying, book-keeping and geography*"; of "extraordinary strength," like his father, who could "throw a stone across Rappahannock"—it is now "no easy matter to find a man, now-a-days, who could do it"; and "as to running, the swift-footed Achilles could scarcely have matched his speed" (20, 21).

Still, one might foreground the literary discontinuity here to argue, as Alexander Cowie suggests, and Abrahams and Walker concur, that the Old World, verse-based epic aesthetic came to an end. But this thought pivots on the literariness of Homer, not on the epic habitus and the reinforcing aesthetics emerging from logic, practice, and performance rooted in the body. If the lens is that of cultural studies, and culture as performance, in particular, the answer is simple: far from being an antiquated genre that is closed and monological, as Georg Lukács and Bakhtin argued in *The Theory of the Novel* (1920) and "Èpos i roman" (1941), respectively, with Homer as their foundation, the epic performance cannot be contained in the form of classical verse.[30]

The Homeric aesthetic ultimately results in a New World epic performance, one with a difference. Just as "Inkle and Yarico" suggests Homeric performativity, the same discursive poetics applies to the creative performance of American literature. Old and New World are interlocked in dialogue and debate, performative mimicry and disavowal at the site of an emergent American epic habitus. Emersonian Transcendentalism may occasion the genesis of F.O. Matthiessen's "American Renaissance,"[31] but it also signifies the robust continuity of what might be usefully termed the "American Homer." Classical archaeologist Philip H. Young charts this territory by quantifying America's intensifying relationship to printed editions of Homeric texts. The five twenty-five-year periods from 1775 to 1901 document well this remarkable transformation (see Table 4.1).

From three editions printed in the last quarter of the eighteenth century, and just eighteen from 1801 to 1825, American print culture rapidly expanded its Homeric catalog. The escalation that occurred in the mid-1840s, during the height of the antebellum era, resulted in a remarkable phenomenon: as Hegel opined, America's epic potential and appetite did, indeed, eclipse that of Europe. Germany dominated Homeric scholarship in the late eighteenth century and competed vigorously with Great Britain in the production of new editions as the nineteenth century began, but the last half of the nineteenth century witnessed the rise of American Homer. From 1851 to 1900, especially 1876 to 1900, American printers were increasingly more apt to print new translations and new reprints of Homer, the *Iliad*, than France, Germany, and Great Britain. During the nineteenth century, these four nations were the most Homeric in their print culture and fascination with Homeric images, as the proliferation of steel engravings based on Romantic-era paintings indicates (see Figures 4.1 to 4.6). In nineteenth-century America, print versions of the *Iliad* clearly outstripped the *Odyssey*: the ratios for the four quarters from 1801 to 1900—exclusive of versions not clearly dedicated to the *Iliad* or *Odyssey*—were 12:7, 31:8, 77:35, and 176:99.

Table 4.1   British, French, German, and American Homer: New Editions and New Reprints Published Quarterly from 1775 to 1900†

Quarter	United Kingdom*	France	Germany	America/ United States
1775–1800	52	27	55	3
1801–1825	123	56	74	20
1826–1850	86	54	71	55
1851–1875	188	49	130	126
1876–1901	276	39	167	292

† Excludes serial reprints published yearly by the same press.
*Includes fourteen Scottish and Irish editions.

Figure 4.1   Ulysses, by L. MacDonald, after painting by J. Brown (1855, steel engraving).

Figure 4.2   Trojan Horse, after oil on canvas painting *Beware of Greeks Bearing Gifts* by Henri-Paul Motte (1846–1922) (1879, steel engraving).

Figure 4.3   Ulysses Defying the Cyclops, by Louis-Frederic Schutzenberger (1887 or 1894, photogravure).

Figure 4.4 *Ulysses Ploughing the Sea Shore,* by C. Cousin, after 1874 oil on canvas painting by Heywood Hardy (1888, steel engraving).

Figure 4.5 *Ulysses Deriding Polyphemus,* after Joseph Mallord William Turner's 1829 *Ulysses Deriding Polyphemus—Homer's Odyssey,* exhibited at the Royal Academy in 1829 and presently at the National Gallery, London (1910, Swantype by the Swan Electric Engraving Co. Ltd., probably first engraved by E. Goodall in 1859–61).

Figure 4.6   Hector et Paris (or *Hector Approaching Paris*), after 1888 painting by Diogène Ulysse Napoléon Maillart (1926, original Heliogravure engraving).

Though causation may not be inferred from this, the data from Young's study suggest a strong correlation between a nation-state's Homeric print performance and its performance on the stages of domestic and geopolitical theaters: "Homeric studies were dominated by the Germans throughout the nineteenth century," Young notes, "and this fact is evident in the list of printings" (127). The veritable explosion of Homeric printings in the nineteenth century (704 editions from 1801 to 1850; 1,374 from 1851 to 1900) reversed itself in the period from 1901 to 1950 (1,047 from 1901 to 1950). Thus, Young observes, "the decrease from the previous half-century illustrates the worldwide damage to civilization done by the wars, financial depression, and widespread cultural changes" (125, 128, 136).

Naturally, the confluence of the literary and performative Homeric epics abounds in the same antebellum era in which Hegel first remarked upon the comparative vitality of epic in America. In July 1849, *The Christian Examiner* published a review of Frederick Douglass' *Narrative* (1845) written by Rev. Ephraim Peabody, an abolitionist and Unitarian minister:

There are those who fear lest the elements of poetry and romance should fade out of the tame and monotonous social life of modern times. There is no danger of it while there are any slaves left to seek for freedom, and to tell the story of their efforts to obtain it. There is that in the lives of men who have sufficient force of mind and heart to enable them to struggle up from hopeless bondage to the position of freemen, beside which the ordinary characters of romance are dull and tame. They encounter a whole Iliad of woes, not in plundering and enslaving others, but in recovering for themselves those rights of which they have been deprived from birth. Or if the Iliad should be thought not to present a parallel case, we know not where one who wished to write a modern Odyssey could find a better subject than in the adventures of a fugitive slave. (62)

Peabody implicitly responds to Hegel, but far beyond what he imagined; Peabody here inaugurates the first cultural studies approach to America's Homer, a radical gesture even as the Homeric referent undermines Peabody's intent. Specifically, Peabody's literary review makes a crucial connection: the literary, poetic Homer and the sublime horrors of America's Homeric performanceare contiguous. The South's early antebellum epical subjectivity was codified by legal and constitutional jurisprudence. Scholarly surveys of southern laws conclude that, collectively, southern opinion leaders, jurists, legislators, and journalists recognized and sought to protect the "impassable gulf" between the races.[32] In this regard, the homonyms "res" (property, a thing) and "race" merge in their imaginary to effect an epical jurisprudential bar.

In an irony Rev. Peabody could not have imagined, Justice Henry Billings Brown constitutionally consecrated the gulf with the landmark 1896 doctrine emerging from *Plessy v. Ferguson*. *Plessy* is a supreme, ironic performance of the epic, for the body of Homer Adolphus Plessy is an enfleshed icon and patronym of America's epic habitus, even as his one-eighth African inheritance tainted him with a res/race that irremediably deformed his body. With the white epic subjectivity now restitched into the constitutional common law by the nation's constitutional arbiter, the epical scale and foundational precursor to southern manliness and emergent white supremacy can be best appreciated.[33]

Of particular relevance in Chesnutt's case is the *res judicata* of the Supreme Court of North Carolina, which policed this gulf—articulated, for example, as "deep rooted and virtuous prejudices," with revulsion for " unnatural and . . . revolting" interracial marriage[34]—from the antebellum era up to and beyond *Plessy* as the white supremacy campaign rapidly progressed to the racial *coup*. Hence, Dr. Miller is Chesnutt's proxy for Homer Plessy, and Homeric is the irony. *Marrow* restages *Plessy*, the laws of the epical gulf written against the body of Dr. Miller and his optimistic diagnosis of the racial problem of Wellington. Naturally, Dr. Miller faces a conundrum: upon whose body—whose house, allegorically speaking—should he make a house-call? Chesnutt refuses to validate modern laws as sound and modernity worthy of access, as Washington's and Du Bois' uplift philosophies held, and seeks the mythic flows and roots of the body-politic. The medical rhetoric implied by Chesnutt's choice of Dr. Miller of *Wellington*—echoed by the juridico-medico "problem" rhetoric Du Bois[35] uses and by Hopkinson's "of one blood" argument—appears in Justice John Marshall Harlan's dissent in *Plessy*:

> Only "nurses attending children of the other race" are excepted from operation of the statute. No exception is made of colored children traveling with adults. A white man is not permitted to have his colored servant with him in the same coach, even if his condition of health requires the constant personal assistance of such servant. If a color maid insists upon riding in the same coach with a white woman whom she has been employed to serve, and who may need her personal service while traveling, she is subject to be fined or imprisoned for such an exhibition of zeal in the discharge of duty. (553)

In this passage Justice Harlan foregrounds the arbitrariness of the Louisiana segregation law upheld by the majority, but it is Harlan's specific medical-related hypotheticals that some black writers seized upon and brilliantly troped. Under such arbitrary circumstances aged and infirm whites, many of whom were founding members of their respective families and communities, assumed a serious medical risk.

Considering the *Plessy* ruling and Harlan's dissent, Chesnutt's literary choices suggest that, for him, no clearer symptoms of a body-politic suffering from a severe case of epic agony could present themselves. The body is the root source from which all the body-politic—laws, traditions, aesthetics, science, religion, philosophy—naturally flowed, thus the need to address ontology. Dr. Miller clearly dramatizes Homer Plessy as "a Chinaman, of the ordinary laundry type" and "a colored nurse . . . with her mistress" (*Marrow* 55) then enter the whites-only passenger car, thus proving the arbitrariness Harlan foregrounds.[36] But if Josh Green is considered Chesnutt's dramatization of Robert Charles, the New Orleans' laborer whose actions precipitated the New Orleans Riots of 1900, the evidence suggests that myth and reality cycle around one another, and *Plessy* restages the cautionary tale arising from Chesnutt's Troy, North Carolina.[37] Truth is better than fiction in this case, for Chesnutt easily enough extends the disease Col. Campbell embodied to the Wilmington and New Orleans events. Both are symptoms of sickness in the body-politic sown, he argues, by the supreme rejection of Plessy and affirmation of white supremacy.

In an American aesthetic space interpenetrated by immigrant poetics, a traditional epic performative essential to understanding those

poetics—often overlooked but ironically *apropos* given the institution
of slavery—is that of West and West Central Africa. New scholarship
into African literatures and retentions allows for a discussion of the role
of the traditional African epic as a possible performative force shaping
African-American culture, including its folklore and arts and letters as
shown in Chesnutt's *Marrow*.

THE EPIC TRICKSTER: E-RES/RACE-ING THE BLACK BODY

Chesnutt's interest in black folk culture is a salient feature of his aesthetic, one he consciously used in the short stories that helped to secure
his literary acclaim. Conjure perhaps gave his fiction its greatest cache,
with titillating promises of dark incantations and deeds constituting a
powerful elixir in America's racialized, gothic Christiandom, especially
since the "angels in the house" constituted the largest body of readers.
The trickster figure aesthetic, like the conjure-telling Uncle Julius McA-
doo of "The Goophered Grapevine" (1887), placed Chesnutt's craft, consciously and not,[38] squarely within the folk tradition emerging from the
slave community. Grounded in decades-old research on the slaves' retention and transformation of African culture, scholarship on the trickster
elucidates its importance to the slaves and their descendants well into the
mid-twentieth century. Far more than being a mere echo of West African
cosmology, the trickster tale, figure, and aesthetic, like the Signifying
Monkey derivative of the Yoruba's Esu-Legba (Gates 1989), the badman arising from African trickster lore (Roberts 1989), or Aunt Nancy
of Ghana's Anansi spider-trickster (Benjamin 2005), not only enriched
African-American aesthetics, but provided a formulary/heuristic for the
enslaved to decode and navigate the peculiar institution and beyond.
Invested with this charge at the height of American slavery, when survival was tenuous at best, the trickster, according to scholars, functioned as a "trickster hero" (Abrahams, "Some Varieties" 341–42) and
"culture-hero" (Roberts 1989). In the postmodern analytics of Gates'
Signifying Monkey, the Yoruba-Esu-trickster-cum-Signifying-Monkey
has the paradigmatic deconstructive, "meta-discourse" potential as the
"trope of tropes, the figure of the figure." The Signifying Monkey's chaos
disrupts linearity and totality, and even the Manichean dichotomies of
white/black and male/female lose ontological priority in the truth of a
third Other-ness performed by Esu, who is "the third principle—neither
male nor female, neither this nor that, but both, a compound morphology" (28–35, 42).

In lieu of a Greco-Roman epic habitus, however, this interrelated but
distinct interpretation, equally applicable though discounted by Levine (and
much earlier by Peabody), is one that recognizes the isomorphic counterpart
to the master of the African short narrative: the traditional African epic.

CONJURING HEALTHY BODIES: GREEN(NESS) FROM
"THE HEART OF DARKNESS" TO *THE MARROW OF TRADITION*

One has to stop and ask a critical question: why would Chesnutt, a new Negro witnessing progress in the form of his own career advances and prospects, turn away from the trickster's socio-aesthetics that brought him to fame, refuse the industrial and classical education models of Washington and Du Bois, respectively, and elevate Green, a clear throwback to slavery and perhaps Africa? Scholars conclude that because of amoral tendencies (Abrahams, "Some Varieties" 341–42), the trickster-proper failed to translate well into a more sophisticated, literate black population and lost cultural traction as the twentieth century matured, storytellers became more "self-conscious," and great "doubts about the appropriateness or efficacy of the trickster's approach" emerged (Levine 112–121, 370–77). By "efficacy," Levine meant the limits of "pre-modern" literacy in an era of common schools. Levine recognized, but left unexplored, a thesis that put folkloric performance on either side of the color-line. In addition to standard trickster tales, Levine observes, "Slave tales are filled with instances of the strong acting as tricksters: Fox asks Jaybird to pick a bone out of his teeth, and once he is in his mouth, Fox devours him"; "Wolf constructs a tar-baby in which Rabbit almost comes to his end"; and "Elephant, Fox, and Wolf all pretend to be dead in order to throw Rabbit off guard and catch him at their 'funerals'" (118–19). At the same time, but as an intraracial dynamic, the duplicity attributed to the trickster is also a feature of the epic figure. In spite of the trickster's potential as a culture hero and radical deconstructive agent under Gates' post-structuralism, a structural dilemma persists: the Homeric epic hero, a "superman" as E.V. Rieu describes Odysseus in his 1945 introduction to *The Odyssey* (19), is also a master of wit and verbal felicity. Along with brutal race riots in Wilmington, New Orleans, and elsewhere, laws and governmental policies, strictly speaking, provide much of the answer: Reconstruction-era law had been uprooted, black codes had been violently imposed in some places, and the United States' imperialist policy in the Philippines paralleled the rapid colonization of Africa and Asia by Western Europe. However, the blackletter law and contemporary policies had uncodified and uncodifiable antecedents predating any of the constitution-based nation-states by centuries.

The *Plessy* court's rejection of Homer Plessy perfected Chesnutt's Troy, North Carolina–based argument regarding epic agony, for though Dr. Miller is a talented physician and "new Negro," he is, like Col. Campbell, beholden to the marrow of tradition or to "The Heart of Darkness." Conrad's novel was serialized, beginning just three months after the Wilmington *coup*, in *Blackwood's Edinburgh Magazine*, which championed empire at a time when events in the Congo were well known to the nascent pan-Africanists. Chesnutt's title, *The Marrow of Tradition*, not only furthers his objective of writing a literary masterpiece critical of racism, but reveals his own understanding of how racial mythology evolves. While Conrad makes the Congo

"The Heart of Darkness," dehumanizing and objectifying the Africans along the way, Chesnutt's *The Marrow of Tradition* signifies against it in a gesture trebly damaging: first, parodying Conrad with a logic and symbolism that forces the West and Africa into an equivalency; second, subsuming Conrad's title under his own, which has the effect of locating "The Heart of Darkness" within *The Marrow of Tradition* and parodying it; and, perhaps most significantly, adducing Wellington, a body-politic and -biologic, as an allegorycal exhibit of epic and empire, and hence of darkness.

Chesnutt substitutes Wellington for Wilmington, merging it into his tradition-based dissent to the *Plessy* majority and Justice Harlan. But this body-politic has its body-biologic: Field Marshal Arthur Wellesley, an Anglo-Irish British aristocrat, soldier, and statesman best known as the first Duke of Wellington. His family roots dating back to the elites leading the 1066 Norman invasion, Wellington was Britain's version of Napoleon Bonaparte, whom he defeated at Waterloo. As the heart of the British Empire that rose in the nineteenth century, Wellington was unparalleled as a military strategist and laurelled for his fighting, as Sir Colin Campbell recounted after the Battle of Assaye:[39] "The general was in the thick of the action the whole time and had a horse killed under him. No man could have shown a better example to the troops than he did. *I never saw a man so cool and collected as he was the whole time*" (Wellington 184–87; italics mine). Though Wellesley did not become emperor, his extensive military career included a captaincy, majority,[40] and generalcy (Corrigan 18, 67; Hibbert 40; Severn 50)—the ranks of Chesnutt's Big Three, the conspirators who dream of empire from the offices of the *Morning Chronicle*. Whereas the biological Wellington is heroic, Chesnutt adds temporality—the past marrow of tradition informing Chesnutt's present and future bodies—to his allegorycal figure to counter overly simplistic Homeric mythmaking: Capt. McBane is robust but low ranking, Maj. Carteret is less vigorous but ranks higher, and Gen. Belmont is a cipher—an effeminate, hard-drinking dullard who is, quite appropriately, the most inconsequential character in the entire novel.

Against *this* West, Chesnutt symbolically looks East toward the Congo and taps an African epic trickster aesthetic, a gesture which enters *Marrow* into the canon of world literature as a brief in dialogue with and dissent to the Homeric diaspora. This strategy, in light of the Congo's *Mwindo Epic*, has the effect of conjuring Mwindic Green(ness) from the heart of Africa. Josh Green offers an indigenous agency which provides Dr. Miller with an herbal, roots-based rejuvenation he needs for himself and, most significantly, a troubled West.

ALL GREEN WITH EPIC POTENTIAL

Study of the epics of Sunjata, Ozidi, and Mwindo debunks the archetype of a monological, idealized epic protagonist who moves from trickster to epic hero. Teleological understanding is useful, but contra the Homeric adulation in which the ends of fully matured epic protagonists are considered worthy of emulation, Chesnutt would be interested in teleological closure to such ideas. Because of the clear potency of epic, and its continuation implied by the epic cycle, ritual invocation of a cooling source is imperative. Featuring a lush rainforest with a quest representing maternal justice's marriage to life-waters, the *Mwindo Epic* begins with justice sold down the river and ends with cooling elements—a cold year spent in the realms of Rain, Moon, Sun, and Star—returned to the story. Each of the MOS-epic protagonists, soon after or even before birth, suffer repeated and intensifying deformations—physical, mental, sociopolitical, and geographical—that ultimately force each one to flee the homeland, into their respective diasporas, for their survival. Mwindo, whose epical abilities earn him the epithet "Little-one-just-born-he-walks," faces death from his greedy father, Shemwindo, immediately after he is born and has to flee down a river; Sunjata is born lame, slow-tongued and -witted, and even loses his royal inheritance through the machinations of a covetous stepmother, who eventually forces him and his mother into exile; and Ozidi is whisked away by his epic-grandmother, Oreame, for the covetous generals that killed his father, also named Ozidi, threaten his existence. Deformities accumulate until the MOS-epic plots erupt into sociopolitical directionlessness and the ironic indirection of the epic trickster: Mwindo's signifying, Ozidi's verbal fighting incantation, and Sunjata's sudden verbal felicity when his epic energies first emerge (Rutledge 74–87).

These deformations are impediments, for their cumulative effect is to metaphorically blacken the potentiality of the epic protagonists and their families to such an extent that they suffer symbolic deaths. In light of this, Cartwright's *Reading Africa* establishes a vocabulary and heuristic that fills a critical gap between the epic metaphor of the social epic and Africa's epic vitality. The African epic force of *nyama*, consisting of *badenya* (mother-child-ness) and *fadenya* (father-child-ness), provides the source of "imperial mother-wit." Sunjata, a transgressive figure, relies upon the Answerer-of-Needs, his mother's and sister's sorcery, at the most critical junctures of his epic ordeal in the "diaspora" away from his Malian homeland (25–34). Consonant with the Sunjatic performance, Mwindo's masculine singularity requires the flows of female justice and the motherland for the successful realization and closing of epic potential.

Fate allows the MOS-epic tricksters to nullify their deformations and their duskiness, but none of them faces the Diaspora-proper and racial deformation of American Homer. Mwindo, Sunjata, and Ozidi each has his own microcosm of an epic community, led by the female Answerer-of-Needs, extra-national helpmates in the diaspora, and native-born inheritance arising from a land free of the racial bar. In contradistinction, Chesnutt's Josh Green epitomizes the African-American epic trickster because he lacks these benefits in a land predicated on an epic cultural performance where whiteness, *a priori*, constitutes the impassable gulf between it and blackness. The metaphoricity of African epic blackness pales next to an American epic *habitus* in which the ontological, God-given black body bears an immutable, res/race-ial character.

Whereas Sunjata, Ozidi, and Mwindo are predestined epic protagonists, no such issue is possible in an American space quickened by an epic-inspired "white supremacy" diametrically opposed to all things African. Dr. Miller, in spite of his "broad shoulders" and "manly instinct," is a cosmopolitan man caught between *noblesse oblige* and Talented Tenth ideologies, faith and Darwinian thought (*Marrow* 62, 282), leadership and "wife and child," action and inaction as the pogrom unfurls. Given Dr. Miller's behavior, Green is not, as Sundquist argues, a "heroic" foil whose heroism is betrayed by his "radical" and even "outlaw" propensities ("Introduction" xlii), but an uncompromising moral force of folk provenance. Like his Old Testament epic counterpart, Joshua of Nun, his African epic trickster forebears, the original transgressive bad men, and even Achilles, Odysseus, and Hector, as part of his inheritance as an epic native son, Green is an emergent folk icon.[41] Though lacking full MOS-epic potential, this "bad man" is nevertheless deployed by Chesnutt as a revolutionary who judges and topples the racist walls of Jericho and Troy located in North Carolina.

But toppling the founders' walls is no simple matter of mortar and stone. The body-politic itself is predicated on the marrow as a living tradition more than capable of replicating itself through the mythologies that inform the most essential common sense. Chesnutt's use of genealogical roots and generational politics may not be as tangled as William Faulkner's Yoknapatawpha County fiction, but they are deeper. Against a historical backdrop featuring the exploration of Cape Fear by William Hilton in 1662 and Hector McAlester's establishment of New Troy in the eighteenth century, Chesnutt provides the history and bloodlines for four generations of founders and their black counterparts: early antebellum figures, like John Delamere and Polly Ochiltree, and Sandy Campbell and Jane Letlow; mid-nineteenth-century figures and current opinion leaders represented by the Carterets (Philip and Olivia), the "Big Three" (Carteret, Gen. Belmont, and Capt. McBane), and the Millers; the postbellum generation that had just reached majority—Tom Delamere, Clara Pemberton, and Jerry Letlow; and, Theodore Felix Carteret ("Dodie") and the Miller's unnamed son, the faces for the dawning twentieth century.

Though the first generations present a solid foundation, *Marrow* extends the logic of "The Sheriff's Children," which presents Col. Campbell— heroic, cultured, and noble—as an inferior species to his son because of breeding. Similarly, Chesnutt makes clear that the Wellington founders are failing: Delamere, who represents the most noble elements of Col. Campbell, is retired to his estate at Belleview, the name of an actual Civil War veterans' cemetery in Wilmington (Bellevue); the finances of the Carterets have forced them into enterprises such as the *Morning Chronicle*; Tom, whose handsomeness is effeminate,[42] is an ethically bankrupt gambler, card cheater, thief, and murderer; and Dodie, who has physical defects—by virtue of a mole below his ear, which augurs future problems—faces death from the opening of the novel. Aunt Jane Letlow and a "new Negro" black nurse— providing the first of two episodes that restage Harlan's dissent—attend to him, but the nurse is fired, and thus Jim Crowed, by Aunt Mammy Jane. Jane Letlow, the Carterets' faithful retainer, despises the nurse's aggressive, progressive attitude because, she tells a concurring Maj. Carteret, "Dese yer young niggers ain' got de manners dey wuz bawned wid!" (43).

If the manhood and womanhood—Olivia Carteret struggled to give birth, and gave birth to Dodie—of the Wellington founders is failing or has failed by virtue of epic agony, why should Chesnutt bother with Green? The "stress of competition," a mantra of white supremacy, seems to have already interred their potency alongside the remains of Mr. Delamere and Polly Ochiltree. Because the marrow is grounded in mythology that is greater than the sum of its parts, Chesnutt looks to the source of the next branch of founders, Capt. McBane. The blue blood generation, for McBane, is a source of epic mimicry: he seeks to equal their status, which requires a mastery of their culture, but not through an *in toto* mimesis, for that would negate his individual, native-born greatness. McBane is not only capable of weathering the stress of competition, but he is a source that foreshadows a new standard. Beyond being a simple "bane," McBane is a pivotal figure, channeling the old mythology of eighteenth-century North Carolina and revivifying it for the new.

McBane offers a vessel by which Chesnutt repackages and literally re- fashions the Trojan classical code in an era that saw the emergence of the gentleman's sports coat, immediately preceded by the "frock coat," which McBane wears with a "slouch hat" (53). The "frock coat" places him either in an informal country setting of the eighteenth century or in the formal- wear occasions of the late-nineteenth, and the hat suggests shady South American business dealings and his involvement in military campaigns. McBane has no *prima facie* correlation with McAlester, but the genealogi- cal roots of McBane capitalize on the denotation of "bane" as curse and the Scottish surname—literally, "son of the fair lad"[43]—to cloak the Homeric epic in the body of an ultra-ambitious lower-class white supremacist. McBane's *parvenu* status represents the new capitalist face that not only competes with traditional old money and the new Negro, but threatens to make the emerging Industrial-Age urban space a New Troy.

Hector McAlester's New Troy will continue with a different branch or bough, and a different name, McBane, which simultaneously connotes the youthful, sublime lightness of the marrow of tradition and, Chesnutt estab- lishes, the bane of the heart of darkness. This parodic treatment of Con- rad's "The Heart of Darkness" may also reflect Chesnutt's similar regard for Sir James Frazer's *The Golden Bough: A Study in Magic and Religion* (1890), a controversial and widely influential source text for Conrad's novella. Chesnutt looks to vegetal myths as did Conrad, but with clear anti-racist and anti-imperialist intent. Just as Frazer's comparative study of old religions as vegetal myths took inspiration from Virgil's *Aeneid*, McBane simultaneously functions as a Homeric (New Troy) and vegetal myth. Residents of McBane's New Troy will worship at the altar of capital, a foundation rising from the Wellington founders' plantation economy and an equally aggressive and rapacious form of white supremacy.

Thus, McBane is the metonymic "hero" whose ascent has to be stopped, but by whom? Since he is richer than the Wellington elite, "had enough money to buy out a half dozen of these broken-down aristocrats" (82), the two natural antagonists are Dr. Miller and Green. Of these two, Dr. Miller is beholden to the Wellington tradition, and bides his time for entry into its ranks. New Negro he may be, but confronted on the Jim Crow train by the new capitalist McBane, his heroism and morality fail, and he, like a dog with its tail between its legs—a point made when a white man enters with a male "dog, an intelligent shepherd, [which] licked" Dr. Miller's hand "as he passed" (60)—slinks back to his assigned place. Chesnutt hereby qualifies the new Negro type, which he divides in twain: the type Dr. Miller represented before the racial massacre and *coup d'état* who died along with the source of New Troy, and a second, *greener* version rising in its stead.

Of the major characters, only Green desires nothing from tradition. His only concern is to care for his mother, "Silly" Milly, and when she dies, get justice or revenge for past wrongs done to her and his father, whose lynching by McBane when Green was young drove her insane. Although Green has been considered a member of the working class (Wagner 329), he differs from other working-class blacks. From his first description and the questionable status of his employment,[44] Green appears to be a representative of the vast underclass Chesnutt's novel otherwise elides.

Green's underclass status is important, for it generally aligns with the position of the trickster-hero proper. However, as Chesnutt's bad man, Green struggles against a trickster-property status, a condition which eliminates the subjectivity required for the epic trickster and, ultimately, the epic hero. Jerry Letlow, recognized as a type of trickster whose "actions convey no benefits . . . to the larger black community" (De Santis 84–85), is the res/race thing, a species of trickster-prop(erty) distinguishable from a trickster-proper that represents the essential survival skills for the self and healthy community. As suggested by his last name—Letlow means to "let" (lease) "low," or to hire cheaply—Jerry is a sycophant who values whiteness and money above all else. Josh boxes him on the ears and gives him a chance to fight to redeem himself, but instead he jumps through the hospital window.

Green's socioeconomic status is also important for the critical social distance and insight it gives him. As a member of the underclass, he is outside of tradition, the color-line, and the false hierarchy they enshrine. Thus, Green is impervious to the rhetoric of democracy, equality, and fusion (party politics) when it is devoid of justice for, as he makes clear, he "ruther be a dead nigger any day dan a live dog" (*Marrow* 284). Green sees the total situation clearly, even if he is educationally and rhetorically unlettered, and is the only character "who holds to principle without duplicity" (Reilly 35–36). Hence, unlike the aforementioned nurse, who is figuratively killed off by being fired, Chesnutt *qua* narrator—contra Dr. Miller's thoughts—introduces Green largely unburdened by his narrative critique.[45] He is heroic, but Green's exact heroic character and complexity relative to Chesnutt's goal of reconceptualizing the black and white marrow remain underappreciated.

Notwithstanding the role Green plays in reconstructing black masculinity in the South and the nation, the global, colonial scale of Chesnutt's allegorycal vision forces him to cast Green in terms at once more non-American and non-Western. Indeed, Green's status and stature bear more than a little resemblance to his African epic predecessors. But the African epic trickster's African-American counterpart faces the complications of a New World order, one with its own epic traditions never countenanced by the epic tricksters of traditional African epics. Whereas the irony confronting the African epic trickster is overturned in a matter of years, slavery forced a profound and prolonged irony into its American incarnation until it had been blackened, fragmented, and reduced to its trickster-proper masquerades. The performances rising out of the Homeric cartography of Troy, North Carolina, which create a tragic and prophetic epical realism, become Chesnutt's rehearsal for geopolitics. Chesnutt's strategy is to use the historical records available to him to ground *Marrow* with an inexhaustible allegorycal subtext that viciously ironizes even the most noble figures.

By all accounts a nobleman, Delamere is simultaneously an actor whose generation is one stratum of the founders' marrow and a patriarchal paragon who set the prototype. William Hilton, Jr., of the New England merchant marine and the one for whom a significant stretch of coastal North Carolina is named, offers one historical source for Delamere, for he navigated the Cape Fear River. The settlement of North Carolina, known as Cape Fear along the coastline, brought the colonizers in direct contact with the indigenous Americans. In November 1662, explorers aboard the ship *Adventure*, led by Hilton, summarized their three-week reconnoitering of the lower reaches of the Cape Fear River (October 4th to the "latter end of October"). Hilton's report, made for their employer, the New England Company for the Discovery of Cape Fear, comments favorably on the abundant fish, flora and fauna, the topography, and the potential for good growing conditions. Perhaps because Hilton knew this report would constitute promotional literature, his description is of an edenic cornucopia which invites readers to sally forth to ultimately colonize the

> abundance of vast meddows, besides upland fields, that renders ye country fit to be a called a Land for Catle, whereby they that dwell there, may enjoy ye freedom from that toyle in other plantations. . . .

And there are besides greatt swamps laden with varieties of great oakes, and other trees of all sorts, and . . . Large grape-vines in abundance, and other fruites. We found also some barren land, and other exceeding good land, most of it very easy to plow up. There is scarce a stone to be seene, *only in 2. or 3. places by ye side of ye river we spied some rocks in a very sandy ground.* We have seen india Corn Stalks as big as a mans wrist, 11. or 12. foot long. . . . There are abundance of Deer, as appeare by ye many tracks, which we cannot avoyd almost, if we go ashoare: We saw two run by us: There are store of Otters; and of fowles there is abundance, . . . [he lists 17 species], and severall sorts of other fowles. We know no fruit or grain that grows in New England, but will grow there very well. Besides potatotes, Oranges, Lemons, Plantines, Olives, Cotton-trees; and we know not, why ye Pine apple will not grow there, and also ye Sugar-cane, for there are excellent tall and strong wilde canes in abundance: Tobacco must needs excell.

Because this 1662 catalog is a looking-glass into the plantation history of the Carolinas, and an economy driven by tobacco and cotton crops for the next two centuries, its status as the first official account of the land, one that historian J. Leitch Wright said went "unnoticed for centuries in the archives of the Royal Society"[46] because his 1663 report was far more influential, makes it useful to Chesnutt as he assembled historical facts for his epic-centered allegorye. Chesnutt pierces the mythological veil, but he seems to have expropriated concrete elements for repackaging under the guise of a seemingly unrelated event, the Wilmington *coup d'état.* He bypasses Hilton's surname, but not the surnames of two of the six co-authors of the November 6, 1662, account, Lucas Enoch *Green*lese and John *Green.* Moreover, Hilton wrote that the American Indians were "very poor and *silly* Creatures" and "very theevish." It follows that since he had observed fewer than one hundred of them, he wished "all Englishmen, that know how to improve and use a plentiful Countrey and condition, not to delay to posses it" (Hilton et al. 99–101; J. Wright 96–98; italics mine).

When one looks beneath the literal surface of the plot and beyond one-to-one allegorical correspondence, a complex web of performances, centered about Mr. Delamere, emerges from the tidewaters—water, silt, and "very sandy grounds"—of this historical reference. Between him and Dr. William Miller, the one whose memory establishes the Silly Milly backstory to Josh Green, lies Hilton's adventure. Green's mother, Milly, is the product of one of the "silly Creatures," and Mr. Delamere's Bellevue estate lies along a "sandy road" away from Wilmington. As noted earlier, this allusion undercuts Dr. Miller's independence and professional status by association with Sandy Campbell, but William—again, the name of Aunt Polly Ochiltree's coachman and the name by which Delamere calls him en route back to Wilmington—and "sandy" link Delamere and Miller to Hilton. "Delamere," an Anglicized Norman word taken from the Latin *mare* ("sea"), literally translates into "of the sea" or pond, a strategy which imports the blood of Norman conquest[47] and Hilton's conquest of the "silly Creatures" into Delamere's past which Chesnutt, in a delicate cue to his readers, links to the "famous pirate Blackbeard" (*Marrow* 196).

Delamere's past is significant, but it is insufficient if Chesnutt hoped to stage a complex living tradition that reaches from the mythological marrow and beyond to reflect itself in the space ranging from the local to the global. Chesnutt includes the full sweep of the Anglophone, past and present, with the noble British lineage of Delamere, one of North Carolina's native sons. Again, the British Empire serves him well, for the peerage of the Barons Delamere—based on their East African presence, which dates to the early 1890s—established a principal estate in Kenya, a British colony.[48] Chesnutt concretizes his analogy through visual allusions. Belleview, the historic estate and "colonial plantation" of the Delameres, is a two-hundred-year-old British import: it "dated from 1750 and was built of brick which had been brought from England. Enlarged and improved from generation to generation, it stood, like a baronial castle, upon a slight eminence from which could be surveyed the large demesne still belonging to the estate, which had shrunk greatly from its colonial dimensions" (196–97). Equally important is the physical stature we should associate with Delamere by extrapolation. Here it is useful to consider Col. Campbell's physical description—

> He was a tall, muscular man, of a ruddier complexion than is usual among Southerners. A pair of keen, deep-set gray eyes looked out from under bushy eyebrows, and about his mouth was a masterful expression, which a full beard, once sandy in color, but now profusely sprinkled with gray, could not entirely conceal. ("The Sheriff's" 75)

—as one we might attribute to Delamere at the same age, and compare it with Capt. McBane's gothic image—

> His broad shoulders, burly form, square jaw, and heavy chin betokened strength, energy, and unscrupulousness. With the exception of a small, bristling mustache, he was clean shaven, with here and there a speck of dried blood due to a carelessly or unskillfully handled razor. A single deep-set gray eye was shadowed by a beetling brow, over which a crop of coarse black hair, slightly streaked with gray, fell almost low enough to mingle with his black, busy eyebrows. (*Marrow* 32)

—one which, owing to his monocular appearance, suggests that he is a Scottish-American Cyclops. Adjust Col. Campbell's/Delamere's image for the two-hundred-year-old Blackbeard[49] legacy and Delamere-family genealogy Chesnutt just stops shy of formally averring as piratical, and the "deep-set gray eye[s]" and virility conveyed by their physical strength and "bus[h]y eyebrows" make Delamere and McBane generational equivalents. Though separated by social class and physical space, the combination of Delamere's family origins with McBane's robust presence suggest that both men were and are capable of being "golden boughs" who translated the past William Hiltons, Lord Carterets, and Baron Delameres into the American present. But the postbellum present represents the failure of the Wellington bloodlines and an uncertain future for it that is fated for gradual—if not precipitous—decline. *Captain* McBane, however, rendered piratical by military and maritime rank, behavior, and appearance, easily eclipses the current generation of Wellington founders—Maj. Carteret, Gen. Belmont—and the prototype of its most glorious past, Delamere. A two-hundred-year throwback, McBane, as an epical golden bough, represents another two-hundred-year epical rejuvenation of the marrow—he is, in contemporary medical terms most appropriate to Chesnutt's *leitmotif*, a Scottish bone marrow transplant. In the years to come thanks to men like McBane, the British Empire will meet and be surpassed by another: the rugged American Empire.

The irony of McBane's role, of course, is twofold. First, Chesnutt implies, through the physical descriptions cited above, ambitious low-class white Europeans and Americans are not much distinguishable, really, from the Africans being colonized by the British Empire. Second, although the body-politic tends toward homeostasis, its continuity based on "an Homeric" performance that is vegetally renewed by a new generation of converts, an extended epic performance disrupts homeostasis by virtue of epic agony. The epic physicality and ambition of a new generation may renew the body-politic, but the ethical decline—Delamere's generation contrasting with his grandson's, and McBane's epic ruthlessness and "masterful duplicity" in contrast yet again—is continuous. In lieu of an Old World, Western European, and Scottish-immigrant bone marrow transplant, a golden possibility that masks an ever-darker epic agony for the body-politic, Chesnutt turns toward an indigenous knowledge equal to the task of confronting the likes of McBane: Green, the *African*-American epic trickster.

Green may not have been a slave, but the deformation which characterizes his first appearance—woolly headed, animalistic, unclean, apparently unemployed—makes him a distinctly blackened figure. The blackened self serves as an important convention in the classical epic narrative, for it functions as a trope which marks the epic figure as a victim of some significant injustice. For example, in the *Iliad*, Homer uses the trope of blackening to externalize his epic hero's internal condition after the trauma of a perceived injustice. When Achilles first hears of Patroklos' death, he pours soot over his head, blackening himself: "And he lay there with his whole body sprawling in the dust, huge and hugely fallen, tearing at his hair and defiling it with his own hands" (Homer/Hammond 310).[50]

Although Green shoulders race, class, and gender burdens as his antebellum inheritance, to consider them "a whole Iliad of woes"—albeit well-intentioned—only deepens the problem. While Peabody's divination betrays the fierce truths of the American epic habitus, one in which the epic sublime and slave sublime are mutually constitutive,[51] its metaphoric fulcrum specifically pivots upon the Homeric aesthetic. Even Peabody's epic metaphors fail, for his reliance on the Homeric epics as the cultural cornerstone reinscribes European hegemony, inextricably represented by Homer, into the form and content of emancipatory poetics. But Homer-inspired sympathy in which, without more, readers identify blacks as humans and civilized in an epic-charged habitus fails as a matter of poetic scale, aesthetic, and episteme.[52] Indeed, the Supreme Court's dismissal of the white-looking body of Homer Plessy forecloses the Homeric route to equal rights Rev. Peabody invokes by judging his appeal under a mythological framework that is steeped in pure, exceptional whiteness.

Scholars like Page DuBois vex the Homeric valence to fathom the intersection of Homeric aesthetics and ancient and antebellum slavery, particularly the implications Hector's fall has for his wife, Andromakhe, and the women of Troy. Not only does the attendant epic subjectivity result in a *sine qua non* performance of a slave- and gender-based aesthetic, as DuBois elucidates, but arguably the aesthetics of the lynching ritual. Achilles' epic contest with Ilios' contest-hero, Hector, establishes the epic consequences—a total, epical dehumanization—facing the hero, and his ethnic group by metonymic liability, who dares lay manly claim to epic beauty:

> So he spoke, and then put glorious Hektor to shameful treatment. He cut through behind the tendons of both feet from heel to ankle, and pulled straps of ox-hide through them which he tied fast to his chariot, so the head would be left to drag. Then he mounted the chariot and lifted the famous armour into it, and whipped the horses on, and they flew eagerly on their way. As Hektor was dragged behind, a cloud of dust arose from him, his dark hair streamed out round him, and all that once handsome head was sunk in the dust: but now Zeus had given him to his enemies to defile him in his own native land.
>
> So Hektor's head was all sullied in the dust. (Homer/Hammond, *The Iliad* 369)

Helen may be the proverbial trophy—although her remarks to Odysseus' son Telemachus in the *Odyssey* problematize such—but Hector's body, the bearer of his epic potential, becomes the trophy on which Achilles enacts a swift and terrible revenge: his epic potential, marked by an ethnic Otherness borne by his "dark hair" and "dark eyes," is the "dust[y]" body Achilles' wrath denudes of epical presence and leaves deformed and dogged.[53] Achilles' ritualized lynching, beginning with his patent display of dragging Hector's body around Ilios, the circumscription of the once-epical Trojan community auguring its assured sacking and enslavement, continues with equal visibility for two weeks afterward. Priam's successful entreaty for Hector's body cannot change the foreordained: Ilios, its contest-hero not just defeated, but lynched of humanity and epic potential in a ritualized, graphic cinema, is "without sanctuary."[54] The Homeric imagery, providing ancient, graphic snapshots of Hector's lynching, is a disturbingly prescient foreshadowing of the lynching photographs, postcards, and plates—often publicly displayed, sometimes copyrighted—whose materiality documents a ritual at once ancient and modern, Greek and American.

Green's dusky and huge body, woolly head, fighting prowess, and biblical significance underscore his epic pedigree as an American figure. Particularly important is Green's role in foregrounding an African epic tradition as coequal to the white (American) epic heroes of the Greco-Roman tradition. Although Chesnutt's blackening strategy masks Green's later significance, this deformed Green shares the total opprobrium suffered by the fatherless Ozidi, lame Sunjata, and aborted[55] Mwindo at the outset of their epic trickster phases. By the time they are forced into exile, they are also relegated to the underclass, or worse. But they are also better situated, ironically, since their respective exiles enable them to see the full corrupt totality.

Though less true of Chesnutt's *Marrow*, Green's outlaw status also gives him the requisite distance needed to exercise proper ethical sight. Sight or insight into the problem is one thing, piercing and expunging it is another, hence the signal difference between the African and African-American epic tricksters. The African-American epic trickster represented by Green faces a total barrier created by the absence of the generative habitus and the presence of a totalized system of slavery that suppresses his full evolution and return. Although Green is part of and thus can theoretically rely upon the African-American community, racism as a legacy of slavery exercises insidious force on this potential constituency. *Marrow* dramatizes how white supremacy impacts the African-American community from its elite members to the most low; in effect, it deprives Green of key, fully supportive individuals without whom the epic cycle can have no successful issue.

Even facing a large and hostile epic community, the protagonists of traditional African epics nevertheless enjoy something Green lacks: a loving, just, and potent microcosm of the epic community. Sunjata, Mwindo, and Ozidi all had strong women—Sunjata's mother and sister; Mwindo's aunt; and, Ozidi's grandmother—supporting them in their formative years. Green, by comparison, has only his mother, and she is the insane Silly "Milly" Green. Moreover, those African-American characters Green does have at his disposal are not even neutral, but directly supportive of the system, as is the case with Jane and Jerry Letlow, or invidiously compromised by it unbeknownst to themselves.

Dr. Miller's and Mr. Watson's interactions with Green during Sandy's impending lynching deserve some attention here. Although Dr. Miller and Mr. Watson profess opposition to white supremacy, because they are so entrenched in the system they work against Green (Reilly 36), their nominal anti-lynching measures notwithstanding. Mr. Watson's and Dr. Miller's law-abiding professionalism establishes the context—modern, professional time regulated by the law—that flattens, infantilizes, and delegitimizes Green. A pre-modern figure who operates to laws attuned to deep time, Green finds himself caught in the precise time and the performance of a professional, juridico-medico discourse issuing from Mr. Watson and Dr. Miller. Chesnutt may allow them this space for legitimate reasons, but their performance is nevertheless disturbing since it mimics the effect of master-servant, white-black legal rhetoric Justice Harlan foregrounds as arbitrary.

While Green embodies direct and immediate action to meet the exigent circumstances, their professional command of the situation effectively arrests him, one after another: first Mr. Watson to Dr. Miller and Green ("We'd better leave Josh here"; "Wait for us here, Josh, until we've seen what we can do"), then Dr. Miller to Green ("and you, Josh, learn what the colored folks are saying, and do nothing rash until I return") (*Marrow* 192, 195). Together, Miller and Watson check Green's subjectivity and epic potential until he literally becomes an inanimate object *that* is, they would prefer, more trickster-prop than epic trickster.

This reading shows the character of the Miller-Watson compromise, for they follow the procedures and rules of order pursuant to democratic, civilized, and professional routes of action when justice commands otherwise. Green is effectively and figuratively exiled, not only by the white supremacist power structure characterized by the Big Three, but by the Big Two of the African-American community. Chesnutt sums up the preordained outcome of their efforts with the chapter title itself: "How Not to Prevent a Lynching."

Heroic, decisive action, not professional compromise with those invested in tradition, ultimately takes center stage after Green is rendered frozen and flat-footed by the procedures of Dr. Miller and Mr. Watson's anti-lynching performance. The stage is set when, the Miller-Watson two-step completed, Green is left without any major support, except for the "small party" of "resolute-looking colored men" he commands in the end (281). These men may be Green's soldiers, a heroic band of fighters for justice, but as established earlier, male power without female magic, *badenya*, results in an inchoate epic hero. Hence the ironic significance of the death of Silly Milly, which both frees for battle his indigenous epic potency and seals his death.[56] His mother's death just before his major war begins with the restaged racial riot in Wellington/Wilmington is similar to Sunjata's story. But unlike Sunjata's mother, Green's mother has been insane throughout all of his formative years. In short, the epic potential Green represents, and the successful issue of the epic journey, are doomed even before he can get started. Still, Chesnutt clearly figures Green as the embodiment of an African-American epic figure, the roots doctor who cures epic excesses, although for most of *Marrow*—from his first appearance under Dr. Miller's gaze—he represents the antithesis. Shunted away from socioeconomic stability, political utility, and even the basic conditions denoting full humanity, Green symbolizes the gerrymandered underclass and Chesnutt's will to transform the entire black body-politic from the bottom up.

Green's demise is far from the end one assumes Chesnutt would give him if he were merely a "militant." Identifying Green as one "with the eye of a general" and "the instinct of a born commander" (299, 301), Chesnutt makes his death nothing less than a sublime blaze of glory. Having coolly survived a hell storm of bullets that kills all of his comrades, just as a "cool and collected" Duke of Wellington survived the 1803 Battle of Assaye, Green stands alone as a towering "black giant." At this moment, he is an epic figure whose native forerunners are Sunjata, Mwindo, and Ozidi:

> Some of the crowd paused in involuntary admiration of this black giant, famed on the wharves for his strength, sweeping down upon them, a smile upon his face, his eyes lit up with a rapt expression which seemed to take him out of mortal ken. This impression was heightened by his apparent immunity from the shower of lead which less susceptible persons had continued to pour at him.
>
> Armed with a huge bowie-knife, a relic of the civil war, which he carried on his person for many years for a definite purpose, and which he had kept sharpened to a razor edge, he reached the line of the crowd. All but the bravest shrank back. Like a wedge he dashed through the mob, which parted instinctively before him, and all oblivious of the rain of lead which fell upon him, reached the point where Captain McBane, the bravest man in the party, stood waiting to meet him. A pistol-flame flashed in his face, but he went on, and raising his powerful right arm, buried his knife to the hilt in the heart of his enemy. (309)

Conjured—then penned—from Chesnutt's imaginary, just before the tragic ending befalls him, Green flings off the veil and flashes his resplendent potential as an epic figure at this moment. A simple militant and empire-builder he is not, for he neither kills indiscriminately nor wields the weapons—guns—calculated to do so, his violence is reasonably tailored for a specific end. He is armed with the American equivalent of a sword, the bowie-knife, through which he is fated to mete out the justice the Civil War represented only symbolically. As only an epic or epic-like figure can, Green uses his size, strength, determination, speed, and folk constitution to "sweep" through destruction toward his destiny.

Clearly, Green has been transfigured, but so has McBane. Having once said that "[o]ne white man can chase a hundred of 'em. I've managed five hundred at a time," and called "Mr. White Man" by Green (250, 302), McBane's confrontation with his lynching victim's survivor brings the bodies Chesnutt places in *Marrow* into sharp focus: McBane is the white epic body to Green's black epic corollary. McBane, as Mr. White Man, is Chesnutt's allegorycal heart of the white heroic, while Green is the allegorycal emblem of the green potential residing within the woolly headed beast implied by white supremacist ideology. Their final confrontation occurs with all the polarities—white is always Good and supreme, black always

Bad and inferior—reversed, and results in a Pyrrhic victory that collapses into a frightful reality: Green defeats McBane, the embodiment of Achilles unleashed, dashing past his flashing pistol flame, the modern version of Bronze-Age swords, and "buried his knife" in the dark "heart" of white supremacy embodied by McBane, politically incorporated by Wellington/Wilmington, and projected globally by the Duke of Wellington's British Empire.

McBane's earlier display of "cool and collected" behavior, after he has defeated Tom Delamere, an incompetent aristocrat who tried to cheat him at cards, and statements to Tom—"I'll give you your revenge another time" and "Luck is against you to-night" (156–57)—serve Chesnutt's strategy of subtly constructing an ironic spyglass through which he objectively judges Wellington, particularly his heroics at the Battle of Assaye. Sir Colin Campbell may have said, "I never saw a man so cool and collected as he was the whole time," but he appended to it a critical proviso: "though I can assure you, till our troops got the order to advance the fate of the day seemed doubtful; and if the numerous cavalry of the enemy had done their duty I hardly think it possible we could have succeeded" (Wellington 184–87). In other words, Campbell suggests that notwithstanding his suave battle demeanor, Wellington's heroism would not have saved them from his vainglorious, risky gamble, but the sheer ineptitude of the Maratha cavalry won the day.

All of this evidence together constitutes an important footnote: Chesnutt attributes Wellesley's success at the Battle of Assaye, his military career, and the rise of the British Empire to historical happenstance in which his gamble paid dividends.[57] For McBane, "revenge" and "luck," God and justice, happen to be against him when he faces a truly competent and heroic opponent; the same is true for Dr. Miller, whose future ambitions, predicated on his wife and child and commitment to succeeding in Wellington's troubled social structure, encounter the deadly hand of Fate. Though the theological implications are beyond the scope of this analysis, suffice it to say that Chesnutt's strategy of foregrounding chance not only rebuffs mainstream American Christianity, which is predicated on the Protestant work ethic, self-determination, and God's fateful blessings of the Republic, but reveals his own distance from this form of Christianity, at the least.

In light of the argument made thus far, that McBane is the convergence of Homeric performance and vegetal rejuvenation, Green, more than any other character, deserves approbation. However, the reality is one in which anti-African marrow provides the infrastructure for the white and black communities, so he is circumscribed as the epic trickster and cannot concretize and fully realize his epic potential. His MOS-epic resemblance gives way to his fate as the black Hector, for "the crowd dashed forward to wreak vengeance on his dead body" (*Marrow* 309). Naturally, although it occurs postmortem, Green's body and his epic potential are lynched in a culminating performance, and the epic event, a racial riot, peters out once its mission has been accomplished.

Hence, McBane's and Green's deaths bring closure to the violence and the epic cycle. In the traditional African epic performances, when the epic conflict has been resolved, the epic hero washes his face of the violence and rejoins the restored community and land. But at the end of *Marrow*, neither of these conditions has been met. Since Green represents the epic potential, yet he is dead, then where does this *nyama* go if the task of transforming the black body-politic is unfinished? In yet another ironic twist which resuscitates the Millers, Chesnutt transforms them. He endows them, by virtue of Green, with epic potential.

CONCLUSION

Notwithstanding the foregoing argument, it is easy to overlook or de-emphasize Green's potentiality, for when the epic tension ends, the best and last chance to prevent it by force, Green, has been killed and disembodied. According to the traditional line of reasoning advanced by many critics, Dr. Miller and his ideals are alive, so Chesnutt must have considered Green's radical, militant approach to be a dead end. But Dr. Miller's ideal of following the Protestant work ethic into Wellington tradition, which his son embodies, also meets a generational dead end. Dr. Miller escapes Green's tragic life and terrible death, but tragedy bedevils him, too, since his son dies as a result of a stray bullet. Though he blames Major Carteret, "fiat justitia," Dr. Miller is substantially at fault as well. His desperate search for his wife and child, the twilight of his life, and three-time rejection of Green, Chesnutt suggests, are symbolic of his constant deferral, equivocation, and inaction in light of a growing crisis.

Confronted with the untenable dilemma of selecting between Green's militancy and Dr. Miller's compromises, some scholars turn to Janet Miller.[58] Dr. Miller's wife does show remarkable magnanimity in the end, but this position is not reached until the Millers, in effect, have been reduced to Green's existential position because they suffer a loss so tragic that it rends their veil of security and exposes them, personally, to the brute face of injustice. The death of their son, whose unnamed status brings into sharp focus the tenuous future they were nurturing, awakens their bodies to the deeper emotions, urgency, and sense of injustice Green unsuccessfully tried to convey to Dr. Miller. Shocked out of their twilight, the total reality of tradition has finally and fatally impressed itself upon the Millers. This explains why Janet Miller now refuses that which she coveted for so long: a sister's love, legal privileges, and Wellington's traditions.

But even the Millers' dawning awareness of the insidiousness of the white body of tradition suggests how Chesnutt uses Green. Although he is disembodied, his death as a transfigured epic figure opens up the additional allegorycal space Chesnutt needs to reshape the marrow of the black body implied by tradition. The Millers, in the person of Dr. Miller, who was incapable and unwilling to assume a more heroic stature, assume some of the potential Green created and the death of their son forced upon them. The old new Negro he was dies along with his son, and a newer, greener, more African new Negro rises to replace the old. At the same time, the great tragedy threatening the Carterets has diminished their bodies and made them face the Other/ing consequences of their tradition. The "horror of the situation" confronts Major Carteret "at Miller's house,—for a moment the veil of race prejudice was rent in twain, and he saw things as they were, in their correct proportions and relations—saw clearly and convincingly that he had no standing here" (321). The violence, horror, and epic agony of Achilles unleashed have come full circle and threaten their future in the form of their son, Theodore Felix Carteret. The diminution of the Carterets-body, concomitant with the ennobling of the Millers-body, is necessary to help reinforce racial equality, per force of justice.

Thus, like the commanding, epic figure Green represented, the Millers now possess some of his moral/personal stature. *Major* Carteret shrinks from Dr. Miller's censure and gaze, "bowing mechanically, as though to Fate rather than the physician"; Olivia Carteret throws "herself at his feet,—at the feet of a negro, this proud white woman,—and was clasping his knees wildly" (321, 324);[59] but Chesnutt makes explicit the reconfiguration of bodies as the two sisters face one another with Dr. Miller looking upon them:

> The two women stood confronting each other across the body of the dead child, mute witness of this first meeting between two children of the same father. Standing thus face to face, each under the stress of the deepest emotions, the resemblance between them was even more striking than it had seemed to Miller when he had admitted Mrs. Carteret to the house. But Death, the great leveler, striking upon one hand and threatening upon the other, had wrought a marvelous transformation in the bearing of the two women. The sad-eyed Janet towered erect, with menacing aspect, like an avenging goddess. The other, whose pride had been her life, stood in the attitude of a trembling suppliant. (325–26)

No longer the aspiring, dusky shadows of the Carterets, the Millers now "towered erect," standing in "marvelous transformation" as equals who can make commands, issue judgments, and rebuff entreaties when morally justified, and yet show leniency for "a trembling suppliant" whom they recognize as an equal, despite the suppliant's previous transgressions.

But why not make Janet Miller an "avenging" *angel*? The answer reveals Chesnutt's final allegorycal strategy of deepening time and mythology. Contra M.A. Dwight's mythology, in which she wrote that ancient Greek "suppliants . . . stood under the protection of the gods," Chesnutt invokes an ancient Egyptian goddess instead. While Dwight discusses how ancient Greeks' "system of morals was on the whole deduced from the fear of the gods" (36),

Chesnutt redirects attention away from the behavior of the Greek pantheon and toward the origins of Greek fertility rites Herodotus called "mysteries." Dwight, following this lead, cites the ancient goddess Ceres, who "had long wandered over the earth before she was received at Eleusis, and erected there her sanctuary. Her secret rites at the Thesmophoria, according to the account of Herodotus, were first introduced by Danaüs, who brought them from Egypt to the Peloponnesus." Chesnutt demonstrates close reading of Dwight's irony—underappreciated, Ceres "wandered" until the Greeks "received" her and she gladly established a "sanctuary" whose rites "exhibited the superiority of civilized over savage life," specifically Greek agency over Egypt's—by sifting through her Eurocentric "interpretations of the sacred traditions" to recover the allegorycal essence: an "instructress in agriculture," Ceres "gave instructions respecting a future life and its nature" (38–39).

This Ceres, known to the Greeks as Demeter, was Isis, ancient Egypt's matron goddess of mothers, healing, and deep compassion who was widely worshipped and beloved; often seen suckling a child, some consider her the source for the Virgin Mary and infant Jesus iconography. More important to *Marrow*, when Isis' husband was killed and his body torn asunder and spread, she recovered the pieces and resurrected him. The African epic spirit is completed by Isis, channeled through Janet Miller thanks to the sacrifice of Green, the spirit of this conjuring not being "cool and collected" in the acquisitive, imperialistic forms of Hilton, Wellington, and tradition, but in the most ancient, *cool* green life-force.

Although Green is the Other-self that gives dimension to an overly rational, vacillating, and compromised Dr. Miller, both are needed for the new body Chesnutt envisions. Green's death makes Miller, and thus the body of African Americans, more commanding and epical in a jurisdiction rooted in a Homeric landscape; Dr. Miller adds the sensibility, intelligence, ambition, and social acceptability Green lacks in a democratic, civilized one. The thin veil between the surreality of Wilmington and Chesnutt's fictional reality of Wellington, both of which exist in a landscape mapped by a Homeric cartography centuries old, invites the reader on the quest to reconstruct the body-politic. The prominent Green and Miller families of Wilmington match Green and Dr. Miller of Wellington, the Josh Green of Wilmington, a coal and wood worker who was a business and property owner recognized as an upstanding citizen,[60] equaled and eclipsed by the epical accomplishments of Josh Green of Wellington.

By effecting these parallels, Chesnutt accomplishes multiple social purposes related to the elevation of Josh Green from stevedore status. First, he argues for the legitimacy of epic potential, when it has meritorious cause, and the propriety of a democracy capable of more fully assessing a body for its merit. Second, he uses his mastery of narrative and analysis of human subjects to specifically make Wilmington an allegorycal case study for how the actual Green and Miller families, and thus all Talented Tenth

African Americans, might need to reconceptualize their own bodies. Third, he proves the epic potential of Green, a gesture at once capable of refuting the Secret Nine's/Big Three's white supremacy, socioeconomic stratification represented by Dr. Miller's stereotypical regard for working-class blacks like Green, and the deep and virulent anti-African sentiment the vast majority of African Americans would feel. Chesnutt's strategy of privileging Hilton's 1662 account as the founding narrative for Carolina instead of the widely disseminated and easily available 1663 narrative must be revisited relative to Green. "Green," among other significations, fixes its historical referent to the 1662 voyage, the previously mentioned Lucas Enoch Greenlese and John Green, both signatories of that account and shipmen aboard the *Adventure*. Josh Green's epic potential unfolds through Chesnutt's construction of a parodic allegorye that effects a near-total reversal: Green, son of a "silly Creature," is the epical figure whose "adventure" is indispensable to the founding of a new body-politic. Finally, but perhaps most importantly, Chesnutt intuitively taps the cautionary aesthetic of the epic, realizing that its transgressiveness, if made the natural law underlying tradition, will lead to excesses that distort all "proportions and relations" of the body. Having received a personal, tragic lesson about the root-calling of the Hippocratic oath from Green, who defended the hospital he abandoned, Dr. Miller is prepared to go forward and treat the marrow of the Wellington body-politic as the novel closes.

Thus, the Miller versus Green dilemma, conflict is a nonesuch, for if a new African-American body is Chesnutt's goal, then the division between them is a red herring. Since Chesnutt seeks to eliminate the entire black body-politic—middle, lower, and underclass, as well as new Negro and pre-modern African—and uplift it into true human status, neither the Millers nor Green is *the* protagonist, for each is just "one of the novel's protagonists" (Nowatzki 65). Chesnutt's new African-American body replaces them, even though it has a near-white bourgeois face and professional training. This new body is now rooted in a more heroic, epic character making it worthy to the larger society—black folk as well as white—as an equal representative who no longer needs to pass or perform in the supreme, urgent, and epical task of healing the Republic.

5   From Dust to Dust to . . . Water?
Native Son, the American Epic, and the Ecological Implications of Wright's Blues-Print

Negro folklore contains, in a measure that puts to shame more delib-
erate forms of Negro expression, the collective sense of Negro life in
America. Let those who shy at the nationalist implications of Negro
life look at this body of folklore, living and powerful, which rose out
of a unified sense of a common life and a common fate. Here are those
vital beginnings of a recognition of value in life as it is *lived*.
>   —Richard Wright, "Blueprint for Negro Writing" (1937)

Your Honor, consider the mere physical aspect of our civilization.
How alluring, how dazzling it is! How it excites the senses! How
it seems to dangle within easy reach of everyone the fulfillment of
happiness! How constantly and overwhelmingly the advertisements,
radios, newspapers and movies play upon us!
>   —Boris A. Max, *Native Son* (1940)

Tribal and indigenous peoples' . . . lifestyles can offer modern societies many lessons in the management of resources in complex forests,
mountain and dryland ecosystems.
   These communities are the repositories of vast accumulations of
traditional knowledge and experience that link humanity with its
ancient origins. Their disappearance is a loss for the larger society,
which could learn a great deal from their traditional skills in sustainably managing very complex ecological systems.
>   —[UN] World Commission on Environment and Development,
>   *Our Common Future* (1987)

INTRODUCTION

For hundred of years up until the late summer of 2005, New Orleans
occupied a unique place in the American imaginary. It was jazz, Mardi
Gras, carnival, the Big Easy—a mecca for tourists, college students, and
music afficionados who wanted to experience the birth place of jazz and

blues. Almost all of this changed in a matter of hours on August 29, 2005, when, at approximately 6:10 a.m., Katrina, a category 3 hurricane with sustained winds equaling or exceeding 125 mph, moved from the waters of the Gulf Coast into the urban spaces of New Orleans. Katrina changed this centuries-old culture in days, if not hours: one thousand people were dead and two-thirds of the city population gone. Another unspeakable tragedy occurred, too, for 320 million trees were destroyed, their destruction perhaps releasing 367 million tons of carbon dioxide—an amount produced by the entire forest ecosystem in the United States in one year (Chambers et al. 318)—into the atmosphere. This reinforced the greenhouse effect which had, scientists and eco-activists like Van Jones—former White House Council on Environmental Quality in the Barack H. Obama Administration and author of the best-selling *The Green Collar Economy* (2008)—widely believe, already "supercharged" (23) the storm and, thus, significantly contributed to the scale of destruction.[1] Located in the eye of this hurricane were Katrina's New Orleans folk, survivors and victims who were disproportionately poor, black native daughters and sons; many of them were scattered to the four corners of the nation into what some have called the Hurricane Katrina Diaspora.

While Americans have moved before en masse, the uniqueness of this exodus re-wrote the political cartography. The 2008 election of Barack H. Obama confirms this. When Hurricane Katrina deluged New Orleans, it created a perfect storm of human and natural disasters—sharecropper-like existence for many blacks in New Orleans, global warming, inadequate government responses at all levels, white supremacists killing desperate blacks—that sank George W. Bush, Jr.'s administration. "Politically, it was the final nail in the coffin," opined Dan Bartlett, White House communications director and presidential counselor (Murphy and Purdum 155). This true story, an horrific account apt for cinematic apocalypses, is but one more fragment characterizing the African-American experience, which is full of exoduses like the one Katrina caused. As Theophus H. Smith observes, since the colonial era Exodus has served as a defining trope that "recurs with prophetic force in the figural context of the earliest African American experience of a biblical Wilderness" (102). This old American story, featuring grand historic homes, racial traditions, and the elements unleashed in a vast metropolis, was Bigger Thomas' story in Richard Wright's *Native Son* (1940). The core of Wright's oeuvre—*Uncle Tom's Children* (1938), "Blueprint for Negro Writing" (1937), *Native Son*, "How 'Bigger' Was Born" (1940), and *Black Boy* (1945)—is a form of "Exodus," or diaspora, literature. After rising up out of neo-slavery in the sharecropping South, blacks found themselves pushed by southern terrorism into an exodus northward that ended in the immense ghettoes of the urban North. Here they confronted a range of existential difficulties: inter- and intraracial hostility and a bewildering, fast-moving northern culture full of competition and rapid, undirected development—progress—that had, on a larger scale, led to the Great War.

Wright's literature, a snapshot of his own life narrative, not only arose out of this exodus, but reflects an ecological sensitivity heretofore never explored. The full scale of Wright's retrospective on the exodus is obscured by his potent anti-racial narrative, the relationship between Wright and the ecological dimensions of migrations to the Great Plains—epitomized by the 1930s Dust Bowl he personally experienced—veiled by the protest litera-ture label attached to Wright by his supporters and fierce detractors.

Spurred on by Hurricane Katrina, the national security threat of global warming led First World governments to begin military planning for what military expert Gwynne Dyer calls "climate wars": rising seas, food and water shortages, mass exoduses on a global scale, and global chaos caused by "failed and failing states, and very probably internal and international wars" (Dyer xii–xiii, 3–27). This climate—the Hurricane Katrina disaster, the rise of President Obama and his post-racial success, the interrelated twin crises presented by Wall Street and global warming, and the frightful prospect of climate wars—forces us to reconsider Dyer's assessment: since no one could have seen these developments, which are the cumulative effect of all "our actions," he maintains, "nobody is to blame for the crisis that looms over us" (44). How does one evaluate Dwyer's assessment and the scale of the climatic "crisis that looms over us" when there are so many variables and we do not have the benefit of hindsight? Given Wright's pro-lific hand and the encyclopedic range of his fiction, second sight and epic performance aesthetics might offer a possibility. While assaying contempo-rary culture is fraught with dangers because we can see it, at best, through a veil darkly, past "theories"—grounded in anthropological and historical data—are available that speak to human nature from time immemorial.

Wright uses his oeuvre, particularly the large scale of *Native Son*, to foreground the absence of folk sense. Although Wright distanced himself from black authors and sociology informed his aesthetic, his social sci-ence is nevertheless grounded in a deep vernacular antecedent. The epic-informed vernacular aesthetic and cultural phenomenon Wright deployed is the "bad man," a figure scholars have traced to an African provenance.[2] Attention should be given here to Josh Green of Chesnutt's *Marrow* and the fortuitous significance of his name relative to *Native Son*, which links past slavery and present racism to the possibility of a gothic future.[3]

If Green is the first "bad man" figure to have a substantive presence in a work of fiction, with ramifications for the extant middle-class ethos (Bryant 27–28), then Wright advances this aesthetic and the lower-class stratum he represents by making him the protagonist. While Josh Green is the forerunner of Bigger Thomas, who is an urban rendering of the trickster and "bad man"/"nigger" (Baker, *Long Black Song* 127, 133, 137), Wright's departure from a black middle-class center is a significant aesthetic and sociopolitical maneuver (Reilly 37). Whereas Green and Dr. Miller both symbolically represent the African-American body Chesnutt attempts to render epical and equal in a violently epic and racist America, Bigger, the lowest common denominator, becomes the body and protagonist.

Though *Native Son* focuses on the bottom of the socioeconomic stratum, Wright tries to speak for everyone, and maybe for all times. He does so by fashioning an adventure story, driven by encyclopedic forces both subjective and objective, and by appropriating tropes from some of the world's earliest literature to ironize the sociopolitical moment. Bigger, the bad man and epic trickster, represents both the fusion of low folk and high epic culture into one. Ross Pudaloff prefaces this very point when he speaks of Wright's aesthetic, which disrupts the "conventional distinction between high art and popular art." Starting with modernist texts such as Gertrude Stein's "Melanctha" and the influence of cinema on literature,[4] Pudaloff maintains, Wright incorporated mass culture (film, newspaper, pulp fiction) to make *Native Son* part of "the world of Superman and tough guys, of popular fantasies of omnipotence" (5–15).[5] Elizabeth Schultz, following Robert A. Bone's lead in his landmark study of *The Negro Novel in America* (1958), centered Wright's use of the epic in her comparative reading of *Native Son* and Herman Melville's *Moby-Dick*. Wright, Schultz argues, "rewrites Melville's epic, parodying or intensifying—signifying on—well-known characters, images, and episodes from *Moby-Dick*, to create an original African-American epic with a new kind of hero, one who, in facing American racism, is challenged as profoundly as any previous epic hero" ("Power" 641). Even with readings like Schultz's, significant space remains to excavate the nonliterary epic aesthetic informing American literature and culture. With the epic habitus as the unit of analysis, *Native Son* is a lens for productively exploring the broader sociocultural conditions far too encyclopedic for any one novel to express. Specifically, traces of the ancient epic antecedents may be teased out and read in conjunction with other literary (epic, folk), political, and cultural elements.[6]

African and European epic traditions both preside over the story as it unfolds in the urban heartland of America. In this epic trickster narrative, race drives Bigger, but Wright reveals the class economy of capitalism as imperialists' latent tool. Indeed, as *Native Son* unfolds, the presence of Homeric mythology and tropes makes Wright's perspective overwhelmingly evident: the modern understanding of ancient Greek epics and capitalism share a radical economy and habitus—epical realism—based on acquisition, possibility, and epic-oriented ontology uprooted from an organic folk context. Although no study indicates that Wright specifically used Homer, the nature of the American epic habitus reflected in literature and the broader culture grounds this reading.[7] When Wright distanced himself from Horatio Alger's fiction "and the warm, Sunday-school glow that bathes his heroes [in] the glow of the dream and its irrational logic" (Wright, "American" 181), he did not only challenge the fetishized myth of American possibility. Instead, George E. Kent argues (1969), Wright foregrounds a folk-centered "cosmic self" who is struggling with the "dominant forms of Western culture," a strategy which "establishes the myth of the heritage of Man, Western Man, as counterpoint to the disinherited condition of Bigger" (323, 324, 328, 336, 339).[8]

While many scholars have addressed the heroic aesthetic—and have even addressed the epic impulse—in *Native Son*, none of them has taken a comparative approach which specifically relates its African and European/American epic aesthetics to one another. Homer's *Iliad* and *Odyssey* set the founding drama Bigger confronts as Wright foregrounds running, sport, siren song, and other Homeric tropes that quicken the urban modernity around him.

At the outset of *Native Son*, Bigger exemplifies the earliest phase of the epic trickster, for he is a dozens-speaking signifier struggling for survival. Faced by a formidable race/class/gender bar, an eighth-grade education, and status as a repeat offender who foreshadows contemporary inner-city gang members, Bigger has little to motivate him. Thus, the loitering that characterizes his daily routine marks him as a late-1930s form of the trickster-prop and bad man. The opening fight of the novel, the warfare between "black boy" Bigger and the "huge black rat" stages this: on the one hand, it establishes an easy parallel, for both are tricksters—Bigger as trickster-prop and the rat as the quintessential urban-jungle trickster—caged together and intent on surviving at all costs; on the other hand, and more significantly, Bigger is an as-yet-dormant epic trickster and all-too-human contest-hero representing the very antithesis of the rat's limited potential and its "huge," vicious will. The rat is an huge, monstrous incarnation of the inhuman terrors comprising Bigger's understanding of the real-world forces intent on continuously reenacting a traumatic event with him as the prop upon which it is restaged. The pathology here is two-fold, for it both defines the individual trauma (Bigger is analogous to a vicious rat) and the pathology of the given society or social context responsible for it. Bigger is both pathological in the clinical denotation of the word and, from Wright's purview, a trickster signifying against normative institutional sources and the national pathology as his adventure unfolds. As trickster-prop and epic trickster then, Bigger corresponds to the epic journey he undertakes as a bad man moving through the epical realism and gothic horrors Chicago and the nation harbor.[9]

GREAT MIGRATION: INTO THE WORLD OF THE FATHERS . . . AND MOTHERS

Wright uses Chicago, the fast-paced metropole sounding the nation's heartland, as the backdrop for his exploration of the American epic habitus.[10] As one of the early and primary sites of the Great Migration,[11] it was a city on the run both as a destination-of-choice for new immigrants and as one of the central hubs of economic expansion and opportunity. By using Chicago as the *situs*, specifically its Black Metropolis, Wright invokes the urban core of the American Dream mythos and the encyclopedic cultural artifacts it signifies. Chicago, a cityscape full of the "sharp precision of the world of steel and stone" (*NS* 16), represents the modern, epic incarnation of possibility. What Bigger faces, as Bakhtin opined, speaking of the epic, was the world of the Fathers. Bigger's Chicago represents the congruence of epic and capitalism, filled with possibility and democracy, transgressiveness and epic excess.

A standard Marxian reading reveals Chicago to be a microcosm of the larger global, imperialistic context working beneath the surface. But Wright makes a significant departure, for he places Bigger in a position such that the world of the Fathers—the patriarchy—is no different, and potentially subordinate to, the world of the mothers. For the racial subaltern, the diachronic is comprised of two synergistic temporalities: ancient myth channeled by male or female desires and a present reality fixed in optic whiteness and its coolly rational privileges.

The ultimate emblem of female power in the traditional epic, the *badenya*-force Cartwright calls imperial mother-wit, has its parallel in the liberal Mrs. Dalton. It is not Mr. Henry Dalton who is the capitalistic force, but Mrs. Dalton's wealth which financed his successful business endeavors (*Native Son* 56; subsequently cited as *NS*). Beyond this, her whiteness and sex, of course, automatically denote the metaphysical—the off- and outer-limits—to Bigger and the general class of black males. The numinous association arises because of the longstanding gyneolatry holding aloft white femininity as saintly, if not divine. Bigger knows this, intuitively, but the threat is so far beyond his reckoning as to present, in Burkian terms, a sublime terror. Thus, more than his awareness of and trepidation about interracial rape, the one crime demanding lynch justice, the taboo of violating such purity is so absolute that Bigger *over*reacts to the idea.

Wright makes Mrs. Dalton, in her ghostly omnipresence, less than St. Mary, whom many white men held to be the ultimate icon of feminine purity. While she, arguably, shares this iconographic role with her daughter Mary, Wright makes Mrs. Dalton's embodiment of a Hebraic epic equally hellenic. E.V. Rieu's introduction to his 1946 translation of the *Odyssey* is useful here, for he says Pallas Athene "commands our attention" as the central Greek divinity in the story. More specifically, "she dominates the *Odyssey*," especially in the way Homer's key characters exercise "the mother-wit which she personifies." Finally, Rieu characterizes "her as a tall and beautiful woman, *with brilliant eyes, clad in a white robe*" (16–17; italics mine). This description of Athene correlates with Mrs. Dalton, whom Wright limits to flowing white robes.[12] Blind she may be—the brilliance of such blind eyes lending themselves to easy irony, her kindness notwithstanding—but Bigger feels the omniscience of her mother-wit with results equally liberating and catastrophic: his odyssey begins in earnest.

Here, Wright demonstrates his insight and literary skill, which enable him to fuse sociology and ancient epic in the persona of Bigger: like the ancient Greek and African epic heroes whose fates are predetermined, he accidentally suffocates Mary despite his own intentions. Unlike the epic heroes, Bigger's initial fearful reaction is very human and expected; but soon enough Bigger would be more as the series of events initiating his second epic trickster phase bring him to the color/battle-line. Instead of running in retreat after he crosses the color-line, Bigger's ideals of racial justice send him running to do battle. In the initial, heady moments of his epic incipience, Bigger thinks, as a classical epic hero would, nothing is impossible. For example, Bigger uses his own wit and signifying, in the form of lying and playing simple to Britain, the Dalton's private investigator. He does the same to the press, making sport of them by cloaking himself in the presupposed intellectual inferiority of his race (*NS* 152–72, 190–215).

However, Bigger soon faces the reality of Chicago's epic scale and the true and terrible possibility it harbors. When a reporter discovers Mary's remains and Bigger flees, the press disseminates his story and face almost as soon as he starts running, indicating there would be "a thousand white policemen" mobilized just to find him. But even worse than Mary's alleged murder, her supposed rape, reported by the major newspapers, sets off a host of events with encyclopedic repercussions: Bigger is objectified and magnified as "the Negro" while police and a volunteer army 3,000 strong are mobilized to search the Black Belt. Meanwhile, a "white heat" of indignation and fear goes through the city as an army of black male suspects is rounded up and black men and women are fired from their jobs. At the same time, Mayor Ditz makes inflammatory radio broadcasts, among other things.[13] The epic chase plays itself out in the larger-than-life newspaper photos and headlines of the *Chicago Tribune* and *Times*, which are "large," "tall," and "black," respectively (*NS* 224, 243–44, 255).

Thus, in Wright's novel, in which muscularity and swift-tongued signifying share narrative space, running becomes the ultimate trope. It functions both figuratively and literally, pivoting and jumping between them: Bigger, Wright suggests, has been running a race, and *running race*, ever since he was born; now, specifically following his rebirth, someone is actually chasing him—and gaining—with Death.

In addition to canvassing Chicago's epic performance, Bigger-*qua-flâneur* also runs deeper into the black community. The running sounds the Black Belt's economic instability—stemming from racism acting in tandem with the Daltons' corporate power—and ideological conflicts. This occurs when Bigger overhears two men, Jim and Jack, debating whether, as Jim maintains, it can be assumed that Bigger is guilty because he is black and simply will not act right. Here, *Native Son* ventriloquises Dr. Miller's "wife and child" mantra from *Marrow*: Jim says he will not fight because, "Ah gotta family. Ah gotta wife 'n' baby" (*NS* 250–51).

Jim voices the pragmatist role, *viz.*, we should get along because there are too many of them, whereas Jack ventriloquizes Josh Green's defiance: "'Ah don' care whut yuh say,' Jack says. 'Ah'd die 'fo' Ah'd let 'em scare me inter tellin' on tha' man. Ah tell yuh, Ah'd die firs'!'" (*NS* 252).[14] In other words, this aside, which delves into conflict at the very hearth of intraracial domesticity, arrays yet another army against Bigger because many blacks think like Jim.

Pinioned between two or more belligerent hosts, Bigger has to work doubly hard just to keep himself away from his fellow ethnic pursuers. But Wright makes this chase nothing in comparison to Bigger's efforts to stay ahead of Chicago's white host. Chicago's "army," quickened by the epic, grows magically, and moves almost as quickly as the action rapidly approaches the climactic battle. Wright actually flattens the objective reality behind the story, which imbues it with Homeric coincidence and immanence even as Bigger's subjective reality—his perception of the threat—reads all too realistically. No sooner than the press has reported, and Bigger has read, about the existence of an army 8,000 strong than it is there, impossibly fast. Given the photographs and headlines, and the subsequent swelling of the army arrayed against him, Wright argues that Bigger's is the face that launched 8,000 men, which surround him with police sirens, cars, and search lights. With this swift-footed army's feet sounding like thunder running up the stairs and the "high, shrill note" of the siren driving Bigger mad, he hopes for divine inspiration to do the right thing and die with honor (*NS* 256–59).

As the foregoing discussion indicates, it is obvious, following Bigger's capture at the end of Book Two ("Flight") and with him facing Book Three ("Fate"), that the Homeric epics inform *Native Son* to no small degree. Wright refracts Homeric tropes into realistic events he forces readers to juxtapose against the urban landscape of modern Chicago. In spite of Wright's obvious adaptation of an epical folk story whose genealogy clearly predates the advent of modern sociology and protest literature, his aesthetic and characters have often been dismissed as static sociological objects. However, just as Houston Baker understood that Wright "had been immersed in the culture of the black American folk" (*Long Black Song* 124), Eugene E. Miller argues that what Wright "osmotically" received from black folklore, which informs black southern theology, were "Epic Laws of Folk Narrative" rooted in "rigid stylization," a "severe economy" of detail, and hence a "flatness" (34, 40–41).[15]

Many of Wright's detractors, including leading black critics, are complicit in reducing his artistry and, more tragically, his sense of agency and knowledge of folk cultures. While Zora Neale Hurston is noteworthy for her objection to *Uncle Tom's Children* as too masculine and violent,[16] Ellison's and Baldwin's critiques establish an important benchmark. In "Everybody's Protest Novel" (1949), James Baldwin poignantly critiqued Wright's most famous character:

In *Native Son*, Bigger Thomas stands on a Chicago street corner
watching airplanes flown by white men racing against the sun and
'Goddamn' he says, the bitterness bubbling up like blood, remember-
ing a million indignities, the terrible, rat-infested house, the humili-
ation of home-relief, the intense, aimless, ugly bickering, hating it;
hatred smoulders through these pages like sulphur fire. All of Bigger's
life is controlled, defined by his hatred and his fear. And later, his fear
drives him to murder and his hatred to rape; he dies, having come,
through this violence, we are told, for the first time, to a kind of life,
having for the first time redeemed his manhood. Below the surface of
this novel there lies, as it seems to me, a continuation, a complement
of that monstrous legend it was written to destroy. Bigger is Uncle
Tom's descendant, flesh of his flesh. (1704)

Bigger and Uncle Tom, Baldwin suggests, rest upon the principles of martyrdom, lack of agency, and ultimately a self-inflicted fatalism. The irony
of Baldwin's protest designation is that it further strips away agency—one
protests only because one has no, or virtually no, agency. Is this Bigger
Thomas? One of the most vivid episodes in *Native Son* occurs in Bigger's jail cell when he rejects God, represented by the Rev. Hammond,
a black minister, his wailing family, morose friends, and, most importantly, their "pity" for him. "Forget me, Ma," he intones three times as he
recoils from—denies—their pity. Bigger literally slams his cell door into
Rev. Hammond's face, knocking him out of the cell, and throws away the
cross the minister had left. Later, Bigger's life is summed up by Mr. Boris
A. Max, Bigger's Communist Party defense attorney, as one of "rugged
individualism" and determination—"In him and men like him is what was
in our forefathers when they first came to these strange shores hundreds of
years ago" (*NS* 299, 339–40, 393).

Baldwin's fallacy of collapsing Bigger's agency and Wright's perspective into protest is understandable, from a strict modernist perspective. But
just as the traditional epic hero depends on the collective whose culture
embodies the epic figure, the same obtains in this case: Bigger is a "native
son," a black "hero in the garden" city of Chicago[17] who swells from justified racial angst and protest; in this capacity he is also a metonym for the
desires of the majority culture. In short, by collapsing our focus into Bigger and his heinous deeds as a member of the black youth toast-culture of
1930s urban America, admittedly a subculture charged with epic badness,
Baldwin obscures the exponentially greater danger of the American desire/
hunger he represents.

For these reasons, Anthony Dawahare, in his examination of Wright's
Depression-era urban novels, moves away from the protest novel designation. Based on Wright's critique of nationalism and imperialism, fascism
in particular, Dawahare argues that Bigger is not meant to be a hero, but
a representative figure imbued with pro-nationalistic, fascist (pro-Hitler)

"infantile desires" and "male fantasies." Because of racism and capitalism, he and other young males are caught in an Oedipal paradox forcing them to hate the father and yet replace him to restore their own masculinity (451–52, 462–64). After noting Wright's prolific, insightful work on the topic of nationalism from 1937 to 1941, Dawahare stakes his claim:

> Remarkably, Wright's literary treatment of nationalism remains avant-garde since he reveals what many contemporary theorists have yet to disclose: a complex insight into the deep psychology of nationalism. . . . For Wright, the danger posed by nationalism was its *unconscious* appeal to the psyches of male workers. His Depression Era works suggests that, since all male workers are raised in a patriarchal society, their feelings of powerlessness can evoke feelings of emasculation. . . . Wright's concern is that black working-class men are apt to heed the call of black nationalists, precisely because they promise a reclamation of manhood and the goal of disposing of the white father—namely, the acquisition of the mother-land. (451–52)

Bigger and Wright's urban characters, in short, must not be reduced to sentimental protest-caricatures: they are already fully capable of actualizing their hungers and desires in ways that ought to be "heed[ed]." Dawahare focuses on Bigger's "dangerous" political (i.e., fascist, imperialistic) capacities as an urban male severed from labor potential associated with the folk's agrarian existence.

As important as this is, Dawahare's frame is also too reductive, for the folk is far more extensive than yeoman farmers' reconnection to the land and their agricultural labor, their blues-singing prowess, or a sentimental, "infantile" adherence to magic and dark belief in witchcraft. Wright's folkloric gesture is not toward knowledge of lore in the form of trickster tales and discrete, quantifiable formulations, but toward a healing cosmology rooted in a different way of seeing the body.

Indeed, beyond the blues, trickster tales, proverbs, spirituals, dancing, and the like, the folk encompasses a way of being in and reading the world, and coexisting with it. It is also the performance of heroic epics and consideration of the ecological ramifications that go along with them. Useful here is the genre theory of Wai Chee Dimock, articulated in *Through Other Continents: American Literature across Deep Time* (2006), which establishes a non-Western foundation set in ancient notions of bodies in performance and uses a "different ontology of time." Dimock's contrapositive to the mask of modernity draws upon notions of syncretism, indeed generic "kinship," to escape the "sovereign state" and the extension of that sovereignty into the literature expressing its founding myths.

Dimock, ecologically sensitive to the "planet's multitudinous life," which is inclusive of human relations, offers "deep time" as a corrective. She defines it as a *"longue durée,"* or "scale enlargement," history not as modern Western linearity, but as "measured in centuries this time: the history of the long, even of the very long time span, of the *longue durée*." Dimock's vision of temporal flows across deep time—which posits the influence of the *Epic of Gilgamesh* on Homer's artistry and Aristotle's *Poetics*, meant to seal off the foreign lexicon (3–4, 82–88)—enjoins literary critics concerned with epic and novel to look beyond the modern/ist critiques.

Dimock's science-to-fiction-to-humanity shift parallels Wright's aesthetic. "I wanted to reveal the vast physical and spiritual ravages of Negro life," he writes in his autobiography, "the profundity latent in these rejected people, the dramas as old as man and the sun and the mountains and the seas that were transpiring in the poverty of black America" (*Black Boy* 336). Dimock's deep-time genre theory is useful, then, for understanding Wright's call for an African folk knowledge of the body that could adequately respond to the American epic performance. Scale enlargement has implicit futurity once the clear and present danger of oncoming climate wars is subjected to Dimock's sense of the larger Western history of epic violence, one inclusive of the Industrial Revolution as just one of countless assaults against the multitudinous life of the earth:

> Scale enlargement along the temporal axis changes our very sense of the connectedness among human beings. It also suggests that different investigative contexts might need different time frames, with no single one serving as an all-purpose metric. Some historical phenomena need large-scale analysis. They need hundreds, thousands, or even billions of years to be recognized for what they are. . . . This is also the case with long-lasting genres, such as epic and novel, with thousands of years behind them, and demanding analytic frames of comparable magnitude. (2–5)

The scientific scale of global warming falls within the purview of ancient genres and thus, contra Dyer, establishes a comparative treatment of past and present, non-Western and Western.

Though few scholars have attended to African-American folk knowledge and issues of slavery and race in the context of eco-criticism, this frame enables a scale enlargement that exponentially expands our perspective. For example, Jeffrey Myers, in *Converging Stories: Race, Ecology, and Environmental Justice in American Literature* (2005), makes the following fundamental association:

> The very existence of the Euroamerican subject depends on imagining not only the racial Other, but a priori on imagining the essential "otherness" of the physical world—of the human body, the bodies of plants and animals, and the body of the earth itself. A recognition that such separation is an illusion—that the "self" is ecologically interconnected with the "other"—threatens to erase individual identity as it is defined

in European metaphysics, an identity "whose sole *essence or nature* consists in *thinking.*" (15)

Labeling the fear that identity could be lost to the "primacy of the natural world as *physiphobia*," Myers makes the threat clear and direct: "I believe there is a fundamental connection between racism and domination of the natural world and that neither of these oppressive forces can be challenged meaningfully on its own" (16). Myers later applies this argument to folk culture and the symbiotic relationship between African Americans and the land, in Africa and both during and after American slavery. His focal author in this endeavor is Charles Chesnutt.

Lisa Woolley's study of Wright's evolving and expanding concern for canines in his prose and haiku likely offers the first truly eco-critical treatment of Wright. Finding Wright's prose works—"Big Boy Leaves Home," *Black Boy*, and autobiographical essays in *Harper's*—to differ markedly from his later haiku, which show a mature appreciation of animals, Woolley begins the critical task of recovering Wright's traditional ecological knowledge ("TEK") aesthetic. Woolley's work, informed by a fundamental, synergistic association between animals, humans, and relationship to the earth, reveals the logic underlying Wright's insight into the same. Whether selling his dog, Betsy, for much-needed money for food, or working in a brickyard or a Chicago hospital where dogs are devocalized, Woolley suggests, like Myers, that far more is at stake than a "discriminatory economic system" impacting race, class, and physical hunger (178–82). The production of bricks that create orderly white homes and neighborhoods, hospitals where dogs are devocalized, and urban tenements also creates hungry, apathetic black workers who are treated like animals. Tragically, as native sons and daughters, they do the same to one another and other humans at the same time they narcotize their own trauma through various forms of consumption. Their protest is Bigger's protest; Wright's perspective on this racial protest, and the loss of TEK inseparable from it, makes reading his eco-cautionary tale alongside the epic performance a most natural and necessary gesture.

Just as Alain Locke privileged the "new scientific rather than the old sentimental interest" and dismissively deployed southern folk culture, "a leaven of humor, sentiment, imagination and tropic nonchalance" (988), as a raw resource to fashion, in a matter of speaking, a *new factory man*,[18] Ellison similarly treats Wright's folk call in "Blueprint for Negro Writing" and *Black Boy*. In his famous essay "Richard Wright's Blues," a searing critique of *Black Boy*, Ellison fashions Wright as "the subject" and fiercely attacks Wright's sociological fiction and call for a folk sense as a way of addressing the blight of racism. Ellison's rhetoric here is a masterful *coup*: he fixes the blues as the folk "impulse" guiding Wright's autobiography and then, later, lyricizes an oft-quoted counter-philosophy: "The blues is an impulse to keep the painful details and episodes of a brutal experience alive in one's aching consciousness, to finger its jagged grain, and to transcend it, not by the consolation of philosophy but by squeezing from it a near-tragic, near-comic lyricism" (1538–39).

Ellison's Enlightenment-based modernism, which informs *Invisible Man*, and his pro-democracy, assimilation/access ideology flatten the performative agency of folk culture, which ceases to function as a root metaphor full of deep-time organicity. On this score, another quote from "Richard Wright's Blues" deserves attention: "The welfare of the most humble black Mississippi sharecropper is affected less by the flow of the seasons and the rhythm of natural events than by the fluctuations of the stock market; even though . . . the sharecropper's memories, actions and emotions are shaped by his immediate contact with nature and the crude social relations of the South" (1545). The obvious, redeeming recourse informing Ellison's essay is migration to the urban North.

In light of the twin catastrophes of the 1930s, the Great Depression and the Dust Bowl, the latter of which arose out of Ellison's Oklahoma and other Southern Plains states, and the twin crises of the 2008 economic depression and global warming, it is clear that the blues is just one aspect of a much larger phenomenon whose ecological dimension is critical to the roots metaphor.

TRADITIONAL ECOLOGICAL KNOWLEDGE: TAKING MEASURE OF THE "PROBLEM"

When the World Commission on Environment and Development proclaimed, in *Our Common Future* (1987), that "[t]ribal and indigenous peoples' . . . lifestyles can offer modern societies many lessons in the management of resources in complex forests, mountain and dryland ecosystems" (12), it established an important benchmark. Over the last couple of decades, both ecologists and humanities scholars have increasingly recognized the validity of the root metaphor undergirding the critical local knowledge produced by many traditional societies. An essential component of this sea change has been their understanding of centuries-old developments in Western Europe—antedating transatlantic slavery and colonization of the New World—leading to the present environmental crises. For example, the shift of the word "environment" away from its original performative is significant, David Mazel argues, for what vanishes as the verb "environs" becomes obsolete is the action of penetrating the land through "discovery, exploration, [and] conquest" (138–40). The evolution Mazel pursues, from oral action/performance-to-textual object, parallels the work of scholar-activists who see the implications of this textual shift manifest on the macrological scale. They locate the present ecological crisis in the precipitous rise of Western democracy, science, and Christianity because of textuality and mass literacy.

For Lynn White, Jr., the "late eleventh century" was a watershed, for the West started its "distinctive . . . tradition of science . . . with a massive movement of translation of Arabic and Greek scientific works into Latin" (7).[19] Even assuming the reliability of literal translation, cultural context is untranslatable. In other words, *Oriental* context, in the hands of Western translators, was reduced to the new *Occidental* text and imaginary context Edward Said excavated. It bears noting here that White roots his ecological perspective in a culture's perspective on the *body* and spirituality: "What people do about their ecology depends on what they think about themselves in relation to things around them. Human ecology is deeply conditioned by beliefs about our nature and destiny—that is, by religion." The roots-source underneath the "beliefs" in modern Western ontology and episte-mology, White adds, is Western Christianity's "victory . . . over paganism," which "was the greatest psychic revolution in the history of our culture," with the subsequent faith in "perpetual progress which was unknown either to Greco-Roman antiquity or to the Orient." The silencing of the ancient Greco-Roman animist spirits—the ancestors—alive among the common people, who believed that "every tree, every spring, every stream, every hill had its own *genius loci*, its guardian spirit" that had to be respected, meant that "Christianity made it possible to exploit nature in a mood of indiffer-ence to the feelings of natural objects" (9–10).

"Nature *is* silent in our culture (and in literate societies generally) in the sense that the status of being a speaking subject is jealously guarded as an exclusive human prerogative," Christopher Manes insists. "The language we speak today, the idiom of the Renaissance and Enlightenment humanism, veils the processes of nature with its own cultural obsessions, directionali-ties, and motifs that have no analogues in the natural world" (15). Animist societies, including pre-Christian Europe, are not inclined to exploit nature, a ubiquitous presence "that speaks to them."[20] Thanks, first, to the rise of literacy and its abstractions, and then to Western Christianity's exegetical tradition, nature comes to be literally read as flat, static, mute allegory: allegory is born in which "behind the *littera*, the literal (often mundane) meaning of a biblical passage, lay some *moralis*, a moral truth established by God." In effect, the Natural Law here, separating thought (Christianity/science) and the biosphere, parallels the "pure will"/"antiwill" dichotomy critical race theorist Patricia Williams associates with the racial economy. The damage from such laws, ultimately punitive to US all in incalculable ways, is treble, as Manes argues: 1) the natural world's *fauna* and *flora* lose their agency as "speakers" and actors in their own rightful place; 2) the *scala naturae* or "Great Chain of Being" shifts, thanks to humanist reason, to privilege humans (18–21); and, 3) though Manes does not address his-torical oppression, he knows all too well that this *scala naturae* privileges a whiteness—God's whiteness or that of rational Western Europeans—felt by the "colored" people around the world. Against modernity, Manes advo-cates a restored appreciation of animism, which he considers an inescapable dimension of our being, and learning a new language, the "language of animals, especially of birds" (17, 25).[21]

Even in this green zone, an eco-hegemony, constructed out of the same racial/ethnic and culture/nature distinctions in national privilege, lurks as a real possibility. Mazel argues that in the long history of environmental concerns, dating back to Thomas Jefferson, "domestic Orientalism" has characterized the movement. National Parks appeared as American Indians were "being evicted" and the "environment" was being constructed out of an imperialistic discourse that avoided the "deeper politics" of how indigenous groups are disallowed from defining the environment even as they are situated in it as authentic representatives.

Carl Anthony, writing in the immediate aftermath of Hurricane Katrina, wrote "African Americans and Environmental History: A Manifesto" (2007) in part because he apprehended the overwhelming tragedy confronting black Americans. Anthony unearthed a disturbing greening of the racial line done at the expense of the people of African descent:

> I came across a very important book by Thomas Berry, called *The Dream of the Earth*. Berry proposed that, in order to get our bearings in terms of our current ecological crisis, we need a new story about who human beings are in relationship to the story of the earth . . . . At the same time, I found I had an uneasy feeling about the book because it didn't appear to include black people at all. There was wonderful talk of Native Americans—the ecumenical spirit, the struggle against patriarchy, etc., were reflected—but where were the black people? In fact, African Americans' experiences were not included in any of the environmental literature I could get my hands on about people's relationship to the land. Thoreau, David Brower . . . none of them reflected black people's experience.
>
> How could this be? What was I to do with this? (186)

Anthony's insight suggests one form of Afro-Orientalism, here a doubly negative comparative: American Indians are Orientalized with all of the colonial baggage Said highlights with the concept, but people of African descent are implicitly considered inferior to this Oriental construct. However, Anthony's dismay arises not only from Orientalism joined with racism, but from the African-American response to racism, *viz.*, an uplift strategy rooted in reimagining ourselves as modern, urban individuals (187). Was the diagnosis of the problem of the "color-line" myopic?

Fortunately, historians Emmanuel Kwaku Akyeampong and James L.A. Webb, Jr., examining West African diseases like malaria and trypanosomiasis (African sleeping sickness), understand the relationship of diagnoses, traditional ecological knowledge, and the historical processes of racial conflict. Because of millennia of migration—across ecological zones, some of the earth's most challenging terrains, characterized by virulent malaria strains and impacted by extreme climate shifts[22]—and notwithstanding wide ethnic and sociopolitical diversity, West Africans developed common cultural patterns and a common storehouse of "ecological knowledge of plants, animals, insects, water supplies and mineral resources" (Akyeampong 189; Webb 34–35). Consonant with a cosmology integrally related to TEK*nowledge*, West Africans valorized "ecological balances that kept local diseases at a lower level of endemicity. Folk environmental knowledge promoted the control of vegetation and game, which kept . . . epidemics and epizootics at bay" (Akyeampong 190–91).

West Africa, as a whole, continued to support TEK balances, even with significant cultural change associated with epic and empire. The transatlantic slave trade started, and the loss of West African autonomy accelerated fundamental shifts relevant to the diagnoses of the problem of race. The loss of slaves is just one aspect of a much larger multifaceted change. The transatlantic slave trade infected Africa with European viral diseases like measles, smallpox,[23] and rubella as well as bacterial diseases such as tuberculosis and syphilis. West Africans now confronted Western European viral and bacterial diseases (contagions with no cures in Europe) in addition to the local ones. The increased interethnic warfare among West Africans because of the slave trade, and the natural human response— "cluster[ing]" together for protection—exacerbated the problem: war toppled long-standing ecological "balances and endemic disease then became epidemic in various parts of Africa" (Akyeampong 191–92).

Once the slave trade ended in the 1830s, West African coastal societies, deprived of income related to the triangle trade, shifted toward export crop production. This change reflected a "new gendered division of labor" based on the West's discrete categorization of the body: vegetable oil/cash crops were produced by men, grain/food crops by women. Export production led to benefits of greater income and development, but it also came at an exorbitant cost: the traditional diversity of farming shifted toward monocultural use of crops in the sahel/savannah (e.g., cotton and peanuts) and woodlands (e.g., cocoa in Ghana) that exhausted soil nutrients and, because of fewer crops, increased the risk of insects and fungus. European racism directly led to dramatic ecological shifts in West Africa, for nineteenth- and twentieth-century European colonials thought the low agricultural productivity resulted from

> less advanced technology, a lack of initiative, and primitive ecological practices. They identified the agronomic practice of "shifting cultivation" (that allowed for long fallow periods) as responsible for environmental degradation. Thus the colonialists, presuming that they had ecological knowledge superior to that of West Africans with centuries of accumulated experience, prescribed an intensification of agricultural production, to be led either by market forces or by coercion. (Webb 46–47)

This change accompanied another articulated by Akyeampong: "European colonial rule changed the praxis of therapy, with African healers being declared illegitimate under the new political dispensation. . . . As Feierman and Janzen accurately observed, the diagnosis of illness is closely connected to power and authority, and 'whoever controls the diagnosis of illness . . . shapes cultural ideas on misfortunes and evil. The power to name an illness is the power to say which elements in life lead to suffering'" (195).[24] It is also the power to define life and the body, and the complex dynamic connecting them.

Fortunately, scholars have begun to recover African TEK. Paralleling important recovery work among indigenous groups in North America that exposes the strengths of TEK and the false universality of Western science (Berkes 10–11), a growing body of scholars have done the same for desertification and savannization debates in North and Western Africa, respectively.[25] The exhaustive work by James Fairhead and Melissa Leach (with research collaboration by Dominique Millimouno and Marie Kamamo), in *Misreading the African Landscape: Society and Ecology in a Forest-Savanna Mosaic* (1999), is exemplary in this regard. Since France colonized Guinée in 1893, French administrators have believed that the forest of Kissidougou, once a humid paradise, has been under assault by the locals. Rotation of cultivation and bush-burning, according to this belief, "progressively" undermined the forest and converted it to "'derived' savanna"—"savannisation"—that threatens widespread ecological harm. Global funds to monitor and protect Kissidougou are plentiful, and criminalization of traditional practices have become policy boilerplate, but Fairhead and Leach argue that the

> elders and others living behind the forest walls provide quite different readings of their landscape and its making. At their most contrasting, they bluntly reverse policy orthodoxy, representing their landscape as half-filled and filling with forest, not half-emptied and emptying of it. Forest islands, some villagers suggested, are not relics of destruction, but were formed by themselves or their ancestors in savanna. And rather than disappearing under human pressure, forests, we were shown, are associated with settlement, and come and go with it. In short, it became clear that by treating forest islands as relics and savannas as derived, policy-makers may have been misreading Kissidougou's landscape, by reading forest history backwards.

From the colonial era onward, the villagers have borne the brunt of the blame, with little attention to the massive climactic shifts in Africa—long dry spells followed by humid ones—ecologists are now just beginning to understand. Post-colonial regimes have marginalized the locals' TEK and blamed them, continuing the post-WWII practice of French colonial botanists who, along with a French forest advisory team and Guinée's existing "national forest plan," created policy based on a misreading of

Kissidougou's past and present forest. A contemporary example is "Environment Awareness Days" promoted by a new nongovernment organization, Friends of Nature, based on the Kissidougou problem and staffed by schoolteachers.

In this climate, and facing "different root assumptions" about ecological science as well as policy shaped to benefit certain groups, Fairhead and Leach recognized that their methodology had to be encyclopedic. Between their review of photos, satellite images, and the documentary record in light of new evidence of massive climate shifts, Fairhead and Leach concluded that the villagers' "indigenous technical knowledge" was correct and the "expert" knowledge was wrong: there was insufficient evidence of savannization (1–16, 24–26, 50–51, 55).

Though TEK practices, like any form of knowledge, can be wrong and ecologically destructive, sometimes subject to exaggerations "of indigenous wisdom of the 'noble savage'" (Berkes 15, 227), experience clearly suggests the wisdom of considering all of the evidence. Given the ancient, deep-time pedigree of epic performance, this raises the linchpin question: what is the specific eco-critical ethos associated with epic performances?

WRIGHT'S EPICAL TEKNOWLEDGE

TEKnowledge, epic culture, and folk wisdom may make more sense in light of this discussion, but reading *Native Son* from an eco-critical perspective confronts the argument that it is modern urban fiction. This encompasses two distinct critiques. First, it addresses the concern that blacks, and Africans more generally, having become the racial trope for anti-modernity, must rebut primitivism and nativism to prove their equality—through ever-more pioneering *firsts* in morality, literacy, and then creative excellence in the arts and sciences. David Lionel Smith writes that because of the problems of race in Western culture, with nature and civilization as opposites and people of African descent assigned to nature, African Americans dedicate themselves to entering civilization as a way of rebuffing the charge that they are in a state of nature. Just as Smith notes that "[t]o write about nature is to invite the invidious associations of presumptive inferiority and backwardness that black writers as a class have been especially anxious to avoid" (1004), the larger black community has focused on urban exceptionalism and sought refuge from southern terrorism by migrating toward the North's promise of equal civil rights. In this regard, central to Ellison's critique of Wright is a species of Darwinian regionalism hedged on a North-is-good/South-is-bad logic: black folk southern culture is a sentimental affect shorn by blacks who migrate to, and thus evolve in, the more rational North. As the TEK evidence suggests, this perspective is premature at best and, worse, quite likely a self-inflicted, fundamentalist supremacy masquerading as objectivity.

A second and equally formidable barrier to reading Wright's *Native Son* eco-critically, specifically as a Dust Bowl epic, stems from his international acclaim: because of *Native Son,* white and black scholars, in spite of Wright's "Blueprint for Negro Writing" and its call for black writers to explore their own roots metaphor, reduce him to an urban writer and disciple of modernity. In effect, according to this reading and its manifold variants, *Native Son* performs on a stage featuring Chicago, a metropole replete with slumlords, corporate empires, cars, abandoned buildings, skyscrapers, and concrete and asphalt jungles. Not only are there no trees, but conspicuous by total absence are any environmental concerns that would recognize nature. Race engulfs Wright's novels and oeuvre, and any environmentalism exists only incidental to his sociological fiction.

Consider Lawrence Buell's *Writing for an Endangered World* (2001), a form of literary eco-criticism tasked with fashioning an organic relationship between "ecocentric" and "anthropocentric ethics." Buell briefly considers Wright's *Native Son* in the context of urban sociology and the ecological dimension contained within the Chicago School of Sociology, specifically Wright's style of describing the urban environment compared to works like Upton Sinclair's *The Jungle* (138–42). Perhaps because Buell focused exclusively upon American literature, notwithstanding his awareness that eco-criticism "should extend from the oldest surviving texts" like the *Epic of Gilgamesh*, his eco-criticism of *Native Son*—despite being the first—creates a modern, urban divide that undermines Wright's eco-critical depth. *Native Son*, a work of "ghetto" or "urban fiction," is "sparse," Buell argues, in "environmental detail." Contrasting Wright's sociological acumen with Gwendolyn Brooks' "sensuous feel of urban blight" and Zora Neale Hurston's "'anthropological' approach to the rhythms and preoccupations of African-American folk-life," Buell reads Wright's aesthetic—conjoining sociology and fiction—as the product of a mind incapable of comprehending the limits of his ability to reconcile them. Hence for Buell, Wright's decision to portray Bigger in a film version though he was twenty years too old and his claim to have "derived Bigger, so he said," from "representative" lives, arises from Wright's use of the "'ecological' approach" of the Chicago School of Sociology, "a confused blurring of categories and pseudoscientific claims about the 'natural' laws of urban structure and growth" instead of a legitimate ecological perspective (1–18, 138–42).

Wright's failing, Buell suggests, is his scientific, urban treatment of art. Implicit here is a near-universal dichotomy: John Steinbeck's Pulitzer Prize–winning *The Grapes of Wrath* (1939) is a Dust Bowl novel of rural America whereas Wright's *Native Son*, which outsold it, is a sociological novel about race, class, and the city. Buell's method, unfortunately, discounts the vast corpus of work on, and Wright's own appreciation of, the folk forms not just predating modern sociology, but dating back to storytelling performance dynamics at least as old as the *Gilgamesh* texts. Bigger is not just a creature of sociology; the bad man folk figure reaches back into the nineteenth century, to the bad slave, and arguably to the original bad men associated with African epic heroes. Reading Wright eco-critically—in the context of the Dust Bowl, the (epic) hero in the garden, and specifically the bad man in Chicago, the City of Gardens—is a necessary recovery.

For centuries, a salient *topos* that informed Europeans' imaginary about the New World was a garden, equal parts Golden Age and paradise. Along with biblical injunctions to mankind to exercise "dominion" and "subdue" it and the animals,[26] Martin D. Snyder points out that the Homeric myth of the Elysian Fields was "essential" to early representations of the continent. One of the functions of this American myth was to "attract men first to America itself, and then to the vast wilderness of the interior. Like a mirage dancing on the horizon, it encouraged men to press ever onward in search of a perfect world." Though the "mirage" had negative consequences related to frustrated desires and unsettled lives, Snyder argues for its benefit: "it could inspire men to creative action. If paradise could not be regained, it could, perhaps only incompletely and imperfectly, be created through heroic human efforts." Eventually, this myth makes over the "rugged frontiersman" into an Achilles figure (144, 149–52, 154–55, 167).

But the heroic man injunction, if one seeks the roots-knowledge beneath modern hagiography and the too-literal interpretation of "dominion" and "subdue," reveals itself to be destructive. The violence is not only against the original Americans and their land rights, or the land subjected to rights of discovery, but ultimately the Anglo-self laboring on the land. The diversity of the land, an allegorye of abundance, tends toward allegorical flatness and a monologic that betokens a dark apocalypse.[27] Consider Achilles' rampage in Book XX of the *Iliad*:

> As through the deep glens of a parched mountainside rages wondrous-blazing fire, and the deep forest burns, and the wind as it drives it on whirls the flame everywhere, so raged he everywhere with his spear, like some god, ever pressing hard on those he slew; and the black earth ran with blood. And as a man yokes bulls broad of brow to tread white barley in a well-built threshing floor, and quickly is the grain trodden out beneath the feet of the loud-bellowing bulls, so beneath great-hearted Achilles his single-hoofed horses trampled alike on the dead and on the shields. (Homer/Murray 403)

The close relationship between warfare, forest fire, whirling winds, and husbandry is unmistakable: Achilles' potential—his fair-haired presence bringing total, bloody darkness in a way inseparable from cultivation of the land—has serious ecological and even, one might argue, climatological ramifications. The organic allegorye of biodiversity, if simplified by epic allegory, literally disappears under the violence of cultivation. Achilles' rage is monological, his own capacity as a farmer who depends on the land intentionally implicated. The threat is literally "everywhere" for Achilles' blackened and bloodied victims—the slain bodies, the earth, and himself. This passage reveals the awful truth of the Sunjatic principle: the hero's creativity is only welcomed on troubled days and that epic creativity also troubles the epic hero.

Faced with an eco-apocalypse, it is not surprising that critics have begun to treat Homeric epics and ecology. In *The Unsettling of America: Culture and Agriculture* (1997),[28] Wendell Berry reads "Creation," and presumably the Genesis garden, from a perspective in which humanity is very much a part of it. The shape society takes depends upon human potential, including epic heroic potential, which in turn depends on the body: "The question of human limits, of the proper definition and place of human beings within the order of Creation, finally rests upon our attitude toward our biological existence, the life of the body in this world. What value and respect do we give to our bodies?" Our bodies are made of the earth and are fed by the earth no matter "how urban our life," Berry argues. "It is hardly surprising, then, that there should be some profound resemblance between our treatment of our bodies and our treatment of the earth" (97).

Consequently, Berry interprets Homer's *Odyssey* as a partial repudiation of the *Iliad*, a "war-obsessed" world too much like our own, and eschews a simplistic oppositional binary between domestic peace and wartime. Odysseus' return, symbolically grounded in the planting of his oar "like a tree" inland on Ithaca, parallels the Bible and allegorically represents, for Berry, the recovery of American marriage and husbandry (Berry 124–29). Berry's method of articulating TEK while deploying his "I" and Western literary greats—the Bible, Shakespeare, William Blake, and Homer (98, 99, 103, 104, 123)—*in lieu* of indigenous stories is a form of Afro-Oriental erasure.

The Odyssey stages the homecoming of Odysseus for Elizabeth Schultz's "Odysseus Comes to Know His Place: Reading *The Odyssey* Ecocritically" (2009) as well, but instead of marriage and a stable household, Schultz focuses on a biomorphic reconnection to the earth. Odysseus evolves from being an anthropocentric exploiter and dominator to one who is a steward of the earth or, in some instances, a part of the complex synergy between human and nonhuman upon which the biomorphic model relies. Implicit to Schultz's reading is a latent orality, manifest in Homeric similes in contrast to metaphor: the similes connect "human characters with the world of animals and birds" while not erasing their distinctiveness; the metaphors, Schultz implies in a manner reminiscent of Benjamin's concern with the outrageous metaphors of textuality, disrupt this synergy.[29] Likewise, the more creative Odysseus is in his anthropocentric mode, the greater the actualization of "disaster and death." His most creative adventure, venturing to Hades, Schultz argues, leads to the ultimate threat, a "sunless state": "Homer envisages an apocalyptic world, one resembling Hades and caused by human irresponsibility, aggression, and greed. . . . The sunless state is the extreme manifestation of the effects of [the] anthropocentric model on the physical environment. No sunless state can nurture life or nature." Odysseus has to be cooled down and humbled, thus his extended seven-year period of relative isolation and "meditation in the wildness of Calypso's island," followed by a ritual act that associates him with olive trees. Finally, Odysseus' storytelling performance with the Phaecians, at its end, presents him as a "hard-working yeoman" biomorphically connected to the land and animals (303–05, 307–08). In short, Schultz argues here that Homer's TEKnowledge functions in a manner akin to how the Sunjatic *maana*—narrative as opposed to *faasa* (praises)—slows and cools down the body.

A "sunless state," of dusty skies instead of green fields, is the eco-critical reality Berry and Michael Pollan[30] have argued as the consequence of past and present monocultures, such as the 1930s Dust Bowl. Race folds into this dynamic naturally, for the creative genius classics scholars attribute to Achilles assumes the existence of his antithesis: objects fit for his mastery, objectives conquered, and humans objectified and othered. The *nigger* epithet is the human form of the coarse, black, Hectored object opposed to Achilles' godlike perfection. Berry, who situates *nigger* as human and natural objects, even extends the trope of blackening to the self-destructive behavior of the American middle class, the same argument Wright made in *Native Son*. Wright's Bigger and Berry's nigger embody allegories in which the actualization of epic mythology in real space unleashes a war against America's oppressed minorities. The American bourgeoisie's "luxury and idleness," Berry argues, is associated with vast profits and desires to escape ecologically sound work and "yet be slender and good looking." It is, for him, the consequence of a progressive, creative, labor-saving enterprise:

> Out of this contempt for work arose the idea of the nigger: at first some person, and later some thing, to be used to relieve us of the burden of work. If we began by making niggers of people, we have ended by making niggers of the world. . . . We have made of the rivers and oceans and winds niggers to carry away our refuse, which we think we are too good to dispose of decently ourselves. And in doing this to the world that is our common heritage and bond, we have returned to making niggers of people: we have become each other's niggers. (12)

Berry labels such consumptive behavior a "fantastical" adherence to "fantasists in government" (13), but he might as well have invoked epic performance, Bigger Thomas, and the Great Migrations—white and black—into and away from the Midwest and Great Plains.

With the frontier moving ever westward, it should hardly come as a surprise that the Dust Bowl is a product of Americans' wartime treatment of the Great Plains of the Southwest and Midwest as an Elysian Field. Though "Food is a weapon" was not spoken until after World War II,[31] the "militarizing of food" was official Washington policy at the outset of America's involvement in the first Great War. When the Turks disrupted Russian wheat shipments west, European governments then turned to the

United States. The Wilson administration complied, its entrance into the war promoting a policy of higher wheat prices as a patriotic duty and military strategy: "Plant more wheat! Wheat will win the war!" Laws such as the Food Control Act of 1917, which set two dollars per bushel as the price of wheat, exacerbated existing homesteading practices by more than doubling the price of wheat (Worster 89; Berry 9). The tragedy of this lies in the underlying logic, which turns upon converting the ecosphere—assumed to be infinite in expanse—into a weapon.

Beginning in the 1920s and propelled by John Deere tractors, paradise grew out of the Plains in ever-golden harvests of wheat. The year 1931 was pivotal, for the Southern Plains had produced an unprecedented, record-breaking harvest, but in the summer of 1931 the rains stopped and the golden mythology of an inexhaustible garden met harsh reality. Wheat died in the fields, but worst of all the winds started and blew dust and sand unabated for a hundred hours. The arrival of the "Dust Bowl"—coined by Associated Press correspondent Robert Geiger, writing from Guymon, Oklahoma, on April 15, 1935, and popularized by the national and international press—quickly advanced from dead crops and livestock to blighted livelihoods and then an epidemic of death that blotted out numerous human lives and entire communities. Eventually the Plains paradise, raped by farmers and U.S. wartime policy, came to "resemble a WWI battlefield" (*American Experience* 3–4).

The fierce dust storms, increasing in intensity and frequency, brought along other disasters: static electricity that cooked crops to cinders, a "plague" of "[h]undreds of thousands of starving jack rabbits" descending out of the hills to devour the remaining crops, and then the April 14, 1935, arrival of the Black Sunday storm—the worst of the Dust Bowl—that lasted for twenty-seven consecutive days. Black Sunday brought with it dust considered by many to be God's blight upon them, and dust pneumonia, which killed animals and up to one-third of the residents in some communities. That same year saw the beginning of the mass exodus Steinbeck captured in *The Grapes of Wrath* and the rise of soil conservation. This new policy shift occurred when Congress, thanks to soil conservationist Hugh Bennett,

> learned that a great dust storm was heading towards the east coast. *The storm had already deposited 12 million pounds of dust on Chicago— four pounds for each person in the city*—and was poised to descend on the nation's capital. . . . For the first time Easterners smelled, breathed, and tasted the dust blowing off the Southern Plains.
>
> For years—before the dust storms—the Federal government had regarded the soil as a limitless, indestructible resource. In a major shift, Washington now put its full weight and authority behind soil conservation. (*American Experience* 6, 9, 10–14, 17–18; italics mine)

The dust moved east,[32] "Oakies" moved west from the Southern Plains, but significantly, the combination of the Great Depression and the Dust

Bowl actually froze the great migration. The immense country-to-city shift, driven by the young and African Americans, fell from six million in the 1920s to two million in the 1930s. However, the Dust Bowl caused the greatest per capita exodus of Americans—Plains refugees—in U.S. history. In 1932, Donald Worster notes, the Plains inflow "reversed, as unemployment peaked," and in 1935 there was a record number of people on farms, a figure driven by a rural baby boom and by urban immigrants "seeking small homesteads where they could weather economic adversity. . . . One sociologist saw at work here 'a great, uncontrolled mass movement to the succoring breast of Mother Earth'" (47–48).[33]

WEST/CENTRAL AFRICAN EPIC PERFORMANCE

Wright could not, of course, invoke MOS-epic performances, but his gesture toward folk knowledge demonstrates a substantive appreciation of the indispensable importance of African folk knowledge in struggles against imperialism. Western epics of conquest may be calamitous, but Wright implicitly recognizes that inorganic, reflexive responses to racism that understand it as a denial of equal access or treatment and foreground exceptionalism[34] will extend the epic performance with greater consequences for everyone. Against this dilemma, Wright's blueprint is a call to recover folk culture which offers deep-time understanding of the excesses of epic performance.

As with other heroic epic traditions, few critics have yet to articulate a relationship between MOS excess and ecology. The one critical exception to this is Isidore Okpewho, who balances between the "subtle but discernible link between art and the landscape out of which it grows" and his effort to foreground African creativity and originality *vis-à-vis* Western European epic traditions. Okpewho attenuates the biomorphic foundation in favor of a Western ontology, but not entirely: "it would appear that much of the aesthetic nourishment of traditional African art derived from the nature of the surrounding landscape and the concomitant throb of animate company within it." Though he artfully begins his description of African "ecology of art" with landscape and aesthetics, and ends well before a fully embodied eco-critical or eco-cautionary epic aesthetic emerges out of the ashes of epic excess, Okpewho provides critical insight. "Environment" determines the "forms or the quality of art," hence the relative poverty of language and "more restricted" heroic deeds manifest in the Sunjatic tradition arising out of the "lean vegetation of the surrounding savanna." Relevant here is the salience of the Sunjatic tradition in West Africa, where fierce battles for resources dominated the area for centuries. Okpewho's description of the forest, a place where "persistent rainfall gives rise to thick vegetation, wildlife in myriad shapes and numbers," is instructive: the African epic heroes of the forest, like Mwindo, show "much greater bravado" and have "hardly any restraints." The "organic environment" of the Nyanga sustains a "luxuriance of life" and art, and "buxom mirth attends the teeming camaraderie." Situated between the savanna and forest is Islam, a world religion, which penetrated indigenous traditions. The savanna has less animism than the forest because Islam "succeeded considerably in suppressing the vigor of traditional life and myth," Okpewho argues, just as Christianity did in Western Europe, though to a significantly greater degree (*The Epic* 19–21).

Though Okpewho's analysis elides excess, the "buxom mirth" and "teeming camaraderie" of Mwindic performances help enhance the artistry and functionality as synergistic complements of TEK. Mwindo's epic begins when his father, Shemwindo, seeks to prevent the birth of any sons, and then tries to kill Mwindo once he is born. What follows is exile, recovery of a paternal aunt, Iyangura, whose name relates to justice, and then a series of epical tasks—warfare against his father's army, a trip to the underworld filled with fantastic feats against the gods, and then the capture of his fleeing father—culminating in Mwindo's coronation as chief. The story should but does not end here, for Mwindo continues to exhibit the same epical behavior. He is not just transgressive, but excessive, for the Banyangan social code frowns upon the ideals that make Mwindo epical: boasting, individualism, wanderlust, competitive aggression, and talkativeness. Thus, when Mwindo kills Kirịmu, a dragon of the forest, and makes sport of his feat by inviting all of his people to see the spectacle and "wagging" his magical scepter (*ME* 133), he has overstepped his boundaries.

But who or what can stop Mwindo, the quintessential survivor who mastered the trickster's wit en route to becoming the ultimate warrior? The answer is a higher authority, the very emblem of an ecologically sound rainforest: Nkuba, the god of lightning and friend of Kirịmu, snatches Mwindo off his throne and sends him on a year-long solo journey. Mwindo's frightful experiences in the realms of Rain, Moon, Sun, and Star—he freezes, he wanders as a nomad, he is thrashed sevenfold times for his insolent heroism, toughness, and pride—make clear the cosmological and ecological threat his unwise policy-bravado entails (*ME* 135–43). After all, the rainforest is the Banyanga's "world." Even though they have villages and fear the forest, they also "love it," too (Biebuyck, "Nyanga Circumcision" 90, and *Hero* 26–27, 62, 98–99).

This summary allows us to answer the paradoxical question regarding Mwindic epicality and Banyangan pacificism *vis-à-vis* other societies with epic performance traditions: the Banyanga's culture, and the synergistic relationship of their bodies to the environment, provides a foundation broad enough for the contradiction to be understood. A hero in the garden who represents the apogee of heroic epic possibility and violence, Mwindo's cause is both righteous and necessary, for Shemwindo is the paradigm of a dictatorial chief in a cosmology in which he is formally recognized as the central functionary (chief) and a crucial earthly link in the *scala naturae*. His corrupt rule portends inexorable progress toward the destruction of Banyangan cosmology, but the Banyanga literally enjoy deep mirth, laughter, in direct proportion to Mwindo's justifiably epical exploits and abilities, which subdue and dominate Shemwindo and, indeed, some divinities important to their teeming rainforest.

The Banyanga, their bodies having far greater allegorycal extension into one another, the forest, and into the spiritual world, can apprehend the apocalyptic violence of epic heroics without being reduced to it. Shemwindo may be the original source of the battle royal, and Mwindo's heroics may double as high comedy, but the Banyangans' second sight is worth noting: their eyes were watching chief Mwindo, for his excesses exceed his father's when he, raising Cain and some, kills the allegorycal emblem of the rainforest's regenerative mystery and life. He, too, like Adam and Eve, is expelled from the Garden, but even though Mwindo kills and himself replaces the Serpent of the rainforest, redemption is possible since the Banyanga's common/sense of the body is extensive enough to permit it. Mwindo's infraction is nothing a little exposure to Rain, Moon, Sun, and Star—the year here symbolically reacquainting him with the "flow of the seasons and the rhythm of natural events"—cannot cure. Thus, epic heroism is part of the Banyangan body-politic, but this performance conforms to a blueprint— human bodies in balance with the biosphere—that makes for healthy, sustainable relationships and the possibility of heroic epic performance.

WRIGHT'S DUST BOWL CAUTIONARY AESTHETIC

Wright's call for a folk-oriented response to American racism implicates an "ecology of art" based on an allegorycal extension of the healthy body. Healthy bodies—as opposed to black and white ones—would be capable of challenging the racial dynamic undergirded by performance of epic mythology. However, in an (under)world of epical realism created by European/American epic tricksters, would-be African-American saviors—trickster-heroes, epic tricksters, and epic heroes—must, logically, rely upon global, eco-critical TEKnowledge. Though full eco-critical treatment of Wright's epic-inspired, Dust Bowl–sensitive literature is not possible, the following select close readings of Wright's primary works should open another chapter in Wright criticism and African-American storytelling during the Dust Bowl.

As the narratives of his own life journey and most famous novel indicate, Chicago is ground zero for Wright's Dust Bowl eco-epic aesthetics. *Native Son* is more fruitful in this regard than Wright's other fiction because of its quality and encyclopedic scale, but the intertextuality between *Black Boy* and *Native Son* demonstrates that the Great Migration that brought Wright to Chicago's Southside ghetto merges into the white great migration of the Dust Bowl. The result, an inobtrusive *leitmotif* overlooked like a fine layer of dust, is appreciated when we realize that the silent, eco-cautionary sediment coats everything, including Wright's journey and Bigger Thomas' relationship with Bessie Mears.

Black Boy is Wright's post-migration autobiography of his own odyssey from hunger, poverty, and brutality in a slavery-haunted South where racialized epical realism existed as a most telling Jim Crow performance. Poverty and starvation, cruel relatives, fundamentalist Christianity, his mother's illness and deteriorating condition, and the ethics of the Jim Crow regime eventually propelled him northward. Originally entitled *American Hunger* (and referred to as such hereinafter), Wright's publisher declined to produce the entire autobiography, instead publishing the first half, which focused on Wright's reflections on his pre-migration life in the South, as *Black Boy*. The second half of *American Hunger* narrates his experience in the northern Midwest and shows his disillusionment with the supposedly free North, an experience foretold by free blacks and fugitive slaves decades earlier.

The fulcrum linking the southern and northern narratives is the Great Migration, a source of hope and wonder for generations of southern African Americans; in Wright's autobiography it becomes a cautionary tale in which white knights and dragons, reality and epic mythology, are one and the same in the North as well as the South. As the narrative moves toward the realization of Wright's northern wonderment, a residual, poetic TEK shadows his southern maturation. Thus, one of the critical features of *Hunger* is the catalog of experiences he uses in his narrative; there are three examples,[35] the first occurring when he is just a young boy, the last when Wright is ten or eleven. Similar to Walt Whitman's free-ranging poetic verse that revels in human nature and nature, Wright's third and last is striking, if not magical:

> Up or down the wet or dusty streets, indoors or out, the days and nights began to spell out magic possibilities.
> If I pulled a hair from a horse's tail and sealed it in a jar of my own urine, the hair would turn overnight into a snake.
> If I passed a Catholic sister or mother dressed in black and smiled and allowed her to see my teeth, I would surely die.
> If I walked under a leaning ladder, I would certainly have bad luck.
> If I kissed my elbow, I would turn into a girl.
> If my right ear itched, then something good was being said about me by somebody.
> If I touched a humpback's hump, then I would never be sick. (*BB* 71)

Bearing in mind David Mazel's cardinal principle that to construct an ecological perspective on literature critics must not confuse nature and environment, that beneath a discrete, objectified surface lies a whole other world, it becomes possible to see that Wright's third catalog reaches for deep ecology through the supernatural—conjure. Stereotype relegates conjure to the domain of dark magic, occult, and voo doo, but as Theophus H. Smith points out, conjure actually recognizes the organic synergy of everything: humans, living and ancestral, the natural world of flora and fauna, and the vast spiritual world. The catalogs are part of the folk or roots metaphor Wright uses at important formative moments of his life in the South. Their occurrence in the first quarter of his narrative offers structural incantations suggesting an expanding awareness of his folk roots, but the critical point is that these incantations, poetic instants comprising diluted lore and deeper folk sense, occur only during his southern journey through the stunting forces of racism. They have long become a receding memory by the time he embarks for the urban North.

Wright's journey north is pivotal to understanding his perspective on urbanity, including spaces like Harlem. As he recalls his 1927 train ride northward to Chicago, Wright makes this observation: "My first glimpse of the flat black stretches of Chicago depressed and dismayed me, mocked all of my fantasies. Chicago seemed an unreal city whose mythical houses were built of slabs of black coal wreathed in palls of gray smoke, houses whose foundations were sinking slowly into the dank prairie" (*BB* 261). The detailed, graphic imagery of the epical realism is evocative, but just as important here is the Negro folk song Wright uses to open the chapter *before* his "first glimpse":

Sometimes I wonder, huh,
Wonder if other people wonder, huh,
Sometimes I wonder, huh,
Wonder if other people wonder, huh,
Just like I do, oh, my Lord, just like I do! (*BB* 260)

Since Wright *after*wards focuses on Chicago's "unreality," "mythical" urbanscape, and sinking "foundations," his call-response dynamic is critical for those entering its incorporated municipal monopoly. The two identical couplets and final, off-rhythm line of the Negro folk song follow the basic structure of the blues. The slow and low minor key implied here is clearly subsonic, just as the colors of the blues metaphor is essentially invisible to hearers' classical sight. Unlike the Odyssean narrator of Ellison's Invisible Man protagonist, whose New York City basement is an open embrace of empowerment, Wright's low-light, low-sound blues-song starts with the folk out in the open. Flowing its cool simplicity is a very natural rhythm guided by sunlight—a direct contrast to the "1,369 bulbs," each one a "klieg light in an *individual* setting," which the Invisible Man proudly, satirically, uses "with the compliments of Monopolated Light & Power" (*IM* 13; italics mine). The readers' gateway into Chicago, then, takes them into and through Wright's blues-deep folk call which, through the repetition of "wonder," urges and even cautions those who would make the odyssey to respond with a responsible, meditative reading.

Wright's oeuvre pivots on Chicago, not on founding issues of race, class, gender, or political ideology, but the ecological parable of Chicago's founding. Eminent historian William Cronon, in his landmark study *Nature's*

Metropolis: Chicago and the Great West (1991), also foregrounds ecology. Cronon argues that the founding of Chicago defined the "midcontinent," from its nineteenth-century perch on the "frontier" into the twentieth century as a global center. Consonant with Wright's fictional mapping of Chicago, Cronon does not lionize its greatness as he attempts to knot together the economic and ecological dimensions to its founding and transformation. Chicago, also known as the White City or "alabaster city," is summed up by Cronon in a way that resonates with much of Wright's explicit and implicit concerns:

> By the end of the nineteenth century, Chicago was filled with temples of commerce that were also, less obviously, mausoleums of landscapes vanishing from the city's hinterland. The grain elevators and Board of Trade celebrated the new speculative furor of the futures markets while simultaneously commemorating the tallgrass prairies being plowed and fenced into oblivion. The acres of sweet-smelling lumber stacked along the South Branch of the Chicago River testified to the fencing of the prairie and the growth of the city itself, but were also graveyards for the white pine forests rapidly disappearing from Michigan, Wisconsin, and Minnesota. Chicago's refrigerator cars and packing plants betokened a revolution in the way its citizens killed and sold animals, but were also monuments to the slaughtered bison herds. Behind each urban structure were the ghost landscapes that had given it birth. In sinking roots into the western soil, the city was remaking the countryside after its own image. (263)

From the outset, ancient folk genre guides his readers: though *Nature's Metropolis* contains histories of Chicago and the Great West, Cronon says, "I intend them as parables for our own lives as well" (xiii–xv).

The fact that Wright wrote about and published accounts of his 1927 "first glimpse" and produces his best-known novel—while invoking folk knowledge—during the worst part, and in the immediate aftermath, of the Dust Bowl[36] must not be underestimated, though scholars have. Historian Donald Worster incorrectly places Wright "[i]n the cotton belt" in the 1930s, but his study of the Dust Bowl nevertheless establishes the link between Wright and the Dust Bowl. Just as Wright deploys "wonder" as a trope for the dystopic possibility of great migrations from the rural South to urban spaces like Chicago, "wonder" guided Pulitzer Prize–winning poet Archibald MacLeish during the summer of 1937 as he penned "Land of the Free" on his Massachusetts farm. Like the eighty-eight photographs published along with MacLeish's poem in *Land of the Free* (1939), Wright's *12 Million Black Voices* (1941) fused literary aesthetics, photography, and politics to document the human cost of 1930s America. MacLeish's topic was America's dusty rural landscape, a poet's migration covering "millions of acres of stumps" from "New England to Wisconsin" instead of Wright's autobiographical approach to Chicago, but Worster's brief analysis of MacLeish's poem enables us to reevaluate Wright and the wide gulf between his Jim Crow urban politics and ecology. Thanks to Worster's invocation of MacLeish's sentiment that "[a]s 'the dust chokes in our throats we get wondering,'" the "wonder"-centered intertextuality between "Land of the Free" and Wright's Negro folk song becomes undeniable:

Sometimes I <u>wonder</u>, huh,	We <u>wonder</u> whether the dream of American liberty
<u>Wonder</u> if other people <u>wonder</u>, huh,	Was two hundred years of pine and hardwood
Sometimes I <u>wonder</u>, huh,	And three generations are up: the years over. . . .
<u>Wonder</u> if other people <u>wonder</u>, huh,	We <u>wonder</u> whether the great American dream
Just like I do, oh, my Lord, just like I do!	Was the singing of locusts out of the grass to the West and the
	West is behind us now. . . .
	We <u>wonder</u> if the liberty is done:
	The dreaming is finished. (46–47; underscoring mine)[37]

As the quotes above indicate, "wonder" aligns Wright and MacLeish, southern agrarianism and racism, Great Plains imperialism and homesteading, and the Dust Bowl. The folkloric wonder is repetitive by comparison to MacLeish's poetic creativity, but Wright's "first glimpse" of Chicago, practically photographic in its clear, potent imagery, is strategically placed so as to elevate the Negro folklore. The interrelationship between the folklore and imagery replicates the synergistic energy of the poetry-photography of *Land of the Free*.

Worster's brief but specific association of Wright's *12 Million Black Voices* with the 1930s photographic works represented by MacLeish's *Land of the Free*[38] is important. Though there is no evidence to suggest the two ever met, there is significant evidence that, for a time, Wright took ideological and poetic inspiration from MacLeish. Wright clearly knew of and admired the poetry of MacLeish[39] and later states that his approach to Bigger Thomas was to "develop the dim negative." "Dim," indeed, for Wright describes Chicago, notwithstanding its eminence as the "pivot" of America's vast continent, as a potential dust bowl because "black clouds shut out the sunshine for seven months of the year" ("How 'Bigger'" 442, 443, 453). Thus, the wintry, snowy landscape of *Native Son* doubles in meaning beyond racial hostility: the red snow that fell on MacLeish's New England in the winter after Black Sunday had, before, fallen on Chicago as twelve million tons of dust, each one a "black voice" that leads Wright to "Wonder if other people wonder." In short, the intertextuality and comparable documentary technique suggest that Wright's sensibility to seasonal cycles, as a writer who knows black sharecroppers, responds to

MacLeish's critique, as a New England poet-yeoman, of the American roots of the Dust Bowl.

Wright's autobiography quickens the eco-critical element, and contains a considerable degree of "sediment" for critics to sift, but *Native Son*, though preceding the writing of the autobiography by five years, is the inheritor of the fullest breadth of Wright's epic aesthetic. Wright's autobiography is his own story, and Bigger, a poor black youth of the South and the North, is the native American essence of the epic trickster, but limiting analysis of *Native Son* to its racial protest function reduces Wright's broad analysis of "How 'Bigger' Was Born" to Bigger's viewpoint. Protest is reflexive, anchored to the past and present, whereas cautionary stories use both as blueprints for potential future difficulties.

Temporality is important here, for if the cautionary ethos is confined to modern, personal time, Bigger's sense of time, the full implications will be obscured by direct and material manifestations. The proto-fascist impulse Wright noted among blacks, who are lured to the tribal spirit nurtured by European fascists and preached by black ministers ("How 'Bigger'" 440, 445), presented immediate manifestations. From this perspective, the looming cautionary threat is the fallout of nuclear winter—the MOS-epic's "almost radioactive" potential and nuclear-family crises. Much of *Native Son* unfolds during winter, the blanket of snow a metaphor for Bigger's consciousness of the everywhereness of whiteness. As he flees the aforementioned army of police and volunteers that grows to 8,000, he is freezing in the snow. Because of racial and other trouble, Wright excavates Bigger out of diasporic, vernacular ignominy and thrusts him into a space resonant with epic—albeit deracinated—potential.

As the epic trickster, Bigger initially shows the swelling, quickening subjectivity (*I am! I am! I am! . . .*)[40] and unbridled potential (*. . . Bigger!*) of the epic hero. For example, Bigger obtains second sight, an ability and trope indicative of epic immanence. Since his second sight enables him to see the absence of strength in his family and girlfriend, Bessie Mears (*NS* 106–08, 138–39), Bigger perceives that he has even greater physical/psychological strength. Consequently, not only does he find his family and former associates to be blind, but those who belong to the world of the Fathers and the Mothers, too. As significant as second sight might be, the actualizing *physical* potential would, unfortunately, be more appealing to urban(e) subalterns who lack the wholeness to contextualize the organic import of spiritual sight. Along with his greater insight, then, Bigger suddenly believes himself capable of amazing physical feats. Although Wright tropes running throughout the novel, its positive denotation climaxes after Bigger's rebirth. Like the lame Sunjata, he evolves from a lackadaisical loafer into a swift and decisive runner. Once he is reborn, Bigger can walk "over the snow," feeling no fear and developing a desire to explore the new world (*NS* 111–13).

Thus, Bigger, who walks "over" snow, is neither an Uncle Tom nor a mere protester. True, Bigger the *black individual* is galvanized by racial protest into an epical mode, but the *folk* Bigger signifies on a far deeper level. Considering the parallels between the role of nature in epic performance and the attempts at weather manipulation beginning in World War II, Bigger's racial fear merges into a cautionary fable. Nationalism and identity concretize the modern expression of this ethos. After all, his snowy isolation from his nuclear family is part of, Dawakare argues, larger forces capable of producing nuclear winters. But this problem can be surgically corrected: eliminate the sociopolitical barriers that feed Bigger's pathological hungers—the white hegemony and legal bars to his equal access to democracy—and America will realize its democratic possibilities for everyone. In short, Bigger's nuclear family will join the middle class.

This analysis, however, cannot account for the Dust Bowl and the ecological blight of Chicago, both of which are independent of Bigger's pathology as a black boy. Nor, more importantly, can it explain the extensive eco-critical details imbedded in Bigger's epic action. As might be expected in an encyclopedic work, a veritable cornucopia of possibilities supports an eco-epical reading of *Native Son*, for the earliest instances of such details start as normative behavior in domestic spaces. Critical to Wright's prize fighter aesthetic is irony, for beneath the sociopolitical tragedy, graphic violence, and action—the Scottsboro Boys cause célèbre, the Great Depression, masturbation in a movie theater, the accidental suffocation of Mary Dalton followed by her gruesome dismemberment, the daring and nerve-wracking extortion plot, Bessie's rape and graphic murder, and final flight from an army of white males conducting a city-wide search—lies a layer of nondescript environmental details that, fittingly, are *apropos* to a fast-moving racial epic. But these interconnected environmental details, the important domestic filler to the action proper, also have an inverse relationship to the specifics of Bigger's story. Though seemingly unimportant, epic deepens the time and implications: the Chicago cityscape folds into the 1930s Dust Bowl of the Great Plains and the modern time of normative American behavior folds into a *longue durée* that augurs future ecological disasters.

Clearly, Wright considers the animal spirits of modernity to be fatally inorganic and civil rights predicated upon access into this modernity a bankrupt strategy; instead, an organic infusion of folk sense—inclusive of TEK and respectful of the pre-modern voices—would re-form the body and its political extension, eradicating the state regimes of blackness and whiteness and the potentially global dimensions of ecological warfare. One of the most critical Dust Bowl–nuanced readings of *Native Son* begins, appropriately, not with the immediacy of epic action, but with the path toward Bigger's reformation: a job interview for a chauffeur opening with the fabulously wealthy Mr. Dalton.

Bigger's first reaction to the Dalton's palatial home—an absolute contrast between the "tiny, one-room apartment" his family occupies on the Southside and the "world of white secrets" hidden in "huge" homes full of "pride, a certainty, and a confidence" (*NS* 4, 43–44)—is stultifying discomfort, reluctance, and resistance. Feeling as if he has exposed himself, he resorts to a ritual performance dictated by Jim Crow and his own survival ethos. The Daltons encourage him to dismiss his mannerisms and, as Mr. Dalton says, "just be yourself" (*NS* 49). Understandably, Bigger does not know how to read the situation or behave. It is a figurative and a literal test, one in which passing the latter, the interview conducted by Mr. Dalton, is literally a no-brainer by comparison to the former: confronting and reading well, although alone and unprepared, the dark, opulent recesses of an impossible reality he could never have imagined. Nevertheless Bigger passes the interview, after which he becomes figuratively—and excitingly, almost dizzily, since it happens so fast—green with potential: Mr. Dalton hires him as the family chauffeur for twenty-five dollars per week, with five for himself and twenty for his family; he is shown a fancy automobile which will be his responsibility; he is rewarded with food, which Peggy O'Flagherty, the Daltons' Irish domestic, serves him; he receives his own large bedroom, which has two radiators; and, of course, he replaces Green. In the wake of all this, Bigger's native-American instinct makes him giddy with the windfall: a job a golem could perform is practically handed him and he is paid so well that he can suddenly afford to dream of replacing his "dollar watch" with a "gold one" (*NS* 58–59). Though we might stereotype Bigger's fantasies as poor people's juvenile fascination with shiny baubles, a more disturbing reading is yoked to this dismissive perspective. But for his black face, his green potential is also a golden harvest shared with and valorized by the majority; just as the Plains homesteaders' very normal but epic-inspired harvest of golden wheat wrought the Dust Bowl, Fa-Digi Sisòkò's TEK-sensitive Sunjatic axiom—"Wealth" is the "Voice of Transgression" (Johnson, *Epic* 22)—enables us to read, and foreshadow, the ecological ruins of Bigger's modern job.

By staging Bigger's fantasy of acquiring gold, *inter alia*, Wright is enabled, with a simple image of cinematic iconography, to invoke the *Iliad*'s *raison d'être*. It is, of course, the photographs he sees in Green's room as he stands "in the middle of the floor, looking at the walls. There were pictures of Jack Johnson, Joe Louis, Jack Dempsey, and Henry Armstrong; there were others of Ginger Rogers, Jean Harlow, and Janet Gaynor" (*NS* 59). Wright's narrative quickly moves on, but this is a powerful moment with equally potent foreshadowing. Although only still photographs, Green's male sports figures and white female celebrities restage Homer's epic, for they present to Bigger the possibility of an ultimate, epic prize (white women) if he, too, is a contest-champion. Of course, the pictures also invoke *im*possibility as well, and between the two is a space of encyclopedic obstacles. For Jack Johnson and Joe Louis, two contest-champions of international acclaim, such prizes are possible. At least Bigger could deduce this in theory, for he is far removed from the imagined and real impossibilities even the world's heavyweight boxing champions face. He is just a black boy, from a poor family, and poorly educated. Because he is not prodigiously talented, the photographic portraits raise the very deadly, epic possibility that one who embarks on this mythical journey confronts the very real prospect of becoming a sport of the gods.[41]

It is only fitting that Green functions as a key metonym representing the interlocked evolutions of mainstream America and the black community's epic trickster from 1900 to 1940. Green's metempsychosis from *Marrow* to *Native Son* and the tragic failures of Green's struggle come into focus once we meditate on the eco-critical significance of the chauffeur named Green. Just as Josh Green's death creates the epic potential Chesnutt uses to transform the Millers and the larger African-American body-politic, Green's absence (invisibility as symbolic death) is also a condition leading, in Robert Stepto's terms, to Bigger's epic ascent. Now, however, the stakes are much higher and forces are much stronger, for this native-son Green, far from the organically whole epic striving of Josh Green the epic trickster, has become, according to Peggy, "a good man" (*NS* 55). In the ironic space of the bad man rhetoric and aesthetic of the black community Wright has appropriated, bad—and good by implication—signifies the very opposite of what it normally connotes and denotes. Although his African etymology of "bad" (or "ba-ad," more precisely) may be suspect,[42] H.C. Brearly nevertheless made this very important point in 1939:

> In many Negro communities, however, this emphasis upon heroic dev-iltry is so marked that the very word *bad* often loses its original signifi-cance and may be used as an epithet of honor. This use of *bad* as a term of admiration is quite likely an importation of Africa, for Herskovitz has found a similar terminology among the blacks of the Surinam district of Dutch Guiana, among the Negroes of the West Indies, and among the natives of the province of Dahomey in West Africa. In some parts of the South, however, there is a change in pronunciation to indicate whether or not the word carries approval. If the speaker wishes to use the term with the ordinary connotation, he pronounces it after the manner of Webster. But if he is describing a local hero, he calls him "ba-ad." The more he prolongs the *a*, the greater is his homage. (75–76)

In short, the bad (read: ethically good) Josh Green has become the good (read: bad because he is capitalistic and egoistic) Green. Moreover, Green, as Peggy's remarks and her surname (O'*Flag*herty) suggest, is the very emblem of patriotism, for he is a "government" man (*NS* 55). Beyond Green's patriotic affiliation and G-man agency, his symbolic significance is also a capitalistic one; after all, "Green" is code for greenback. The roots metaphor underlying the epic performance is uprooted, processed, and then papered over for modern consumption.

Bigger the individual intuits enough of this to refuse Green's path and access into the state regime, but he is incapable of fully apprehending and articulating his disquiet, and thus cannot see the nondescript details for what they are. Even as he performs to type, as a black criminal on the lam or, perhaps, an epical ba-ad man, Wright has him act out the American Dream of marriage and castles literally rooted in the dusty sediment auguring future ecological woes. Bessie Mears, the domestic who is Bigger's girlfriend, half-hearted accomplice to extortion, and then murder victim, is essential. Beneath the epic-scale action and her graphic death lies the normal narrative of the American Dream, along with the details of its ecological unsoundness. The dilapidated tenement where their epic flight occurs—"a tall, snow-covered building whose many windows gaped blackly, like the eye-sockets of empty skulls"—also suggests the very opposite of these gothic details: an old three-story "house," long abandoned. Bigger and Bessie mimic the American Dream like a typical, nuclear middle-class married couple who have moved into a new home. Their home has a "wooden floor" and is "carpeted," presumably on the first level; after they ascend to nuptial bliss on the third floor, they roll out "bedclothes" and fashion a bed with "pillows near the window." Eventually, when they "lay down" together—Bigger "tense with desire"—they even have intercourse (*NS* 231, 232). Together, as a man in his castle and an angel in her house, Bigger and Bessie reenact modern Chicago's version of the classical code and the its ecological crime.

Of course, Bigger and Bessie's domestic bliss is nothing more than shadow and act, though Bigger's tenseness, "numbed" by smoking, whisky-drinking, and sex, speaks well enough to modern times and middle-class anxieties. But disturbing details from these dreams anticipate disturbing acts, and the deepening of that time as the past grandeur of that house is symbolically extended into the future. That future, represented by Bigger and Bessie's compressed time together, belongs to the Other middle classes who, seeking access in a state predicated on epic ontology, are green with potential and golden desires. But sedimented beneath putative domestic bliss are more interconnected details: the "sharp scent of rot," "scurrying" vermin, the aforementioned "*wooden* floor," and the "slight creak, as of a tree bending in wind," as he mounts wooden stairs. Furthermore, the "airshaft" of their third-story bedroom "stank of old timber" and its "floor was *carpeted* with black dirt and he saw two bricks lying in corners" (*NS* 231; italics mine).

When Bigger later decides to kill Bessie, using the brick instead of the gun because it "would make too much noise," Wright's past, the epic action, the underlying layer of detail, and the dangerous future all swirl around one another. Wright and Bigger, from this perspective, partially act out each other's role, first in life, then fiction, autobiography, and finally the cinematic version of *Native Son*. Wright and Bigger lived in Chicago during the Dust Bowl, its sedimentation—*twelve million pounds of dust on Chicago—four pounds for each person in the city*—deposited like heavy snow in 1935, two years before he published "Blueprint for Negro Writing" and roughly three years before he, in 1938, apparently conceptualized, wrote the outline of, and completed a draft of *Native Son*.

Indeed, the blueprint for the ecological, Dust-Bowl sensitivity Wright metaphorized in *Native Son* lay in his "Long Black Song" short story from *Uncle Tom's Children*. A tragedy featuring a cuckolded black share-cropper, Silas, and his young wife, Sarah, the racial drama unfolds in an unspecified rural landscape that could be the Deep South, the Southwest, or Midwest. There, just before the fiery climax of the story, death speeds toward Silas because he has killed the white man who slept with Sarah. The queue of cars racing toward their home to lynch him is not surprising, but Wright's description of its appearance is, for it sutures together impending racial terror and ecological horror: "A dull roar came from the south. They both turned. A long streak of brown dust was weaving down the hillside" ("Long Black Song" 153). Multiple readings of this northbound, roaring "streak" of dust overlap to convert an ostensibly single, simple cause into a complex relationship of race, class, gender, and ecology: the fictionalized queue of dust directly created by the cars provides cover for the arrival of the immense dust clouds of the Dust Bowl, ending Silas and Sarah's middle-class American Dreams, which had simultaneously exposed them to the travails of middle-class aspirations and the ecological consequences of rap-ing the land to maximize crop yield and market returns.

Dust from 1930s Chicago must have shocked and awed the city and Wright, a country boy scarred by southern terrorism who found the north-ern, urban(e) terrorism more frightening because its deep-seated racism was coded and gentrified. However, the bricks add yet another layer of complex irony here, one that makes Wright's knowledge—based on inductive (experi-ential) and deductive (academic, book-based) learning—more essential than the role Lucious Brockway plays as the black, basement-situated core of Elli-son's Liberty Paints factory. This is rooted in exceptional ability, but one fully able to identify with rural and working-class struggles: Wright knows the heft of the literary brick. Indeed, Wright also worked a southern brick-yard as a youth, his dog-bite experience there—the dog was vicious; the black workers threw bricks at it—extending into Bigger's use of one of the bricks to murder Bessie, who is asleep on the floor "carpeted with black dirt":

> Then he took a deep breath and his hand gripped the brick and shot upward and paused a second and then plunged downward through the darkness to the accompaniment of a deep short grunt from his chest and landed with a thud. *Yes!* There was a dull gasp of surprise, then a moan. No, that must not be! He lifted the brick again and again, until in falling it struck a sodden mass that gave softly but stoutly to each landing blow. Soon he seemed to be striking a wet wad of cotton, of some damp substance whose only life was the jarring of the brick's impact. (*NS* 237)

Graphic it is, but also quite workmanlike. Bigger "grunt[s]" like a worker wielding a sledgehammer to build a home, and then strikes repeatedly until his bloody action collapses epic violence into a southern sharecropper's cleaving of arable land. This episode is graphic cover for an interconnected web of ecological disasters with truly global, tower-razing implications that Wright places below the sociopolitical unrest of revolution, fascism, anarchy, or world war: inhumane treatment of animals; brick-laying and home-building that rely upon converting trees to wood; farming based on a monoculture of cotton which, like the wheat monoculture of the Great Plains, rapes nutrients from the soil and symbolically murders the biosphere; and the response of the earth. Or, more specifically, Wright concerns himself with the *non*-commen/sensical response to nature's voice—the Dust Bowl, colder winters and hotter summers in the city, more devastating floods, stronger hurricanes, melting glaciers, and rising seas—as the American body-politic, its bodies quickened, appetites intensified, and senses foreshortened by modern times, fails to appreciate deep-time knowledge and the cautionary ethos of TEK.

Once we factor in the chain of ecological being and the remarkable parallel between Bessie, who has "round, helpless black eyes," and Betsy, Wright's "little female poodle" who became his "pet and companion" (*BB* 66; *NS* 145), the full scale of Bessie's murder reveals itself. Although one of the most singularly brutal literary episodes—accounting for changing (de) sensitivity—in all of American literature, Bessie's murder is the result of a sequence of events set in motion by a nuclear detonation of an ecological, epical sort. This startling event merges cruelty to humans and animals as part of a *scala naturae* in which whites' cruelty to blacks is passed along by the victims as cruelty to their own children, who take the violence out on hapless, helpless animals like Wright's "stray kitten."[43] The human-animal web of cruelty Wright expresses in *Native Son* and *American Hunger* is exemplified by brick-throwing at the "snapping, growling" dog of the brickyard, or dogs "devocalized" by Jewish doctors in Chicago hospitals while apathetic black workers fought like dogs, if the animals are not mercifully "crushed to death," like Betsy, "beneath the wheels of a coal wagon" (*BB* 10–14, 71, 162, 306–309).

The implication here, consistent with Wright's perspective, is that the real racial "Problem" is not epic mythology, patriarchy, or the nation-state, but a modern epic ontology insufficiently related to folk sense. Treating the TEKnowledge implicit in Wright as part of a deep root metaphor may help to explain a problem attributed to him *vis-à-vis* Hurston's more robust use of folklore: why does Wright dismiss black folk culture? Houston Baker addressed this argument, specifically Wright's and Bigger's disavowals of black folk culture in "How 'Bigger' Was Born" and Wright's autobiography, when he says,

> the manner in which Wright's experiences were transmuted into art remains unexplained even by himself. When Wright speaks of Bigger's estrangement from black folk culture and religion there is a high

degree of critical myopia involved; he reduces folk culture to little more than folk religion. Hence, in *Native Son*, Bigger is estranged from Mrs. Thomas and Reverend Hammond (her minister), who embody the author's perception of his own folk religion. Wright knew that black folk culture was more than otherwordly hymns and humble Hebraism, but in an attempt to explain the genesis of *Native Son* he did not reveal his broad wisdom.

Thus, Baker concludes, even as he portrayed black religion as "passive, escapist," still "Wright adopted several fully developed strategies from black folk culture that have little to do with humble passivity" (*Long Black Song* 137).

The scholarly confusion over Wright's folk sense may stem from a tendency to collapse Bigger's folk sense, Hurston's more robust and sharp-tongued—but still deeply inchoate—mother-wit, and Wright's knowledge that folk knowledge entails far more. In short, we must not mistake folk ruins or fragments for a cultural performance bearing a healthy relationship to a root metaphor nourished by deep time. Clearly, Bigger's engagement in the dozens sounds like, and signifies, the existence of black folk culture, a vestige of the roots metaphor perhaps underestimated in *Native Son* because of the role of the black church and Christianity within Chicago, a racially charged urban center. Both are folk forms, but neither amounts to more than a mask for cultural rituals and forms bearing the imprints of a roots metaphor. For this very reason, Wright's experience in Seville, Spain, particularly the "Holy Week festival" Christian rituals and iconography, captured Eugene E. Miller's attention:

> As in Ghana, he was struck by similarities between what he saw in this ritual and things he had seen back in the United States, except this time the similarities existed between Old World practices and the behavior of white Americans of the Old South. Attending the statue of the [Blessed] Virgin were marchers dressed in long robes and tall, pointed hoods that suggested the garb adopted by the Ku Klux Klan. The function of these marchers also suggested the Klan to him [as Wright indicated in *Pagan Spain* (1957)]:[44]
>
> These hooded penitents had been protecting the Virgin, and in the Old American South hooded Ku Kluxers had been protecting "the purity of white womanhood." Even if the White South . . . had copied their tactics and costumes from here, it did not explain why men loved to march in defense of what they felt was female purity. Some underlying reality more powerful than the glittering Virgin or southern white woman had gripped these undeniably primitive minds. They were following some ancient pattern of behavior and were justifying their actions in terms that had nothing whatever to do with that pattern. (44)

Although Wright is not in a position to channel or reconstruct the roots metaphor, his common/sense nevertheless directs him toward it. But Wright likely knew—even if the painful memories scarred his recollections of the rural South until near the end of his life, and even though he "adopted several fully developed strategies from black folk culture"—that he did not possess a "broad wisdom." His travels to the Third World, particularly the Gold Coast of Africa, may have been his unfinished quest.

Or, for Wright, it was an impossibly tragic odyssey, the tragedy all the more painful because of Wright's keen second sight into *American Hunger.* From our vantage point of MOS-epic-attuned second sight, made possible by a black studies movement Wright did not live to see, this is clear enough: Wright never knew of the traditional African epic performance and what it would offer to make it possible to resist a racial epic without losing one's soul. With TEKnowledge rooted in the body, healing, resistance, and cautionary performances, Wright's Dust Bowl aesthetic amounts to a call for action: heroic epic performance against imperial hegemonies of race, class, and sex must provide a broad blueprint for restoring an essential, traditional epic semantics to overly simplistic, even if modern and herculean, anti-supremacy efforts.

CONCLUSION: KATRINA'S "FOLK" & SANDY'S JOKE

> WEDNESDAY, 6 JULY 2011—Phoenix residents awoke on Wednesday to a thick layer of dust . . . [covering cars, streets, and everything] . . . after a giant sandstorm more than a mile high roared through the city.
>
> The storm . . . grounded airplanes, led to traffic tie-ups and set off a wave of coughing across the Valley of the Sun.
>
> —Timothy Williams, *New York Times*

More than seventy years after the publication of *Native Son* at the close of the decade-long Dust Bowl, forty years after ecological devastation in Africa gave us HIV/AIDS and the nightmarish Ebola, twenty years after global warming became an international problem, and five years after Hurricane Katrina signaled the inauguration of a period of extreme weather and economic instability around the world, the outcome of the Wright prophecy remains uncertain. On Wednesday, March 31, 2010, virtually at the same time new emission-reduction standards went into effect, President Obama announced a new oil drilling plan. "The answer is not drilling everywhere all the time," President Obama explained at Andrews Air Force Base in Maryland. "But the answer is not, also, for us to ignore the fact that we are going to need vital energy sources to maintain our economic growth and our security" (Feller A1). President Obama announced his plans in front of an F-18 jet fighter and a light armored vehicle, both to be powered by a mixture of biofuels previously, and successfully, used by the Army and Marine Corps. The Navy fighter jet, called a Green Hornet, was to be flown for the first time on April 22nd, the fortieth annual Earth Day, using a mix of biofuels.

On the evening of Tuesday, April 20th, however, just two days before the Green Hornet could fly again for Earth Day, the Deepwater Horizon oil rig exploded in the Gulf of Mexico, fifty miles away from Louisiana. Eleven workers died in the explosion and two days later, on the fortieth anniversary of Earth Day, the oil rig sank, but there were assurances—by the international oil conglomerate that rented the rig, BP Oil, by Transocean Ltd., the corporation owning it, and the U.S. government—that there was no oil spill. There were such reassurances every day, including Friday, but on Saturday the U.S. Coast Guard did an about-face and announced that it was a serious spill. Weeks later, with millions of gallons of oil still gushing every day and BP pumping millions of gallons of chemicals into the waters to disperse the oil, the question was not whether there was an ecological disaster, but how extensive it would be. Corporations dodged responsibility, in the media and before Congress. President Obama, facing the possibility of a natural and political disaster on the scale of Hurricane Katrina, hurried to the Gulf Coast and put a moratorium on the expansion of drilling. The oil spread rapidly on the surface and on the sea floor a mile deep: it penetrated delicate wetlands, reached deep currents, closed shrimp fisheries and hundreds of miles of beaches, and formed plumes—gelatinous blobs rolling on the sea floor in subzero temperatures—destined to advance up the food chain.

Yet lost again is TEKnowledge as well as the voices of those who have the greatest stake from the epic excesses manifest as the threats of climate change, wars, and chaos central to *Native Son*: "Who knows when some slight shock," says Boris A. Max in his closing argument, "disturbing the delicate balance between social order and thirsty aspiration, shall send the skyscrapers in our cities toppling?" (*NS* 402).

Keeping in mind the 1930 to 1940 Dust Bowl that provides an eco-critical backdrop to Wright's *Native Son*, the 2005 Katrina tragedy leaves behind race and speeds US toward a global warming disaster that threatens to dim all of our lives. Recall Baldwin's comments on Bigger's "bubbling" hatred as he gazed on the jet. Bigger, indeed loitering and seething with racial blues, watches a "weaving motion in the sky [that] made him turn his eyes upward; he saw a slender streak of billowing white blooming against the deep blue. A plane was writing high up in the air. . . . Noiselessly, the tiny plane looped and veered, vanishing and appearing, leaving behind it a long trail of white plumage, like coils of fluffy paste being squeezed from a tube; a plume-coil that grew and swelled and slowly began to fade into the air at the edges. The plane wrote another word: SPEED." When finished, the plane has written "Use Speed Gasoline" (*NS* 16, 17) on the tablet of blue sky.

With this Chicago before us, the Chicago Wright confronted in the past as the black Southside ghetto, it is relatively easy to see that in the sixty-five years between *Native Son* and Hurricane Katrina, the unthinkable had happened. Modern epic weapons like the F-18 Green Hornet had gone "green" while African Americans, urbane middle and working class, had internalized consumption as access, and valued their purchasing power as an equal right long denied them. Just as Wright taps Bigger's love of fast cars and the "color and style" and "feel" of the Daltons' "dark blue Buick, with steel spoke wheels and . . . a new make" (*NS* 62, 63),[45] contemporary blacks valorize their "rides." Blacks love their automobiles so much that they will put rims on anything, as comedian Chris Rock blackly joked: "Black people, we love rims. We will put shiny ass rims on any piece of shit car in the world" (2004).

Shiny rims seem to have nothing to do with epic, but the black-American Hectors are, for reasons related to race and native impulses, forever chasing the swift-footedness epitomized by Achilles' fair eyes and hair. Herein lies the Negro folk song "wonder," a simple but profoundly ironic bluesy response, Wright invokes in *Hunger*: Achilles may have trampled on the dead like bulls treading on white barley, and "all the trees in the forest trembled and splintered" following Ozidi's "cry of slaughter" (*OS* 189), but their individual epic bravado is just one aspect of the performance. Indeed, even the "wrath of Achilles" and "Achilles heel" take on additional meaning literally conveyed through the existence of Western Yarrow, *Achillea millefolium*.[46] The literal meaning of this root metaphor—Achilles, a Bronze Age cyborg (killing machine), was also an healer—is not lost on Ursula K. Le Guin, whose classical novel, *A Wizard of Earthsea* (1968), is an epic mythology and allegorye grounded in an epic diaspora equal parts West Africa and West (Europe/America). A cautionary tale directly attuned to the MOS-epic mode of excess, and an odyssey toward power and then toward the healing resulting from self-inflicted excesses, a most remarkable moment unfolds near the conclusion when the protagonist, the sorcerer Ged, is introduced to a fellow-sorcerer's younger sister: "'Yarrow she's called. Yarrow, this is Sparrowhawk, the best of us and my friend'" (156). Hailing from the Eastern part of Earthsea, this Eastern Yarrow, owner of a dragon common to Asian lore, is the female, black-skinned personification of this flower. Their meeting is fateful, for Sparrowhawk is a name for Sunjata just as Yarrow makes her an healing Achilles heroine. Indeed, instead of "wrath," her presence signals, just before he begins the last and most dangerous journey of his odyssey, the full healing of his whole self.

Le Guin's novel is epic fiction and, like MOS-epic performances, a metafiction in which past myth is brought into the present imagination, but that epical realism is lost in a world where the dark-complexioned Ged/Sparrowhawk and Yarrow are whitened, allegorized, as the organic allegorye is flattened into standard Western fantasy.[47] In a modern world, Le Guin's *Earthsea* is just a novel set against the real things of value. Tragically, its whole value, and reliance upon TEKnowledge, becomes a weapon against those like Bigger Thomas—inner-city residents of 1930s Chicago, black and poor New Orleans natives scattered into the Hurricane Katrina Diaspora—and, ironically, the poor and wealthy whose homes and lives became the watery ruins Hurricane Sandy left in New York and New Jersey in November 2012, just weeks before the presidential election.

Thus the mantra of Van Jones sums up my argument: "Green the ghetto first." The ecological tragedy that struck the ghetto of New Orleans in 2005 as Hurricane Katrina had already struck innumerable times and against innumerable peoples looking like, sounding like, and understanding Bigger Thomas because their story has been his story; only now, all of US, including European Americans, appear to be minorities—Biggers/niggers—as Mother Earth warms up in her anger.

In other words, Jones argues that using centuries of lost TEKnowledge, which Wright foregrounded decades earlier when he said "for the Negro to try to save himself he would have to forget himself and try to save a confused, materialistic nation from its own drift toward self-destruction" (*BB* 298), to help the descendants of Africans recover this sense of human/nature, and self, will help address many lingering ills. Jim Crow segregation may end, and many folks like Bigger Thomas may access Ivy League educations and dazzling careers, becoming important "firsts," including black Green Hornet pilots and *Columbia* shuttle astronauts, and governors and black presidents. But what matters formal knowledge and "firsts" if the folk knowledge—needed to end American epic performance and prevent global ecological disaster, climate wars, and "the skyscrapers in our cities [from] toppling"—is dismissed?

6 A *Beloved*, "Ten Times Better" Community
The Epic Trickster and Morrison's post–Civil Rights Common/Sense

Sixty millions of whites are in no danger from the presence here of eight millions of blacks.

—Associate Justice John Marshall Harlan, 1896

It was not a story to pass on. . . . It was not a story to pass on. . . . This is not a story to pass on. . . . Beloved.

—Toni Morrison, *Beloved* (1987)

Blacks have to be "ten times better" than whites.

—A popular African-American common/sense

Notwithstanding the flying African mythology of *Song of Solomon* (1977), a novel many critics considered to be Toni Morrison's best, *Beloved* (1987) quickly established itself as Morrison's *magnum opus* and a "thunderbolt" (Longinus 4) in the African-American canon. The epic aesthetic, situated in a black folk tradition and rigorously racial ideology, as one might expect, leavens the novel: the historical case of Margaret Garner's slavery-induced infanticide furnishes the backdrop for the plot; Morrison's stylistics moves the experience from passive reading of an historical novel to active, visceral witnessing; and, Africa provides the deep cultural source underlying the mythological poetics motivating the action and characterization.

Exegeses that examine *Beloved* and the epic aesthetics are not new, just as critics, like Louise Cowan, have recognized Morrison's *Beloved* as an epic for women and demonstration of an older, female-oriented wisdom operating in conjunction with masculine energies (9, 18–21).[1] Though Morrison's own description of her craft holds much in common with the African epic performance, only a handful of critics have examined *Beloved* and the influence of the traditional African epic. Deborah Ayer (Sitter), in her study of the construction of masculinity and Paul D, briefly discusses the "ideal of manhood" represented by Sixo and the "tree" on Sethe's back in the context of the baobab tree of D.T. Niane's *Sundiata* (196–97). More recent work has treated the epic subject matter more extensively, although primarily through a feminist hermeneutic. Linda Krumholz situates *The Mwindo Epic* as an African epic "analog" both informing Morrison and revealing a male-centric "contamination" against which she writes ("Dead Teachers" 216–20). Kathryn Rummell reads *Beloved* against the Nyanga and Mande epic traditions, the *Mwindo Epic* and *Sunjata*, respectively. Unlike Rummell, who found Morrison's "borrowings of African folklore [to be] intentional and conscious" (1), Keith Cartwright fills in a critical methodological aporia by locating *Beloved* within the continuity of the Africa-to-America genealogy of *Sunjata* (*Reading Africa* 222–28).[2]

Notwithstanding these scholarly excavations, critical space exists to build upon their work. Specifically, Morrison's racial uplift and text-as-performance strategies enable scholars to articulate the aesthetic and socio-political roots necessary to construct a theory for how the epic trickster motivates Morrison's aesthetic, which vexes what she considers to be the novel's genesis as a bourgeois genre (Morrison, "Rootedness" 340). Her discursivity is at once postmodern and, as Morrison has iterated, resistant to any modern(ist) critique that does not privilege a black experiential lens (S. Blake 188–89; Morrison, "Rootedness" 342).[3] The logical, literary, and performative space to begin decoding such problematics is the folk story-telling tradition.

EPIC STORYTELLING

Arguably, the crossroads between Levine's genealogy of African lore, in *Black Culture*, and a rigorously conscious craft exemplified by the best of the African-American canon, meets in *Beloved*, a confluence of the formal (academic) and informal (folkloric) epic. The 1950s work of Djibril Tamsir Niane and Daniel P. Biebuyck introduced Western readers to the African epic traditions of Mali and the Belgian Congo. *Sundiata* and *Mwindo* entered the canon of world literature as classics in their own rights and provided the critical framework for much scholarship produced in the 1970s and afterward.

Coincidentally, Morrison's storytelling career began in this era, a cultural crossroad uniting the arrival of the African epic tradition, Levine's watershed study on the African/American trickster genealogy, and the myth-consciousness of the Black Power/Arts era. Although Morrison distances herself from the "instant and reactionary myth-making" of the Black Power/Arts movement ("Behind the Making" 88), mythology nevertheless motivates her storytelling, from Western racial mythologies to the mythologies of black folklore whose provenance is in Africa. Indeed, Morrison's early life makes her an ideal candidate for bardic enterprise because it gave her an interest in mythology and her longing for "places where we can hear those stories," where parents can "sit around and tell their children those classical, mythological archetypal stories that we heard years ago" ("Rootedness" 342).[4] Storytellers like Morrison, according to Hegel, enjoy the optimum position for creation of epics: close enough to the "bar of history," which instantiates an epic spirit into the tribe, but far enough removed to lyricize it (*Aesthetics* 1061). Morrison's Depression-era birth gives her a wide lens on the subject matter and lore ripe for epical poetics. The WPA Federal Writer's Project of the 1930s preserved slave-era stories for subsequent generations, but Morrison's grandparents and parents made slave folklore part of her homestead and "neighborhood." Morrison mines and channels the spirit and lore of this folk era, her "ancestors";[5] through her professional editing and storytelling, especially in *Beloved*, Morrison makes the excavation of black myth her own special storytelling project.

As mentioned earlier, although numerous studies have examined Morrison's fiction, little attention has been given to the commonality between African epic performances detailed in scholarship and the performative aesthetic Morrison inherited and consciously appropriates for her "village literature" (Morrison, "Interview" 26). Missing are the actual dancers, drummers, performers, and audience of the epic performance, but hers is a polyphonic vocality that vexes the sedentary, disembodied novelistic enterprise of the post–Industrial Age. In simplest terms, Morrison's oral model here involves a poetics of communal participation in which audience engagement was *a priori*. Indeed the dynamic intermixture of folklore and neoclassical studies makes the chorus Morrison's stories feature a lively multivocality that oftentimes explodes into song.

But akin to the African epic bards' performances, Morrison's multivocality never ruptures into the cacophonous because, as Yvonne Atkinson observes, "[i]n the Black English oral tradition the storyteller and the audience are symbiotic" (250). Call-and-response exemplifies the symbiotic space the storyteller and audience enter to negotiate the con/text. The aesthetic domain, true to its poetics of communal participation, even occasionally thwarts the epic bard's narrative mastery, as with the frequent admonitions to Okabou Ojobolo, the aged narrator-performer of *The Ozidi Saga*, to get "On with the story, man," "Tell it on, man!" and "Go on!" (272, 312, 362).[6]

Indeed, though the Homeric tradition informs gendered notions of heroic epics, the matrilineal cultural background and the performative context enable female spectators to be just as or more aggressive in their interjections or corrections.[7] Participant-auditor interruptions like this, no matter how frequent, never threaten the integrity of the narrator and narrative because, ironically, of the power of silences embodied somatically, sensually, and sociopolitically. Morrison attempts to saturate her story with "the inclusion of nonverbal gestures and tonal inflections"; since writing this would entail "a great deal of awkwardness," she says "implied meaning fills in the gaps caused by the limitations of written language." Beginning with the *in media res* opening Morrison prefers ("The Opening" 91),[8] readers must, Atkinson surmises, "listen to the spaces" if they are to fully participate in the storytelling event (247–48).

Hence, Morrison fills the spaces with meticulously chosen sights (e.g., colors, objects natural and synthetic) and sounds (Morrison, "Interview" 28–29). *Beloved* is unique in this regard, for Morrison considers it more performative and experiential than any of its predecessors. With its *in media res* opening the reader, Morrison declares, "is snatched, yanked, thrown into an environment completely foreign. . . . Snatched just as the slaves were from one place to another, from any place to another, without preparation and without defense" ("The Opening" 91–92). Through a story viscerally and experientially instructive, not merely contemplative or hedonistic, Morrison advances the concept of realism by populating her story with bodies biologic, politic, and (post-)traumatic: those of the readers, who must stand naked in foreign space (i.e., without customary novelistic cues as guides) to grasp the experience; those of the characters on whom brutal, racial violence becomes enfleshed, and their desperate attempts to make sense of or escape it, or both; and, the black body-politic, a "beloved" embrace of all those bodies and their "unspeakable" trauma, which possesses its own ability to haunt contemporary spaces and bodies.

BELOVED AND EPICAL REALISM

Thanks to the rich audiovisual field that is *Beloved*, its realism makes its imagery graphic, arresting, and impossible to resist once the readers fully enter Morrison's performative space. *Beloved*, like Wright's *Native Son*, polarizes readers, inclining their entire bodies toward the polemical and either high encomium or fierce spleen. Ironically, *Beloved*, *Native Son*, and epic classics like *The Iliad* may have ageless potency because of their ability to transport readers beyond modern-day ennui into oblivion itself—vicariously, of course—and then back.[9] The retelling of *Sunjata* at Kangaba and *The Ozidi Saga* at Orua stages the same for its African auditor-participants: in the former, the Keita youths' protection of the *bara* and the sacrosanct Kamabolon sanctuary at its center, a very real danger, likewise contributes to the mysticism; as Ojobolo retold and re-enacted *The Ozidi Saga*, the real threats to his person from other members of the troupe swept up into the mythological register made the complementary relationship between epic and realism most transparent.

Since the 1970s, reviewers and critics have occasionally associated Morrison's version of realism with the magical realism of South American writers such as Gabriel García Márquez.[10] Indeed, Morrison is critically conversant with and admittedly influenced by Márquez. Nevertheless, Morrison's aesthetic operates within an African provenance (Jennings 1–15; Wilentz 137–38)[11] and deep, epic traumas peculiar to an African-American experience. Thus, whereas magical is a rubric broadly applicable to Morrison's aesthetic, and perhaps defining in some texts, it diffuses the fusion of high mythology and staggering realism that informs her aesthetic.[12]

It is more useful to approach *Beloved* from the graphic realism and epic mythology of the Margaret Garner story and "the seething Hell of American slavery" that made it possible in the first place.[13] The flying African mythology lending *Song of Solomon* its aesthetic of magical realism is reprised, albeit in a far more limited way, in *Beloved*. Sethe, whose act of successful escape and birthing of a child has been likened to the Homeric (Argyros 141–42, 148–54),[14] is sent by Morrison flying like a "hummingbird" to scoop up her children as slavery, just as it did Garner, descends upon them with the apocalyptic authority of "four horsemen." Faced with an impossible dilemma, she is only partially checked in her efforts to commit the "unspeakable" act of infanticide (*Beloved* 69, 175, 192; *Playing* 37).

Paul D is pivotal here, for he establishes, *in media res* and at the beginning, the measure of exceptional potential as he exorcises the spiritual venom of the spiteful baby haunting 124 Bluestone. Although Paul D's early heroic feat of "beat[ing] up a ghost" and his miraculous escape from Alfred, Georgia, with the help of Hi Man, allegorically invoke the epic possibility of Old Testament interventions, Morrison's deployment of the epic comparative makes his reddish-brown, "hazelnut" complexion[15] pale next to the deeds of other characters. Of course, Beloved's resurrection and ability to clean-jerk a rocking chair with one arm and unman him, move him out of 124 against his will when he was one who "could snap like a twig" the white guards of the chain gang, require no comment. As the enfleshed representation of the "sixty million and more" victims of trans-Atlantic slavery, Beloved outmatches him by a factor that amounts to a sublime both qualitative and quantitative (*Beloved* 67, 79, 191).[16]

Beloved aside, Paul D enables Morrison to deepen the epicality of two of the Sweet Home men. Imagined as an "angel man" by Denver (*Beloved* 246), Halle more than measures up as a perfect emblem of the true Protestant work ethic. His excellence, which provides freedom for his mother, Baby Suggs, and thus leads Sethe to choose him as the most marriage-worthy of all Sweet Home men, is deserving of the praise his name invokes. But no mortal character in the novel—and perhaps in Morrison's oeuvre—approaches Sixo's sublime blend of discredited knowledge, difference, and ability, and his unparalleled resistance to slavery. "Indigo with a flame-red tongue" (*Beloved* 21), his peculiar actions epitomize the mystical. Even Beloved is hard-pressed to compete with his archetypal moment of defiance, a signature event that occurs, after their abortive escape attempt and with Paul D trapped and looking on,

> when Sixo turns and grabs the mouth of the nearest pointing rifle. He begins to sing. . . . Schoolteacher is saying, "Alive. Alive. I want him alive." Sixo swings and cracks the ribs of one, but with bound hands cannot get the weapon in position to use it any other way. All the whitemen

have to do is wait. For his song, perhaps, to end? Five guns are trained on him while they listen. Paul D cannot see them when they step away from the lamplight. Finally one of them hits Sixo in the head with a rifle, and when he comes to, a hickory fire is in front of him and he is tied at the waist to the tree. Schoolteacher has changed his mind: "This one will never be suitable." The song must have convinced him. . . .

By the light of the hominy fire Sixo straightens. He is through with his song. He laughs. A rippling sound like Sethe's sons make when they tumble in hay or splash in rainwater. His feet are cooking; the cloth of his trousers smokes. He laughs. Something is funny. Paul D guesses what it is when Sixo interrupts his laughter to call out, "Seven-O! Seven-O!"

Smoky, stubborn fire. They shoot him to shut him up. Have to. (*Beloved* 266–67)

As this graphic excerpt demonstrates, Sixo exemplifies the epic trickster as one who approaches the classical epic paradigm and yet epitomizes complementarity, contradiction, and ultimately ambivalence.[17] Indeed, his appearance is also doubly epical by standards of color-coded belief among the Ijo and in the Mande: blue and indigo represent "intractable" character in the *Ozidi Saga* performance, and red denotes female epicality in *Sunjata* (Clark-Bekederemo, "Introductory" xliv).[18]

In addition to the trickster aesthetic and ideology that enliven Sixo, as discussed later, Morrison draws from the mold of Jake Solomon and Pilate to portray him, and uses the classical device of the epic comparative to enter him into legend. Hence, when Paul D, reflecting on Sixo, thinks, "Now *there* was a man. . . . Himself lying in bed [next to Sethe] . . . didn't compare," the effect is to elevate Sixo into mythology by direct comparison and temporal distancing. Paul D's memory ritually invokes a time— called "absolute" by Bakhtin and "remote" by Bieubuyck—where men like the years-dead Sixo could do the unbelievable, if not the impossible.[19] As a mythical creature more time out of mind than a mind comfortable in the personal, modern time of the West, the funny irony, most suitable and explanatory for those who critique CP-time, is that he was never on time (*Beloved* 25–26).

Notwithstanding its sublime poetics, the most radical potential for *Beloved* lies in understanding it not only in the context of long narrative, male or female epic heroics, and the sublime terror of the real, but in its poetics of scale that ranges from epic performativity to a short narrative of *common/sense*.[20] In other words, its epic performativity is most appropriately understood not within the limitations of canonical artistry, which fails to consider the place of the real world Morrison acknowledges (*Playing* 3–6; "Rootedness" 343–45), but the performative sociohistorical context. True to its encyclopedic nature, *Beloved* develops an epic trickster aesthetic through a two-step process linking the internal and external worlds of the novel. Morrison does not dismantle individualism or even hypermasculinity, but instead envelops them within a range borne of the epical milieu in and against which she makes her texts perform. Thus the black community, as admitted by Morrison and addressed by various scholars, is the aesthetic centerpiece. However, consideration of the revolutionary potency of Morrison's aesthetic theory, one which would not offer "dreams of subversion or rallying gestures at fortress walls," achieves novelty if the contemporary black community is given voice as Morrison's ancestors (*Playing* 3).

What might it say that is useful for explicating the epic trickster? Through its common/sense wisdom, this epic community, literally and figuratively a body of knowledge, would perhaps whisper, with less authority than the canon but more sense than a "sth" of the tongue, "ten times better." That is, the post–Civil Rights era, perhaps post-modern but a classical continuation of epical violence nevertheless, requires its members to be ten times better than whites if they are to succeed. Explication of this expression invites the community into the Ivory Tower to co-interpret *Beloved* and, more importantly, suggest a common/sense strategy for abrogating the epic performance.

Because its "discredited knowledge" and "difference"[21] is seldom given attention by scholars, unlocking its meaning as a form of common/sense requires finding the diamond in the rough. The road there begins with the literary genre recognized foremost as the domain of common sense, the proverb.

COMMON SENSE DEFINED

Common sense, by all accounts, is a modern contradiction in terms. As a store of received wisdom, oral and traditional, the scholarly consensus foregrounds its amorphous, contradictory, illogical, and unreliable character. But in a watershed moment, cultural anthropologist Clifford Geertz, in "Common Sense as a Cultural System" (1975), took aim at a central hallmark of the modern/pre-modern, traditional/modern divide. Disavowing modernists for whom the divide is one of "primitivity," presumptively enfleshed, Geertz posits the difference as one of "degree." Thus, instead of arguing that "traditional" societies have high canons of thought and technology, an endeavor Geertz considers "miscast," he looks beyond the fortuities of modern sophistication to our most meaningful similarities; common sense, he argues, is a "systematized" form of culture that reveals the commonality between all societies. Under Geertz's consideration, common sense takes form as a unit of analysis, a "genre" every bit as worthy of study—and more totalizing—as the genres of art, philosophy, and religion, for example. Common sense is not an "antipodal extreme" of art, or "the simple truth of things artlessly apprehended; plain fact acknowledged by plain men," but "a cultural system; a loosely connected body of belief and judgment" that instructs us in a world of material, ideas, and everything in between. Not just an *a priori*, biological fortuity, common sense is a "special frame of mind" that differs between cultures and yet has a set of canonical features (Introduction 10–11; "Common Sense" 74–75, 84–85).

Modernity and its sciences have common sense, too, Steven Shapin suggests. This "vulgar knowledge," as Shapin argues in his controversial defense of common sense, begins to expand as a cognitive and artistic heuristic when it is approached through the ancient genre of the proverb. The dismissive rubric of "vulgar knowledge" unravels as Shapin explores the cognitive reflectivity and figurative function of context-dependent "proverbial economies," and essays to expose the proverbial penchant and unsystematic behavior of the sciences. "The learned," he quips, "are in the same boat as the vulgar" (755–61).

Geertz's and Shapin's arguments are useful, for they foreground the generic and particular, common sense and proverbs, in an organic manner critical for understanding Morrison's radical aesthetic on its own and as a logical extension of Chesnutt's and Wright's aesthetics. These proverbs are commonly defined as short sentences of traditional oral wisdom anonymous in origin (see, e.g., Owomoyela 1; Prahlad, *African-American* 34; Shapin 736).[22] They express with unlimited metaphoricity a wide range of time-tested cultural knowledge, problem-solving formulas, and psychosocial dispositions: the wisdom of the ancestors in general, and the common-sense outlook of a given social group based on its sociopolitical circumstances; experiential wisdom for situation-specific advice, counsel, critique, and diffusion of conflict; efforts to explain and understand the natural and social worlds; a means of passing time and reinforcing social cohesion; and, when sufficient contextual data permits, an individual's psychological temper associated with a particular proverbial speech performance (Obelkevich 46–47; Owomoyela 13, 15–20; Prahlad, *African-American* 25–28; Roberts, "Slave Proverbs" 130, 133, 137–38; Shapin 743–49; T. Smith 3–4, 140–58). Add to this African-based spirituality and its continuation in African-American proverbial aesthetics (Prahlad, *African-American* 28–33; Roberts, "Slave Proverbs" 132, 136), and the result is a divine close-cousin to common sense, what Sw. Anand Prahlad calls "shamanistic" ("Chickens" 268) and theologian Theophus H. Smith calls "wisdom, or *sapientia*" (141).

The sociocultural base shaping a group's shared understanding of a proverb, along with the role of the antebellum southern church as an acculturating institution, gave slaves and their descendants a sizeable store of biblical sense. John W. Roberts, in his seminal study of "Slave Proverbs: A Perspective" (1978), extracted from within the short narrative of the proverb the encyclopedic range of its habitus. Consonant with its reflection of "what the group sees as moral or ethical truths," proverbs ventriloquize "their religious beliefs as expressed in the spirituals in a number of ways" (136). Two of the most common proverbs are the cautionary prophecy, "You reap what you sow,"[23] and its secular, even militant analog made famous by Malcolm X, "All chickens come home to roost" (Blassingame 98; Prahlad, *African-American* 49–59, and "Chickens" 275–76).[24]

The point worth iterating here is that big things also come in small, nondescript packages. The proverbial economy, most often poured into a grammatical container of ten to twelve words (Shapin 736), may be mistaken for simplicity; however, its "polyvalent, all-purpose register" (Obelkevich 47) enables a variability that approaches its own version of Kant's sublime, romantic (qualitative) and mathematical (quantitative). The likeness Prahlad reveals between Gates' Esu-inspired Signifying Monkey and the African-American proverbial economy becomes one of unlimited possibility far beyond a disruption of Cartesian binaries and Manichean foils. The range of proverbial meaning and artistry, Prahlad makes clear, is a metaphorical factor extending from the complex interrelationship between literal or grammatical construction, context, sociocultural interpretation, and an individual's specific psychological ("symbolic") association (*African-American* 23–28, 31, 41; "Chickens" 272).[25]

COMMON SENSE VERSUS *A* COMMON/SENSE: A HIP HOP UNDERSTANDING

Broadly speaking, characterizing common sense as "folk thought" literally misses the beat, the skip, the hip, and the hop. Common sense denotes a body of wisdom, or knowledge, but Geertz and (especially) Shapin suggest a dynamic meaning rooted in a common people's sense-making. It is active, kinetic, at once the domain of know-what and know-how and sensual knowledge; it is abstract and empirical, deductive and inductive (Geertz, Introduction 11; Geertz, "Common Sense" 85–93; Shapin 743–49). The oldest English-language understanding of common sense, obsolete to be sure, hearkens back to ancient notions of consciousness that arise from our human ability to sense the world.

In *A History of the Senses: From Antiquity to Cyberspace* (2005), historian Robert Jütte confirms the sensual and communal[26] as original epistemologies of common sense reflected in ancient India, China, and Greece. A universal, cosmic common sense can be said to be reflected in the ancient written documents of these societies, which associated each sense with a different element (e.g., the eye could detect light and darkness because it contained both fire and water in it, respectively). Even though Aristotle, in *De Anima* [*On the Soul*], was not the first to divide the senses into five separate entities, he nevertheless became the authority on the senses, a place he retained, Jütte notes, "well after the Christian Middle Ages." Most significant here is Aristotle's *sensus communis*, or "common sense": "'But in the case of the common sensibles there is already in use a general sensibility which enables us to perceive them directly; there is therefore no special sense required for their perception.'"[27] The "common sensibles" (*sensibilia communia*) reflect traits one would associate with human subjectivity—"movement, rest, number, shape and, not least, size"—that seems to contrast to the five senses' apprehension of more static objects (20–31, 38–46, 55).

If, as the *Oxford English Dictionary* suggests, common sense and "common wit" are synonymous, the classical Aristotelian definition prevailed until about 1621, while the second, limited definition of common sense as "ordinary, normal or average understanding" begins and strengthens at about this time. Thus, Jütte notes, Descartes' theorization of the *sensus interni*, the desires such as "hunger or thirst" natural to the "human machine," replaced Aristotelian thought. The *sensus interni* apprehended the external world without the "intelligent sensorium" of the *sensus communus* (Jütte 52–53).[28]

As a corollary of this post-oral evolution, in which European/American communal sense is flattened, the dynamism of West African ethnic groups collapses into blackness. However, instead of undifferentiated blackness, this collective is a polyphonic, poly-optic, poly-somatic hero(ine) of a thousand faces whose harmonics generate a soulful *nyama* that is bad—"superbad," James Brown attests in his 1970 hit—and then some.[29] Whether she considers the community "transcendent," as Joy James argues (32), or its common cause because of unspeakable threats, Morrison clearly locates wonder within the ancestral formations of discredited knowledge. Akin to the caustic interjection such as "On with it, man!" in the *Ozidi Saga* (320), Morrison's artistry involves participation in a larger, grander common/sense. *Beloved* relies not only on call and response, though it sounds an individual-community participatory dynamic of African provenance, but call and be *called out*, too. Thus, Morrison's epic community has agency, for its polyphonic voice is oneness in harmony—synergistically, not hierarchically—with the broadcast-voice of the epic hero(ine).[30] When African-American congregants sing, "It is well, it is well with my soul," the spiritual refrain is the solo and the chorus, the solo *sotto voce* by comparison to the mass-produced, epic broadcast of 1970s soul music, but this mass is at once older, deeper, and more common.

Hence, common to both the spiritual and secular soul concerts is a jump, a circle, a cakewalk and shuffle, a tap tap, and a "hip!"[31] and a hop, to boot. The signifying genius of the tongue—of tales and proverbs, the short narratives of signifying monkeys and "proverb masters" (Prahlad, *African-American* 125)[32]—meets its match in the artistry, synchronic and out-of-sync, of the body-politic. The embodied rhythm of participatory storytelling complements the disjunctive shout-out and the singular genius of all-out physical expression that is almost heroic as a matter of course: "The dancers range themselves," missionary George T. Basden observed of the Ibo tribe in the early 1900s,

> and begin slow rhythmic movements, unconsciously swaying their head in time with the music. As the dance proceeds they appear intoxicated with the motion and the music; the speed increases, and the movements

become more and more intricate and bewildering. . . . The twistings, turnings, contortions and springing movements executed in perfect time, are wonderful to behold. . . . For these set dances . . . the physical strength required is tremendous. The body movements are extremely difficult and would probably kill a European. (Blassingame 23)[33]

The hyperbolic conclusion aside, this excerpt is witness to a vigorous artistry of embodied common/sense, ranging from the dancing noted above to the slaves' "extraordinary" language, "a kind of genius" (Blassingame 99)[34] surely reflected in wisdom, lore, song, and dance. Indeed, because of the long association of race, senses, and the European imaginary, which manifested itself as slavery and forged whites into a *sensus communis* in which "lynching was an aesthetic performance,"[35] slaves and their Jim Crow–era descendants held to the common-sense "notion that their senses could be used to resist bondage" and segregation (Castronovo 1451; M. Smith 29–39, 106–114).

The West African epic performance strives toward a quintessence of this common/sense, which assumes a bounty of participatory configurations involving narrational, musical, and theatrical elements. Defined at its core by the storytelling circle, the common/sense of the epic performance may be too massive to quantify and assay in a manner that is not grossly reductive. In the *Ozidi Saga* performance, the common/sense stems from an epic performance which begins in earnest at the "stream washing the feet of every Ijo village." Led by the ozi master-drum and accompanying drums, the *ogele* dance begins, women following the men, more people joining by voice, step, and hands all the way to the market. This momentum established, the *ogele* gives way to the *agene* or *kene-kene-koro* ("one-one-you-may-drop") dance, which asks men and women alike to genuflect forward from the waist, extend their arms frontward with the elbows bent, and move their feet in a rhythmic pattern so quickly that it looks as if they are dancing above ground. In the public square ringed by spectators on three sides, and filled with a troupe of actors, a chorus of male dancers, a group of women providing rhythmic handclapping, and musicians, "things enter" the actors.[36] Ojobolo, the narrator-protagonist, simultaneously shows his knowledge of the "root of the story" and invokes the Ijos as his collaborators: "I will not speak again, I have covered it, / the story is finished" (*OS* 100).

Small wonder, then, that between a swift-footed "little antelope" dance of Denver in Sethe's womb (*Beloved* 36), and the swift-footed poetics of racial domination, emerges the common/sense rhythms of the African-American soundtrack: the harmonizing sway of spirituals and gospels, like that of the women who exorcise Beloved; the blues, jazz, ragtime, and intoxicating dances like the cakewalk, which "Parisian critics pronounced the acme of poetic motion" (Johnson, *Autobiography* 63);[37] the rhythmic gliding and stepping of the Temptations, the Four Tops, the Spinners, the Supremes, the Impressions, and others; James Brown, "the hardest workin' man in show business," "doin' it to death"[38] in the form of "the Good Foot" and other signature dances; and, most recently, the transgressive muscularity of contemporary break dancing and hip hop.

It is the Other-ing of the common/sense that lies as the source for the dismissal of those things African. The result is a creation, particularly in America's Romance era, of a sublime horror and divinity that kept pace with the modernization of the New World. The consequence for African Americans during and after slavery is the silencing of its witnessing agency as the horrors unfurled.[39] The reality of this history not only occasions the self-inflicted racial and cultural lobotomies satirized by Pauline Hopkins as the "Hidden Self" and James Weldon Johnson as an "ex-colo(u)red man," but a self-inflicted negation of traditional Western common sense and the rise of its racial, epical, modern continuity.

COMMON/SENSE AS EPICAL, RACIAL SENSE AND THE OTHER'S "DISCREDITED KNOWLEDGE"

"The genius, wit, and spirit of a nation are discovered in its proverbs," historian James Obelkevich quotes Francis Bacon as opining (Obelkevich 49) as exemplification of a key juncture in British linguistic history: the proverbial base of common sense waned, revived, and ultimately decayed as modern nationalism, ultimately considered the antithesis of a common sense, achieved its acme. Bacon's obscure expression is telling, for "the vanity and illusions of a nation are discovered in its writings about proverbs. The English," Obelkevich continues, "congratulating themselves on the manly and moral quality of their own sayings, found less to praise in other peoples'" (50).[40] Documented here is the violent process of modernization as English and Europe shifted from a proverb-based linguistic economy, in the sixteenth century, to a literate one by the nineteenth. The separation occurs at several junctures: print culture and Enlightenment principles led early modern English elites to dismiss their previous enchantment with proverbs, which the "educated classes" used as much "as anyone else"; the orality and intertextuality of the proverb, the essence "of a society's common sense," shifted toward individualism (Obelkevich 44–45, 56, 65–66); proverbs split between those "sayings embodying official, orthodox values . . . without metaphorical flourishes and hardly distinguishable from maxims," used by teachers and preachers for the service of the nation-state, and the vulgar "wisdom" that characterized the highly metaphoric realm of the common people, who were "[s]keptical of official pieties, . . . cynical, amoral, coarse and obscene"; and, the mastery of proverbs as the measure of learning faded against the "Romantic realm, with its apotheosis of the creative self" (Obelkevich 48–49, 55–59).[41]

But "modernisation," Obelkevich argues, is an insufficient explanation for the decline of the proverb (46). Instead, it may be a selective decline traced in the shifting sociopolitical fortunes of Europe, one that may reflect a common-sense shift to a heroic culture. The beginning traces lay with the British elites and their adherence to the "old 'high' code of manners, with its aggressive sense of 'honour.'" This code, Obelkevich argues, "had a conversational style to match, in which competition, 'raillery' and display were the aims and proverbs one of the means" (57). Along with linguistic economies, economies of very different scales led to creation of capitalist proverbs in the eighteenth century and nineteenth-century proverbial novelties evidencing "a certain strong-willed and hard-working Victorian culture hero" (53). Though Obelkevich limits his discussion to Europe, he decries the modern (and scholarly) penchant against "collective wisdom," for "in viewing proverbs as a linguistic 'other', associated with peasants, plebeians and the petty-bourgeois, they [moderns] ignore their historic role in elite culture itself" (65–66).

The British shift away from the "linguistic other," with its "honour" and "Victorian culture hero" mainstays, provides a sensible proverbial genealogy that leads into the epicality of a more western, wilder American culture. Indeed, the founding myths, poured into the "hot state" of the unincorporated body-politic of colonial America, arise from the dismissal of the common/sense as a Constitution-al. The U.S. Constitution directly relates to this proverb-to-literature, common-tongue-to-elite-textuality process, for the founders relied upon theorists like John Locke, who strongly distrusted common understanding and thus favored reason-based knowledge.[42] At the level of the proverb, the process engendered the discrediting of common knowledge and relegation of the proverb to linguistic Other-ness; at the level of the epical process of concretizing a nation-state and establishing the U.S. Constitution as a high-minded, modern, democratic text, the embodied Other faced a broad, encyclopedic discrediting that ranged from low (proverbs) to high (jurisprudence).

America's epic semiotics shift the register into even more literal, violent Truths of white exceptionalism that render the Other's exceptionalism out of sight, out of mind. American college students' use of "proverbs" such as "No guts, no glory" reveal a "preoccupation" with—not necessarily endorsement of—mainstream American values such as competition, machismo, achievement, higher "levels of performance," and "overwhelming emphasis on appearance, public image, and social status." As the official maxims, "mottos or inspirational phrases" of the mainstream, the "literal" (Prahlad, "No Guts" 291–95) quality reflects the official simplicity Obelkevich identified in association with Britain's grand narrative.

The proverbial literalization Obelkevich and Prahlad foreground represents the twin process of epistemic simplification and subjective expansion into the paranormal, if not epical. As the Anglo-national character approaches the epical sublime, it becomes less a "relative" truth, "relativity" a staple characteristic Oyekan Owomoyela notes of *òwe*, Yoruba proverbs (21–23),[43] and more a simpler Truth imaginatively envisioned as the inherent, blood-based essence of national and racial character. In this nation-building process, extreme violence is done to the proverb, a short canonical narrative whose generic and thematic universality is generally accepted among paremiologists (e.g., Obelkevich 48–50; Owomoyela 5; Roberts, "Slave Proverbs" 130).[44] Proverbs, the arms, legs, eyes, ears, and tongues of our common human heritage, are truncated as an "impassable gulf" and a vertical taxonomy of US/them Truths replace them. The rich metaphorical terrain of a universal imaginary, in short, empties itself of proverbial complexity, contingency, and reflective thinking, and literally replaces it with alienating, Other-ing, racializing economies borne by mottos, maxims, and simplest of all, half-expressed thoughts, sententiae.[45] Sententiae, perhaps even more than the "epigraphs, apothegm, and didactic poetry" Hegel recognized as the earliest "elementary" epics, would seem to be the purest—and most disturbing—distillation of epical common sense.

Morrison's "American Africanism," the ideation at the root of the American racial imaginary, in large measure operates at the level of sententia. It goes far in explaining her penchant for primer-type openings—the "Dick and Jane" parody of *The Bluest Eye* (1970) and "124 was spiteful" of *Beloved*—and the significance of "schoolteacher." In fact, four sententiae, jurisprudential-religious-epical in nature, help Morrison to open and plumb the Margaret Garner story. The "miscegenation, sexual bondage, and the black woman as alluring and dangerous Other" of the Garner case forced it into "code[d]" language symbolized by Kentuckian Thomas Noble's "The Modern Medea" portrait. The result, according to Steven Weisenburger, was "Margaret Garner's translation into myth" (7–8).

But myth begins with mere thoughts that accumulate and concretize into the social contract. Thus, four fragments open *Beloved*: the title, the "Sixty Million / and more" dedication, the Romans 9:25 epigraph,[46] and the three-word first sentence, "124 was spiteful" (xi, 3). As Yvonne Atkinson states, the formal narrative beginning is the dedication (248), although *Beloved* is its (female/African) referent as title and epigraph. This formal beginning is also, however, the middle and ending, as it signifies unions of quantitative/qualitative, past/present/future, and individual/collective. The individual/collective dyad invokes Sixo's name (Ayer [Sitter] 196)—Sixo is the male/African counterpart to Beloved—and the estimated number of enslaved Africans, respectively. But this *social* epic, and centuries-old prelude to the Garner incident, has a future jurisprudential parallel of Homeric character. Morrison's "Sixty million / and more" dedication also becomes a *threat*—using Justice John Marshall Harlan's dissent that "Sixty millions of whites are in no danger from the presence here of eight millions of blacks" (*Plessy* 1147) as precedent—awaiting the characters, especially young ones like Denver, as the novel closes. This "sixty millions" promises the West-migrating eight-to-ten million blacks living in 1896 unprecedented levels of violence. This violence was *un*holy and imperial, as the epigraph from Romans 9:25—a poetic repetition—makes clear even as it chides Christians for violating the principle that *all* of God's children are "beloved." Finally, the three-word first sentence domesticates epic immanence with simple arithmetic: 124, added together, equals seven, a number long associated with epic.

This structure suggests that for Morrison, epic is not only a long/grand/master narrative, but also its very antithesis: the elemental (spiritual) and elementary (informal and formal) institutions. Consequently, the figure who represents familial and formal instruction epitomizes evil in *Beloved*. Unnamed for good reason, schoolteacher, along with his two unnamed nephews, signifies nothing and everything at the same time. They are not great, historical figures, but the social contract nevertheless valorizes the greatness of their whiteness and the uncommon reasonableness of their senses.[47] In this manner, *Beloved* poignantly reveals the privileged fault-line of modernity. In *Playing in the Dark: Whiteness and the Literary Imagination*, Morrison offers up a compelling analytic that explicates her own *raison d'être* as a writer-critic, and gives insight into her primer-thematic. "Africanism," she explains in significant part, is

> a term for the denotative and connotative blackness that African peoples have come to signify, as well as the entire range of views, assumptions, readings, and misreadings that accompany Eurocentric learning about these people. As a trope, little restraint has been attached to its uses. As a disabling virus within literary discourse, Africanism has become, in the Eurocentric tradition that American education favors, both a way of talking about and a way of policing matters of class, sexual license, and repression, formations and exercises of power, and meditations on ethics and accountability. Through the simple expedient of demonizing and reifying the range of color on a palette, American Africanism makes it possible to say and not to say. (6–7).

The "denotative and connotative" Truths of race arise, she argues, from the function of America's Romance genre, and its "imaginative entertainment of violence, sublime incredibility, and terror—and terror's most significant, overweening ingredient: darkness, with all the connotative value it awakened" (35).[48] Morrison's invocation of Homer, and her explanation of her own griotte-like aesthetic (Morrison, "Rootedness" 340–41, and *Playing* 3),[49] together suggest that purging the Homeric violence requires a coordinate aesthetic as deep and as broad as the epic white *sententiae* supporting it.

Morrison, her aesthetic theory working its magic from the roots of black folk's common/sense, starts from the premise that European/American divisions and hierarchies are fictions themselves. These fictions, among other things, create a species of "metaphorical condensation" that "allows the writer to transform social and historical differences into universal differences" (*Playing* 68). In other words, the rich performative context that enlivens metaphors for each and every society collapses and disappears into stripped-down tropes. These abstract, concretized metaphors are then mistaken for universals, Morrison suggests, because the context that would prevent such vanishes into literal textuality. Morrison's understanding is significant for she, as an African American, writes and thinks from the intersection of the African and European/American common sense. It is also critical, for this perspective enables us to see that imperial mother-wit, the *badenya-* and Hellenistic-centered mytho-"gumbo erotics"—identified by Cartwright on behalf of Sugulun Konde and Sugulun Kònate/Kulunkan,[50] and Rieu on behalf of Athena—closes a critical gap between epic and common sense. "Mother Wit," as folklorist Alan Dundes recognized, is the rubric for the whole range of African-American folkloric expression.[51] Indeed, according to Dundes, "Mother wit is a popular term in black speech referring to common sense. Mother wit is the kind of good sense not necessarily learned from books or in school. Mother wit [bears the] connotation of collective wisdom acquired by the experience of living and from generations past [and] is often expressed in folklore" ("Preface" xiv).

Morrison's own self-described soul-phonic approach to narrative, one that sounds the role of "black music" as the center figuration for African/American common sense, crafts an incantation of imperial mother-wit with griottic second hearing and mother-wit with folk-literate in-sight.[52] Instead of a poetics of enlightenment, predicated on the normalized violence of unjustifiable privilege,[53] Morrison's imperial mother-wit, as *Beloved* reveals, probes the true sense—sights and sounds—of American Africanism because she realizes that lying at its core is the dynamic power that should not "be pass[ed] on" (*Beloved* 323–24). The antidote is not mythmaking, or counter-mythmaking for propagandistic broadcast-narratives and proprietary mythologies, for in both lie a racialized, epic-minded common sense of equal parts Adolf Hitler and Holocausts, American Slavery and "Blackness" ("Behind" 88; *Playing* 6, 15–17).[54] Instead the solution, tapped by Chesnutt and Wright,[55] among others, as this study shows, is simple: excavating, evaluating, and (re)assembling the organic knowledge and cultures of the common folk that have been buried beneath modern civilizations.

The right aesthetic, for sure, is a polyphonic voice bearing epic-trickster sense. Found in a blues woman here, Ella and the "singing women" using "the sound" to exorcise a haint in front of 124 Bluestone (*Beloved* 305, 308), or a toasting male on a jazzy street corner there, this polyphonic voice begins not in high-epic poetics of individuated possibility, epic novels by Wright, Ellison, or even Morrison, but in the community poetic voice, barely heard on any frequency. That voice, too seldom spoken among the Talented Tenth, but nevertheless one that is many times seen, heard, and sensed, is but a mere discredited whisper: "It just don't make no sense" to be "ten times better."

"IT JUST DON'T MAKE NO SENSE"

Used by many an African American to be blunt about this, or a little bit of that, "It just don't make no sense" lays irony, especially, upon "white folks!" behavior, race-ism, or more general matters of the color-line.[56] The greater irony is that the perceived grammatical transgression has traditionally been placed at the feet of the vulgar, uninformed, and unenlightened. In effect, the sense is turned back on the speaker and the speaker's community, the folk and its common/sense, to suggest the absence of truer, educated, and modern sense, and the prevalence of a defining, darkening, sense-you-all: a racial sensuality perceivable and understood by whiteness to be ontologically defined by natural musicality, hypersexuality, venality, collective mimicry, uncleanliness, and anything but an empirically based sense of logic.

But "It just don't make no sense," as a short narrative and representative of that common/sense, signifies against its implied vulgarity, for within it abides sophisticated thought and witness to and signification against America's epic performance. Morrison's aesthetic in *Beloved*, doing double-time between the narrative rhythms of the epic and trickster, reality and epical history, epical heroics and epical community, (post-)modern and pre-modern, male and female, and America and Africa, takes up the common/sense to narrate and perform a transcendent poetics of scale. This *Beloved* poetics of scale, centered upon the common/sense folk, allows for the logical extension of the epic-hero aesthetic into the epic community and invites critical methodology. Unlike typical critical methods that foreground the thinking individual, here the real folk, the past ancestors and their present adherents, serve as partners in the project to level a playing field marked by exceptional hierarchies and the traumas of an American epic performance.

In this regard, "It just don't make no sense" exemplifies an existential utterance addressing itself specifically to the domain of reason, and the lack thereof more significantly. Plaintively sounding the divide between real reason, real ethics, and the ugly aporia—perceived as an impassable gulf—of reasoned hypocrisy, the common sentiment saturates much of African-American vernacular discourse. Its frequent use within the community itself taps the common/sense, the multitudinous and often anonymous wisdom arising from the experiential being of the whole community. For African Americans, the rich range of utterances comprising this common/sense is less a signification directed against its members—although there is plenty of this, too—than a reflection of its status as a form of discredited knowledge. As such, it often functions as a reservoir of experiential knowledge, static and shifting, that holds its own heuristic integrity as a form of commentary on Western hegemonies.

Although a totalizing cultural critique, "It just don't make no sense" is incomplete as folk common/sense if its full diagnosis remains discredited. Racism, of course, is irrational, but adhering to self-destructive exceptionalism presents—beyond the mind-body problem—a tenfold threat to the body-politic. An even shorter sententia, "ten times better," conjoins the body with the formal common/sense to signify on epic potentiality and the power—and limitations—of ten.

THE POWER OF TEN

The number ten occupies a special place in the American imaginary. Perhaps more than any number, it serves both the humanities and the sciences—the qualitative and quantitative, individual creativity and mathematical factors—to equate the multitude.[57] In spite of the commonality of ten fingers and toes, this ten is often construed as a factor that inscribes and measures difference: the emblematic Ten Commandments, God's covenant with the Hebrews, has for centuries been taken as God's contract with America, a sanction of the natural law and its violent ordering; "ten feet tall" is the standard measure and metaphor of giant being; the "ten-foot pole" creates a proverbial divide between oneself and another person, event, or situation; and "top ten" lists magnify "the one" at the top, of course, but also multiply this by a factor of ten. This "top ten" hierarchy deserves more attention, for it simultaneously creates a dialogic of distance and possibility: distance between "the one" and other competitors both through the consumers' anticipation as the list unfolds and the competitors' increasing exceptionalism, and the possibility for the consumers not just to vicariously share the glory, but to marshal their own genius, engage in battles royal, and remake the top ten, and themselves, in the process.

Confronted with the implications of the power of ten as metonym for white supremacy, Du Bois responded, in kind, with his own power of ten. His Talented Tenth,[58] comprising the African-American vanguard, is a mathematical and humane attempt to resolve "the problem of the color-line" as it impacted the ten million black Americans (*Souls* 5). The geniuses of the race or ethnic group, he argues in *Souls*, were always the innovators; hence, African America needed to cultivate its talented elite, through higher education and advanced degrees, to eradicate the color-line. The "pull" and "surging forward of the exceptional man" will result in "the lifting of his duller brethren slowly and painfully to his vantage-ground" (*Souls* 66).

While not exclusive of other segments of the black community, namely the working class championed by Booker T. Washington, Du Bois nevertheless insisted on a Talented Tenth formula for reaching social equality with all due celerity. Without black policy leaders, Du Bois argues, the entrenched white supremacy of the South and complicity of the North would ensure the reification of the feudal dialectic of "white" overlords and "black" chattel (*Souls* 62–74, 105–19). Not surprisingly, critics have assailed Du Bois' formula. Beyond Washington's utopian critique, *viz.*, that Du Bois' solution to the racial problem served up a neoclassical entrée that "butters no parsnips,"[59] subsequent critics resist its elitism both in terms of class privilege and masculine hegemony.

Though Du Bois' Talented Tenth warrants such critiques for its Hegelian idealism of progress through Enlightenment, his arguments against those modern Atalantas who are in pursuit of the "golden fleece" evidence an honest ethos for elevating the folk. Du Bois' fundamental concern for moral truth and his southern black folk are crucial factors. Contra Washington, who was born a southern slave while Du Bois had postbellum, genteel origins in the North, he became, in his own words, "more broadly human" when immersed[60] in their company, culture, and "the atmosphere of the land, the thought and feeling, the thousand and one little actions which go to make up life" (*Autobiography* 213; *Souls* 115).

Two non-mulatto, *bottom*-tenth tragedies, one a quasi-biographical vignette and the other a short story, are the result: Josie, the exuberant woman-child of a sharecropping family who has a "certain fitness, the shadow of an unconscious moral heroism," and who faces, and succumbs, to the Herculean task of uplift in "Of the Meaning of Progress"; and John Jones, the protagonist in "Of the Coming of John," who rises up although seeming "unfit for any sort of moulding," being "loud and boisterous, always laughing and singing." John acquires education and enlightenment, but tragically loses his soul and his soulful connection to his folk and the land. Hating his Southern roots, John's symbolic death occurs when he visits the "bright," "brilliant," and "changelessly changing" New York City and hears the epic strains of Richard Wagner's opera *Lohengrin*. The music begins "when, after a hush, rose high and clear the music of Lohengrin's swan" (*Souls* 146–47), Du Bois implying the transformation of John from ugly duckling into a sublime, white transcendence. Du Bois foreshadows the end for as the vignette—and John's life—approaches a close, the "twice-told" intersection of race, gender, racial uplift, and southern violence unfolds to the tragic sounds of *Lohengrin*.[61]

The critical question for the black community, which produces working-class achievers like Josie and John, is even more pressing than for Du Bois, who lost a son: faced with racial, class, and gender problems, how good does the bottom tenth have to be to succeed in the white world? How much more excellent must they be when even Du Bois overlooks their common/sense? The answer, its post–Civil Rights–era commonality in the African-American community making it an anti-American Africanism, if not a truism, is both the corollary and radical revision of Du Bois' Talented Tenth strategy: they must be "ten times better."[62]

TEN TIMES BETTER

In some respects, the sententia is an ancient, communal genre like any other. More pithy than tales, proverbs, parables, and nursery rhymes, and yet containing their wit and wisdom, sententiae reflect anonymous observations on life by members of a community, who embrace its truth. Bourdieu's thoughts on "common sense" are useful here, for "[e]very social order systematically takes advantage of the disposition of the body and language to function as depositories" to write its values. From birth to childhood onward, "childhood learning" is full of "implicit pedagogy" contained in the "rhythm of a line of verse whose words have been forgotten," "rules of thumb," and staples of domestic etiquette—"sit up straight" is one such "injunction" (60–69). If, as Bourdieu suggests, nursery rhymes have the capacity to reify the political mythology, a form of the grand narrative writ small, by the same token, and through similar processes of transmission, the black community of the post–Civil Rights era appropriated and popularized "ten times better" to comment on the epic challenges facing the individuals and community.[63]

"To succeed, you have to be ten times better than they are" was common enough by the mid-1980s that the expression was part of the black folklore passed on by the older generations to the young as a matter of course.[64] Even more than their Civil Rights–era descendants, African Americans from the late-nineteenth to early-twentieth century exemplified this ethos. Post–Civil Rights–era scholars, students of history in particular, see the parallels between earlier civil rights icons whose careers or lives were eclipsed by the people and events of the 1960s.[65] Various critics and artists iterate the prevalence and wide range of "ten times better."[66]

One could easily imagine that Morrison's maternal grandparents (Ardelia Willis and John Solomon Willis) and parents (George Wofford and Ramah Willis Wofford) shared this same rhetoric. Though Morrison is a midwesterner by birth, southern black folk traditions were mainstays in the Wofford family[67] history. Morrison's maternal grandparents were Alabama expatriates who brought with them Afro-centric love and cosmology: "Her parents told her ghost stories. Her grandmother used a dream book to play the numbers" (Blake 188). The family cosmology consisted of equal parts dedication to fighting racial oppression and an ethos of racial self-determination and uplift approaching the superhuman. The "truth is stranger than fiction" axiom ascribed to magical realism is actualized in *Song of Solomon* (1977), for John Solomon Willis "learned how to read through his own efforts and those of his sister," taught himself the violin, "inherited eighty-eight acres of land from his Native American mother," lost it to "unscrupulous white men," and eventually fled a harsh sharecropping existence in Kentucky for Ohio (Jimoh 2002). Just as the Willises and Woffords exemplified the belief that they had to be ten times better, Morrison imbibed this ethos:

Her father, George Wofford, a shipyard welder, worked three jobs simultaneously for most of seventeen years and was proud enough of his workmanship that he wrote his name in the side of the ship whenever he welded a perfect seam. Her mother, Ramah Willis Wofford, sang in the church choir, reasoned with the bill collectors, and, when the family was on relief and received bug-ridden meal, wrote a long letter to Franklin D. Roosevelt. . . .

As her father was an exacting workman, Morrison is an exacting stylist who continues to revise, she says, even after her books are bound. (S. Blake 188)

The mythological, storytelling, and racial context of her youth, combined with Morrison's "exacting" standard as an African-American novelist, constructs a ready association between the racial urgency to be ten times better and the particular poetics of her craft. Moreover, the popularity of this expression in the post–Civil Rights era is significant. Morrison reaches full adulthood and emerges as a storyteller, immersed in black folklore, who valorized black language during the heyday of Civil Rights efforts.

Like proverbs, spirituals, trickster tales, and similar genres, ten times better has a rich texture. Even as sententia, the shortest genre of common/sense, its performative dimension gives it a poetics of scale that matches the classical epic narrative in pragmatic terms, and may even exceed it in some ways unique to it. Grand it is, as well, but instead of an *official* master narrative, it offers the inexhaustible richness of the common/sense: collective memory, sense-making, artistry, and language, but also, true to the polyphonic, call-and-response aesthetics of African origin, the creative individuality operating within the larger whole.

The close scrutiny of ten times better to unlock its potency is a literary analog to splitting the atom to produce atomic energy. In fact, a European form of this sententia is arguably a precursor since modern European/American cultural performance enacts the process of transforming epic mythology into material, mass-producible reality. The godly provenance of Achilles' new armor allegorizes the modern world of swift, sublime technological upgrades. This phenomenon is one in which Longinus' *technê*, the artistic craft needed for producing epic poetry, takes on a performative dimension in which the ancient epic imaginary is concretized as modern reality. Considered as allegorye, such "independent fragments of speech," Walter Benjamin explains, operate through a "disjunctive, atomizing principle" in which each fragment "acquires a dignity equal to that of gods, rivers, virtues and similar natural forms" (208). Black folk, in this regard, too often unseen and taken for granted, or patronized as the disabled or unable in the stress of modern competition, like a humpback or the halt, are atomic beings, too, capable of *being, becoming,* and *producing* ten times better.

As with traditional African performances, the long/grand narrative of the epic heroine or hero is just an element; the epic community encompasses and defines the heroic, which is a ten times better transgressiveness welcomed only on troubled days. Paul D's exorcism of the spiteful ghost is a necessary, though insufficient, catalyst for the song of Ella and the other black women who finally exorcise the enfleshed spirit. His *fadenyic* transgressiveness is a welcome interruption to the very troubled and falling household comprising only *badenyic* energy; Ella and the other women's soulful *badenya* is welcome, too, after the Paul D–exorcised 124 Bluestone becomes an even more troubled trinity of women that "nobody saw . . . falling." Through these, along with Stamp Paid's intercession and Denver's independent action (inspired by the spirit of Baby Suggs), Morrison creates an heroic synergy whose soulful *nyama* results in a harmonic poetics of scale ranging from female to male, individual to communal, and narratives of trauma to epical responses. In short, the common/sense is, per force, ten times better.

Here, the literal meaning obtains, and much of the success of *Beloved* stems from the characters' elevation of their response to meet the exigencies of America's racialized epic performance. Because of its brevity, ten times better seems to foreground the literal meaning. But as indicated earlier through explication of proverbial common/sense, literal constructions are often improper because of the metaphorical subtlety of the expression, the community's experience-driven common understanding, and an individual's particular, context-specific association. While *Beloved* is a novel, applying Morrison's insight to the real-world usage of ten times better enables us to thrust *Beloved* into the interpretive richness of becoming and being epical. Hence, in addition to serving as benchmark, a measure of the epical or superhuman in body or deed, ten times better is both a protest against conditions necessitating such performance and, most significantly, a cautionary tale meant for contemporary American readers—white and black, especially—"not to pass on."

"TEN TIMES BETTER" AS PROTEST AND CAUTIONARY TALE

Beloved, read as a post–Civil Rights novelization of ancestral common/sense, performs this cautionary element. Clearly, as critique of the grand narrative, ten times better decries the past and continuing performance of the white epic; *Beloved*, as Morrison's fictionalized voice of the ancestors—including Margaret Garner, the novel's characters, and "sixty million and more"—presumptively participates in this critique as a neo-slave narrative.

Although America's racialized common sense motivates Morrison's writing and thinking, and thus becomes a *sine qua non* for a proper exegesis of her novels, the African-American lens through which she narrates forces the reader to construct meaning by using the history, culture, and experiences of the ancestors. The ancestors are not those nationally sanctioned as ten times better because of epic whiteness, nor the mulatto/a-complexioned Talented Tenth whose his-and-her-stories continue to establish the ontological benchmark for all African Americans. Morrison's aesthetic reveals, contra the canon of belles-lettres, the virtually untapped beauty of the common/sense, which is often dismissed by the black elites in fiction and fact as the simple, pre-modern element that drags the race down.

Though heroic, avant-garde, and pro-education narratives such as *Invisible Man* have their place in the black canon, particularly in response to an overwhelming epic performance that has historically required, and assumes, exceptionalism as an ontological norm, Morrison's oeuvre problematizes this norm and the enlightened, Talented Tenth rejoinder. In *Beloved* the more complex cautionary tale speaks to working-class African Americans, particularly the "eccentrics" Morrison favors (Morrison, "Interview" 28), those whose lives are often foreshortened narratives to a whiteness construed to be ten times better ontologically.

Out of the slave community, and from among the field hands, Morrison realistically imagines these multihued individuals—singularly, in harmony, and in discord—to create a polyphonic poetics out of the black epic community.[68] Baby Suggs, holy, conjures up a feast out of famine, as one blackberry "grew to a feast for ninety people."[69] Paul D, shipped down south after the failed escape from Sweet Home, miraculously escapes Alfred, Georgia, the chain gang, and a flood of rain, mud, and snakes; condemned to work "the ditches," which were "one thousand feet of earth—five feet deep, five feet wide, in which wooden boxes had been fitted," after eighty-six days, when his "Life rolled over dead," he emerges like Lazarus from the grave. Ella, who "considered love a serious disability," survived a "puberty . . . spent in a house where she was shared by father and son, whom she called 'the lowest yet'" and "against whom she measured all atrocities." It was she, a hardened, "practical woman," who "convinced the others that rescue was in order" against Beloved's spiritual "invasion."

For the love of mother, slave wife, and mate, the novel's men performed the amazing. Not only did he learn to read and write and do arithmetic, but Halle, "Baby Suggs' eighth and last child, . . . rented himself out all over the county to buy her away from" Sweet Home. Joshua forgave his wife and changed his name to "Stamp Paid," and collected black folks from the Ohio, where "the dragon swam . . . at will." And, Sixo, just to see his lover, fourteen-year-old Patsy, the Thirty-Mile Woman, walked a marathon: "He left on a Saturday when the moon was in the place he wanted it to be, arrived at her cabin before church on Sunday and had just enough time to say good morning before he had to start back again so he'd make the field call on time Monday morning. He had walked for seventeen hours, sat down for one, turned around and walked seventeen more" (*Beloved* 26, 29, 79, 125–31, 274–75, 301–02).

And just as amazing as any of these is Sethe's odyssey. Although she was pregnant with Denver, sexually assaulted and whipped, Sethe managed to escape from Sweet Home, travel through the forest, and reach the Ohio River without Paul D, Halle, Sixo, and the other Pauls, all of whom were caught or killed, and only with Amy Denver's timely help, while Denver's "antelope dance" kept a fading Sethe going.[70]

The complexity of ten times better keeps these individuals and the community from being labeled icons of victimization or romantic essentializing, for Morrison's narrative deploys the common/sense as both and neither of these: as a rich signifier unto itself that is both ahistorical and historically determined, and as a state of being and performance always shifting between a tricky reality and sublime epic mythology. In short, Morrison accomplishes this by collapsing the protest novel, epic, and trickster aesthetic into a cautionary tale whose implied message about striving to make—or deny the realities of—myth and its long master narrative is simple: the cost of being ten times better is tricky, indeed risky, even if historically necessary. Thus, though *Beloved* is a slave narrative, one that reveals the archetypal abilities and struggles of its characters, it also responds to blacks' Civil Rights/Black Power–era ethos that boldly claimed, at the expense of their slave ancestors, "Not me."[71]

Morrison does this by using her open-ended, community-centered novel to create a counter-performance to Western epic excessiveness for readers to enter and experience. What the attentive will find, contra classic uplift narratives, are irreducible paradoxes. Slavery is one of the unspeakable horrors in human history, but the wonderful paradox that is humanity warrants that even the oppressed, trying to be ten times better, must be sublimely cautious and ever mindful of the common/sense. Just as anger and "disapproval" arose against Baby Suggs, holy, and 124 Bluestone because the miraculous feasts "were His powers" (*Beloved* 161), Morrison's communal aesthetic creates space in which every action and reaction, however socially necessary, frivolously indulgent, or patently horrific, has to be judged by its impact on the common/sense. *Beloved* provides a centerpiece in which actions of heroic necessity expose the dangers to the self and the community to which one belongs. The black atomism is perhaps inescapable, but the *coolness* implied by or associated with being *bad* demands consideration of fateful questions: can the community support your action to protect you and, most importantly, itself from the nuclear fallout of your actions *and* you? And, assuming this to be true, can the community protect itself from the excellence—introduced into its midst and separate from the causal agent? Badness and coolness may define the ideal responses to the epical moment, but the paradox, evident from MOS-epic performances, also obtains as a cautionary parable: because badness is dangerously transgressive, a hair-trigger remove from excessiveness, one has to know the far more important lessons of coolness as containment. In short, epic effect must be matched—probably exceeded—by an understanding of epic semantics; for Morrison's *Beloved* community, the exercise of ten times better is a form of epic agony to be performed with judicious common/sense.

Numerous characters—Baby Suggs, the Sweet Home slaves—exemplify the cautionary character of ten times better, but none more appropriately, perhaps, than Halle, Sixo, and Sethe. Taken together, Halle and Sixo, the most exceptional of Morrison's male characters, reveal the twin face of the epic trickster: Halle, whose name is literally a shout[72] to biblical excellence, represents the Judeo-Christian ideal of Job-like dedication and possibility, and Sixo, whose very name is a trickster-like signification against the normative knowledge and ethos Halle represents, and schoolteacher corrupts, has already been identified as Sunjata-like in his epic potency and defiance. In them, one finds ahistorical, personal exceptionalism, an epical response to the yoke of slavery, but severe consequences as well. Recall that Halle's fate is one of "squatting in butter"—this following their abortive bid for freedom—and watching, helplessly, from the barn loft as Sethe's milk was stolen by schoolteacher's nephews (*Beloved* 264). Halle's excellence, of being ten times better to meet epistemic and biblical standards, and making and revising excellent plans of escape, results in insanity.

Use of the trope of insanity, for those blacks who achieve exceptional formal knowledge that pierces the veil, is far from new.[73] Of course, this racial melancholia—what Anne Anlin Cheng identifies as the "melancholy of race"—is and remains controversial. But the stigma of racial inferiority, criminal pathology, and self-victimization only has traction in a modern consciousness characterized by an allegorically flat and classical sense of exceptionalism. Wright's and Morrison's challenge is not predicated on equal exceptionalism (which they assume), but its inherent dangers.[74]

Contrary to Wright's and Ellison's uses of this trope, Halle's insanity does not stem from knowledge, or the denial of it, but he nevertheless reveals the limitations of formal (epistemic and ethical) excellence, and thus the limitations of a system built upon them. Knowledge and formal ethics are necessary, in other words, but insufficient. Sixo, the quintessence of the epic trickster, is a character alive with proofs of the insufficiency. Of course, he rejects formal education, and then the very *lingua franca* upon which it is based. Hence, Halle and Sixo would seem to be at ideological odds, but it is significant here that Morrison places Sixo and schoolteacher in conflict. More than a racial/ethnic divide sanctioned by American culture, though it is central, their divide arises over the privileged uses of knowledge, enlightened and empirical *vis-à-vis* discredited common/sense. Halle's knowledge might not appeal to Sixo, but its use is common-sensical and necessary; schoolteacher's knowledge divides commonality—Sethe's in this case, for the formal education of his nephews—into "her human characteristics on the left; her animal ones on the right" (*Beloved* 228). Out-of-sync temporally, Sixo is also out-of-sync in a more fundamental way critical to Morrison's common/sense poetics and an epical realism that suggests that common/sense is not simply fiction or superstition.

The clash between schoolteacher and Sixo—ostensibly over a stolen shoat but really between a white man and an enslaved African, one of "the definers" and "the defined," and between two epics, one modernized by Enlightenment, the other rooted in a discredited knowledge—is a given,

as is the result, a beating and a lynching, for Sixo, though seldom recognized as a trickster-proper for good reasons,[75] is nevertheless an epic
trickster (*Beloved* 224–25). His name is a "six"-o that subverts the West's
system of patronymics, which renames and re-identifies the enslaved as
"negro" chattel, disrupting its qualitative and quantitative certainty. "Six"
also implies the centuries-old association, in Europe's Christian imaginary, of the paganism of antiquity Walter Benjamin describes as "a purer
natura deorum [nature of the gods], embodied in the pantheon," and the
darkness of Satan. Centuries before the Enlightenment and the modern,
nation-state-based notions of race of the nineteenth century, *necro-*, negro,
blackness, and Satan ("666") foreordained Africans as Satan-spawn in a
simplified Christian imaginary collapsed into matter—the body—easier to
espy and thus control. Morrison conflates her Sixo and 666 to draw attention to Sixo's laughter, an epical performance Benjamin would have championed inasmuch as it is an allegorycal signification against "the triumph
of matter." Sixo, indeed, has what Benjamin calls the "devilish jocularity
of the intriguer, his intellectuality, his knowledge of significance." He has
a "scornful laughter of hell. Here, of course, the muteness of matter is
overcome. In laughter, above all, mind is enthusiastically embraced by matter, in highly eccentric disguise. Indeed, it becomes so spiritual that it far
outstrips language. It is aiming higher, and ends in shrill laughter. However
brutish the external effect may be, the inner madness is conscious only of
it as spirituality" (227). Nevertheless, Sixo is still a tragic diminutive that
portends, in the final analysis, a foreshortened narrative because neither his
life-narrative nor his name has the potential of Seven-O, his son.

Seven, of course, has broad significance relative to this study.[76] Sixo, a
trickster-hero whose very name reinforces this status and manner (Krumholz, "The Ghosts" 401), may not be the epical seventh, but he is the father
of the seventh-one. Thus *Seven*-O, representing Sixo's resumption of and
signification against English, is a defiant patronymic gesture that names
into being his epic trickster legacy and signifies against the West's qualitative and quantitative (mathematical) sublime.

If Halle and Sixo together offer a double-tongued rejoinder to the "not
me" ethos of black militant masculinity, the "me, myself, and I" ethos of
assimilating, or the gradualism that would seek safety in nonexceptional
moderation, all troubled by ten times better, Sethe's her-story is the house
giving structure to the *sententia*. Indeed, the consequences of Sethe's
actions, pursuant to a maternal need to be excellent that reflects Morrison's
perspective on "contemporary issues about freedom, responsibility, and
women's place" ("Foreword" xvii), begin the novel: "124 was spiteful. Full
of a baby's venom." *Beloved* begins *in media res* most appropriately, then,
for it both starts the narrative and also locates, architectonically, Sethe's
epic-related dysfunctions as the beginning, middle, and end of things.

Akin to Morrison's epical crafting of Halle and Sixo, Sethe's her-story
claims its own glory, for she, an illiterate black woman, successfully

escaped slavery by herself, a doubly remarkable feat since the obstacle that prevented women from fleeing slavery was maternity, all too often resulting from the planters' use of them as breeders.[77] Thus, the twin, contradictory narratives of success and trauma occasion her remark to Paul D:

> I did it. I got us all out. Without Halle too. Up till then it was the only thing I ever did on my own. Decided. And it came off right, like it was supposed to. We was here. Each and every one of my babies and me too. I birthed them and I got em out and it wasn't no accident. I did that. I had help, of course, lots of that, but still it was me doing it.

Likewise, when schoolteacher, as one of the "four horsemen," arrives at 124 Bluestone to capture the fugitives, Sethe took wings and "just flew." Significantly, in both instances, Morrison uses Sethe as the focal point for choice—coded as "selfish pleasure" and "selfishness"—conjoined with an urgent necessity that simultaneously creates and destroys it. The paradox of a barren present and vibrant "rememory" is the result of this will-to-exceptionalism, even in the face of historical exigency. Sethe's "selfishness" and "selfish pleasure," then, round out the complexity of ten times better, and renders Sethe, a female "counterpart" of Sixo, as Morrison's quintessential female epic trickster.[78]

In mythical terms, Sixo may eclipse Sethe and her actions, as do other sublime events and characters, but just as a dysfunctional house starts the narrative, the historical complexity of Margaret Garner's choice structures the story. Hence, notwithstanding the role selfish choice plays in the critical passage above, which occurs just before a "forest sprang" up between Sethe and Paul D (very near the center of *Beloved*), Morrison reveals the ultimate theme. As Sethe considers Paul D's nuptial offer, a robust "rememory" and barren present collapse into a moment pregnant with all this time, and the future:

> She thought quickly of how good the sex would be if that is what he wanted, but mostly she was frightened by the thought of having a baby once more. Needing to be good enough, alert enough, strong enough, *that* caring—again. Having to stay alive just that much longer. O Lord, she thought, deliver me. Unless carefree, motherlove was a killer (*Beloved* 155, 190–92, 194).

To simply love as a mother, to be "good," "alert," and "strong enough," in other words, required Sethe to go beyond motherly love to be, and face a future rememory because of being, ten times better.

It is this paradox that Morrison found to be a "riveting" idea for *Beloved*. Morrison says her imagination failed her for example, but the memory of her ancestors did not as an epiphany from *The Black Book* occurred to her. In a moment which documents that the genius of her aesthetic is not the mythmaking she decries, but plumbing the artifacts and wonders of black

238 The Epic Trickster in American Literature

life, a "newspaper article" in this instance, Morrison remembered Margaret Garner. Garner exemplifies ability, necessity, and dire consequences for
she, according to Morrison, "was certainly single-minded and, judging by
her comments, she had the intellect, the ferocity, and the willingness to risk
everything for what was to her the necessity for freedom." But what moved
Morrison, ultimately, was not the "fascinating" history, but the subjectivi-
ties resulting from being ten times better: "So I would invent her thoughts,
plumb them for a subtext that was historically true in essence, but not
strictly factual. . . . The heroine would represent the unapologetic acceptance of shame and terror; assume the consequences of choosing infanticide; claim her own freedom" ("Foreword" xvii).

The Margaret Garner her-story, then, is Morrison's "canvas" for medi-
tating on contemporary feminine vigilance, choice, and the failings of the
Civil Rights era.[79] Slavery, by contrast, occurred during the earnest, epical
exigencies of an historical epoch, Morrison seems to imply, when assert-
ing maternal will as a black woman was difficult enough, but becoming
ten times better to challenge it, as was necessary for the betterment of US
all, required a unique personality, perhaps an epical one. To explore the
contradictions inherent in American slavery, Morrison appropriately collapses time, space, events, and character. While this ingenious strategy
serves to create an historical novel about a fugitive slave, *Beloved* nevertheless resonates so deeply with audiences because Morrison intertwines the
consequences of Margaret Garner's epic performance with post-1960s civil
rights efforts related to race and gender.

CONCLUSION

Morrison's aesthetic theory of common/sense, a poetics of scale between
epic narrative and *sententia*, offers a revolutionary solution to the deep
divides of American epicality and modern hegemonies separating the West
and the Rest. Against canons of exceptionalism, literariness, modernism,
and complexion-based privileges, Morrison valorizes the genius common
to and constituting US all. Baby Suggs' ritual circle in the Clearing effects
a *tabula rasa*, not to reify the now-debunked Western common sense that
people of African descent had no original culture, or "to clean up their
lives or to go and sin no more," but as a means of clearing away layers of
racialized, epic-minded Africanisms, "Africanist idiom" (James 38), and
loss of a common/sense. In the epic space of the novel, slavery's dehumanizing, Othering common sense is culturally and Constitution-ally written
and read onto the bodies of former slaves. Hence, when Baby Suggs intones
"we flesh; flesh that weeps, laughs; flesh that dances on bare feet in grass.
Love it. Love it hard. Yonder they do not love your flesh" (*Beloved* 103), her
"ancestral" spirituality works to excavate a wholesome, soulful, embodied common/sense. African/American in origin, it arises from a common

guns. Thanks to the Internet, military technology, and government policy, domestic surveillance of Americans dovetailed into a "War on Terror" that now includes extrajudicial military strikes on suspected terrorists and even Americans suspected of—but not formally charged with—plotting against US. The U.S.-led Odyssey Dawn Operation toppled Libya's Muammar Gaddafi, Operation Geronimo led to the extrajudicial killing of Osama bin Laden, considered the 9/11 mastermind, and American Indians protested the use of Geronimo as a military code name.

Perhaps more important than any of these developments is the rise of Asia and recent events that augur America's lost global influence. Japan's economic hegemony may have lapsed, but it has been replaced: China's recent rapid economic, militaristic, and technological growth parallels the same national arcs for Germany in the nineteenth century and for the U.S. from the mid-nineteenth to the twentieth century. Celebrated film director Zhang Yimou's "epic" opening ceremony for the 2008 Summer Olympics in Beijing stunned the Western world by staging China's majestic and ancient cultural history (Gong 204). After eclipsing Germany and Japan as the world's largest exporter in 2009 and second largest economy in 2010, respectively, China has captured the global imaginary—especially among Europeans: most nations believe China has already topped or will top the U.S. as the world's leading superpower and economy (Pew Research Center, "China" 3, and "Global" 5). In 2008, Asian immigration into the U.S. surpassed that of Spanish-speaking immigrants (Pew, "Rise" 11, 30).

Despite decades of Afro-Oriental cultural and political alliances dating back to at least the 1920s, these developments may present a *deepening* of the global racial divide. China, like Europe of the 1890s, initiated a second "scramble for Africa" by buying land (Polgreen A6). Although the 2010 emergence of Spanish speakers as the largest "ethnic" group in the U.S. has critical political and economic implications for African Americans, Asian immigration may be equally significant. Spanish-speaking immigrants, who have aligned themselves with the experiences of minority Americans, are projected to become the largest ethnic group in the nation by 2050. The Asian immigrants represent a very different demographic. Although they tend to lean democratic and prefer a more active government, Asian immigrants' higher salaries—their technical expertise commands top dollar—and higher rates of college and graduate degrees compared to the populations of their countries (Pew, "Rise" 27, 35) put them at a far remove from African Americans, the U.S. ethnic group they are least likely to marry.

The marriage gap between people of Asian and African descent relative to higher rates of inter-racial marriage between people of Asian descent and other American ethnic groups is not surprising. Although the cultural and linguistic difference is the same with other groups, differentials in level of education, Asian American's higher mobility because of their socio-economic status, and, most importantly, global and U.S. racism multiply the cultural divide. The effect of Asian countries' greater discrimination against people African descent and the recent rise of the economic power of Asia amplify the cultural divide in the U.S. This results because immigrants from Asia into the U.S. enjoy higher global stature than most other immigrants, often have technical or professional degrees that remove them from mainstream American culture, and they dismiss the materiality of a centuries-old racial performance that would allow them to evaluate stereotypes.

African Americans, because of the history of slavery, bear a particular burden that peole of African descent from other nations do not bear. For African Americans, epic, irony, and Asian Americans date back to Chesnutt's satirical reading of and dissent to *Plessy*, which he restages with Dr. Miller's train ride from the North to North Carolina: "At the next station a Chinaman, of the ordinary laundry type, boarded the train, and took his seat in the white car without objection" (*Marrow* 55). Chesnutt plays the stereotype,[2] 1896 American jurisprudence and 1850s Chinese railroad slaves—"coolies"—perhaps collapsing into a new-age tragedy Chesnutt, a sure-sighted apostle of modernity, *sees* for Africa and its Diaspora.

Some Asian Americans, aware of this divide, have actively sought to address it for years. For example, Korean-American novelist Chang-rae Lee, in *Native Speaker*, in the wake of the L.A. riots, maps out the decades-old history behind tensions between African and Korean Americans in the late 1980s and early 1990s. Byong-Ho "Henry" Park (박 병호), his narrator, sums up the tension as one in which his father, a South Korean with an engineering degree from the best South Korean university who has to settle for life as a "green grocer" does try, "[f]or a time, . . . not to hate" African Americans. Mr. Park hired several African Americans, but when they all proved unreliable he resorted to immigrants alone, "even blacks from Haiti or Ethiopia," under a rule of thumb that became inviolate: "The most important thing was that they hadn't been in America too long" (186–87).

Here Lee, showing that he is most astute student of African-American literature, carefully and methodically approaches this delicate subject. Relying upon a seemingly objective gesture—yes, African American work habits are inferior to immigrants, and yes, privileged Asians like Mr. Park are harder, more disciplined workers—that seems to justify African-American resentment toward Koreans, Lee effectively establishes a disquieting moral and ethnic dilemma of his own. Since both ethnic groups are equally right *and* wrong, then a fundamental contradiction lies within the social structure itself that brought them together. Faced with this paradox, Lee changes the joke and slips the yoke by leaving behind the sidewalks of New York City realist fiction to recover the mythical terrain, and common/sensical lore, the Parks have sacrificed in their Korea-to-America emigration.

Though Lee's narrative voice and technique remind most critics of Ellison's *Invisible Man*, Lee writes toward the cautionary ethos of *Native Son* and critique of America's production of exceptionalism. Against a post-Korean War backstory and a favorable immigration policy of internationalism turned toward Asia, especially Korea, *Native Speaker* takes direct aim at Ellison's underlying strategy of foregrounding an exceptional African-American whose narrative frame (beginning and end) is a protest against his invisibility and unrecognized individuality. In contrast, Lee suggests that the talented, well-educated, and articulate South Korean immigrants who embody the heroic "lore" of rugged individualism suffer a greater burden directly associated with the internalization of such ideals and, ultimately, the repudiation of folk common/sense. Instead of an African-American Green, the absent model of successful education and enlightenment who moved on up, Bigger Thomas learns in *Native Son*, from chauffeur for the Daltons to government man, Lee relies upon a Korean-to-America green grocer immigrant who also moves on up, eventually to the wealthy Westchester suburbs. Henry Park, carries Wright's Green-based uplift and generational projection into Henry's work as a G-man: a private spy for Glimmer & Company. Lee's strategy, of casting off Ellison's reliance upon the totalized, claustrophobic voice to make Henry the spy a feeling person, follows naturally from a cultural critique that places the locus of imperial authority in epic myths motivating the elites—like Wright's Daltons and Lee's Boswells, the parents of Lelia Park née Boswell, Henry Park's wife. Instead of an after-the-fact protest from a subterranean space of privilege isolated from the folk-sense on the loose in New York City, Lee rejects Ellison's categorical critique of folk forms just as Henry, ultimately, rejects the ethos of perfectionism and hyper-rationality that reduces itself, ultimately, to overwork. After all, in addition to the "Massive global stroke" and multiple strokes of Mr. Park (mentioned at the end of chapter 3), his mother, "an impossible woman," dies of liver cancer, and Henry's Ajumah literally drops dead from pneumonia brought about by overwork—one night she "collapsed" while trying to care for the stroke-stricken Mr. Park (77, 80, 221), In short, Lee turns not away from traditional knowledge, and epic lore, but *toward* it in a most essential gesture: it is necessary to save Henry because neither his perfect speech, marriage to an European-American woman of exceptional pedigree, elite education, inherited wealth, "honorary white" status as a Korean, nor his individual will (to be bigger and not invisible) can.

Against the racial frustration that engulfed their communities, numerous Korean- and African-American scholars, artists, and activists, like Chang-Rae Lee, Elaine Kim, and Spike Lee realized the white/Other divide as their common enemy. Indeed, Spike Lee's *Do the Right Thing* is most poignant: Sonny, a Korean shop owner facing angry black rioters following a police officer's killing of an unarmed black youth, shouts, "I no White! I Black! You, me, same! We same!" Sonny's solidarity is recognized and rewarded on screen, but the U.S. Asia-oriented immigration policy, in place since the 1960s, strategically undermines that solidarity and interethnic cooperation in real-world terms. South Korea has become one of the world's wealthiest nations and the high number of Koreans entering elite American universities/colleges means lost jobs and income, along with dwindling democratic leverage, for all Americans. This is most true for African Americans, who are less affluent than Americans of Asian, European, and Hispanic descent (Pew, "Rise" 12).

African-American novelists confront a post-globalization racial problem comprising centuries of Western/white Othering that is potentially becoming centuries more—Mother Owl[3] allowing—of Eastern/"honorary white" Othering. Against this dilemma and the epic trickster sensibility of Chesnutt, Wright, and Morrison, how do authors who have foregrounded a cautionary ethos as an answer to epic performance measure up? James McBride's *Song Yet Sung* (2008), Colson Whitehead's *The Intuitionist* (2000), and Paul Beatty's *The White Boy Shuffle* (1997) represent three interim voices.

McBride's *Song*, set largely in the marshlands of antebellum Maryland, fuses together a neo-slave novel, cowboy mythology, and African/American epic mythology. McBride's gritty epical realism—replete with seers (its protagonist has visions of our hip hop present), a giant, an infamous gun-slinging cowgirl, a feared bounty hunter, and a Sixo-like "Woolman"—is deceptive. McBride's epic aesthetic, a *Song* that signifies against the type of singing Ella and the women of *Beloved* represent, folds into a Christian-based cautionary ethos: all of these epical characters, including the protagonists, meet violent ends because of their hatred and greed. Freedom is about choice, about "being decent," says Amber, a slave, as he interprets the protagonist's dreams (162–63). Amber's anthem, a rejection of sociological fatalism, strictly adheres to American-styled Judeo-Christian optimism.

Whitehead's plot for *The Intuitionist* is a temporal-spatial grayscale set in an unidentified urban-American landscape and an indeterminate time. Instead of the epical milieu McBride selects, Whitehead combines hard-boiled, crime-noir detective realism, elevator "lift" technology as a Tower of Babel *leitmotif*, and racial uplift heroics. Swirling sabotage and election politics around his protagonists, an unassuming black woman whose dedication to her profession eclipses all, Whitehead uses *The Intuitionist* to critique the classical racial uplift strategy of attaining intellectual excellence at all costs. Whitehead conflates technology, atheism, "genies"/"djinns," and "mythology" en route to directing toward the protagonist (and Ivy League–based uplift strategies) the novel's most critical question: "Was it worth it? All the stuff they put on you?" (92, 226, 234–42).

Despite their virtuosic insights, Whitehead's and McBride's Christian allegories do not engage racial mythology as an epical performance that foregrounds *present* culture. America's fluid epic performance mythology has never been reducible to Wild West mythology, white supremacy, antebellum slavery, mental superiority, technology, or Christianity. Instead, it literally encompasses "everything" between the ancient genesis and the imperial future.

While the traditional epic performance is encyclopedic, in the racially charged modern form of Homeric epic performance, it is also a cannibalistic black hole that devours everything: epicality, of course (Geronimo, who fought imperialism, became an American celebrity), but also natural resources from scorched earth to scorched sky, human resources that make us most human, and even Time. Clement Hawes defined eighteenth-century Britain's temporal cannibalism, a rewriting and thus conquest of the Past, as *metalepsis*, a trope involving the "retrospective fabrication of origins" in which "effects are retrospectively constituted as origins and causes" (148).[4] In addition to this, the Homeric American performance cannibalizes a *future-metalepsis*, a development Afro-futurist writers and scholars see as a disturbing whitening and colonization of the future; this, of course, is equivalent to Britain's and Germany's imperial dreams to equal and surpass the duration of the Roman Empire.

Beatty's *The White Boy Shuffle* responds to the bi-millennial challenge with the allegoryçal ferocity of MOS-epic hipness: Beatty sews epical cool into the French-made soles of "high-tech Adidas Forum II's, an outrageously expensive pair of plain white basketball shoes, computer-designed for maximum support." He then laces them up with neo-imperial satire so hilariously keen that the users of "basketball courts in ghettos throughout the world"—beneficiaries of Adidas donations, the salesman says (89)—will hip hop with Mwindic and Ozidic laughter until they keel over. Gunnar Kaufman, a mind-body genius who slams sublime poems down just as easily as he does basketballs, does exemplify black exceptionalism and late-capitalist commodification (Murray 215; Rambsy 643), but more than this he represents Beatty's epic-attuned insight into America's epic performance and the cautionary ethos he combines with a satirical take on blacks who (un)intentionally subscribe to it.

Hence, *White Boy* enhances African-American literature with a *fresh* Afro-Orientalist aesthetic. Converting a neo-slave novel steeped in the Kaufman men's Uncle Tom devotion to British and German exceptionalism into a *new-yo!*-slave narrative that is Gunnar's inheritance, Beatty deploys Hip-Shogun and Afro-Korean women in the L.A. era of the Rodney King riots. *White Boy*, a "poet's hip-hop epic" ("First" 154), rambles through the Afro-Asian-Latin back lot of America—Hollywood Western mythology, rap video shoots, gangsta and urban legends, fetishization of Nazi gear and weapons, professional sports celebrity obsessions, faux multiculturalism, inner-city violence, and the bourgeois affectations of the African-American elite—en route to returning to, reinvigorating, the "roots" of traditional folk soulfulness.

A wicked-smart and scathingly hilarious novel like no other in the African-American canon, *White Boy* does not surrender the mass(ive), hip (hop) folk potency of epicality even as Beatty refuses to essentialize and romanticize. He recognizes that sophisticated, modern theories and discourses fail to credit folk tradition as a reservoir of generations-deep insight into human nature. Contra the classical Christian allegories of *Song* and *Intuitionist*, the most vivid personality in Beatty's novel is its international, cross-temporal, transgressive/excessive allegorycal character. Thus, *White Boy* closes with an ongoing communal ritual in a public L.A. park, a place where his mail-order Japanese wife, Yoshiko Katsu, gives birth to an Afro-Japanese daughter.

Though Afro-Orientalism represents Beatty's carnivalesque quest for traditions, epic agon(y)—from an inescapable epical performance—explains the existential vertigo that closes the novel, and opens it: in the Prologue, Gunnar, a bestselling poet-minstrel, represented by the 126 million copies he sold of *Watermelanin*, a poetry collection, announces himself qualified as a "messiah" for blacks; Chapter 1, which begins his memoir, immediately debunks his qualification by erroneously placing his ancestors' origins in East Africa (Mount Kilimanjaro, in Tanzania) and lamenting his lack of a seventh-son inheritance (1, 5). Like Huck at the close of Twain's riotous coming-of-age-in-an-epic-performing-America story, Beatty's conclusion suggests that Gunnar has not learned the lessons of epic excess. After all, Yoshiko is Japanese (an "honorary white" whose exceptionalism was fetishized by many European Americans in the 1990s), the public park is surveilled by a police helicopter, and the communal ritual is a *real* live telecast.

Beatty's television-sensitive satire puts him on sound footing. Chesnutt foregrounded newsprint as the mass medium of 1890s white supremacy, and Wright achieves his epical realism in part by using both Chicago newspaper headlines and the silver screen to make *Native Son* bigger, more cinematic. The wild popularity of "movie palaces" before the Great Depression occurred because cinema achieved epic quality—spectacular sights and sounds—that devoured reality. In such an epic habitus, reality merges into possibility because Americans fetishize celebrity culture until reality becomes increasingly elusive. In *Native Son*, the titillating newsreel Bigger sees of Mary Dalton and other rich white debutantes became *Trader Horn*; for Slavoj Žižek, the merger is between 9/11 and *The Matrix* (1999).

Inspired by 9/11 coverage and the social commentary of *The Matrix*, Žižek points to the "passion of the Real" as the defining trait of late capitalism in significant part because everyday social reality has become insufficient and the only "authenticity resides in the act of violent transgression." Under late capitalism, Žižek argues, life loses its material substance and becomes a "spectral show" consisting of television reruns and a social life in which our neighbors behave like actors and extras. Hollywood has conditioned us with the Real until the repeat televising of the 9/11 attack—"the collapsing tower . . . reminiscent of the spectacular shots in catastrophe movies, a special effect which outdid all others"—loses its social meaning. Here, Žižek rewrites Marshall McLuhan's classic dictum to posit the spectacle—not the medium—as the message: it cannibalizes television and Hollywood cinema. The 9/11 terrorists did not attack the towers for the "material damage," he argues, "but *for the spectacular effect of it*" (7–18; italics in original).

Consider here Boris A. Max's closing remarks at Bigger's criminal trial, which warned of "skyscrapers . . . toppling." Wright's prophesying here is less the prediction of collapsing towers in the service of the revolution than the collapse of the fictions upon which the edifices are built. In Beatty's *White Boy*, the Afro-Oriential folk recovery actualized by the communal ritual fails because America's epic performance is inescapable even for persons exceptional of mind and body. Gunnar's ritual anticipates reality television and the day when even Weather Channel anchors could report "wildfires of 'epic proportions'" and "epic flooding" virtually at the same time—and with professional cheerfulness.[5]

The question of the success of the epic trickster ultimately becomes moot in this instance as the "reality" behind the epic habitus, too tenuous for its inhabitants to exercise any discerning judgment, consumes itself. As that happens, many more of US, not just Bigger or Gunnar types, may wake to a sunless day and greet one another with the only appropriate words for the occasion: *Welcome to the desert of the real.*

52. See, in particular, Žižek 7–18.
53. The Enemy Way ceremony, also known as the "Navajo War (or Warrior) Dance" and the "Navajo Squaw Dance," are frequently performed continuously for a period lasting nine days during the summer and autumn months (Gill 102; Schwarz 310).
54. Cf., e.g., Haile: "We may not agree with those who make Monster Slayer subject to weakness so that he was eventually forced to become the first patient of Enemy Way" (19).
55. Odysseus' traits, according to the ancient Greek tragedians, all of them war veterans, are the following: "'quibbling, unscrupulous, corrupt, ambitious, self-serving, sophistic, rejoicing to make the worse argument appear the better'" (*Odysseus* 78, quoting W.B. Stanford, *The Ulysses Theme: A Study in the Adaptability of a Traditional Hero* [New York: Barnes & Noble, 1968], 110).
56. For a similar perspective on how slavery corrupts and perverts, see Jacobs 44, 112.
57. See also Conrad, "Introduction" 4.
58. Equilbecq did betray some ambivalence toward the Manden lore, which includes his encounter with *Sunjata*: it represented the "supreme vestiges of the primitive beliefs of the black race and, on this basis, deserve to be saved from oblivion." For this and comments on the ambivalence of Maurice Delafosse, an instructor at the Ecole Coloniale in Paris, see Bulman 233, 236, 239.
59. The Mwindo epics are so different, Belcher emphasizes their discontinuities as preeminent (*Epic* 41).

NOTES TO CHAPTER 3

1. Alan Dundes reports that Hurston's work may be nothing more than "poetic license" (*Mother Wit* 542).
2. For example, Abrahams' Davy Crockett is an epic trickster prototype, for he is a frontier hero whose life "shows . . . the biographical pattern of epic heroes" and yet "his adventures and pranks all express adolescent and even occasionally childish (*trickster*) values" ("Some Varieties" 343, 357–58; italics mine).
3. To his credit, Abrahams' thought continued to evolve. His subsequent scholarship, such as *African Folktales: Traditional Stories of the Black World (Fairy Tale and Folklore)* (1999), contained African heroic epics. Indeed, although it meant nothing to me at the time, my first encounter with the *Mwindo Epic* was through this volume.
4. For the importance of the moving, dancing body to storytelling, see Levine 16, 88–89.
5. This summation comes from Levine 6–10, 16, 31–32, 36–37, 82, 88–89, 90–99, 102–24.
6. See Levine 420–29.
7. Levine agreed with Ruth Finnegan regarding epic in Africa. See Levine 86–88, fn12.
8. Cf. Sir Walter Rodney's comparative perspective on Shaka Zulu versus what he might have been as a slave in the Diaspora. See Rodney 131–32.
9. Of course, there are traditional musical instruments often used by the epic performers, such as the kora, balafone, ngoni (lute), and *jembe* drum. There is also Mwindo's adze and conga-scepter, but again Biebuyck's scholarship does not designate them as epic-specific implements. Indeed, I could find no pre-colonial or colonial-era *indigenous* representations of epic figures in sculpture or any other plastic form.
10. Though the focus here is on the Manden and the Niger Delta, names are, of course, important to the Nyanga, too. See Biebuyck, *Hero* 95.

11. Primary archival sources and secondary resources document these examples and are included in the bibliography. Also, see Newbell Niles Puckett, who compiled a list of 10,954 slave names from 1800 to 1865 and compared it with the names of contemporary black female and male college students. Among the top one hundred most common names was *Helen*, a name which was not given to *any* female slaves on his 1800–1865 list but was the *fourth* most popular name among black female college students (477, 479–81, 489).

12. A full investigation of all slave names, a difficult task if not all but impossible, is outside the scope of this study. Moreover, the irregular orthography characterizing English well into the nineteenth century, combined with epic variants (e.g., Sundiata, Sonjata, Sonjara), means that searches through various electronic databases are speculative.

13. In versions of Sunjata not influenced by the patriarchal bent of Islam, Tumu Maniya, a female, is considered to be Sunjata's first *djeli*, the one who first travels with him and who composes "Song of the Bow" (S. Belcher 109).

14. Various instances of Soso/Sosso (male and female), Bala (a male), and Balla are in the Afro-Louisiana History and Genealogy 1699–1820 online database and among the names I collected from the Registers of Liberated Africans made in Sierra Leone, Havana, and Rio de Janeiro (between 1819 and 1845).

15. Cartwright stipulates, on this point, that "only a trace of its imperial memory and a stronger vein of the Mande/Senegambian semiotics at work in it seem to have survived the transformations of American acculturation in familiar form" ("Reading Roots" 36–38).

16. See Abrahams, *Deep Down* 97–172; Brown 177–83; Levine 382–83.

17. For more of Roberts' work in this regard, see "The African American" 98–101, and "Stackolee" 180–183, 187–189.

18. See, e.g., Krumholz, "Dead Teachers" 563–67, and Peach 65. However, these studies concentrate on how recent recuperation of traditional African epics has influenced contemporary writers, not on transmission through slavery.

19. Indeed, inspired by Detienne, who maintains that in ancient "Greece no less than elsewhere, myths are perpetually retouched, rearranged, revised, and corrected" (16), classics scholar Thomas J. Sienkewicz used comparative methodology to explore the Sunjatic tradition in "The Greeks Are Indeed Like the Others: Myth and Society in the West African *Sunjata*" (1991).

20. Schein foregrounds gender more than race. For a precursor to his essay, focusing on slavery, see Paul Cartledge's "Rebels and Sambos in Classical Greece: A Comparative View" (1985).

21. For similar thoughts on Mwindic and Sunjatic performances, see Biebuyck, *Hero* 19, 23–24, 41–42, and Conrad, "Introduction" 3, 8–9, 12.

22. Newton's allusion to "moving picture" is echoed by Ousmane Sembene's thoughts on film and African oral tradition. See, e.g., Anny Wynchank, "The Cineaste as a Modern Griot in West Africa," in *Oral Tradition and Its Transmission: The Many Forms of Message*, eds. Edgard Sienaert, Meg Cowper-Lewis, and Nigel Bell (Durban, Natal: U of Natal, 1994).

23. Belcher argues for an indigenous, *badenya*-inspired occult as antithesis to Islamic patronymics. See S. Belcher 107, 109.

24. See Ford 33–53 for similar efforts to reconstruct the Homeric *allegoresis*.

25. Scholars are keen to note the rejection of "slavish imitation" by the colonial Americans. See Reinhold, *Classica* 236, and *Classick* 1, 3, 130; Richard 44–45. This ethos is not only indicative of a break with Old World "hobgoblins," as Emerson quips in "Self-Reliance" (1131), but an epic mimicry of greatness in which the "Ancients" served as a point of comparison. Other self-reliant Transcendentalists follow suit. See López 122–51.

26. Turner's reading of medieval Europe's folk theater parallels Benjamin's and Bakhtin's studies. See "Images" 28–29.
27. Patterson argues, specifically, that Virgil appropriates but also rejects Homer to "inscribe a redemptive Roman difference" (162–64).
28. For example, Thoreau, author of *Walden* (1854) and the essay "On the Duty of Civil Disobedience" (1849). For Thoreau's "Homer worship," see López 123–24.
29. Cited in Abrahams, "Some Varieties" 354, n.13.
30. The American Virgil was Joel Barlow, author of *The Vision of Columbus* (1787), and Philip Freneau, author of various lyrics and satires, was the American Horace.
31. For analysis of the ancients versus moderns debate, and its America versus Old Europe version, see Aldridge 99–118, and Richard 28, 30, 51–52.
32. See Richard 21, 30 for discussion of the role of Homer in the grammar school education of John Adams, Alexander Hamilton, and Charles Pinckney.
33. Pope followed John Dryden's translation ethos. Dryden exercised poetic license to convert the originals into material resonant for contemporary audiences. Thus, classics scholar Richard Bentley is reported to have told Pope, "It is a pretty poem, Mr. Pope, but you must not call it Homer."
34. The quote is from 1751, by a promoter of the College of Philadelphia (McLachlan 86).
35. For discussion of private libraries, see Reinhold, *Classick* 9, and Richard 26–27, 31.
36. Probably Angelica Kauffman's famous and oft-copied *Hector Taking Leave of Andromache*, exhibited at the Royal Academy in 1769.
37. For more on how this "self-reliance" argument allowed for favorable uses of Homer and yet rebuffed the British nobles' arguments for the "hereditary rule" of ability, see Richard 204–07, 217–18.
38. For more on numismatic controls, see W. Benjamin 173.
39. For more on contemporary textbooks, monuments, and heroic treatment of Washington, see Loewen 18–32, 255–57.
40. Historians differ on whether he inherited it, earned it in the French-Indian wars, or gave it new meaning. *Conotocaurious* is a name Washington used for himself in his own correspondence in 1755. Washington's great-grandfather, John Washington, had himself earned a similar or identical appellation because of his seventeenth-century dealings with American Indians. "Town Destroyer" is also translated as "Burner of Towns," "Devourer of Villages," or "Town Taker."
41. According to *Webster's New World Dictionary*, 2nd College Edition (1986): "to•pon•y•my (tə pän⌐ə mē) n. [<Gr. *topos*, a place (see topic) + *onymia*, a naming < *onyma*, NAME] 1. the place names of a country, district, etc., or the study of these 2. [Rare] Anat. the nomenclature of the regions of the body"; and "top•o•nym (täpə nim⌐) n. [back-formation < TOPONYMY] 1. the name of a place 2. a name that indicates origin, natural locale, etc., as in zoological nomenclature."
42. For more on the Croakers, see Maar 155–56.
43. The case of Troy Davis became an international cause célèbre. A former sports coach in Georgia present on the night (August 19, 1989) an off-duty Savannah, Georgia, police officer (Mark MacPhail) was shot and killed, Davis faced murder charges in *State v. Davis*, which resulted in conviction and a death sentence. Davis always maintained his innocence and evidence corroborated his claims. In light of these circumstances as well as Georgia state and federal courts' continual denial of his petitions for another trial or release, Davis' case garnered widespread public support. Supporters

included Nobel laureate Archbishop Desmond Tutu, Congressman John Lewis (D-GA), former President and Nobel laureate Jimmy Carter, Rev. Al Sharpton, Pope Benedict XVI, former FBI director and federal judge William S. Sessions, Harry Belafonte, and representatives from the Council of Europe and European Parliament.

44. For example, the novels of the premier African-American novelists are illustrative. In addition to Chesnutt's and Hopkins' aforementioned novels, Sutton E. Griggs' *Imperium in Imperio* (1899) offers an anti-folk, high-literacy, epical Christian martyr as the response.

45. On February 20, 2009, a white police officer shot and killed an unarmed seventy-three-year-old, Bernard Monroe, a black man left mute by cancer, on his own porch. As Mr. Monroe attempted to check on his wife, who was inside their home with policemen who had chased their son inside, Officer Tim Cox fired seven shots into him.

46. The naming history is not absolute, with some sources indicating Zebulon and Centerville predated the 1838 deed while others suggest Troy followed these two names before becoming official. The city officially considers 1843 to be its founding. Troy has the distinction of perhaps being the only city in the United States with a monument—erected in 1906—honoring John Wilkes Booth, Abraham Lincoln's assassin.

47. For example, from June 15 to July 22, 2000, performance artist Andrew Arnaoutopoulos' "Trojan Horse" art installation ran at the Institute of Modern Art. Arnaoutopoulos' work was a critique of modern Western libraries and their history of expropriation. For more, see Stelzer (2000).

48. The deadliest computer program that, unlike a virus, does not attack immediately, but lies dormant, working covertly to destroy files or hardware, or give hackers control of the computer and access to sensitive information.

49. *Quoting* Fernand Braudel, "Histoire et sciences sociales: La longue durée," *Annales d'histoire économique et sociale* 4 (October–December 1958): 725–53. Translated as "History and the Social Sciences: The *Long Durée*," in *On History*, trans. Sarah Matthews (Chicago: University of Chicago Press, 1980), 25–54; quotation from 27.

50. Even among leading African-American scholars, this reading of Twain's Jim obtains. See Lewis 91–93.

51. From *Webster's New World Dictionary*, 2nd College Edition (1986).

52. Stark argues in "*Invisible Man*: Ellison's *Black Odyssey*" (1973) that Rinehart "is a Proteus who continually changes his form. Odysseus knew how to improvise and trick, but the doctrine of invisibility is a revelation to Ellison's hero" (62–63).

53. He has inspired others, such as Kerry James Marshall and Kara Walker (Powell 63).

54. "Few realize that he was inspired by the classic black silhouettes on Greek vases, such as *The Return of Hephaistos*, a masterpiece by Lydos in the sixth century B.C.," Romare Bearden and Harry Henderson note (133).

55. Or, I am tempted to say, the years *formally* considered the Black Power era. In fact, the logic of epic mimicry not only predates Black Power and its earlier incarnation in the 1920s, but goes back to the 1870s, when the sartorial needle went in motion. After all, the 1870s saw the birth of the New Negro, the rise of black epicality in the form of John Henry and Stagolee, and the emergence of sports attire. Tom Delamere, in Chesnutt's *Marrow*, is illustrative. Delamere makes sporty use of blackface performance in a way that reflects minstrelsy *tradition* and *future* forms of epic mimicry as expropriation.

56. I am referencing, of course, television "sets" and the movie *Pleasantville*, dir. Gary Ross, with Tobey Maguire and Reese Witherspoon (New Line, 1998).

57. Fla. Stat. Ann. §§ 316.2951–316.2957 (1984).
58. Published in 2002, the actual completion date is unknown. Scholars suggests that it was completed between 1853 to 1865.
59. Quoting Friedrich Nietzsche, *Die Geburt de Tragodie* [*The Birth of Tragedy*], from *Basic Writings of Nietzsche*, trans. and ed. by Walter Kaufmann (New York: Modern Library, 1972), 115.
60. With regard to South Korean *gwarosa* (과로사), it is an exceptional performance in its own right. South Koreans "put in far more time on the job than citizens of any other free-market democracy," according to the 2008 *Factbook* of the Organization for Economic Cooperation and Development (OECD), which included thirty developed countries in May 2008 (Harden 9A).

NOTES TO CHAPTER 4

1. Paul Robeson, "Joshua Fit de Battle of Jericho," Rec. 29 Dec. 1945, *The Power and the Glory* (Columbia, 1991).
2. Some of Chesnutt's family members were eyewitnesses. See Pickens 51.
3. The "bar sinister" is Chesnutt's metaphor for illegitimate, interracial birth. See *Marrow* 66; Sundquist, "Introduction" xi.
4. Albion Tourgée's *A Fool's Errand* (1879) is also significant. See Sundquist, "Introduction" x, and Andrews, "Introduction" xxi.
5. See Andrews, "Introduction" xli. Cf. Gates, "What Is" xii–xv.
6. In "Of Our Spiritual Strivings" from *Souls,* Du Bois reiterates "power" as the solution to the color-line. Chesnutt, who is closer to folk traditions as a southerner with roots in North Carolina, voices traditional wisdom.
7. Mary Ann Dwight's *Grecian and Roman Mythology,* ca. 1849.
8. See Brodhead 87–88.
9. See Chesnutt, "Journal" 12, 18, 22–26, 29.
10. For more evidence of Chesnutt's preference for the ancient Greeks, see "Journal" 23–25.
11. See note16, infra. Basically, Chesnutt uses the plot in "The Sheriff's Children" for the first part of *Marrow* and the Wilmington massacre for the second.
12. See chapter 3, pages 95 to 101, for James McLachlan.
13. The town of Troy, Montgomery County, North Carolina, was first settled by Scottish immigrants. It was renamed after John B. Troy, a "popular attorney and solicitor of the judicial district." For more Troy lore, see http://troy.nc.us/town_information.htm.
14. See Chesnutt's "Charles Chesnutt's Own View of His New Story, *The Marrow of Tradition,*" *Cleveland World*, 20 October 1901, in *Charles W. Chesnutt, Stories, Novels, and Essays*, ed. Werner Sollors (New York: Library of America, 2002), 872–73, at 873. Josh Green may be based on a New Orleans figure, Robert Charles. See 1898 Wilmington, Appendix M, 16, fn.16.
15. The names of Josh Green and Dr. Miller, for example, are loosely appropriated from prominent African American families, the Greens and Millers. See 1898 Wilmington, Appendix A, 7.
16. Cf. George and Pressman 287.
17. John Delamere, Esq., Sandy Campbell, and Dr. Miller have much in common with Col. Campbell, although Dr. Miller is also similar to Tom Campbell.
18. Chesnutt's "Journal" reveals his sharp disdain for Paris' similar behavior when he, in single combat against Menelaus, had to be rescued by Venus, who wrapped him in a "cloud, and conveys him from the field to the nuptial bower." He is being "dragged" (46–47), presumably through the sand, when she spirits him away.

19. See Watson 162–69, 177–79, and Hutteman 9, 48, 49, 52 for information on Wilmington's classical culture.
20. By "masterful duplicity," J. Allan Taylor, prominent Wilmington business-man and member of the Secret Nine, meant "the ability of white leadership in Wilmington to develop long-range plans for instigating violence, a strategy to quell that violence and their subsequent ability to call the affair a riot—implying a sudden break in peacefulness rather than reveal its true character, that of a planned insurrection" (1898 Wilmington, "Front Matter," 12–33).
21. Chesnutt uses this quote near the end of both works. See "The Sheriff's Children" 87, and *Marrow* 321.
22. Pauline Hopkins, one of Chesnutt's contemporaries, deploys the same approach in *Of One Blood; or, the Hidden Self* (1902 to 1903).
23. Contra "The Sheriff's Children," *Marrow* depends heavily on historical fig-ures and events in colonial America and the United Kingdom, including the geopolitics of the British Empire as it pertained to colonial Africa. It would have required considerable research and awareness of literary venues such as *Blackwood's*. Chesnutt's decision to close his stenography business in Sep-tember 1899 to become a full-time author and lecturer probably coincided with his access to the serialized form of Conrad's novella. For discussion of *Blackwood's* status, elite readership, and pro-imperialist policies, see Alling-ham (2000), and W. Atkinson (2004).
24. See Felsenstein 12, and Horejsi 201
25. For discussion see Horejsi 201–17, contra Felsenstein 12–13.
26. See Mize (1971).
27. The number of Homeric printings spiked considerably in 1776 (approxi-mately twenty). Curiously, almost none of these were of British origins (Young 110).
28. Emerson, calling for "self-reliance" and "non-conformity," invokes mythol-ogy and whiteness. See Emerson 1128, 1130, 1131, 1137.
29. The 1808 date represents the publication of the manuscript most commonly read today. See Cunliffe xv–xvii.
30. For discussion of the encyclopedic significance of Homeric and African epics, see Frye 315–26, and Johnson, "Yes, Virginia" 320.
31. F. O. Matthiesen, *American Renaissance: Art and Expression in the Age of Emerson and Whitman* (New York: OUP, 1941).
32. See Gross 180, and Kennedy 1151.
33. Cf. Sundquist, "Introduction" xxvi–xxvii.
34. See *Barden v. Barden*, 14 N.C. 548 (1832), at 549–50, and Justice Rodman's majority opinion in *State v. Pink Ross and Sarah Ross*, 76 N.C. 242 (1877), at 245. The North Carolina Supreme Court abided by its own separate but equal doctrine years before *Plessy*. See *Britton v. Atlanta & Charlotte Air-Line Rail-way Co.*, 88 N.C. 536 (1883) (public transportation), and *Puitt v. Commission-ers of Gaston County*, 94 N.C. 709 (1886) (public school education).
35. "What seems to be the problem?" is a standard question an attorney or doc-tor might ask clients and patients.
36. See *Marrow* 53–59. The first appearances of the "white supremacy" mantra in the North Carolina press occurred in 1892 and 1895, but became com-monplace in 1898 as the November 1898 gubernatorial elections neared.
37. Also known as the Robert Charles Riots, its similarities with the *coup d'etat* in Wilmington more than support the parallel. For detailed treatment of Charles and the New Orleans riots, see William Ivy Hair, *Carnival of Fury: Robert Charles and the New Orleans Race Riot of 1900* (Baton Rouge: LSU Press, 1976).

38. Chesnutt "distinguished between folklore on the one hand and literature based on folklore on the other" and singled "The Goophered-Grapevine" out as the only folklore in his oeuvre (Dundes, *Mother Wit* 369). However, Chesnutt also discovered that the divide was far more difficult to determine. See "Superstition and Folklore of the South" 372.

39. The Battle of Assaye, part of the Second Anglo-Maratha War, began on August 8, 1803, when Wellesley ordered an attack on a Maratha fort in spite of the overwhelming number of soldiers ranked against him. Just four days later, on August 12, 1803, the fort surrendered. Wellesley considered this the fiercest battle and greatest victory of his military career.

40. Wellesley also earned the rank of colonel in late 1805 or early 1806 (Corrigan 92; Severn 206).

41. He may also be modeled after Judge Joshua Wright, a popular figure in North Carolina politics, who lived during the Revolutionary War (Preik 57–61; Watson 228, 233). Chesnutt's naming strategy strongly suggests his own debt to this idea. For recent historicism, see Watson 228, 233, and Hutteman 45.

42. See *Marrow* 16.

43. The McBane surname comes from the Picts, an ancient Scottish tribe. McBane etymologically derives from the Gaelic word *Beathan* (or *betha*), which translates into "life." Transcribed as McBean (Bain), it literally translates into "son of the fair lad." In the early eighteenth century, McBanes began migrating to the New World to take advantage of the opportunities to improve their lot. McBanes went to South Carolina (John Baine, 1716), Maryland (Alexander Bain, 1774), and Georgia (Alexander Bean, 1775).

44. Green's socioeconomic aspirations, unlike those of the Letlows or Millers, fall outside of those sought by "respectable" European-American members of Wellington. See *Marrow* 109–10, 114, 283.

45. Even Green's use of a racial epithet, "dagoes," which one scholar considers indicative of Green's racism *vis-à-vis* Dr. Miller's philosophy of racial equality (Knadler 442), is precipitated when the sailor called him "a damn' lowdown nigger" (*Marrow* 110).

46. For more on the Carolinas before the 1663 grant, particularly Hilton's journeys in 1662 (supported by New England merchants) and 1663 (supported by Bardadian merchants), see J. Wright 96–97.

47. This name, of French origin, was probably introduced into England during the Norman Invasion of 1066. It hails from a locale in Normandy called La Mare, from the Olde Norman-French *la* (the) plus *mare* (a pool or pond).

48. Baron Delamere, of Vale Royal in the County of Chester, is a title in the Peerage of the United Kingdom. It was created in 1821 for Thomas Cholmondeley, a former Member of Parliament for Cheshire. Hugh Cholmondeley inherited the title from his father in 1855. His eldest son, also named Hugh Cholmondeley (1870–1931), the third Baron Delamere, was an outspoken white supremacist.

49. Blackbeard (Edward Teach or Edward Thatch, ca. 1680–1718), an Englishman who sailed the Caribbean and the Atlantic seaboard, became America's most famous pirate. Named because of his long black beard, he used his physical appearance to intimidate. According to reports, he lit fuses beneath his hat to create a fearful aspect.

50. The same trope is also evident in the *Odyssey* and the New Testament. See Homer, *The Odyssey* 105–08, and *Holy Bible* I Timothy 6:15.

51. For more detailed exegesis of the neoclassical antecedents of slavery, see David Brion Davis, *The Problem of Slavery in Western Culture* (Ithaca, NY: Cornell UP, 1966), 62–90.

52. Imani Perry (100, 104–09) faults Cartesian dualism as the source of double-consciousness. In contrast, I contend that the American epic habitus vexes the mind-body analytic.

53. For more on dog metaphors in the *Iliad*, see Redfield 159, 199. For a spirited defense of Achilles' behavior and the Heroic Age code of chivalry, see Samuel Eliot Bassett, "Achilles' Treatment of Hector's Body," *American Philological Association* 64 (1933), 41–65.

54. See J. Allen (2000).

55. This symbolic abortion is paternal, as Shemwindo wishes to have his wives give birth to daughters only.

56. See *Marrow* 111–13, 283–84.

57. Chesnutt's "Journal" dwells upon this theme far more than any other, although his admiration of heroism has not yet undergone the critical turn that underlies his Homeric allegorye. Against Sweden's Charles XII, the "Arbiter of the North," he cites true military men as George Washington, Ulysses Grant, Robert E. Lee, John Churchill (1st Duke of Marlborough), and Horatio Nelson (1st Viscount Nelson). See "Journal" 38–42.

58. See, e.g., Giles and Lally 267–68; Knadler 443; McGowan 69–72.

59. Chesnutt's "Journal" has a parallel episode. On behalf of her son Achilles, Thetis "clasps Jove's [Zeus'] knees" in entreaty. Zeus has just returned from "a visit to Ethiopia." See "Journal" 8–9.

60. For more, see 1898 Wilmington, Appendix A.

NOTES TO CHAPTER 5

1. Human development also dramatically weakened the natural habitat by destroying more than 20,000 acres of marsh, swamp, and native pine trees. See Burdeau A6, and Chambers et al. 318.

2. *See* Chapter 3 for my discussion of this genealogy.

3. Here I call attention to the gothic as an aesthetic linking much of the African-American canon. For an isomorphic link connecting Wright, Marx, and the gothic, see Smethurst 29–40.

4. Other high literature influenced Wright. For example, Kenneth Kinnamon (1969) read *Othello* into *Native Son*, and Robert Butler (1991) believed two of Zola's novels influenced *Native Son*. For a listing of Wright's library and readings, see Fabre, *Richard Wright* (1990).

5. The influence of mass culture, particularly horror movies, is also advanced by Smethurst. See Pudaloff 13–14 and Smethurst 32, 35–36.

6. Baker (1972), Kent (1969), and Blyden Jackson (1969) argued for a significant folk influence. Baker, in particular, linked Bigger to the folk aesthetic and such figures as Brer Rabbit, Stackolee, and Nat Turner. See *Long Black Song* 133–38.

7. Thanks to the work of Wright biographer, Michel Fabre, we know that one of Wright's favorite texts was Joyce's *Ulysses*, which he read in the mid-1930s and discussed with his literary club (*Richard Wright* 83; *Unfinished Quest* 111).

8. For a reading of the "Minoan Monster," of ancient Greek heroic mythology, as the recurrent motif informing *Native Son*, see Bullock-Kimball 42–46.

9. Wright echoes Rousseau, Hegel, Nietzsche, and other intellectuals, albeit from an African-American perspective, when he attributes to modernity the dehumanizing of individuals. See Kent 336.

10. For full treatment of Homer and *Native Son*, see Rutledge 245–310.

11. Robert S. Abbott's *Chicago Defender*, according to James R. Grossman, was the source that put momentum behind the Great Migration (84–96). See also Jackson 295–96.

12. Indeed, when she is out in public, Wright avoids describing her apparel as he sustains the image, substituting other objects instead. At the inquest, for example, Bigger sees "white bones," "white sheets of paper," and "Mr. Dalton, white-faced, white-haired" (*NS* 312).

13. There are also random beatings, street searches, and school closings as a general hysteria grips Wright's Chicago.

14. Green proclaims, "I'd ruther be a dead nigger any day dan a live dog!" (*Marrow* 284). See Chapter 4 for discussion of Chesnutt's critique of Dr. Miller contra Green.

15. Miller relies upon Alex Olrik's essay "Epic Laws of Folk Narrative" ("Epische Gesetze der Volksdichtung"), *Zeitschrift für Deutsches Altertum* 51 (1909), 1–12. Reprinted in Dundes *Mother Wit* 129–41.

16. Hurston, "Stories of Conflict," review of *Uncle Tom's Children*, by Richard Wright, *Saturday Evening Review of Literature* 2 April 1938: 32.

17. In the nineteenth century Chicago was known or advertised as the "City of Gardens," among other things. As I discuss later, the "Garden" trope characterized early European perspectives on the New World and lasted well into the nineteenth century.

18. See, e.g., *Invisible Man* 245, where Ellison's protagonist is referred to as a "new man" after his experience at the "factory hospital."

19. White counters Greco-Roman cultural lineage by inserting the East as the reason behind the modern West: "Our science is the heir to all the sciences of the past, especially perhaps to the work of the great Islamic scientists of the Middle Ages, who so often outdid the ancient Greeks in skill and perspicacity: al-Rāzī in medicine, for example; or ibn-al-Haytham in optics; or Omar Khayyám in mathematics" (6).

20. Manes quoting Hans Peter Duerr, *Dreamtime: Concerning the Boundary between Wilderness and Civilization*, trans. Felicitas Goodman (Oxford: Basil Blackwell, 1985), 92.

21. Manes quoting Mircea Eliade, *Shamanism: Archaic Techniques of Ecstasy* (Princeton, NJ: Princeton UP, 1972), 98.

22. Climatologists now know that long periods of arid and humid climates, and recent climatic changes, have compelled migration and changed environmental conditions, Webb notes (35). Droughts, one of the extreme climatological events, are alternatively dubbed "mega-droughts" or "epic dry spells" by *New York Times* reporter Andrew C. Revkin (A11).

23. Recall that Ozidi the Younger faces the Smallpox King, an end to the *Ozidi Saga* that would seem to double as a post-colonial allegorycal critique.

24. Quoted from Steven Feierman and John M. Janzen (eds.), *The Social Basis of Health and Healing in Africa* (Berkeley: U of California P, 1992), 18.

25. For an example of research on TEK and the "desertification" debate in North Africa, see, e.g., Diana K. Davis, "Indigenous Knowledge and the Desertification Debate: Problematising Expert Knowledge in North Africa," *Geoforum* 36 (2005), 509–524.

26. See Genesis 1:26 and 1:28.

27. Laurence Coupe reads the "garden" myth through the teleological logic of the Bible, the linearity from Genesis to the "Terrestrial Paradise" of Revelations resting upon linear, progressive time (182–83).

28. For an eco-critical reading of *The Epic of Gilgamesh* in the context of fertility myths, see Coupe 188–90.

29. Indeed, the first among several reasons scholars have overlooked the ecocritical dimension of Homer's *Odyssey*, Schultz argues, is the privileging of Homer's creativity and the epic's "setting as 'the landscape of the imagination' or 'the fairy-tale world of [Odysseus'] adventures' or a 'wonderland'" (300).

30. See Pollan 65–66.
31. Spoken by Earl Butz, Richard M. Nixon's secretary of agriculture. For comment, see Berry 8–11, and Pollan 62, 64.
32. The dust storm that struck Chicago reached the East Coast two days later. In addition to Washington, D.C., Dust Bowl clouds reached major metropoles like New York City, Boston, and Buffalo. The dust, which blew into the Atlantic Ocean and landed on ships 300 miles off the coast (Stock 24), caused red snow to fall in New England that same winter.
33. Worster 48, quoting Edmund Brunner and Irving Lorge, *Rural Trends in Depression Years* (New York: Columbia UP, 1937), 5.
34. Cf. Toni Morrison's "instant and reactionary myth-making" ("Behind the Making" 88).
35. See *Black Boy* 7–9, 45–46, 71–73; subsequently cited as *BB*.
36. While he lived in Chicago, Wright wrote and published the first autobiographical sketches he would incorporate into "The Ethics of Living Jim Crow" (1937) and *Black Boy* in 1945..
37. MacLeish, *Land of the Free* (New York: Harcourt, Brace, 1938), 80, 83–84; quoted in Worster 46.
38. *See* Worster 248, fn.3.
39. See Fabre, "From Revolutionary" 35, 43, and *Richard Wright* 102, 187–88.
40. From the *Ozidi Saga* 28.
41. In addition, of course, to Paul Laurence Dunbar's 1901 novel, *The Sport of the Gods*, I am also alluding to Homer's *Iliad* in two instances: The Greek gods' constant forays into battle often made sport of the combatants, particularly the Trojans, and Homer himself included a section, called "Funeral Games for Patroklos," which were organized by Achille(u)s and comprised a series of olympic challenges in honor of the death of Achille(u)s' close friend.
42. See Roberts, *From Trickster* 176, 180.
43. Wright, a mere boy, kills the stray to spite his father when he, a fearful presence who worked as a porter in Memphis, commanded Wright to "Kill that damn thing!" Wright's description of their home in Memphis shows the evolution of his thought and ecological range: "In Memphis we lived in a one-story brick tenement. The stone buildings and the concrete pavements looked bleak and hostile to me. The absence of green, growing things made the city seem dead" (*BB* 10).
44. Miller, quoting Richard Wright, *Pagan Spain* (New York: Harper, 1957), 237.
45. Cf. Malcolm X 27–28.
46. For a brief description of this plant, see Clenten E. Owensby's *Kansas Prairie Wildflowers* (Ames, Iowa: Iowa State UP, 1980), 14.
47. A Japanese animated feature, *Tales from Earthsea* (2006), and an older U.S. television mini-series, *Earthsea* (2004), commit this racial re-imagining.

NOTES TO CHAPTER 6

1. On *Beloved* and the "epic intricacies" of slavery, see Crouch 71.
2. See also Brenner (1987), Awkward (1990), Argyros 141.
3. Morrison's M.A. thesis in English at Cornell University explicated the theme of suicide in William Faulkner's and Virginia Woolf's works (S. Blake 189). For discussion of Faulkner's limits, see Argyros 150.
4. See also Morrison, "Interview" 26–27.

5. For Morrison's understanding of the "ancestors," see "Rootedness" 343.

6. These are just two of numerous instances throughout the transcription. See *Ozidi Saga* 60, 61, 314, 316, 320, 340, 362. For more on the audience contributions Okpewho calls "endorsements" of the storyteller, see Okpewho, "Critical Introduction" xviii–xxi.

7. For example, *The Ozidi Saga* storyteller-protagonist, Okabou Ojobolo, reveals that his most assiduous heckler is a female spectator named Owayei (338–39).

8. Atkinson extrapolates from Morrison's use of this feature. See Atkinson 248–49. It should also be pointed out that *The Iliad* begins *in media res*, a feature some eminent Western theorists identify as a particularly advanced stylistic that sets Homer apart. Recall that Mwindo, in Rureke's version, is born *in media res*, which is the source of his epithet, *Kabutwa-Kenda* ("Little-one-just-born-he-walked"). For comment, see Rummell 6.

9. In cinema, Marxist psychoanalyst Slavoj Žižek theorizes, this filmic trace of the desire for self-destruction stems from a vicious cycle of the "irreal." See Žižek 7–18.

10. See, e.g., S. Blake 194, and Morrison, "Interview" 25.

11. Specifically, one should look for socioreligious forms of West and Central Africa as antecedents. See Jennings (2008), and T. Smith 3.

12. Several scholars note Morrison's conflation of mythology and realism in *Beloved* outside the frame of magical realism. See, e.g., Rigney 71, and Rummell 12.

13. The quoted passage is taken from a statement made by John Jolliffe on behalf of Garner in the federal courthouse in Cincinnati, and recorded in the *Cincinnati Gazette*. Remarks excerpted from Weisenburger 124.

14. Cf. Joseph Campbell on childbirth and epic journey in Campbell 124–26.

15. Denver's description. See *Beloved* 14.

16. Paul D's cryptic exclamation during intercourse with Beloved, "Red heart. Red heart. Red heart" (138), suggests the presence of *nyama* as a female energy, for "red," in the Manden, is "central to girls' rites of passage, including the excision ritual and marriage." See Conrad, "Mooning" 212.

17. Sixo's laughter reflects the very intensification of Bakhtinian "ambivalence," for "laughter is ambivalent: it is gay, triumphant, and at the same time mocking, deriding. It asserts and denies, it buries and revives" (*Rabelais* 200, 209). Since African masquerade presents a more fluid synthesis of the sacred, secular, and profane than Bakhtin's description of Western Europe's medieval carnival, Morrison intensifies and Africanizes the laughter in an episode archly comical *and* epical. Little wonder, then, that Sixo embodies and deepens Bakhtin's "positive and negative poles of becoming (death-birth)" (211): his death by burning-lynching is simultaneously an *embrace of the epic* and rebirth carried in his shout-out to "Seven-O!"

18. For a discussion of the significance of red in Mali, see note 16.

19. This ritualized distancing occurs throughout the *Iliad*, where Herakles establishes the benchmark for heroic deeds. See, e.g., Homer/Hammond 117, 118, 123, 312. *The Lord of the Rings* achieves much of its effect through J.R.R. Tolkien's appropriation of such comparatives from his vast readings in English, Welsh, and Celtic lore. See, e.g., Tolkien, *Fellowship* 250–61, and *Two Towers* 408, 429.

20. Though I elaborate on this concept later, I am drawing a distinction here between contemporary American understanding of common sense privileging individuality and the mind, and common/sense, which is an inclusive concept in which the senses of the body and the body-politic create communal sense.

21. I take these terms, "discredited knowledge" and "discredited difference," from Morrison's "Rootedness" 342, and *Playing* 10.

22. For a structural definition approach to proverbs, see Prahlad, *African-American* 33.

23. Works Progress Administration interviews often featured this biblical proverb. For a list, see Prahlad, *African-American* 248–51.

24. For some literary examples, see Chesnutt's *Marrow* 241, 278, 304; see 321, too.

25. Roberts, noting the "verbal indirection" of slave proverbs, likened them to trickster tales. See "Slave Proverbs" 130, 136–37.

26. See "common sense" in the *Oxford English Dictionary,* 2nd ed. 1989 (2007).

27. Jütte 39, quoting from Aristotle's *De Anima.*

28. For Europe's pre-Cartesian sense of the body, featuring a "grotesque realism" that was "universal," "ancestral," and "collective," see Bakhtin, *Rabelais* 204–05.

29. For examination of the African polyrhythmic intertextuality of "Superbad," see David Brackett's "James Brown's 'Superbad' and the Double-Voiced Utterance," *Popular Music* 11.3 (1992): 309–24.

30. By "broadcast," I am suggesting the need for the epic voice to be larger than life—massive in other words. This trope is common to traditional epics, American literature, and American cinema. See, e.g., Niane *Sundiata* 63, 64; Douglass, *Heroic* 28; Hopkins 85; see also Ridley Scott's epic film *Gladiator* (2000), one of the best-known films of this type.

31. I am referencing hip hop, of course, but also the "hip, hip, hip!" applause of the auditor-participants in the *Ozidi Saga* 311 and 370. For comment, see Okpewho, "Critical Introduction" xxi.

32. Prahlad cites Denver, from *Beloved,* as the kind of child who could become a "proverb master." See *African-American* 125.

33. Blassingame quotes George Thomas Basden's remarks on "sports and pastimes" in Among the Ibos of Nigeria: *An Account of the Curious and Interesting Habits, Customs, and Beliefs of a Little Known African People by One Who Has for Many Years Lived amongst Them on Close and Intimate Terms* (Philadelphia: J.B. Lippincott, 1921).

34. Citing Edward A. Pollard, "The Romance of the Negro," *American Missionary* XV (Nov. 1871), 241–48.

35. See James K. Allen, *Without Sanctuary: Lynching Photography in America* (Santa Fe, NM: Twin Palms, 2000).

36. For detail on the septennial Kamabolon ceremony, see Jansen, "Hot" (1998), and "Sunjata" (2001). Clark-Bekederemo provides performance details for *The Ozidi Saga* in his Preface xx–xxxiv and Introductory Essay xxxv–xxxvi, xxxviii, and xl–xlv, in particular.

37. James Weldon Johnson brilliantly establishes racism as "selfish" and "reason[able]" common sense in this context. See *Autobiography* 103–04, 106–07.

38. I appropriate "doin' it to death" from Geoff Brown's *James Brown: Doin' It To Death* (London: Omnibus P, 1996).

39. For example of rumors of medical school raids of black cemeteries, see H. Washington 118–19, 125, and Blassingame 41, 44–45.

40. "Italian proverbs, for example," according to Obelkevich, "were marked down for their cynicism, despite winning points for style" (50).

41. Cf. Bakhtin, *Rabelais* 195–209, 220–21, and W. Benjamin 181.

42. Locke expressed this distrust in *An Essay Concerning Human Understanding* (1690). For Morrison's thoughts on national literature and the new "social contract," see *Playing* 8, 15, 47–48.

43. On non-Western exceptionalism, see Owomoyela 23–26.
44. But see Prahlad, *African-American* 5–11, which argues against assumed, noncontextual themes or "base meaning."
45. Sententia, lying as it does between grammatical completeness and mere thought, hardly figures in the scholarship. It is defined by the *OED* as a "sentence"; the modified use, which I privilege here, is "a thought or reflection." Shapin lists "sententiae" among synonyms for proverb, but his use of the consensus criterion that a proverb must be a complete sentence nullifies this possibility (735). Indeed, to the extent paremiologists limit their efforts to "true proverbs," sententia might be classified as a "proverbial phrase," which Prahlad defines as clausal modifications (Owomoyela 1; Prahlad, *African-American* 34).
46. The epigraph, on page xv of the 2004 Vintage edition of the novel, reads as follows: "*I will call them my people, / which were not my people; / and her beloved, / which was not beloved.* Romans 9:25."
47. For observations on race and smell, see M. Smith 13–14, and Malcolm X, *Autobiography* 278.
48. Morrison, in particular, faults Ralph Waldo Emerson and his "call for" a "new white man" (*Playing* 39). Cf. Ellison, *Invisible Man* 182–92.
49. The analog between Morrison's self-described aesthetic and the epic griot is detailed by Rummell. For a discussion of griottes, see Hale 217–43.
50. Iyangura, the "arbiter" whose absence occasions *The Mwindo Epic* cycle, and Oreame, the grandmother-tutor of Ozidi the Younger, function in similar capacity.
51. I owe Prahlad credit for equating "common sense" and "mother wit" (E-mail to Author 2007).
52. Spirituality, song, and folk sensibility are in relationship here. See Biebuyck, *Hero* 70, and W. Benjamin 200–02.
53. Morrison, in her interviews, makes clear that her tradition-centered understanding does not abrogate all hierarchy. See Morrison, "An Interview" 49.
54. Benjamin's genealogical method is most telling here. His discussion of the "spoken language" as free and "written language" as enslaving immediately precedes a genealogy of how German language was seen in "first place among the 'major languages'" and as 1) descended from Hebrew or, more radically, 2) the origin language for Hebrews, Greeks, and Latin speakers. This was accomplished, Walter Benjamin argues, by "an extreme foreshortening of the historical perspective. Everything is placed in the same rarefied atmosphere" (202–03).
55. Though Morrison suggests that Wright "had great difficulty with that ancestor" ("Rootedness" 343), probably meaning his tyrannical maternal grandmother and father, she is clearly aligned with Wright's valorization of the ideological and aesthetic utility of black folklore as articulated in his "Blueprint for Negro Writing" (1405). Cf. Ellison's appropriation and critique of folk common sense—"conscious thought," "common people," and for "the uncommon people"—in *Invisible Man* 67–68, 74, 91, 94, 342.
56. The expression is common enough among African Americans that Melvin Van Peebles, in his 1971 musical, *Ain't Supposed to Die a Natural Death: Tunes from Blackness*, entitled the opening song "It Just Don't Make No Sense" to give folksy voice to a common sentiment. Likewise, "Yeah, well, it don't make no sense to me" and "It don't make no sense," says and thinks Roscoe Crandel as he ponders his place in hell in Reginald McKnight's 1988 short story, "Roscoe in Hell" (343, 360).
57. See "ten" (from Old English *tien, -e*, with parallel roots in Anglican and Teuton) in the Oxford English Dictionary Online, <http://www.oed.com> (accessed 16 July 2007), especially definitions A.1.b. and c., B.1.a., and C.

58. For my purposes here, I rely upon Du Bois' *Souls*. For Du Bois' explication of this concept, see "The Talented Tenth" (1903).
59. So argued Walter Hines Page, an education reformer, in his "Introduction" to *Up from Slavery* (1901), xvi. See Washington, *Up from Slavery* 59–60.
60. For Du Bois' southern "immersion," see Stepto xvi, 80.
61. Du Bois' last chapter in *Souls*, "Of the Sorrow Songs," paratactically instantiates the epic into the spirituals via a comparative: Lohengrin, the epic opera Wagner created from folk elements and Arthurian lore, gives way to Du Bois' exegesis of the "Sorrow Songs," which arose from the lore of the slave community.
62. "Ten times better," of course, is a fairly common qualitative/quantitative measure. Some early instances of it in literature pertaining to matters of race date back to the nineteenth century. See, e.g., the attack on abolitionism, ostensibly published by Harrison Berry, called *Slavery and Abolitionism, as Viewed by a Georgia Slave* (Atlanta: M. Lynch & Co., 1861), 23 (*Documenting the American South*, University of North Carolina at Chapel Hill, <http://docsouth.unc.edu/imls/berry/berry.html> 5 July 2007).
    Many other twentieth-century uses, both related and unrelated to race, abound. For the *Chicago Daily Tribune* alone, from 1900 to 1979, I found sixty-nine references using the ProQuest Historical Newspapers Database. The pieces using "ten times better" included advertisements, hard and feature news articles, theater reviews, letters to the editor, sports news, poetry, and ephemera (wisdom, advice).
63. For one of the earliest instances of "ten times" used in connection with racial struggle, see Hannah Allen's Federal Writers' Project interview in *Born in Slavery: Slave Narratives from the Federal Writers' Project, 1936–1938*. The Library of Congress. American Memory. (5 July 2007) <http://memory.loc.gov/ammem/snhtml/snhome.html>.
64. Indeed, my own mother, who came of age during the height of the Civil Rights/Black Power era, passed on this folk wisdom to me and my sisters as we grew up in Bradenton, Florida. A resident of Bradenton all of her life, she had heard it herself, she declares, as a commonplace often used in the black schools.
65. See, e.g., Yeakey 489, arguing that Paul Robeson intellectually, physically, artistically, and ethically eclipsed the "belief that a black man had to be literally ten times better than a white man."
66. See, e.g., Lee 28, 29; Vargas (1999); Vaught 22; Scherman 278; Evans 26; Calloway 11 (theater review of "Man and Boy," featuring Bill Cosby, about freed slaves who, heeding the call to go west during the southern violence of the 1870s and finding "racial prejudice" already present, learned that "[t]heir only survival was to be the 'badest' and fastest gunslinger and to be ten times better than whites"); Myles 115; Collins 59.
67. Born Chloe Anthony Wofford in 1931, Morrison changed her name in the 1950s while a student at Howard University.
68. In addition to these, Morrison deploys her own version of an indispensable form of the epic, the encyclopedic catalog to document the atrocities of slavery. See, e.g., *Beloved* 78, 114, 128, 131, 213, 234.
69. The "miracle" orchestrated here by Baby Suggs, holy, echoes the New Testament narrative, of course. However, this event has a Sunjatic parallel. See Conrad, "Mooning Armies" 197, 216, and Johnson, *The Epic*, lines 2750–2764.
70. Denver is Mwindic in this regard. Sethe says, "'she pulled a whitegirl [Amy Denver] out of the hill' to save both of them" (*Beloved* 50). For analysis of Sethe and Amy Denver relative to the (Homeric) epic, see Argyros 148–54.

71. See Morrison, "Foreword" xvi–xvii. For similar thoughts, see Octavia Butler's in Rowell 51 and Malcolm X's in *Autobiography* 243–48, 262, 277, 290.
72. "Halle, Halle, Halleluja," for example, is a traditional Caribbean spiritual. See Hoyt L. Hickman (gen. ed.), *The Faith We Sing* (Nashville: Abingdon, 2000), 2026.
73. Indeed, Halle's mastery of formal knowledge and processes is decades old. See, e.g., the university student in Wright's *Native Son* 342–43; Wright, "How 'Bigger'" 436 ("Bigger No. 4"); and the "crazy" neurosurgeon in Ellison's *Invisible Man* (21, 35).
74. Cheng recognizes a bilateral effect in which the "racialized minority is as bound to racial melancholia as the dominant subject" and argues that "it is surely equally harmful *not* to talk about this history of sorrow" even if "the implications . . . are . . . inconvenient to a racist culture and . . . potentially threatening to . . . traditionally conceived" racial uplift (14–15, 19).
75. See, most notably, Kathleen M. Ashley's "Toni Morrison's Tricksters," in *Uneasy Alliance: Twentieth-Century Literature, Culture and Biography*, ed. Hans Bak (Amsterdam: Rodopi, 2004), 269–84, and Jeanne Rosier Smith, *Writing Tricksters: Mythic Gambols in American Ethnic Fiction* (Berkeley: U of California P, 1997).
    Of course, Sixo's reasoning in his debate with schoolteacher reprises the tale of John the trickster slave, "Just Possum," with a difference: schoolteacher beats Sixo and unmans and unarms the Sweet Home men by confiscating the guns Mr. Garner had given them to hunt game (*Beloved* 224).
76. For example, the seven nights of the *Ozidi Saga* performance; Ozidi's seven-pronged sword; Mwindo is Shemwindo's seventh child born; and Niane-Kouyaté's Sundiata is prophesied to be "the seventh star, the seventh conqueror of the earth" (6). See also Blight and Gooding-Williams, "Notes" 197, n.5.
77. Though not explicit in *Beloved*, Morrison draws an analog between breeding animals and slaves when schoolteacher's nephews steal her milk. For historical commentary, see, e.g., Deborah Grey White, *Arn't I a Woman? Female Slaves in the Plantation South* (New York: W.W. Norton, 1985), 70.
78. For Sixo as analog to Sethe, see Plasa 127.
79. For Morrison, Civil Rights celebrity resulted in *cinéma vérité*. See Morrison, "An Interview" 52–53. Cf. Malcolm X, *Autobiography* 286.
80. Using Stamp Paid as proxy, Morrison literally roots the cause of Baby Suggs' soul-sickness, the racial trauma that lays waste to her belief in the common/ sense, in the "marrow" of her body. See *Beloved* 212.
81. A vodu(n) reading of Beloved offers important parallels. See Jennings 62–71 for Morrison's use, and Thompson, *Flash* 164–91, and Gomez 57 for information on its place in the Diaspora.
82. For a compelling reading on Beloved as trickster and Beloved as ritual, see Krumholz, "The Ghosts" 397.
83. The circumcisor, or an assistant, may carry as one of the symbolic tools a "short scepter-like stick topped with the chest feathers of a sacrificed chicken (*nkóma yá bukiriite*)" (Biebuyck, "Nyanga Circumcision" 86).

NOTES TO CHAPTER 7

1. See Houston Baker, "Failed" (1999).
2. For a suggestion that Chesnutt uncritically stereotypes, see Sollors 40, fn.1.
3. Mother Nature. See the beginning of Chapter 1.

4. Hawes cites Martin Bernal, who designates the "late eighteenth-century fabrication of Ancient Greece as the origins of the 'West'" as the quintessence of the metaleptic trope (148).
5. On the morning of Wednesday, 27 June 2012: about massive forest fires burning in the West, particularly Colorado, and Tropical Storm Debby, which formed in the Gulf of Mexico and spent a week deluging Florida.

Working Bibliography

HISTORICAL ARCHIVES

Afro-Louisiana History and Genealogy 1699–1820 on-line database. <http://www.ibiblio.org/laslave/> 23 June 2006.

Cordes, John, 1718–1756. John Cordes Estate, Account Book, 1764–1937. Robert Scott Small Library, Special Collections, College of Charleston (South Carolina).

DeSaussure, Charles Alfred, 1846–1935. Charles Alfred DeSaussure Memoirs, "The Story of My Life up to the Beginning of the War Between the States," ca. 1931. Robert Scott Small Library, Special Collections, College of Charleston (South Carolina).

Grimball, John Berkly, 1800–1892. Diary of J. B. Grimball, 1832–1938. Robert Scott Small Library, Special Collections, College of Charleston (South Carolina).

Heyward and Ferguson Family Papers, 1806–1923. Robert Scott Small Library, Special Collections, College of Charleston (South Carolina).

Nwokeji, G. Ugo. Liberated African Registers. 1,541 Female Names of Women and Girls Taken from the Bight of Biafra, compiled for Ugo and David Eltis' "Characteristics of Captives Leaving the Cameroons for the Americas, 1822–37," *Journal of African* History 43.2 (2002), 191–210. File sent via e-mail to author, 18 June 2006.

Registers of Liberated Africans made in Sierra Leone, Havana, and Rio de Janeiro between 1819 and 1845. The National Archives, United Kingdom.

Torrans, John, ca. 1702–1780. John Torrans Letters, ca. 1775. Robert Scott Small Library, Special Collections, College of Charleston (South Carolina).

TEXTS: PRIMARY AND SECONDARY

Aardema, Verna. *Why Mosquitoes Buzz in People's Ears: A West African Tale.* 1975. New York: Dial-Penguin, n.d.

Abrahams, Roger D. *Deep Down in the Jungle: Negro Narrative Folklore from the Streets of Philadelphia.* Chicago: Aldine Pub. Co., 1970.

———. "Some Varieties of Heroes in America." *Journal of the Folklore Institute* 3 (1966): 341–62.

Abrams, M. H., gen. ed. *Norton Anthology of English Literature.* 5th ed. vol. 1. New York: W.W. Norton, 1986.

Adorno, Theodor. *Minima Moralia: Reflections from Damaged Life.* 1951. Trans. E. F. N. Jephcott. London, New York: Verso, 1999.

Akyeampong, Emmanuel Kwaku. "Disease in West African History." *Themes in West Africa's History*. Ed. Akyeampong. Athens: Ohio UP, 2006. 186–207.

Aldridge, Owen A. "The Concept of Ancients and Moderns in American Poetry of the Federal Period." Eadie, 99–118.

Allen, James. *Without Sanctuary: Lynching Photography in America*. 2000. Santa Fe, New Mexico: Twin Palms, 2005.

Allingham, Philip V. "The Initial Publication Context of Joseph Conrad's Heart of Darkness in Blackwood's Edinburgh Magazine ('Maga'): February, March, and April, 1899." *The Victorian Web* (Dec. 2000): n. pag. 14 June 2010. <http://www.victorianweb.org/authors/conrad/pva46.html>

American Experience: Surviving the Dust Bowl. Prod. Chana Gazit. PBS, 2010.

Anderson, Martha G. "Bulletproof: Exploring the Warrior Ethos in Ijo Culture." Anderson and Peek, 91–119.

———. "From River Horses to Dancing Sharks: Canoes and Fish in Ijo Art and Ritual." Anderson and Peek, 133–61.

Anderson, Martha G. and Philip M. Peek, eds. *Ways of the Rivers: Arts and Environment of the Niger Delta*. Los Angeles: UCLA Fowler Museum of Cultural History, 2002.

Andrews, William L. Introduction. *The Portable Charles W. Chesnutt*. Ed. Andrews. Gen. Ed. Henry Louis Gates, Jr. New York: Penguin Classics, 2008. xvii–xliv.

———. *The Literary Career of Charles W. Chesnutt*. Baton Rouge and London: Louisiana State UP, 1980.

———. *To Tell a Free Story: The First Century of Afro-American Autobiography, 1760–1865*. Urbana and Chicago: U of Illinois P, 1986.

Anthony, Carl. "African Americans and Environmental History: A Manifesto." *From Timbuktu to Katrina: Readings in African-American History, Vol. II*. Comp. Quintard Taylor, Jr. Boston: Thompson Higher Ed., 2007. 185–87. Excerpt from "Reflections on the Purposes and Meanings of African American Environmental History." *To Love the Wind and the Rain: African Americans and Environmental History*. Ed. Dianne D. Glave and Mark Stoll. Pittsburgh: U of Pittsburgh P, 2006. 200–208.

Argyros, Ellen. "'Some Epic Use for my Excellent Body': Redefining Childbirth as Heroic in Beloved and 'The Language of the Brag.'" *This Giving Birth: Pregnancy and Childbirth in American Women's Writing*. Eds. Julie Tharp and Susan MacCallum-Whitcomb. Bowling Green, OH: Bowling Green State U Popular Press, 2000. 141–56.

Aristotle. *Poetics*. Trans. Malcolm Heath. New York: Penguin, 1996.

Armstrong, Robert G. "The Etymology of the Word 'Ògún.'" Barnes, *Africa's Ogun* 29–38.

Aronson, Lisa. "Tricks of the Trade: A Study of *Ikakibite* (Cloth of the Tortoise) Among the Eastern Ijo." Anderson and Peek, 251–67.

Arrested Development. *Zingalamaduni*. CD. Chrysalis Records. 1994.

Asante, Kariamu Welsh, ed. *African Dance: An Artistic, Historical and Philosophical Inquiry*.
Trenton, NJ: Africa World P, 1996.

Ater, Renée. "Creating a 'Usable Past' and a 'Future Perfect Society': Aaron Douglas's Murals for the 1936 Texas Centennial Exposition." Earle, 95–113.

Atkinson, Willliam. "Bound in Blackwood's: The Imperialism of 'The Heart of Darkness' in Its Immediate Context.'" *Twentieth Century Literature* 50.4 (2004): 368–93.

Atkinson, Yvonne. "The Black English Oral Tradition in Beloved: 'listen to the spaces.'" Solomon, 247–60.

Awkward, Michael. "'Unruly and Let Loose': Myth, Ideology, and Gender in *Song of Solomon*." *Callaloo* 13.3 (1990): 482–98. Rpt. in Solomon, 67–93

Austen, Ralph A. "Criminals and the African Cultural Imagination: Normative and Deviant Heroism in Pre-Colonial and Modern Narratives." *Africa* 56.4 (1986): 385–98.

———. Ed. *In Search of Sunjata: The Mande Oral Epic As History, Literature, and Performance*. Bloomington: Indiana UP, 1999.

———. "Social and Historical Analysis of African Trickster Tales: Some Preliminary Reflections." *Plantation Society* 2.2 (1986): 135–48.

Ayer (Sitter), Deborah. "The Making of a Man: Dialogic Meaning in Beloved." African American Review 26 (1992): 17–29. Rpt. in Solomon,189–204.

Babalola, S. A. *The Content and Form of Yoruba Ijala*. Oxford: Clarendon P, 1966.

Babcock-Abrahams, Barbara. "'A Tolerated Margin of Mess': The Trickster and His Tales Reconsidered." *Journal of Folklore Institute* 11.3 (1975): 147–86.

Baird, Keith E., and Mary A. Twining. "Names and Naming in the Sea Islands." *The Crucible of Carolina: Essays in the Development of Gullah Language and Culture*. Ed. Michael Montgomery. Athens: U of Georgia P, 1994. 23–37.

Baker, Houston. *Modernism and the Harlem Renaissance*. Chicago: U of Chicago P, 1989.

Baker, Houston A. "Failed Prophet and Falling Stock: Why Ralph Ellison Was Never Avant-Garde." *Stanford Humanities Review* 7.1 (1999). 4 May 2005. <http://www.stanford.edu/group/SHR/7–1/html/body_baker.html>

———. *Long Black Song: Essays in Black American Literature and Culture*. 1972. Charlottesville: UP of Virginia, 1990. 122–41.

Bakhtin, Mikhail Mikhailovich. "Epic and Novel: Toward a Methodology for the Study of the Novel." *The Dialogic Imagination: Four Essays*. Trans. Caryl Emerson and Michael Holquist. Ed. Michael Holquist. Austin, Tx: U of Texas P, 1994. 3–40. Trans. of "Èpos i roman." 1941.

———. Bakhtin, Mikhail. *Rabelais and His World*. 1965. Trans. H. Iswolsky. Bloomington: Indiana UP, 1984. *The Bakhtin Reader: Selected Writings of Bakhtin, Medvedev and Voloshinov*. Ed. Pam Morris. London: Edward Arnold, 1994. 195–244.

Baldwin, James. "Everybody's Protest Novel." *Zero* 1 (Spr. 1949). Rpt. in *Partisan Review* 16 (1949): 578–85. Rpt. in Gates, Jr. and McKay, *Norton* (2004), 1699–1705.

Ballantyne, Archibald. *Lord Carteret: A Political Biography 1690 to 1763*. London: Richard Bentley & Son, 1887.

Barboza, David. "China Passes Japan as Second-Largest Economy." *New York Times* 16 Aug. 2010: B1.

Barnes, Sandra T., ed. *Africa's Ogun: Old World and New*. Bloomington: Indiana UP, 1989.

Bearden, Romare, and Harry Henderson. *A History of African-American Artists: From 1792 to the Present*. New York: Pantheon, 1993.

Beatty, Paul. *The White Boy Shuffle*. New York: Picado-Henry Holt, 1997.

Beissinger, Margaret, Jane Tylus, and Susanne Wofford, eds. *Epic Traditions in the Contemporary World: The Poetics of Community*. Berkeley: U of California P, 1999.

Belcher, Wendy Laura. "Consuming Subjects: Theorizing New Models of Agency for Literary Criticism in African Studies." *Comparative Literature Studies* 46.2 (2009): 213–32.

Belcher, Stephen. *Epic Traditions of Africa*. Bloomington: Indiana UP, 1999.

Benjamin, Walter. *The Origin of German Tragic Drama*. 1928. Trans. John Osborne. *Ursprung des deutschen Trauerspiels*. 1963. London: Verso, 1998.

Benjamin, Shanna Greene. "Weaving the Web of Reintegration: Locating Aunt Nancy in *Praisesong for the Widow.*" *MELUS* 30.1 (2005): 49–67.

Bercovitch, Sacvan. "New England Epic: Cotton Mather's *Magnalia Christi Americana.*" *ELH* 33 (1966): 337–50.

Berkes, Fikret. *Sacred Ecology.* 1999. 2nd Ed. New York: Routledge, 2008.

Berry, Wendell. *The Unsettling of America: Culture and Agriculture.* 1986. San Francisco: Sierra Club, 1997.

Biebuyck, Daniel P. "The African Heroic Epic." *Heroic Epic and Saga: An Introduction to the World's Great Folk Epics.* Ed. Felix J. Oinas. Bloomington: Indiana UP, 1978. 336–67.

———. *Hero and Chief: Epic Literature from the Banyanga Zaire Republic.* Berkely: U of California P, 1978.

———. "Nyanga Circumcision Masks and Costumes." *African Arts* 6.2 (1973): 20–25, 86–92.

Biebuyck, Daniel and Kahombo C. Mateene, eds. and trans. *The Mwindo Epic: From the Banyanga (Congo Republic).* By Shé-kárisi Candi Rureke. Berkely: U of California P, 1969.

Bird, Charles. "The Production and Reproduction of *Sunjata.*" Austen, *In Search,* 275–95.

Bird, Charles, Martha B. Kendall, and Kalilou Tera. "Etymologies of Nyamakala." Conrad and Frank, 27–35.

Bird, Charles, Mamadou Keita, and Bourama Soumaouro, trans. *The Songs of Seydou Camara.* Bloomington, IN: African Studies Center, 1974.

Blake, Susan L. "Toni Morrison." *Dictionary of Literary Biography: Afro-American Fiction Writers After 1955.* Vol. 33. Eds. Thadious M. Davis and Trudier Harris. Detroit, MI: Gale, 1984. 187–99.

Blake, William. "The Tyger." 1794. *The Norton Anthology of English Literature.* 5th ed. vol. 2. Gen. Ed. M. H. Abrahams. New York: Norton, 1986.

Blassingame, John W. *The Slave Community: Plantation Life in the Antebellum South.* 1972. New York, Oxford: Oxford UP, 1979.

Blight, David W. and Robert Gooding-Williams. "Notes." *The Souls of Black Folk.* By W. E. B. Du Bois. Eds. Blight and Gooding-Williams. Boston, New York: Bedford/St. Martins, 1997. 196–219.

Bone, Robert A. *The Negro Novel in America.* New Haven: Yale UP, 1958.

Bourdieu, Pierre. *The Logic of Practice.* 1980. Trans. Richard Nice. Stanford: Stanford UP, 1990.

Bramble, Dennis M. and Daniel E. Lieberman. "Endurance Running and the Evolution of *Homo.*" *Nature* 432 (18 Nov. 2004): 345–52.

Brearly, H. C. "Ba-ad Nigger." *South Atlantic Quarterly* 38 (1939): 75–81.

Brenner, Gerry. "*Song of Solomon*: Rejecting Rank's Monomyth and Feminism." *Studies in American Fiction* 15 (1987): 13–24. Rpt. in Solomon, 95–109.

Brodhead, Richard H., ed. *The Journals of Charles W. Chesnutt.* Durham and London: Duke UP, 1993.

Brown Ruoff, A. LaVonne, and Jerry W. Ward, Jr., eds. *Redefining American Literary History.* New York: MLA, 1990.

Brown, Cecil. *Stagolee Shot Billy.* Cambridge: Harvard UP, 2003.

Bryant, Jerry H. *Born in a Mighty Bad Land: The Violent Man in African American Folklore and Fiction.* Bloomington: Indiana UP, 2003.

Buchan, Mark. *The Limits of Heroism: Homer and the Ethics of Reading.* Ann Arbor: U of Michigan P, 2004.

Buell, Lawrence. *Writing for an Endangered World: Literature, Culture, and Environment in the U.S. and Beyond.* Cambridge, MA: Belknap-Harvard UP, 2001.

Bullock-Kimball, Susanne. "The Modern Minotaur: A Study of Richard Wright's Native Son." *Notes on Mississippi Writers* 20.2 (1988): 41–48.

Bulman, Stephen P.D. "*Sunjata* as Written Literature: The Role of the Literary Mediator in Dissemination of the *Sunjata* Epic." Austen, *In Search*, 231–51.

Burdeau, Cain. "Stakes run high in Katrina flooding trial." *Lincoln Journal Star* Mon., Apr. 20, 2009: A6.

Butler, Robert. *Native Son: The Emergence of a New Black Hero.* Twayne's Masterwork Studies. Gen. Ed. Robert Lecker. Boston: Twayne-G. K. Hall, 1991.

Calloway, Earl. "'Man and Boy' premieres at the Oriental Theatre." *Daily Defender* 14 Dec. 1971: 11.

Campbell, Joseph. Interview by Bill Moyers. *Joseph Campbell: The Power of Myth.* New York: Doubleday-Bantam, 1988.

Cartledge, Paul. "Rebels & Sambos in Classical Greece: A Comparative View." *Crux: Essays in Greek History Presented to G.E.M. de Ste. Croix on his 75th Birthday.* Eds. P. A. Cartledge and F. D. Harvey. London: Duckworth, in association with Imprint Academic, 1985. 16–46.

Cartwright, Keith. *Reading Africa into American Literature: Epics, Fabes, and Gothic Tales.* Lexington: UP of Kentucky, 2002.

———. "Reading Roots—From Sunjata to Kunta Kinte and Milkman Dead." *Yearbook of Comparative and General Literature* 43 (1995): 31–51.

Caspari, Rachel, and Sang-Hee Lee. "Older Age Becomes Common Late in Human Evolution." *PNAS* 101.30 27 (July 2004): 10895–10900.

Castronovo, Russ. "Beauty along the Color Line: Lynching, Aesthetics, and the *Crisis*." *PMLA* 121.5 (2006): 1443–59.

Chambers, Jeffrey Q., Jeremy I. Fisher, Hongcheng Zeng, Elise L. Chapman, David B. Baker, and George C. Hurtt. "Hurricane Katrina's Carbon Footprint on U.S. Gulf Coast Forests." *Science* vol. 318 16 Nov 2007: 1107.

Champlin, Drew. "Ex-Husker Dixon trying to run with second chance at Troy." *Lincoln Journal Star*, Fri Aug. 21, 2009: D2.

Cheng, Anne Anlin. *The Melancholy of Race.* Oxford: Oxford UP, 2000.

Chesnutt, Charles W. Journal Entry for August 13, 1878. MS. Spec. Collections. John Hope and Aurelia E. Franklin Library. Nashville: Fisk U. 49 pages.

———. *The Marrow of Tradition.* 1901. New York: Penguin, 1993.

———. "The Sheriff's Children." *Independent* Nov. 7 (1888/1889). Rpt. In *The Portable Charles W. Chesnutt.* Ed. William L. Andrews. Gen. Ed. Henry Louis Gates, Jr. New York: Penguin Classics, 2008. 71–88.

———. "Superstition & Folklore of the South." 1901. Dundes, 369–76.

Clark, J. P., trans. *The Ozidi Saga.* By Okabou Ojobolo. Ibadan, Nigeria: Ibadan UP and Oxford UP, 1977.

———. Preface. *The Ozidi Saga.* By Okabou Ojobolo. Ibadan, Nigeria: Ibadan UP and Oxford UP, 1977. xxix–xxxiv.

Clark-Bekederemo, J.P. Introductory Essay. *The Ozidi Saga.* By Okabou Ojobolo. Ibadan, Nigeria: Ibadan UP and Oxford UP, 1977. xxxv–lvii.

Collins, Lauren Nicole. "The Impact of Father-Absence on Self-Concept Formation in African-American Women." B.A. Thesis. Philosophy. School of Interdisciplinary Studies. Miami University, Oxford, OH. 2004.

Conrad, David C. "Introduction: The Land of Mande and Its Oral Traditionists." *Epic Ancestors of the Sunjata Era: Oral Tradition From the Maninka of Guinea.* Ed. Conrad. Madison, WI: African Studies Program, 1999. 1–14.

———. "Mooning Armies and Mothering Heroes." Austen, *In Search*, 189–229.

———. "Note on the Map of the Mande Heartland (Map A)." Conrad, *Sunjata*, xxxvii–xxxix.

———. Trans. *Sunjata: A West African Epic of the Mande Peoples.* Perf. by Djanka Tassey Condé and Mamady Kouyaté, 1994. Indianapolis: Hackett Pub., 2004.

Conrad, David C. and Barbara E. Frank. "Introduction: *Nyamakalaya*: Contradiction and Ambiguity in Mande Society." *Status and Identity in West Africa:*

Nyamakalaw of Mande. Eds. Conrad and Frank. Bloomington and Indianapolis: Indiana UP, 1995. 1–22.

Corrigan, Gordon. *Wellington: A Military Life*. London: Hambledon & London, 2001.

Coupe, Laurence. *Myth*. 2nd. ed. London and New York: Routledge, 2009.

Cowan, Louise. "Introduction: Epic as Cosmopoeisis." *The Epic Cosmos*. Ed. Larry Allmus. Dallas: Dallas Institute Publications, 1992. 1–26.

Cowie, Alexander. "John Trumbull as Revolutionist." *American Literature* 3 (1931): 287–95.

Crafts, Hannah. *The Bondwoman's Narrative*. Ed. Henry Louis Gates, Jr. New York: Warner, 2002.

Cronon, William. *Nature's Metropolis: Chicago and the Great West*. New York: W.W. Norton, 1991.

Crouch, Stanley. "Aunt Medea." *New Republic* 197.16 (1987): 38–43. Rpt. in Solomon, 64–71.

Cunliffe, Marcus. Introduction. *The Life of Washington*. 1808. Mason L. Weems. Ed. Cunliffe. Cambridge, Mass, London: Harvard UP-Belknap P, 1999. ix-lxii.

Dawahare, Anthony. "From No Man's Land to Mother-land: Emasculation and Nationalism in

Richard Wright's Depression Era Urban Novels." *African American Review* 33.3 (1999): 451–66.

Deardorff, Daniel. *The Other Within: The Genius of Deformity in Myth, Culture, & Psyche*. Ashland, OR: White Cloud, 2004.

Del Franco, Mark. "Toy Story." *Multichannelmerchant.com*. Multichannel Merchant, 1 Oct. 2005. Web. 5 Nov. 2006.

Delmar, P. Jay. "The Moral Dilemma in Charles W. Chesnutt's *The Marrow of Tradition*." *American Literary Realism* 14.2 (1981): 269–272.

De Santis, Christopher C. "The Dangerous Marrow of Southern Tradition: Charles W. Chesnutt, Paul Laurence Dunbar, and the Paternalist Ethos at the Turn of the Century." *Southern Quarterly: A Journal of the Arts in the South* 38.2 (2001): 79–97.

Detienne, Marcel. *Dionysos Slain*. Trans. Mireille Muellner and Leonard Muellner. *Dionysos mis à mort*. 1977. Baltimore and London: Johns Hopkins UP, 1979.

Dimock, Wai Chee. *Through Other Continents: American Literature Across Deep Time*. Princeton: Princeton UP, 2006.

Do the Right Thing. Screenplay and Dir. Spike Lee. Perf. Danny Aiello, Ossie Davis, Ruby Dee, Spike Lee, John Turturro. Universal, 1989.

Douglass, Frederick. *The Heroic Slave*. 1853. *Three Classic African-American Novels*. Ed. William L. Andrews. New York: Signet-Penguin, 2003. 23–69.

———. *Narrative of the Life of Frederick Douglass, An American Slave, Written by Himself*. 1845. Eds. William L. Andrews and William S. McFeely. New York: Norton, 1997.

———. "What to the Slave Is the Fourth of July?: An Address Delivered in Rochester, New York, on 5 July 1852." Gates and McKay, 462–73.

Drewal, John Henry. "Celebrating Water Spirits: Influence, Confluence, and Difference in Ìjèbú-Yorùbá and Delta Masquerades." Anderson and Peek, 193–215.

DuBois, Page. *Slaves and Other Objects*. Chicago and London: U of Chicago P, 2003.

———. *Trojan Horses: Saving the Classics from Conservatives*. New York and London: New York UP, 2001.

Du Bois, W.E.B. *The Autobiography of W.E.B. Du Bois: A Soliloquy Viewing My Life from the Last Decade of Its First Century*. 1968. New York: International Publishers, 1997.

———. "Criteria of Negro Art." 1926. Gates and McKay, 777–84.

———. *The Souls of Black Folk*. 1903. Eds. Henry Louis Gates, Jr. and Terri Hume Oliver. New York: Norton Critical Edition, 1999.

Dundes, Alan. Preface. *Mother-Wit from the Laughing Barrel: Readings in the Interpretation of Afro-American Folklore*. Ed. Dundes. Englewood Cliffs, NJ: Prentice-Hall, 1973. xi-xiv.

———. *Mother Wit from the Laughing Barrel: Readings in the Interpretation of Afro-American Folklore*. Englewood Cliffs, NJ: Prentice-Hall, 1973.

Dwight, M. A. *Grecian and Roman Mythology*. 2nd Ed. New York: Putnam, 1849.

Dyer, Gwynne. *Climate Wars*. Toronto, Ontario: Random House Canada, 2008.

Eadie, John W., ed. *Classical Traditions in Early America*. Center for Coördination of Ancient and Modern Studies. Ann Arbor: U of Michigan P, 1976.

Earle, Susan, ed. *Aaron Douglas: African American Modernist*. New Haven: Yale UP; Lawrence, KS: Spencer Museum of Art, U of Kansas, 2007.

Earle, Susan. "Harlem, Modernism, and Beyond: Aaron Douglas and His Role in Art/History." Earle, 5–51.

1898 Wilmington Race Riot Commission. 1898 Wilmington Race Riot—Final Report, May 31, 2006. North Carolina Department of Cultural Resources, Office of Archives and History. http://www.history.ncdcr.gov/1898-wrrc/report/report.htm 8 June 2010.

Ellison, Ralph. "Change the Joke and Slip the Yoke." *Partisan Review* 25.2 (1958): 212–22. *Shadow and Act* by Ellison. New York: Vintage-Random, 1972. 45–59.

———. Invisible Man. 1952. New York: Vintage-Random, 1995.

———. "Richard Wright's Blues." Gates and McKay, 1535–48.

Emerson, Ralph Waldo. "Self-Reliance." 1841. *Norton Anthology of American Literature*. 5th ed. Vol. 1. Gen. Ed. Nina Baym. New York: Norton, 1998. 1126–43.

Evans, Howie. "Sort of Sporty." *New York Amsterdam News* Feb. 14, 1970: 26.

Eyen we Langa, Wopashitwe Mondo. *The Black Panther is an African Cat*. Van Nuys, CA: House of August, 2006.]

Fabre, Michel. "From Revolutionary Poet to Haiku." *Studies in Black Literature* 1.3 (1970): 10–22. Rpt. in *The World of Richard Wright* by Michel Fabre. Center for the Study of Southern Culture Series. Jackson: UP of Mississippi, 1985. 34–55.

———. *Richard Wright: Books and Writers*. Jackson: UP of Mississippi, 1990.

———. *The Unfinished Quest of Richard Wright*. 1973. Trans. Isabel Barzun. Urbana and Chicago: U of Illinois P, 1993.

Fairhead, James, and Melissa Leach. *Misreading the African Landscape: Society and Ecology in a Forest-Savanna Mosaic*. 1996. Cambridge: Cambridge UP, 1999.

Falkner, Thomas M., Nancy Felson, and David Konstan, eds. *Contextualizing Classics: Ideology, Performance, Dialogue; Essays in Honor of John J. Peradotto*. Lanham, MD: Rowman & Littlefield, 1999.

Farrell, William R. *Classical Place Names in New York State: Origins, Histories and Meanings*. Jamesville, NY: Pine Grove, 2002.

Feller, Ben. "Obama Opens Taps on Offshore Drilling." *Lincoln Journal Star* 1 Apr. 2010: A1-A2.

Felsenstein, Frank. *English Trader, Indian Maid: Representing Gender, Race, and Slavery in the New World; An Inkle and Yarico Reader*. Baltimore and London: Johns Hopkins UP, 1999.

"First Novels." *The New Yorker* 24 June 1996: 154–55.

Foley, Charles J. County of Manatee District Twelve Medical Examiner. Rutledge, George Sip. Autopsy Report. File No. AB-84–67. 25 May 1967.

Ford, Andrew. "Performing Interpretation: Early Allegorical Exegesis of Homer." In Beissinger, Tylus, and Wofford, pp. 33–53.

Frye, Northrop. *Anatomy of Criticism: Four Essays*. 1957. Princeton: Princeton, UP, 1973.

Furman, Jan, ed. *Toni Morrison's Song of Solomon: A Casebook*. Oxford, New York: Oxford UP, 2003.

Furstenberg, François. *In the Name of the Father: Washington's Legacy, Slavery, and the Making of a Nation*. New York: Penguin, 2006.

Garland, Robert. "Deformity and Disfigurement in the Graeco-Roman World." *History Today* 42.11 (Nov. 1992): 38–44.

Gates, Henry Louis, Jr. *The Signifying Monkey: A Theory of African-American Literary Criticism*. Oxford: Oxford UP, 1989.

———. "What Is an African American Classic?" *The Portable Charles W. Chesnutt*. Ed. William L. Andrews. Gen. Ed. Henry Louis Gates, Jr. New York: Penquin Classics, 2008. vii-xvi.

Gates, Henry Louis, Jr. and Nellie Y. McKay, gen. eds. *The Norton Anthology of African American Literature*. 2nd ed. New York: W.W. Norton, 2004.

Gates, Henry Louis, Jr. and Terri Hume Oliver, eds. Introduction. The Souls of Black Folk by W. E. B. Du Bois. 1903. New York: Norton Critical Edition, 1999. xi–xxxvii.

Geertz, Clifford. Introduction. *Local Knowledge: Further Essays in Interpretive Anthropology*. New York: Basic, 1983. 3–16.

———. "Common Sense as a Cultural System." *Antioch Review* 33.1 (1975): 5–26. Rpt. in *Local Knowledge: Further Essays in Interpretive Anthropology*, by Clifford Geertz. New York: Basic, 1983. 73–93.

George, Marjorie and Richard S. Pressman. "Confronting the Shadow: Psycho-Political Repression in Chesnutt's *The Marrow of Tradition*." *Phylon* 48.4 (1987): 287–298.

Gikandi, Simon. "Picasso, Africa and the Schemata of Difference." *Modernism/modernity* 10.3 (2003): 455–80. Rpt. in Nuttall, 30–59.

Giles, James R. and Thomas P. Lally. "Allegory in Chesnutt's *Marrow of Tradition*." *Jour. of Gen. Ed.* 35.4 (1984): 259–269.

Gill, Sam D. *Sacred Words: Study of Navajo Religion and Prayer*. Westport, Conn.: Greenwood, 1981.

Gilman, Sander L. *Making the Body Beautiful: A Cultural History of Aesthetic Surgery*. Princeton, NJ: Princeton UP, 1999.

Gilroy, Paul. *The Black Atlantic: Modernity and Double Consciousness*. Cambridge: Harvard UP, 1994.

Gleason, William. "Voices at the Nadir: Charles Chesnutt and David Bryant Fulton." *American Literary Realism* 24.3 (1992): 22–41.

Glotfelty, Cheryll and Harold Fromm, Eds. *The Ecocriticism Reader: Landmarks in Literary Ecology*. Athens: U of Georgia P, 1996.

Gomez, Michael A. *Exchanging Our Country Marks: The Transformation of African Identities in the Colonial and Antebellum South*. Chapel Hill and London: U of North Carolina P, 1998.

Gong, Jie. "Re-Imagining an Ancient, Emergent Superpower: 2008 Beijing Olympic Games, Public Memory, and National Identity." *Communication and Critical/Cultural Studies* 9.2 (2012): 191–214.

Green, Doris. "Traditional Dance in Africa." Asante, 13–28.

Griggs, Sutton E. *Imperium In Imperio: A Study of the Negro Race*. 1899. Sioux Falls, S.D.: Nu Vision, 2008.

Gross, Ariela J. "Litigating Whiteness: Trials of Racial Determination in the Nineteenth-Century South." 108 *Yale L.J.* (1998).

Grossman, James R. "Blowing the Trumpet: The Chicago Defender and Black Migration During World War I." *Illinois Historical Journal* 78.2 (1985): 82–96.

Grottanelli, Cristiano. "Tricksters, Scapegoats, Champions, Saviors." *History of Religions* 23.2 (1983): 117–39.

Hackenberry, Charles. "Meaning and Models: The Uses of Characterization in Chesnutt's *The Marrow of Tradition* and *Mandy Oxendine*." *American Literary Realism* 17.2 (1984): 193–202.

Haile, Father Berard. *Origin Legend of the Navaho Enemy Way: Text and Translation*. New Haven: Yale UP, 1938.

Hale, Thomas A. *Griots and Griottes: Masters of Words and Music*. Bloomington: Indiana UP, 1998.

Hammond, Martin. Introduction. *The Iliad: A New Prose Translation*. Trans. Martin Hammond. London: Penguin, 1988. 7–46.

Harden, Blaine. "S. Koreans abuzz over work habits." *Lincoln Journal Star* May 12, 2008: 9A.

Hart, Joseph. "L.A.R.K. Toys—Tin Toys, Wood Toys, Carousel Animals—A magical place to shop and . . ." *Larktoys.com*. Minnesota Monthly, Dec. 1999. Web. 5 Nov. 2006. Havelock, Eric A. *The Muse Learns to Write: Reflections on Orality and Literacy from Antiquity to the Present*. New Haven and London: Yale UP, 1986.

Hawes, Clement. "Leading History by the Nose: The Turn to the Eighteenth Century in *Midnight's Children*." Modern Fiction Studies 39.1 (1993): 147–68.

Hazzard-Gordon, Katrina. "Dancing Under the Lash: Sociocultural Disruption, Continuuity, and Synthesis." Asante, 101–30.

Hegel, G.W.F. *Aesthetics: Lectures on Fine Art*. Trans. T. M. Knox. Oxford: Clarendon P, 1975. Trans. of *Vorlesungen über die Aesthetik*. Ed. Heinrich Gustav Hotho. 3 vols. 1835–38.

Hegel, Georg Wilhelm Friedrich. *The Philosophy of History*. Trans. J. Sibree. New York: Dover, 1956.

Herbert, Anne T. *Robert Harpur's New York: His Role in Its Growth From Province to State*. Binghamton, NY: Broome County Historical Society, 2003.

Hibbert, Christopher. *Wellington: A Personal History*. London: HarperColllins, 1998.

Hilton, Jr., William, et al. "Ye Relacion of Ye Late Discovery Made in Florida." 1662. Rpt. in J. Leitch Wright, Jr.'s "William Hilton's Voyage to Carolina in 1662." 105 *Essex Institute Historical Collections* (1969): 96–102.

Hoffman, Barbara G. "Power, Structure, and Mande *Jeliw*." Conrad and Frank, 36–45.

The Holy Bible. The Authorized (King James) Version. Camden, NJ: Thomas Nelson, 1958.

Homer. *Iliad*. Vol. II. Trans. A.T. [Augustus Taber] Murray. 1925. Loeb Classical Library. Cambridge: Harvard UP, 1999.

Homer. *The Iliad: A New Prose Translation*. Trans. and Intro. Martin Hammond. London: Penguin, 1988.

———. *The Odyssey*. Trans. and Intro. E. V. Rieu. New York: Penguin, 1959.

Hoover, Susan. Home page. "Susan Hoover's LEGO Trojan Horse." *Ourworld. compuserve.com*. n.d. Web. 5 Nov. 2006.

Hopkins, Pauline. *Of One Blood; Or, the Hidden Self*. 1902–1903. New York: Washington Square P, 2004.

Horejsi, Nicole. "'A Counterpart to the Ephesian Matron': Steele's 'Inkle and Yarico' and a Feminist Critique of the Classics." *Eighteenth-Century Studies* 39.2 (2006): 201–226.

Hughes, Langston. "The Negro Speaks of Rivers." 1921. Gates and McKay, 1291.

Hurston, Zora Neale. "High John de Conquer." The American Mercury 57 (1943): 450–58. Rpt. in Dundes, 541–48.

Hutteman, Ann Hewlett. *Wilmington, North Carolina: Postcard History Series* . Charleston, SC: Arcadia, 2001.

Itayemi, Phebean and P. Gurrey, comps. *Folk Tales and Fables*. London: Penguin, 1953.

Jackson, Blyden. "Richard Wright: Black Boy from America's Black Belt and Urban Ghettos." *CLA Journal* 12 (1969): 287–309.

Jacobs, Harriet. *Incidents in the Life of a Slave Girl*. 1861. Eds. Nellie Y. McKay and Frances Smith Foster. New York: W.W. Norton, 2001.

James, Joy. "'Discredited Knowledge' in the Nonfiction of Toni Morrison." *Women of Color and Philosophy: A Critical Reader*. Ed. Naomi Zack. Malden, MA: Blackwell, 2000. 25–43.

Jansen, Jan. "Hot Issues: The 1997 Kamabolon Ceremony in Kangaba (Mali)." *International Journal of African Historical Studies* 31.2 (1998): 253–78.

———. "The Sunjata Epic—The Ultimate Version." *Research in African Literatures* 32.1 (2001): 14–46.

Jennings, La Vinia Delois. *Toni Morrison and the Idea of Africa*. Cambridge: Cambridge UP, 2008.

Jimoh, A. Yemisi. "Toni Morrison." *The Literary Encyclopedia*. The Literary Encyclopedia, 25 Oct. 2002. <http://www.litencyc.com/php/speople. php?rec=true&UID=3214> 18 April 2008.

Johnson, James Weldon. *The Autobiography of an Ex-Colored Man*. 1912. New York: Penguin, 1990.

Johnson, John William. "Annotations to the Text." *The Epic of Son-Jara: A West African Tradition*. By Fa-Digi Sisòkò, performer, and John William Johnson, trans. Bloomington: Indiana UP, 1992. 102–40.

———. Introduction. *The Epic of Son-Jara: A West African Tradition*. By Fa-Digi Sisòkò, performer, and Johnson, trans. Bloomington: Indiana UP, 1992. 1–15.

———. Trans. *The Epic of Son-Jara: A West African Tradition*. By Fa-Digi Sisòkò, performer. Bloomington: Indiana UP, 1992. 102–40.

———. "Yes, Virginia, There is an Epic in Africa." *Research in African Literatures* 11.3 (1980): 308–26.

Jones, Van (with Ariane Conrad). *The Green-Collar Economy: How One Solution Can Fix Our Two Biggest Problems*. New York: HarperOne, 2008.

Joyner, Charles. *Down by the Riverside: A South Carolina Slave Community*. Urbana and Chicago: U of Illinois P, 1984.

Jütte, Robert. *A History of the Senses: From Antiquity to Cyberspace*. Trans. James Lynn. Cambridge, England, and Malden, MA: Polity, 2005.

Kennedy, Randall. "Racial Passing." 62 *Ohio St. L.J.* 1145 (2001).

Kent, George E. "Richard Wright: Blackness and the Adventure of Western Culture." *CLA Journal* 12 (1969): 322–43.

Kinnamon, Kenneth. "Richard Wright's Use of Othello in Native Son." *CLA Journal* 12 (1969): 358–59.

Kirschke, Amy Helene. *Aaron Douglas: Art, Race, and the Harlem Renaissance*. 1995. Jackson, Miss.: UP of Mississippi, 1999.

Knadler, Stephen P. "Untragic Mulatto: Charles Chesnutt and the Discourse of Whiteness." *American Literary History* 8.3 (1996): 426–48.

Krishna, Valerie. "The Alliterative Morte Arthure." In *The Romance of Arthur*. James J. Wilhelm and Laila Zamuelis Gross, eds. New York and London: Garland, 1984. 211–13.

Krumholz, Linda. "Dead Teachers: Rituals of Manhood and Rituals of Reading in *Song of Solomon*." *Modern Fiction Studies* 39.3–4 (1993): 551–74. Rpt. in Furman, 201–29.

———. "The Ghosts of Slavery: Historical Recovery in Toni Morrison's *Beloved*. *African American Review* 26.3 (1992): 395–408.

Kunene, Daniel P. "Journey in the African Epic." *Research in African Literatures* 22.2 (1991): 205–23.

Lee, Chang-rae. *Native Speaker*. 1995. New York: Riverhead, 1996.

Lee, Spike. Black History Month Address. University of Florida. The O'Connell Center. Gainesville, Florida. Transcript. 1 February 2006. 18 April 2008. <http://sg.ufl.edu/accent/transcripts/020106.txt>

Le Guin, Ursula K. *A Wizard of Earthsea*. 1968. New York: Bantam, 2004.

Levine, Lawrence W. *Black Culture and Black Consciousness: Afro-American Folk Thought from Slavery to Freedom*. New York: Oxford UP, 1977.

Lévi-Strauss, Claude. *The Origin of Table Manners, Introduction to a Science of Mythology*. Vol. 3. Trans. J. and D. Weightman. London: Cape, 1978.

Lewis, David Levering. "Twain's Gilded Age, and Ours." Rev. of *Autobiography of Mark Twain: Volume I*, by Harriet Elinor Smith, ed. *DemocracyJournal.org*. Spring 2007: 86–93. Web. 17 March 2012.

Locke, Alain. "The New Negro." Gates and McKay, 984–93.

Loewen, James W. *Lies My Teacher Told Me: Everything Your American History Textbook Got Wrong*. New York: Simon & Schuster, 1995.

Longinus. *On Great Writing (On the Sublime)*. Trans. G. M. A. Grube. Indianapolis & Cambridge: Hackett Publishing Co., 1991.

López, Robert Oscar. "Thoreau, Homer, and Community." *Nineteenth-Century Prose* 31.2 (2004): 122–51.

Lott, Eric. *Love and Theft: Blackface Minstrelsy and the American Working Class*. New York, Oxford: Oxford UP, 1995.

Lukács, Georg. *The Theory of the Novel*. 1920. Trans. Anna Bostock. Cambridge, MA: MIT P, 1971.

Maar, Charles. "Origin of the Classical Place Names of Central New York." *Quarterly Journal* 7.3 (1926): 155–68.

MacLeish, Archibald. *Land of the Free*. New York: Harcourt, Brace, 1938.

Malcolm X (with the assistance of Alex Haley). *The Autobiography of Malcolm X: As Told to Alex Haley*. 1964. New York: Ballantine, 1999.

Manes, Christopher. "Nature and Silence." In *The Ecocriticism Reader: Landmarks in Literary Ecology*. Eds. Cheryll Glotfelty and Harold Fromm. Athens and London: U of Georgia P, 1996. 15–29.

The Matrix. Screenplay and Dir. by Andy and Larry Wachowski. Perf. Keanu Reeves and Laurence Fishburne. Warner Bros., 1999.

May, Christopher. "The Denial of History: Reification, Intellectual Property Rights and the Lessons of the Past." *Capital & Class* 30.1 (Spring 2006): 33–56.

Mazel, David. "American Literary Environmentalism as Domestic Orientalism." *The Ecocriticism Reader: Landmarks in Literary Ecology*. Eds. Cheryll Glotfelty and Harold Fromm. Athens: U of Georgia P, 1996. 137–46.

Mbele, Joseph. "The Hero in the African Epic." Diss. U of Wisconsin-Madison, 1986.

McBride, James. *Song Yet Sung*. New York: Riverhead-Penguin, 2008.

McGowan, Todd. "Acting without the Father: Charles Chesnutt's New Aristocrat." *American Literary Realism* 30.1 (1997): 59–74.

McKnight, Reginald. "Roscoe in Hell." *Black American Literature Forum* 23.2 (1989): 339–60.

McLachlan, James. "Classical Names, American Identities: Some Notes on College Students and the Classical Traditions in the 1770s." Eadie, pp. 81–95.

Miller, Dean A. *The Epic Hero*. Baltimore and London: Johns Hopkins UP, 2000.

Miller, Eugene H. *Voice of a Native Son: The Poetics of Richard Wright.* Jackson and London: UP of Mississippi, 1990.

Mills, Donald H. Preface. *Classical Place Names in New York State: Origins, Histories and Meanings.* By William R. Farrell. Jamesville, NY: Pine Grove, 2002. xi.

Mize, George E. "Trumbull's Use of the Epic Formula in *The Progress of Dulness* and *M'Fingal.*" *Connecticut Review* 4.2 (1971): 86–90.

Morrison, Toni. "An Interview with Toni Morrison, Hessian Radio Network, Frankfurt, West Germany." *Critical Essays on Toni Morrison.* By Rosemarie K. Lester. Ed. Nellie Y. McKay. Boston, MA: G.K. Hall, 1988. 47–54.

———. "Behind the Making of *The Black Book.*" *Black World* (Feb. 1974): 86–90.

———. *Beloved.* 1987. New York: Vintage-Random House, 2004.

———. Foreword. *Beloved.* 1987. New York: Vintage-Random House, 2004. xv–xix.

———. Interview by Thomas LeClair. "'The Language Must Not Sweat': A Conversation with Toni Morrison." *New Republic* 184 (21 March 1981): 25–29.

———. "The Opening Sentences of Beloved." Solomon, 91–92.

———. *Playing in the Dark: Whiteness and the Literary Imagination.* 1992. New York: Vintage-Random House, 1993.

———. "Rootedness: The Ancestor as Foundation." *Black Women Writers (1950–1980): A Critical Evaluation.* Ed. Mari Evans. Garden City: Doubleday, 1984. 339–45.

Morley, Catherine. *The Quest for Epic in Contemporary American Fiction: John Updike, Philip Roth and Don DeLillo.* New York and London: Routledge, 2009.

Murphy, Cullen, and Todd S. Purdum (with the assistance of Phillippe Sands). "Fairwell to All That: An Oral History of the Bush White House." *Vanity Fair* Feb. 2009: 88+ (88–101, 148–60).

Murray, Rolland. "Black Crisis Shuffle: Fiction, Race, and Simulation." *African American Review* 42.2 (2008): 215–33.

Myers, Jeffrey. *Converging Stories: Race, Ecology, and Environmental Justice in American Literature.* Athens, GA: U of Georgia P, 2005.

Myles, L. Renae. "The Absence of Color in Athletic Administration at Division I Institutions." Diss. (M.Ed.) Northwestern State University of Louisiana, 2005.

Nagy, Gregory. "Epic as Genre." Beissinger, Tylus, and Wofford, pp. 21–32.

———. "Homer and Plato at the Panathenaia: Synchronic and Diachronic Perspectives." Falkner, Felson, and Konstan, 123–50.

"Necro." *Webster's New World Dictionary.* 2nd College Edition. 1986.

"Necromancy." *Webster's New World Dictionary.* 2nd College Edition. 1986.

"Negro." *Webster's New World Dictionary.* 2nd College Edition. 1986.

Neihardt, John G. *Black Elk Speaks: Being the Life Study of a Holy Man of the Oglala Sioux.* The Premier Edition. Albany, NY: Excelsior-State U of New York P, 2008.

Newton, Robert C. "Out of Print: The Epic Cassette as Invention, Reinvention, and Commodity." Austen, *In Search,* 313–27.

Niane, D.T. *Sundiata: An Epic of Old Mali.* By Mamoudou Kouyaté. 1965. Trans. G.D. Pickett. London: Longman, 1977.

Nowatzki, Robert. "'Sublime Patriots': Black Masculinity in Three African-American Novels." *Journal of Men's Studies* 8.1 (1999): 59–72.

Nuttall, Sarah. "Introduction: Rethinking Beauty." *Beautiful/Ugly: Africa and Diaspora Aesthtetics.* Ed. Nuttall. Durham, NC, and London: Duke UP, 2006. 6–29.

Obelkevich, James. "Proverbs and Social History." *The Social History of Language.* Eds. Peter Burke and Roy Porter. Cambridge: Cambridge UP, 1987. 43–72.

Ong, Walter J. *Orality & Literacy: The Technologizing of the Word.* 1982. London and New York: Routledge, 1999.

Okpewho, Isidore. *African Oral Literature: Backgrounds, Character, and Continuity.* Bloomington and Indianapolis, IN: Indiana UP, 1992.

———. *The Epic in Africa: Toward a Poetics of the Oral Performance.* New York: Columbia UP, 1979.

———. *Myth in Africa: A Study of Its Aesthetic and Cultural Relevance.* Cambridge, London: Cambridge UP, 1983.

———. *Once Upon a Kingdom: Myth, Hegemony, and Identity.* Bloomington & Indianapolis: Indiana UP, 1998.

———. "*The Ozidi Saga*: A Critical Introduction." *The Ozidi Saga.* By Okabou Ojobolo. Tran. J. P. Clark. Ibadan, Nigeria: Ibadan UP and Oxford UP, 1977. vii–xxviii.

Owomoyela, Oyekan. *Yoruba Proverbs.* Lincoln, NE, and London: U of Nebraska P, 2005.

Page, Walter H. Introduction. *Up From Slavery: An Autobiography.* By Booker T. Washington. N.p.: Association P, 1901. xi–xxiii.

Painter, Nell Irvin. "Soul Murder and Slavery: Toward a Fully-Loaded Cost Accounting." *U.S. History as Women's History: New Feminist Essays.* Eds. Linda K. Kerber, Alice Kessler-Harris, and Kathryn Kish Sklar. Chapel Hill, NC: U of North Carolina P, 1995. 125–46.

Parks, Suzan-Lori. *Topdog/Underdog.* 2001. New York: Theatre Communications Group, 2003.

Patterson, Lee. *Negotiating the Past: The Historical Understanding of Medieval Literature.* Madison: U of Wisconsin, P, 1987.

Peabody, Ephraim. "Narratives of Fugitive Slaves." *The Christian Examiner* 4th ser. 12.1 (1849): 61–93.

Peach, Linden. *Toni Morrison.* 2nd ed. New York: St. Martin's P, 2000.

Perry, Imani. "Occupying the Universal, Embodying the Subject: African-American Literary Jurisprudence." *Law and Literature* 17.1 (2005): 97–129.

Pew Research Center. "China Seen Overtaking U.S. as Global Superpower: 23-Nation Pew Global Attitudes Survey." *Pew Global Attitudes Project.* Pew Research Center, 13 July 2011. <http://www.pewglobal.org/files/2011/07/Pew-Global-Attitudes-Balance-of-Power-U.S.-Image-Report-FINAL-July-13–2011.pdf> 29 June 2012.

———. "Global Opinion of Obama Slips, International Policies Faulted." *Pew Global Attitudes Project.* Pew Research Center, 13 June 2012. <http://www.pewglobal.org/files/2012/06/Pew-Global-Attitudes-U.S.-Image-Report-FINAL-June-13–2012.pdf> 29 June 2012.

———. "The Rise of Asian Americans." *Pew Social & Demographic Trends.* Pew Research Center, 19 June 2012. <http://www.pewsocialtrends.org/files/2012/06/SDT-The-Rise-of-Asian-Americans-Full-Report.pdf> 23 June 2012.

Pickens, Ernestine Williams. *Charles W. Chesnutt and the Progressive Movement.* New York: Pace UP, 1994.

Plasa, Carl. "'It's Not Over Just Because It Stops': Post-Colonialism, Psychoanalysis, History." *Toni Morrison: Beloved.* Ed. Carl Plasa. New York: Columbia UP, 1988. 116–42.

Plessy v. Ferguson. 163 U.S. 537, 16 S.Ct. 1138, 41 L.Ed. 256. Maj. Op. by Justice Henry Billings Brown. Diss. Op. by Justice John Marshal Harlan. Supreme Court of the US. 1896.

Polgreen, Lydia. "As Chinese Investment in Africa Drops, Hope Sinks." *New York Times* 26 Mar. 2009: A6.

Pollan, Michael. "An Open Letter to the Next Farmer in Chief." *New York Times Magazine* [*The Food Issue*] Oct. 2008, in *New York Times* Oct. 12, 2008, late ed.: 62+.

Powell, Richard J. "The Aaron Douglas Effect." Earle, 53–73.

Prahlad, Sw. Anand Prahlad. *African-American Proverbs in Context.* Jackson, MI: UP of Mississippi, 1996.

———. "'All Chickens Come Home to Roost': The Function of Proverbs in Gloria Naylor's *Mama Day.*" *Proverbium* 15 (1998): 265–81.

———. "'No Guts, No Glory': Proverbs, Values and Image among Anglo-American Universitiy Students." *Southern Folklore* 51.3 (1994): 285–98.

———. Message to the author. 24/25 June 2007. E-mail.

Preik, Brooks Newton. *Haunted Wilmington and the Cape Fear Coast.* Wilmington, NC: Banks Channel Books, 1999.

Price, Richard. *Maroon Societies: Rebel Slave Communities in the Americas.* 1973. Baltimore: Johns Hopkins UP, 1979.

Puckett, Newbell Niles. "Names of American Negro Slaves." *Studies in the Science of Society Presented to Albert Galloway Keller in Celebration of his Completion of Thirty Years as Professor of the Science of Society in Yale University.* Ed. G.P. Murdock. New Haven: Yale UP; London: Oxford UP, 1937. 471–94.

Pudaloff, Ross. "Celebrity as Identity: Richard Wright, *Native Son*, and Mass Culture." *Studies in American Fiction* 11.1 (1983): 3–18.

Rambsy, Howard, II. "The Vengeance of Black Boys: How Richard Wright, Paul Beatty, and Aaron McGruder Strike Back." *Mississippi Quarterly: The Journal of Southern Cultures* 61.4 (2008): 643–57.

Redfield, James M. *Nature and Culture in the Iliad: The Tragedy of Hector.* 1975. Durham and London: Duke UP, 1994.

Redmond, Eugene B. "The Black American Epic: Its Roots, Its Writers." *Black Scholar* (Jan. 1971): 15–22.

Reed, Ishmael. *Mumbo-Jumbo.* 1972. New York: Scribner, 1996.

———. "Neo-HooDoo Manifesto." *Conjure; Selected Poems, 1963–1970.* By Ishmael Reed. Amherst: U of Massachussets P, 1972. 20–25. Rpt. in Gates and McKay, 2062–66.

Reilly, John M. "The Dilemma in Chesnutt's *The Marrow of Tradition.*" *Phylon* 32 (1971): 31–38.

Reinhold, Meyer. *Classica Americana: The Greek and Roman Heritage in the United States.* Detroit: Wayne State UP, 1984.

———. *The Classick Pages: Classical Reading of Eighteenth-Century Americans.* University Park, PA: Pennsylvania State U, 1975.

Revkin, Andrew C. "Study Finds Past Mega-Droughts in Africa." *New York Times* Fri April 17, 2009: A11.

Richard, Carl J. *The Founders and the Classics: Greece, Rome, and the American Enlightenment.* Cambridge: Harvard UP, 1994.

Rieu, E.V. Introduction. *The Odyssey.* Trans. E. V. Rieu. New York: Penguin, 1959. 9–21.

Rigney, Barbara Hill. "'The Disremembered and Unaccounted For': History, Myth, and Magic." *The Voices of Toni Morrison.* Columbus: Ohio State UP, 1991. 61–81.

Roach, Joseph. *Cities of the Dead: Circum-Atlantic Performance.* New York: Columbia UP, 1996.

Roberts, John W. "The African American Trickster as Hero." Ruoff and Ward, 97–114.

———. *From Trickster to Badman: The Black Folk Hero in Slavery and Freedom.* Philadelphia: U of Pennsylvania P, 1989.

———. "Slave Proverbs: A Perspective." *Callaloo* 4 (1978): 129–40.

———. "Stackolee and the Development of a Black Heroic Idea." *Western Folklore* 42.3 (1983): 179–90.

Robeson, Paul. "Joshua Fit de Battle of Jericho." Rec. 29 Dec. 1945. *The Power and the Glory.* CD. Columbia, 1991.

Rock, Chris. *Chris Rock: Never Scared*. DVD. HBO Home Video, 2004.

Rodney, Walter. *How Europe Underdeveloped Africa*. Washington, D.C.: Howard UP, 1982.

Rowell, Charles H. "An Interview with Octavia E. Butler." *Callaloo* 20.1 (1997): 47–66.

Rummell, Kathryn. "Toni Morrison's *Beloved*: Transforming the African Heroic Epic." *The Griot* 21.1 (2002): 1–15.

Rutledge, Gregory E. "The Epic Trickster: From Sunjata to Jim Crow." UW-Madison Diss., 2005.

Saunders, William L. Preface. *The Colonial Records of North Carolina*. [Binding Title: *The State Records of North Carolina*.] Vol. I. Ed. William L. Saunders. Raleigh, NC: P. M. Hale, 1886. iii–viii.

Saunders, William L., ed. Preface. *The Colonial Records of North Carolina*. [Binding Title: *The State Records of North Carolina*.] Vols. I and II. Raleigh, NC: P. M. Hale, 1886.

Schein, Seth L. "Cultural Studies and Classics: Contrasts and Opportunities." Falkner, Felson, and Konstan, 285–99.

Scherman, Robert. "What Are Our Kids Buying?" *Journal of Popular Culture* 3.2 (1969): 274–80.

Schultz, Elizabeth. "Odysseus Comes to Know His Place: Reading *The Odyssey* Ecocritically." *Neohelicon* 36 (2009): 299–310.

———. "The Power of Blackness: Richard Wright Re-Writes *Moby-Dick*." *African American Review* 33.4 (1999): 639–54.

Schuyler, George Samuel. "The Negro-Art Hokum." 1926. Gates and McKay, 1221–23.

Schwarz, Maureen Trudelle. *"I Choose Life": Contemporary Medical and Religious Practices in the Navajo World*. Norman, OK: U of Oklahoma P, 2008.

Scott v. Sandford. 60 U.S. 393, 15 L.Ed. 691. Maj. Op. by Chief Justice Roger B. Taney. Supreme Court of the US. 1857.

Severn, John. *Architects of Empire: The Duke of Wellington and His Brothers*. Norman, OK: U of Oklahoma P, 2007.

Seydou, Christiane. "A Few Reflections on Narrative Structures of Epic Texts: A Case Example of Bambara and Fulani Epics." Trans. Brunhilde Biebuyck. *Research in African Literatures* 14.3 (1983): 312–31.

Shaffer, Jason. *Performing Patriotism: National Identity in the Colonial and Revolutionary American Theater*. Philadelphia: U of Pennsylvania P, 2007.

Shapin, Steven. "Proverbial Economies: How an Understanding of Some Linguistic and Social Features of Common Sense Can Throw Light on More Prestigious Bodies of Knowledge, Science for Example." *Social Studies of Science* 31.5 (2001): 731–69.

Shay, Jonathan. *Achilles in Vietnam: Combat Trauma and the Undoing of Character*. New York: Atheneum, 1994.

———. *Odysseus in America: Combat Trauma and the Trials of Homecoming*. New York: Scribner, 2002.

Sienkewicz, Thomas J. "The Greeks Are Indeed like the Others: Myth and Society in the West African *Sunjata*." *Myth and the Polis*. Eds. Dora Carlisky Pozzi and John Moore Wickersham. Ithaca: Cornell UP, 1991. 182–202.

"Sir Gawain and the Green Knight." Abrams, 233–88.

Smethurst, James. "Invented by Horror: The Gothic and African American Literary Ideology in *Native Son*." *African American Review* 35.1 (2001): 29–40.

Smith, David Lionel. "African Americans, Writing, and Nature." *American Nature Writers*. Ed. John Elder. 2 vols. New York: Scribners, 1996.

Smith, Mark M. *How Race is Made: Slavery, Segregation, and the Senses*. Chapel Hill: U of North Carolina P, 2006.

Smith, Theophus H. *Conjuring Culture: Biblical Formations of Black America.* New York, Oxford: Oxford UP, 1994.

Snipe, Tracy D. "African Dance: Bridges to Humanity." Asante, 63–77.

Snyder, Martin D. "The Hero in the Garden: Classical Contributions to the Early Images of America." *Classical Traditions in Early America.* Ed. John W. Eadie. Center for Coördination of Ancient and Western Studies. Ann Arbor: U of Michigan P, 1976. 139–74.

Sollors, Werner, ed. *The Marrow of Tradition.* By Charles W. Chesnutt. New York: Norton, 2012.

Solomon, Barbara H., ed. *Critical Essays on Toni Morrison's Beloved.* New York: G. K. Hall, 1998.

Stark, John. "*Invisible Man*: Ellison's *Black Odyssey.*" *Negro American Literature Forum* 7.2 (1973): 60–63.

Steele, Richard. "Male Hypocrisy: The Story of Inkle and Yarico." *Spectator* No. 11 (1711). *Selections from The Tattler and The Spectator.* By Richard Steele and Joseph Addison. Comp. and Ed. Angus Ross. New York: Penguin Classics, 1988. 463–67.

Stelzer, Cameron. Review. "Andrew Arnaoutopoulos: Trojan Horse." *Artlink. com.* Artlink, 20.3 (2000): n. pag. <http://www.artlink.com.au/articles. cfm?id=2504> 5 Nov. 2006.

Stepto, Robert B. *From Behind the Veil: A Study of Afro-American Narrative.* Urbana & Chicago: U of Illinois P, 1979.

Stock, Catherine McNicol. *Main Street in Crisis: The Great Depression and the Old Middle Class on the Northern Plains.* Chapel Hill: U of North Carolina P, 1992.

Sundquist, Eric J. Introduction. *The Marrow of Tradition.* By Charles W. Chesnutt. New York: Penguin, 1993. vii–xlvii.

Talvi, Silja J.A. "Overworked, Vacation-Starved America Ranks #1 in Depression, Mental Health Problems." *AlterNet.org.* AlterNet Newsletter, 13 Nov. 2008. <http://www.alternet.org/story/106830/> 13 Nov. 2008.

Thompson, Robert Farris. "An Aesthetic of the Cool: West African Dance." *African Forum* 2.2 (Fall 1966): 88–90.

———. *Flash of the Spirit: African & Afro-American Art & Philosophy.* New York: Vintage-Random House, 1984.

Tolkien, J. R. R. *The Fellowship of the Ring.* 1954. New York: Ballantine-Random House, 1985.

———. *The Two Towers.* 1954. New York: Ballantine-Random House, 1985.

"Toponymy." *Webster's New World Dictionary.* 2nd College Edition. 1986.

Turner, Victor. "The Anthropology of Performance." *The Anthropology of Performance.* New York: PAJ Publications, 1986. 72–98.

———. "Images and Reflections: Ritual, Drama, Carnival, Film, and Spectacle in Cultural Performance." Turner, *Anthropology,* 21–32.

Twain, Mark. 1885. *Adventures of Huckleberry Finn.* Ed. by Susan K. Harris and Lyrae Van Clief-Stefanon. Boston, New York: Houghton Mifflin, 2009.

Vargas, Lucila. "When the 'Other' Is the Teacher: Implications of Teacher Diversity in Higher Education." *The Urban Review* 31.4 (1999): 359–83.

Vaught, Sabina. "The Talented Tenth: Gay Black Boys and the Racial Politics of Southern Schooling." *Journal of Gay & Lesbian Issues in Education* 2.2 (2004): 5–26.

Wagner, Bryan. "Charles Chesnutt and the Epistemology of Racial Violence." *American Literature* 73.2 (2001): 311–37.

Walker, Jeffrey. *Bardic Ethos and the American Epic Poem: Whitman, Pound, Crane, Williams, Olson.* Baton Rouge and London: Louisiana State UP, 1989.

Washington, Harriet A. *Medical Apartheid: The Dark History of Medical Experimentation on Black Americans from Colonial Times to the Present.* New York: Doubleday, 2006.

Washington, Booker T. *Up from Slavery: An Autobiography.* 1901. New York: Gramercy, 1993.

Watson, Alan D. *Wilmington, North Carolina, to 1861.* Jefferson, NC: McFarland, 2003.

Webb, Jr., James L. A. "Ecology & Culture in West Africa." In *Themes in West Africa's History.* Ed. Emmanuel Kwaku Akyeampong. Athens: Ohio UP, 2006. 33–51.

Weems, Mason L. *The Life of Washington.* 1808. Ed. Marcus Cunliffe. Cambridge, MA and London: Harvard UP-Belknap P, 1999.

Weisenburger, Steven. *Modern Medea: A Family Story of Slavery and Child-Murder from the Old South.* New York: MacMillan, 1999.

Wellens, Marc. "Playing and Playthings." Accessed 5 Nov. 2006. <http://www.musee-du-jouet.com/europe/ancient.com>

Wellington, 1st Duke of [Arthur Wellesley]. *The Supplementary Despatches and Memoranda of Field Marshal the Duke of Wellington.* Vol. 4. London: John Murray, 1858–1872.

White, E.B. *Charlotte's Web.* 1952. New York: Harper & Row, n.d.

White, Lynn Jr. "The Historical Roots of Our Ecological Crisis." Glotfelty and Fromm, 3–14.

Whitehead, Colson. *The Intuitionist.* New York: Anchor-Random, 2000.

Whitherspoon, Gary, and Glen Peterson. *Dynamic Symmetry and Holistic Asymmetry in Navajo and Western Art and Cosmology.* New York: Peter Lang, 1995.

Wilentz, Gay. "Civilizations Underneath: African Heritage as Cultural Discourse in Toni Morrison's *Song of Solomon.*" *African American Review* 26.1 (1992): 61–76. Rpt. in Furman, 137–63.

Williams, Patricia. *The Alchemy of Race and Rights: Diary of a Law Professor.* Cambridge: Harvard UP, 1991.

Williams, Timothy. "Phoenix Dusts Off After Giant Sandstorm Whips Through." *New York Times* 6 July 2012: A13.

Willis, Cheryl. "Tap Dance: Manifestation of the African Aesthetic." Asante, 145–59.

Wilson, August. *Fences.* New York: Penguin, 1986.

Wolkomir, Michelle J. "Moral Elevation and Egalitarianism: Shades of Gray in Chesnutt's *The Marrow of Tradition.*" *College Language Association Journal* 36.3 (1993): 245–59.

Wood, Peter H. *Black Majority: Negroes in Colonial South Carolina from 1670 through the Stono Rebellion.* New York: Knopf, 1974.

Woolley, Lisa. "Richard Wright's Dogged Pursuit of His Place in the Natural World." *Interdisciplinary Studies in Literature and the Environment* 15.1 (2008): 175–88.

World Commission on Environment and Development. *Our Common Future.* Oxford and New York: Oxford UP, 1987.

Worster, Donald. *Dust Bowl: The Southern Plains in the 1930s.* New York: Oxford UP, 1979.

Wright, Jr., J. Leitch. "William Hilton's Voyage to Carolina in 1662." 105 *Essex Institute Historical Collections* (1969): 96–102.

Wright, Richard. "American Capitalism's Greatest Propagandist: Horatio Alger, Jr." Rev. of *Struggling Upwards and Other Works,* by Horatio Alger, Jr. *PM* 16 Sept. 1945: m8. Rpt. in Fabre, *Richard Wright,* Appendix A, 181–82.

————. *Black Boy (American Hunger): A Record of Childhood and Youth.* 1945. New York: Harper Perennial Modern Classics, 2006.

————. "Blueprint for Negro Writing." 1937. Gates and McKay, 1403–10.

————. "How 'Bigger' Was Born." 1940. *Native Son,* by Richard Wright. New York: Perennial Classics, 1998. 431–62.

————. "Long Black Song." 1938. *Uncle Tom's Children: Four Novellas.* Rpt. as *Uncle Tom's Children.* New York: Harper Perennial Modern Classics, 2008. 125–56.

————. *Native Son.* 1940. New York: Perennial Classics, 1998.

Yeakey, Lamont H. "A Student Without Peer: The Undergraduate College Years of Paul Robeson." *Journal of Negro Education* 42.4 (1973): 489–503.

Young, Philip H. *The Printed Homer: A 3,000 Year Publishing and Translation History of the Iliad and the Odyssey.* Jefferson, NC: McFarland, 2003.

Žižek, Slavoj. *Welcome to the Desert of the Real.* New York: Wooster, 2001.

Index

Page numbers in *italics* refer to illustrations.

allegorycal. *See* allegorye
allegorye: defined, 15, 31–33; African
    allegorycal spirit and hip hop,
    34; African masks and mod-
    ernism, 46; body and relation-
    ship to world, 33, 193–94;
    creation and destruction, 38;
    epical realism, 48; epic bards
    as allegorysts, 37; Europe's
    eleventh-century translations
    and ecology, 182; Fisk Jubilee
    spirituals, 111; New World bio-
    diversity flattened by Homeric
    myth, 188–89; potency of
    speech fragments, 231; so(u)l
    and epic, 51, 84–85; and teleol-
    ogy, 66
allegoryst. *See* allegorye
American Dream, 121, 174, 203
American epic, 59. *See also* Homeric
    Diaspora, epic, epic performance,
    race and racism, and slavery
American Homer: generally, 80–129;
    and white supremacy, 2; as cul-
    tural code, 4; American social
    contract, 4, 107, 126
American Hunger (Wright), 180–81,
    194–96
American Indians. *See* Native
    Americans
American Revolution, 4, 24, 92, 94,
    96, 100–103, 141
Anansi, 149
ancestors: African, 11, 53; the Greco-
    Roman ancients as, 94; in the
    Ozidi Saga, 11. *See also* Toni
    Morrison
Ancients versus Moderns, 87, 93,
    96–97, 103, 113–14, 256n25
Anderson, Martha G., 38, 46–48
Andrews, William, 111
animism, 182
"An Ode to Simeon DeWitt, Esquire"
    (Croaker & Co.), 103–04
Anthony, Carl, 183
Arabic, 79
archetypes, 2, 70
Aristotle: *De Anima*, 219; *Poetics*, 4,
    11, 179; Homer as exemplar, 11,
    252n11; against foreign words,
    179; *sensus communis*, 219–20
Armstrong, Robert G., 56
Aronson, Lisa, 46
Ashanti, 252n19

atambga (Ijo magical knowledge),
    33–34, 38
Atkinson, Yvonne, 224
Austen, Ralph, 44, 253n34,
Ayer (Sitter), Deborah, 211

B
Babalola, S.A., 64
Bacon, Francis, 222
badenya (mother-child-ness): 40,
    78–79, 152
badman, 72, 77, 114–15, 128, 153,
    171–72, 173, 203
Baker, Houston: Afro-Modernism and
    African lore, 67; deformity,
    67–68; folk influence on Rich-
    ard Wright, 176, 205–06
Bakhtin, Mikhail: carnival, 35,
    265n17; on epic, 141; Homer's
    absolute distance from moder-
    nity, 23–24; laughter and
    ambivalence, 265n17; parallel
    and distance from Walter Benja-
    min, 252n11; epic and modern
    capitalism, 174
Baldwin, James, 176–77, 208
Bamana, 22, 27, 67
Banyangan: allegorye, 34–35, 51,
    63, 194; circumcision ritual,
    240–41; common epic owner-
    ship, 22; dragon, 35, 51, 54,
    193; heteroglossia, 22; nyama,
    34–35; hero/chief and nature,
    35, 53, 193; hero's morals, 36,
    62, 193
Barlow, Joel, 96, 257n30
Barnes, Sandra, 4
Battuta, Ibn, 9
Beach Boys, 126
Beatty, Paul, 246–49
Belcher, Stephen, 22, 25–26, 31, 37,
    253n27, 255n59, 256n23
Belcher, Wendy Laura, 4, 80
Beloved: generally, **211–41**: Afri-
    can influences, 211–12, 240;
    Beloved embodies 60 million
    and more, 216, 240; Beloved as
    trickster, 240; cautionary aes-
    thetics, 232–38; community res-
    cues individuals, 231–32; Civil
    Rights/Black Power bravado
    rejected, 234, 236; cool and hot
    thermometrics in, 234, 239–40;
    dancing in, 241; discredited

knowledge in, 215, 227, 235; as epic for women, 211; epic hero/ine defined by community, 231–32; epigraph and *Plessy v. Ferguson*, 224; circumcision and epic performance, 240–41; female/male epic equivalency, 224, 233–34, 236–37; fragments of opening, 224; infanticide and slavery, 215; *in media res* opening meant to disorient readers, 214; insanity trope in, 235; male protagonists' exceptionalism, 233; and *Mwindo Epic*, 212, 240–41; poetics of scale, 216–17, 227, 231; protestant exceptionalism, 215; rememory and motherhood, 237; ritual and healing, 238–41; schoolteacher's knowledge and epic, 236; Sethe as Sixo's counterpart, 237; Sethe's odyssey, 233–34; Sixo as Beloved's male counterpart, 224; and *Sundiata* and *Sunjata*, 211–12; ten times better, 216, 227–31; and traditional African epic, 211–12. *See also* Toni Morrison

Benjamin, Walter: allegory, 32; Trauerspiel, 32; fragments and ruins, 32, 41, 231; German metalepsis, 83, 267n54; chirography and performance, 84–85; philosophical allegory, 6, 32–33; philosophical allegory parallels with African epic performance, 32, 41, 62;

Benston, Kimberly, 8

Bercovitch, Sacvan, 83

Bernal, Martin, xiii

Berry, Wendell: Homer and ecology, 189; race and ecology, 190–91

Bhaba, Homi K., 84

Bible, 92, 153. *See also* Christianity

Biebuyck, Daniel, 42–43, 63, 240–41

bifocalism, 41, 48, 120. *See also* second sight

"Big Boy Leaves Home" (Wright), 180

Bird, Charles, 35, 60

Blackbeard, 158, 261n49

Black Boy (Wright). *See American Hunger*

blackface minstrelsy. See minstrelsy

Black Panthers, 125

Black Power, 125

Blake, William, 59

"Blueprint for Negro Writing" (Wright), 180, 187

Blues, 180–81, 226

Bonaparte, Napoleon, 51, 151

Bond, James, 128

The Bondswoman's Narrative (Crafts), 127

Bone, Robert, 172

Boondocks, 9 Mar. 2005 (Fig. 7.1), 242

Bourdieu, Pierre, 91, 138–39, 230

Brearly, H.C., 202

Brecht, Bertolt, 32

Brer Rabbit, 69, 79–80, 262n6

British, German, and American Homer: Quarterly Reprints from 1775 to 1900 (Tab. 4.1), *142*

Brodhead, Richard H., 132–33

Brown, Henry Billings, 146

Brown, James, 220–21

Bryant, Jerry H., 54

Buchan, Mark, 43, 253n34

Buell, Lawrence, 187

Buffalo of Do/Du. See Ginda.

Bulman, Stephen, 65

Bush, George W., Jr., 170

Butler, Robert, 262n4

C

call and be called out, 5, 25, 213, 220

call-and-response, 5, 25, 99, 213, 220

Campbell, Joseph, 34

capitalism, 91–92, 118–21, 125, 155, 204

carnival, 34–35, 248

Carter, Jimmy, 257–58n43

Carteret, John, 140

Cartesian dualism, 33

Cartwright, Keith: and epic trickster, 78–80; erotic, 253n27; exceptionalism, 111; Mother Africa, 8; nyama as trope, 112; patronymics, 27; second sight, 138; Sunjata among enslaved Muslims, 74; tree as Manden trope, 41

cautionary aesthetics, 52, 59, 126–27, 253n37. *See also* epic agony and epic performance

Chanel, Coco, 125

"Change the Joke and Slip the Yoke" (Ellison), 70

double-consciousness, 6–7, 86, 115; epic and *Souls*, 79, 111; classical education and power rhetoric, 131; race as juridico-medico problem, 148; Sunjatic performance, 111; Talented Tenth paradigm, 111, 115, 136, 153, 226, 228–29
Dunbar, Paul Laurence, xv, 264n41
Dundes, Alan, 69, 226, 255n1
Dust Bowl, 181, 187–88, 190–92, 197–200
Dwight, Timothy, 93, 96
Dyer, Gwynne, 171, 179

E
Earth Day, 208
ecology: and African-American literature, 181–210; America's farming monocultures, 204–05; Dust Bowl and America's WWI policy, 190–9; and Gwendolyn Brooks, 187; Christianity fostered exploitation of nature, 181; environment etymology, 181; European misreading of African TEK, 184–86; and Zora Neale Hurston, 187; *Iliad* versus *Odyssey*, 189–90; American Midwest as Elysian Field, 190–91; national parks and orientalism, 183; New World colonization reduces biodiversity, 188–89; in Homer's *Odyssey*, 189–90; rise of science in West, 182; and city-based racial uplift paradigm, 186
Ellison, Ralph: on Blues and Richard Wright, 180–81; Darwinian regionalism, 186; *Invisible Man* as epic 122; on Richard Wright, 176, 180–81; Rinehart and invisibility, 121–22; on Odysseus as trickster 70–71; Ras the Destroyer, 122–23; on stock market and folk knowledge, 181
Emerson, Ralph Waldo, 141, 256n25
empire: American, 159; British, 64, 158–59; Duke of Wellington, 151; African female role, 27; and epic, 24–25, 64, 102, 159, 164
Enlightenment, 45, 55, 76, 181, 222, 229, 235–36

epic: *Adventures of Huckleberry Finn*, 113–14; and classical verse, 141; as closed genre, 141; colonial American desire for, 141; elementary epics, 224; *Marrow of Tradition*, 137; New World break from old, 141–42; as short narrative, 225; European versus African, 192. *See also* epic performance
epic agony, 54–59, 126, 128–29, 134, 148–49, 159; insanity and Black exceptionalism, 235; purification rituals, 56–58; soul murder, 58–59
epical realism, 48, 109–110, **116–21**, 127–29, 172–73, 195–96, 203, 214, 231,
epic cool, 23, 125, 247
epic habitus, 16–17, 65, 67, 75, 77–79, 84, 88, 91, 98, 123, 138–39, 141–42, 147, 149, 153, 159, 172–74, 248–49
The Epic of Gilgamesh (Anonymous), 3, 179, 187
epic performance: acting, 48; adaptability and fluidity, 21, 28, 82–83, 114, 141; African, 16–17, 21; African bards' anti-antiseptic habits, 43; African diaspora, 80; African ecology foregrounded, 53; African postcolonial vitality, 65; African proverbs, 20, 48; African and European body, 28; allegorycal spirit, 31, 33–35, 37, 48; allusion and indirection, 36; American civic texts as, 98–102; American football, 108; antebellum civil rights, 105–06; artistic and poetic skill, 38, 253n30; audience corrections and interventions, 25, 251n5; auditor-participants danger, 214; beauty/ugly dyad, 45; burlesque and parody, 114–15; capitalism, 91–92, 118–19, 125; cautionary aesthetics, 52–54, 59, 126, 128, 193–94, 253n37; and Christianity, 73, 77, 93, 113–14, 132–33, 153, 189–91, 235, 245, 258n44, 261n50; cinema, 256n22; classical and teleological readings, 18, 23, 43, 62, 66, 160, 253n34;

Stark, John, 122
Star Wars (film), 34
State v.[Troy] Davis, 107
Steele, Richard, 139–40
Stein, Gertrude, 172
Steinbeck, John, 14, 187, 191
Stepto, Robert, 7, 202
Stowe, Harriet Beecher, 131
Sugulun Kòndè. See Sogolon.
Sugulun Kulunkan, 78
Sundiata: An Epic of Old Mali
    (Niane), 65, 253n31
Sundquist, Eric, 136, 153
Sunjata: American Creole, 78; badenya
    foregrounded, 78; bards' anti-
    antiseptic habits, 43; call-and-re-
    sponse, 25; colonial-era vitality,
    65; colonization (French) and
    mistranslation, 61–63, 255n58;
    crippled child, 47; epithets trans-
    gressive and excessive, 51–52;
    food and symbolism, 41, 78;
    George Washington parallel, 94,
    98–99; heteroglossia and plural-
    ism, 22; Louisiana, 78; among
    maana similar to Homer's TEK,
    189; Muslim slaves, 74; physi-
    cal deformities, 19, 152; post-
    colonial Mali, 22, 65; septennial
    kamabolon ceremony, 9–10, 12;
    orthography, 251n8; hot/cool
    thermometric flows in perfor-
    mance, 29, 55; maternal traits,
    40; naamusayer's role, 39; new
    media/technology, 60, 65, 82;
    ruins and mother's death, 39–41;
    sorcerers' physical anomalies,
    43–44; translation limits, 60;
    wealth and ecological ruins, 200
Swift, Jonathan, 140

T
Teach, Edward. See Blackbeard
TEK. *See* traditional ecological
    knowledge
ten times better, 230–38, 268n62
Thompson, Robert Farris, 74
"Thoughts on Prosody" (Jefferson),
    95–96
toasts, 71, 76
Tolkien, J.R.R., 265n19
Topdog/Underdog (Parks), 29, 127
toponymy, 103, 257n41
tortoise, 45–48, 51

Tourgée, Albion, 259n4
traditional ecological knowledge (TEK):
    Achillea millefolium (Western
    Yarrow) plant, 209; and Africa,
    183–86; African-American resis-
    tance, 186; modern American
    insensitivity, 204–05; breadth
    of folklore, 178–79; Homer's
    similar to West African, 189; les-
    sons for moderns, 181; limits of,
    186; monocultures imposed on
    Africa, 184; wealth and ecologi-
    cal ruins, 200
tragic mulatta/o, 126
transgressiveness, 20, 23, 40, 42, 174
translatio imperii, 87, 94
trickster: African cultural retention,
    68–69; African-American
    trickster hero, 68, 150; Anansi,
    and Aunt Nancy, 149; Banyan-
    gan turtle trickster, 47; binary
    and trinary, 76, 80; blackened
    and deformed by slavery, 67; the
    body and storytelling, 71; Brer
    Rabbit, 69, 262n6; deconstruc-
    tive logic, 76, 149; Esu-Elegbara,
    76; European-American master-
    ful duplicity, 138, 159, 260n20;
    literary presence, 76–80, 123,
    137, 149, 235–37, 240; long
    narrative versus trickster tale, 51;
    mask for African epic, 64; orality
    and literacy, 76–77; postbellum
    decline, 150; and proverbs, 219;
    signifying monkey, 51, 72, 76,
    149, 219–20; slave masters as,
    72, 150; compared to trickster-
    prop(erty), 155, 173; in urban
    black lore, 70–71; urban-jungle,
    173; Yoruba trickster, 76. *See
    also* epic trickster
trickster-hero: 2, 44, 72; African-
    American, 68, 138, 149–50,
    236; liminality, 45; and super-
    man, 46; tortoise, 45–48, 51
Trojan Horse. See Homeric
    iconography
Trojan Horse, 144
Trojan Horse (Fig. 4.2), 144
Troy (Fig. 3.4), 90
Troy (Alabama), 108, 258n46
Troy (New York), 103, 105
Troy (North Carolina), 135, 148,
    259n13